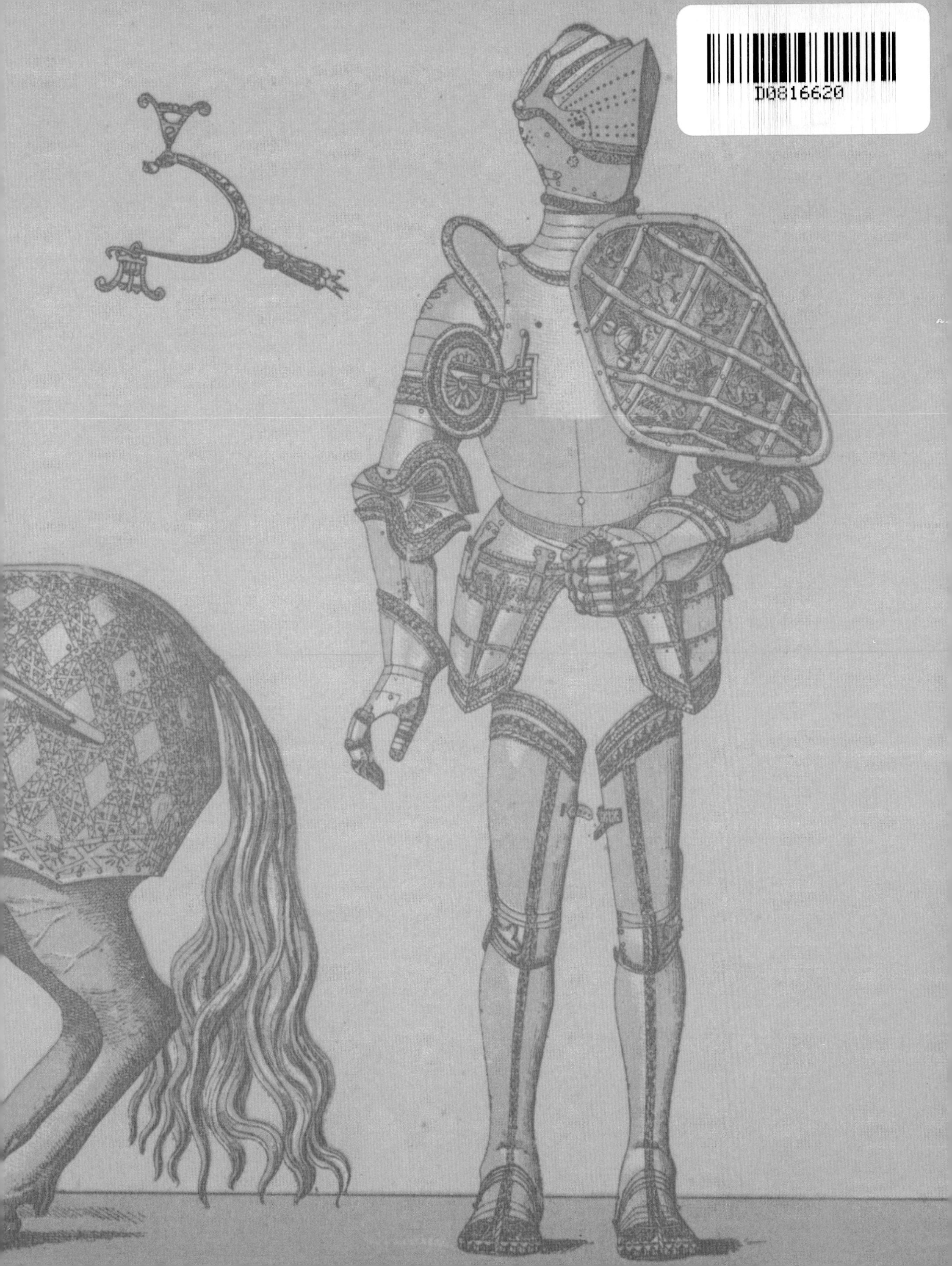

FIGHTING TECHNIQUES OF THE MEDIEVAL WORLD

AD 500 ~ AD 1500

EQUIPMENT, COMBAT SKILLS, AND TACTICS

FIGHTING TECHNIQUES OF THE MEDIEVAL WORLD

AD 500 ~ AD 1500

EQUIPMENT, COMBAT SKILLS, AND TACTICS

MATTHEW BENNETT JIM BRADBURY KELLY DEVRIES IAIN DICKIE PHYLLIS JESTICE

THOMAS DUNNE BOOKS
ST. MARTIN'S PRESS NEW YORK

THOMAS DUNNE BOOKS
An imprint of St. Martin's Press

FIGHTING TECHNIQUES OF THE MEDIEVAL WORLD.

For information, address St. Martin's Press, 175 Fifth Avenue, New York, N.Y. 10010.

www.thomasdunnebooks.com
www.stmartins.com

Library of Congress Cataloging-in-Publication Data
on file at the Library of Congress

ISBN: 0-312-34820-7

EAN: 978-0-312-34820-5

First U.S. Edition 2006

Reprinted in 2007

Editorial and design by
Amber Books Ltd
Bradley's Close
74–77 White Lion Street
London N1 9PF
United Kingdom
www.amberbooks.co.uk

Project Editor: Michael Spilling
Design: Zoe Mellors
Picture Research: Natasha Jones

Printed in UAE

10 9 8 7 6 5 4 3 2

CONTENTS

CHAPTER 1

The Role of Infantry

Medieval infantry tactics underwent significant changes between 500 and 1500. New tactical formations and weaponry brought success to armies such as the English and the Swiss, but inevitably their enemies countered with innovations of their own.

The period AD 500–1500 is often called the 'Age of Cavalry', yet this description is only partly true. In the Byzantine East the heirs of the Roman legions lived on until the empire weakened around AD 1050. True, in the West after 400 the military elite rode to battle, but in Scandinavian cultures they then dismounted to fight. The frontier regions of Europe both external and internal (such as the mountainous areas of Iberia and Switzerland) continued to provide specialist infantry which were eagerly recruited as mercenaries. The rising urban population of Europe, especially in Flanders and northern Italy, produced troops with a corporate sense of

AN ENGLISH FOOT *soldier takes a French nobleman captive at the Battle of Agincourt in 1415. This image symbolizes the superiority that infantrymen could exercise over their social betters.*

identity, which enabled them to challenge the assumed superiority of the chivalric classes. This has often been called an 'infantry revolution', referring to the period around 1300 onwards, but is better seen as a process of evolution.

The development of missile weapons also increased the fighting power of the foot soldiers. First the crossbow, then longbow, then gunpowder, made it possible to strike down the better-armoured and more mobile cavalry from a distance. By the fourteenth century even the knights dismounted to fight, while in the fifteenth century, 'modern armies' contained a balanced mixture of horse, foot and missile-armed men which anticipated the 'pike and shot' of Renaissance warfare.

BYZANTINE HEAVY INFANTRYMEN *of the 10th century wore a helmet, a coat of mail above a padded tunic,* lamellar vambraces *(lower arm), leather* pteruges *(upper arm) and padded cloth greaves (shins). The leather strapping around the upper torso may have been meant to reduce the drag of the heavy mail coat, which is also supported by the sword belt.*

Early Infantry

In the sixth century the most sophisticated practitioners of the art of warfare on foot were the Byzantines. At Taginae in 552, their general Narses laid out a defensive battle line with foot archers on the wings and a centre of dismounted heavy cavalry and spearmen. Behind this line were stationed other cavalry units who remained mounted. His Italian-Gothic enemies had a similarly structured force of lancer cavalry, foot spearmen and bows. However, the Gothic infantry were weak, so their king, Totila, placed his emphasis on a massed mounted assault. Decimated by Byzantine arrows and unable to penetrate the dense hedge of spears by repeated charges, the Goths broke and, pursued by Narses' mounted reserve, fled the field.

The victory was a vindication of the Byzantines' tactics and a combination of arms remained a feature of their tactics until the twelfth century. The late sixth-century tactical manual, entitled the *Strategikon,* delineates the approach to war used by the Byzantines from 500 onwards. Infantry were used to support the cavalry by acting as a defensive base that the cavalry could retire to and reform upon, or, in emergency, retreat behind. The infantry combined spearmen and bowmen, deploying in special formations to resist cavalry charges:

'The first three men in each file form *foulkon*, interlocking their shields with their spears fixed firmly in the ground, holding them inclined forward…the third and fourth men hold their spears like javelins so they can use them for thrusting or throwing. The light armed infantry use the bow.' Once the enemy had been repelled, baulked by the hedge of spears, the Byzantine cavalry sallied out and put them to flight.

The widely accepted date for the fall of the Roman Empire was never recognized by the Romans. Although in AD 476 Rome had fallen under the domination of a 'barbarian' kingdom in Italy, the re-incorporation of the lost provinces remained a strategic goal of the East Romans, as the Byzantines referred to themselves. In 493, a Gothic army had been despatched to remove the barbarian king and return Italy to the fold. However, Theoderic the Great, leader of the Goths, struck out for himself and created an independent kingdom while always recognizing that Italy was culturally part of the empire. Following Byzantium's crushing of the Vandal kingdom in Africa in 533–4, the Byzantine emperor, Justinian, turned his attention to Italy. The Vandals had proven to be a house built upon sand, and he expected dissension within the Gothic royal house to deliver Italy as easily.

'The Byzantines, pushing with their shields and thrusting very rapidly with their spears, defended themselves most vigorously against their assailants; and they purposely made a din with their shields, terrifying the enemy's horses.'

— *Procopius,* The Gothic Wars

Justinian put together a three-pronged assault. A force based upon the army of Illyricum would attack from the Balkans, an alliance with the Frankish kings of Gaul would produce pressure upon the frontiers of Provence and Belisarius, his ex-bodyguard and favourite general would take lightly held Sicily and then invade from the south. The Balkan attack was stalled when its general was killed, the Franks failed to do more than steal southern Gaul, but Belisarius moved north from Sicily, took Naples, defended Rome for a year and took Ravenna, deposing the Gothic king Witiges in 540. Imperial meanness converted the triumph into failure (as it had almost done in Africa), and before long the Goths were resurgent under Totila, winning smart victories in the field and confining the Byzantines to a few cities. Finally, in 552 Justinian provided the funds and an army under Narses entered Italy from the northeast, the traditional invasion route.

Narses' large army was an amalgam of Roman regulars and the elites of allied German tribes, the Lombards and Heruls. Advancing into Italy, Narses evaded the Goth blocking forces by bridging the river mouths and relieved the garrison of Ravenna. Totila, recognizing the threat posed by Roman siege technique and efficient logistics, sought open battle to decide the issue. He placed his army across the Via Flaminia, relied upon the charge of his cavalry and was totally defeated. Teias, his successor, was penned in the south of Italy and died fighting at the head of his men at Mons Lactarius. The only Gothic survivors were now in isolated garrisons. In desperation, they invited the Franks of Gaul to intervene, take Italy for themselves and then sub-let it to the Goths. The Frankish king Theudebald allowed two of his 'dukes', Lothar and Butilin (who ruled the Alamanni to the east of the Rhine), to undertake the expedition.

Narses was by then besieging Cumae, where Aligern (Teias' brother) was defending the Gothic royal treasure. Failing to take the fortress by mining, Narses set off north to Tuscany as word reached him that Lothar and Butilin had crossed the Po. He sent a force to observe the Alamans and set about the siege of Lucca.

Unfortunately for the Byzantines, Butilin successfully ambushed Narses' Herul auxiliaries (who were meant to be observing his movements). Meanwhile, Lucca surrendered on terms, allowing Narses to move to winter quarters in Ravenna while his troops were distributed to fortresses around Italy.

The Byzantine foulkon, *an infantry formation formed of spearmen with interlocking shields, was designed to hold enemy cavalry at bay. As the thwarted enemy withdrew, the Byzantine cavalry charged through gaps in the infantry line to scatter the retreating horsemen.*

At Ravenna, Narses received Aligern who brought the keys of Cumae. He also learnt that the Warni, a German tribe allied to the Goths, wished to transfer their allegiance to the emperor. Narses travelled to Rimini to cement this alliance, and while he was there an enemy foraging force approached the city. Narses led out his personal guard of about three hundred cavalry to intercept them. The Alaman force was estimated at 2000 strong, but it is likely that they had few cavalry, because otherwise the invaders' tactics seem overly defensive. They formed up with a line of locked shields with cavalry on the flanks between two woods that protected them against outflanking. Perhaps the Warni were also present on the field to inhibit them from attacking. Led by Narses in person, the Byzantines skirmished for a while, before performing a feigned flight, which the Germans followed up in disorder. Narses' guard turned and butchered the disordered infantry while the cavalry fled back to their camp.

The Battle of Casilinum: 554

In the spring of 554, Narses concentrated his troops at Rome and carried out training for his army. Meanwhile Lothar and Butilin by-passed the city and moved south, ravaging as they went. Butilin, with the larger force, took the western flank and Lothar the eastern. The Germanic army was reputedly 75,000 strong. This seems an improbably high figure, but may be the reason why it split into two columns, so as to subsist in the war-ravaged south of Italy. Lothar now decided to head back north to lodge his booty, accompanied by many prisoners taken in the raids. Reaching Fano his advanced guard was attacked by a Roman force with Hun auxiliaries. While the Germans stood to arms their prisoners escaped with much of the booty. Lothar's force slipped north crossed the Po and was quartered in Venetia when an outbreak of plague decimated them, rendering their leader powerless to continue the campaign.

It was now early autumn and Butilin was heading towards Rome, looking for Narses. With dysentery ravaging his army, he needed a decisive victory before his strength was also eroded away.

He reached Campania and encamped on the north bank of the Casilinus (River Volturno). Here he built a camp surrounded by earthworks and ramparts made with the wheels of his wagons half-buried in the ground. The bridge over the Volturno was fortified with a tower. Narses arrived from Rome with his army and encamped nearby. In a skirmish Narses drove in Butilin's foragers and burnt the tower that guarded the bridge which the Romans now took, cutting the Germans off from any retreat south. Unable to forage, and so faced with starvation, Butilin was forced to lead his army out into battle.

The Armies

Butilin was an Alaman noble who had won the trust of his new Frankish overlords. He saw the possibility that he could take over the vacant Gothic throne, probably as a sub-king under Theudebald. He probably had considerable military experience; after all he fortified his camp and was the guiding hand behind the ambush of the Heruls outside Fano. The Greek historian Agathias claims that the Germanic army was 30,000 strong.

It may have been considerably smaller, perhaps 20,000 or 15,000. This can be deduced as, when it was deployed deep in a central column, and with extended flanks, it only covered the front of a Roman infantry formation of perhaps 10,000 to 12,000 men. Agathias describes the army as Frankish, which is true only in part. The main contingents were the Alamans, a German tribe, less Romanized than the Franks who now controlled Gaul and with much fewer cavalry than a Frankish army would have deployed. Agathias provides detailed description of their armament:

'Their style of fighting-equipment is simple and does not require a variety of mechanical skills for its maintenance.... They are ignorant of the use of body armour and greaves and most fight with their heads unprotected, though there a few who wear helmets. Back and chest are bare as far as the waist; they wear linen or leather trousers. Rarely, if ever, do they use horses, being experienced infantry fighters which is the customary mode of warfare of their nation. Bows, arrows, slings and other distance weapons form no part of their equipment. Axes and angos are their typical arms. Angos are spears of medium length but can either be used as javelins or for thrusting in close combat. They have long iron heads...and iron butt spikes. At the point there are curved barbs on either side. The "Frank" throws his ango as he closes. If it strikes any part of the body the barbs prevent it being pulled out and its removal disables the victim. If it pierces a shield it remains attached, the butt trailing...the victim is unable to pull it out of the shield because of the barbs and the iron shank prevents him cutting it off. Seeing this, the Frank steps on the shaft and pulls down the shield. He then finishes off his victim with either the axe or another spear.'

This is quite an accurate portrait. Another commentator, Procopius, speaks of the Frankish throwing axe splitting enemy shields, but modern research indicates that the axe was generally kept

A BYZANTINE MILITARY *manual of the middle of the 10th century depicts this 'square infantry formation keeping the cavalry inside', which enabled the two arms to co-operate to best effect. The text is usually associated with the soldier-emperor Nikephoros Phokas II, who led the revival of imperial fortunes from the 950s until his assassination in 969.*

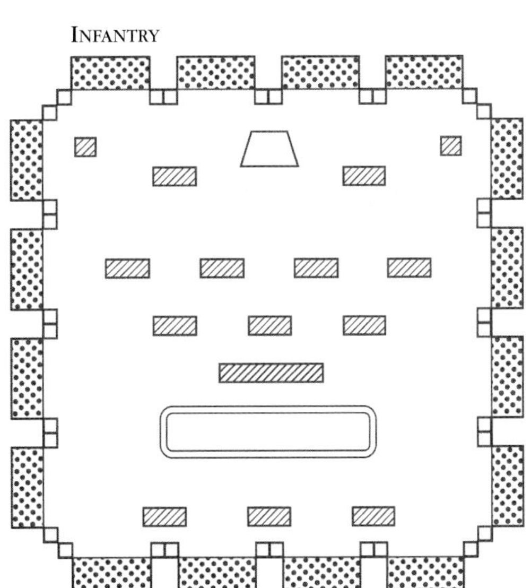

in the hand for use. No differentiation of troop types is given for the Alamanic force, but there must have been a small cavalry element. It was probably dismounted to add its fighting power to the ordinary footmen, and stiffen their resolve. The Franks in Gaul certainly possessed archers, but, even if they were present, the chosen tactical deployment left no room for their use

Narses was certainly more than 60 years of age when called upon to command in Italy. He was a eunuch and a civil servant, but exceptionally able and trusted implicitly by Justinian. Perhaps this was because no matter how victorious he was he could never presume to aim for the throne and thus pose a threat to the emperor. Agathias describes him as 'of diminutive stature and abnormal thinness; yet his courage and heroism were incredible'.

His army was a polyglot, but also a tough and experienced force typical of the Byzantine army of this period. It consisted of Byzantine cavalry, some with javelins, some with bows and some with lances that were used with two hands. There were Byzantine infantry units of heavy armed foot, some, the *antesignani*, wearing cavalry armour of long mail-coats and some with spear, javelins and large spiked shield. These infantry units may have had integral archers and their specialized units of bowmen, javelinmen and slingers.

As auxiliaries, Narses had a force of fierce Germanic Herul cavalry (which he had used dismounted at Taginae), Huns and Persians in imperial service, and Goths under Aligern. (The unruly Lombards had been found to be uncontrollable and been sent home after the victory over Totila.)

> *'The Franks stood firm and immovable behind a wall of shields, protected on every side since they stood next to a thick forest. Now they even began to fight back, hurling their* angons, *as they call their weapons.'*
>
> – *Agathias,* The Histories

The Battle

Narses set out with a defensive blocking force of infantry and dismounted cavalry. In the centre were the *antesignani* and on their flanks the other heavy infantry. Behind the infantry were slingers and bowmen, ready to fire overhead into the advancing enemy, and a body posted as rearguard. If Narses followed the same practice as at Taginae, the rearguard was composed of cavalry, and not (as depicted in some reconstructions) an infantry line. The Herul troops were in dispute with their general at the time, one of their number having murdered a servant and been executed by Narses' order. The Heruls were near mutinous but were calmed down by Sindual, their leader, and were marching up to fill a gap left for them, possibly behind the *antesignani*.

Narses arrayed his cavalry on both flanks. He took post at the tip of the right wing. This was probably to control it and perhaps also to take advantage of a good view from rising ground. On the left flank he concealed cavalry in a wood with orders to emerge only when the enemy was in contact with the centre. The plan was to hold the German charge and then turn the flanks with cavalry.

Butilin formed his men into a line with a 'boar's head' (wedge) formation at the centre, with units echeloning back either side. The whole formation was like an inverted 'V' with the strike force at the head. The Alamans charged, yelling their battle cry as they advanced. The Byzantines braced themselves while shooting their bows and slings at the onrushing wall of shields. Before impact there will have been a volley of angos from the Germans who then crashed into the Roman line. As shield battered against shield, the din would have been terrific. In the centre, where the Heruls should have stood, the line staggered back and broke. The dense wedge pushed through and on past the rearguard, heading towards the Heruls, who were by now advancing. Meanwhile, Narses advanced the Roman cavalry on both wings so

ENGLISH SHIELD WALL, *mid 11th century. The troops are mainly spearmen, although some might hold axes and swords. The formation depended upon the mutual support of men within it for its strength.*

that they could shoot their bows at the unprotected rear of the Germans on the flanks. While the Roman infantry wings held back the bulk of Butilin's army, the Heruls counter-charged the wedge, which had attempted to turn and take the Byzantines in the rear. Butilin was surprised by this fresh force, because intelligence from Herul deserters had suggested their tribe would not fight. The wedge broke, and was pushed back as the Heruls forced their way into the gap in the line left for them. Narses then released his cavalry to sweep around the wings and take the Germans in the rear. This disposed of the wings that were still fighting. Surrounded, the invaders were massacred, with only a handful making it back to their homes across the Alps.

Narses was obviously confident that his line would hold and also had a rearguard to act as insurance. The enemy breakthrough only occurred because the Heruls were not in position. Therefore the Germans must have come on very fast and seized the tactical initiative. Once the 'boar's head' wedge formation had broken through, the cavalry and archers on the flanks coolly turned and shot up the troops in its rear. Narses must have seen that the Heruls were arriving, and in any case the rearguard (whose composition we do not know), was not yet engaged. The infantry on the Roman flanks held up well against the fierce charge. Overall, the Byzantine army reacted flexibly to the tactical requirements of the battle.

In contrast, the Germans were one-paced and they did not deploy any cavalry. This is probably because they were dismounted to stiffen the lightly armed foot, and add weight to their charge. In so doing the elite warriors shared the perils of the common soldier (in contrast to the action at Rimini, when the mounted nobles had escaped back to camp). The charge exploited the homogeneity of their army, but only achieved success for a moment because the Heruls were not in line when Butilin charged.

He had no reserve to cope with any failure of the plan. While the Alamanic tactics look primitive, a fast, frightening charge by brave men was a fearsome event. The outcome of the battle illustrates the strength of a well-led, combined-arms force that can trust its infantry and cavalry to perform their job.

Later Byzantine Armies

Although cavalry were of higher status in Byzantine armies, the infantry had specialist skills

Battle of Casilinum

554

The Byzantine general Narses deployed his troops carefully, dismounting the vast majority and allowing for mutual support and the most effective use of missile fire. The infantry were deployed in the centre with the cavalry on both flanks and largely hidden by surrounding woods. Butilin's Germans also dismounted and formed up for one great rush against the enemy centre, designed to rupture it and hurl back the Byzantine in flight. Initially this seemed to have worked, as the centre of the Byzantine infantry buckled under the ferocity of the German charge, led by their nobles in the 'boar's head' wedge formation. Then the Byzantines' allied Herul troops – held in reserve – came into the line just in time to restore the situation. Meanwhile, Narses, having drawn the Germans into his trap, closed the door on any retreat by manoeuvring his cavalry into outflanking positions. Butilin's men were surrounded and massacred, bringing an end to their rampaging campaign through Italy.

The Battle of Casilinum was fought beside the River Volturno. The Germans, having raided Campania, were returning to their base, but found Narses' Byzantine army astride their path.

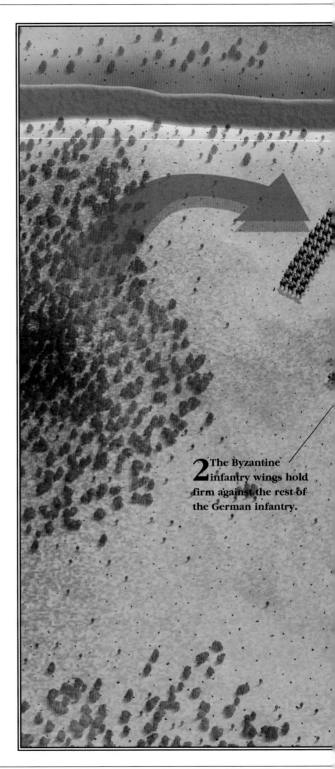

2 **The Byzantine infantry wings hold firm against the rest of the German infantry.**

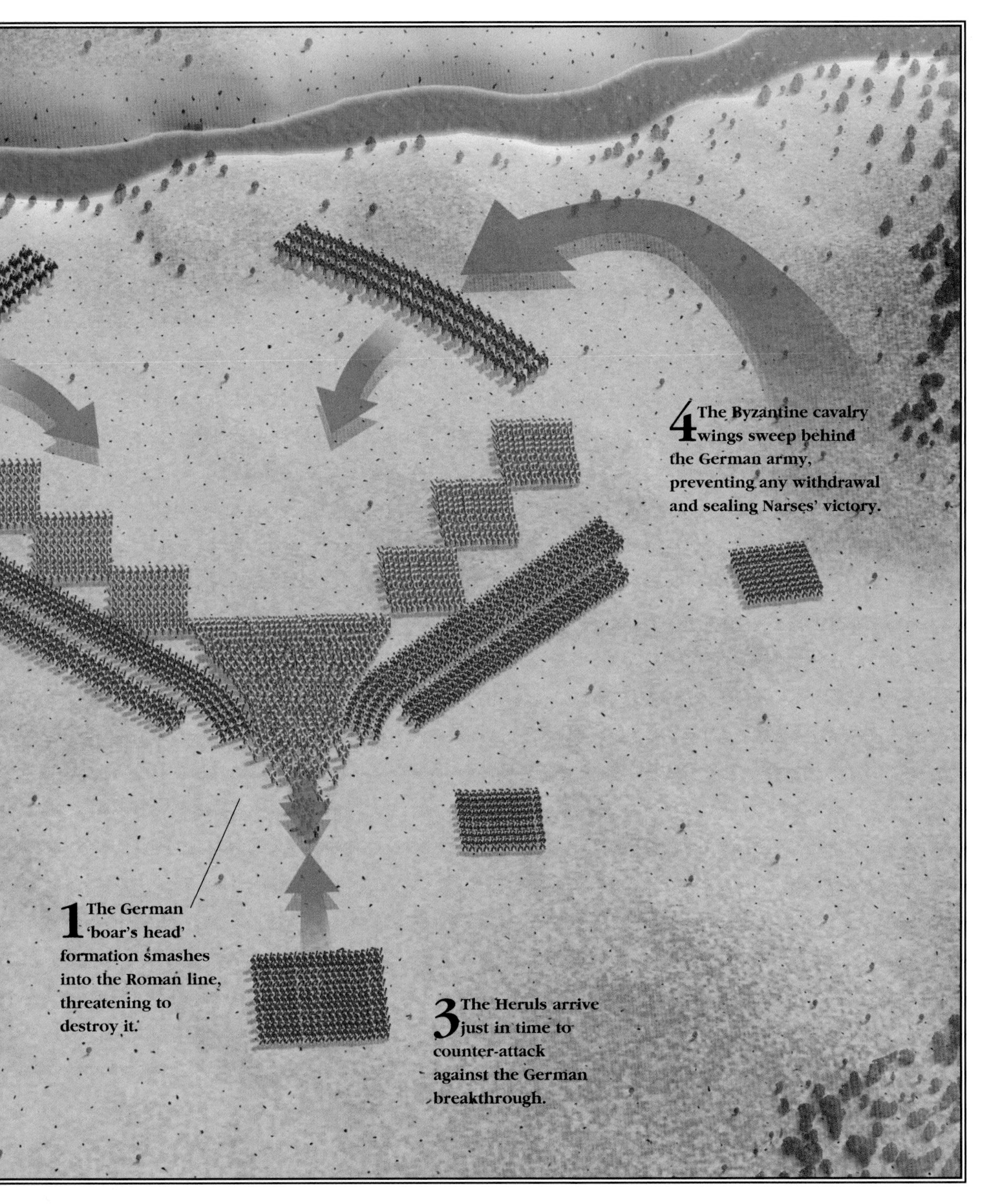
4 The Byzantine cavalry wings sweep behind the German army, preventing any withdrawal and sealing Narses' victory.
1 The German 'boar's head' formation smashes into the Roman line, threatening to destroy it.
3 The Heruls arrive just in time to counter-attack against the German breakthrough.

BERBER INFANTRY FORMATION *of the 10–11th century was widely used by the Arabs. Kneeling spearmen hold back cavalry, while standing javelinmen and archers shoot overhead to inflict casualties on the enemy and disrupt his attacks.*

and weaponry and sophisticated training for their deployment. Tenth-century manuals describe the formation of an infantry square made up of spearmen backed by archers as the main component, but with aisles left for the cavalry to emerge. These gaps were covered by specialist javelinmen (recruited from Slavs) and slingers, all lightly equipped troops able to fill or vacate the gaps quickly, as the tactical situation demanded. Within the infantry formation were units of *menaulatoi*.They wielded a heavy throwing spear and were designated to repulse assaults by enemy *kataphraktoi* (cataphracts – armoured men on armoured horses) whose assault would be invulnerable to archery and might break the long spears of the square's defensive wall of foot.

Byzantine infantry were not just a defensive asset. Against enemy infantry the tenth-century *Taktika* of Nikephoros Ouranos advocated that the main body of spearmen and archers should receive the attack while the menaulatoi and javelin throwers advanced on the wings, curving inwards to maximize the number that could shoot and break up the enemy flanks.An artillery component was provided by *cheiromangana*, catapults shooting giant arrows, and siphons, man-portable tubes for projecting incendiary Greek Fire.

The fundamental attitude of the Byzantine infantry was defensive.This was because their own cavalry force of cataphracts, armoured lancers and light scouts was used as the offensive force against their enemies and was expected to break their front. At the battle of Dorostolon in 971, the Byzantine infantry engaged in close combat over several days of fighting with the Rus. This Scandinavian-style foot had formed a long line of well-armed infantry with spear, axe and bow and were holding off the Byzantines with their rear protected by the fortress of Dorostolon.After days of grinding down the enemy, the decisive breakthrough came when the emperor himself led the Byzantine cataphracts, in a large wedge formation, to break the weakened Rus line.

From the 960s onwards, the empire's armies contained many Norse and Rus mercenaries. Some of these were formed into the Varangian Guard, an armoured unit wielding two-handed axes. They provided both a cutting edge to the Byzantine infantry and a personal guard for the emperor. At Dyrrachium in 1081, Emperor Alexios Komnenos was fighting to repel an invasion of the south Italian Normans under the formidable Robert Guiscard. The Varangians formed the centre of the battle line, acting in concert with units of archers. 'These (the archers) Alexios intended to send first against Guiscard, having instructed Nampites (the Varangian commander) to open his ranks quickly for them (by moving to right and left) whenever they wanted to advance out against the Normans; and to close ranks again and march forward in close order, when they had withdrawn' (*The Alexiad*). This tactical deployment is an example of the sophisticated combination of missile and shock troops in Alexios' army. The Varangians advanced successfully, their archers deterring Norman cavalry attacks and the axemen defeating the infantry opposed to them. Only when they had advanced too far were the Varangians surprised by an infantry flank attack and repulsed.

> *'Keep the cavalry away from us with your arrows and let them not come upon us from the rear. If you see us collecting booty, do not join us, and if you see us being slain do not help us.'*
>
> – *The Prophet Mohammed*

The Arab Conquests

The main enemies of the Byzantines from the seventh to the eleventh centuries were the Arab states that first deprived the empire of its eastern provinces and then became its most dangerous neighbours. The Arabs were famous for their cavalry and for the quality of their steeds. However, they also had a strong tradition of infantry warfare going back to the pre-Islamic period.

Arab infantry were crucial to the Islamic Wars of Conquest, when, mounted on camels, they were able to cross deserts, launch destructive raids on Byzantine and Persian provinces and then disappear back into the desert, frustrating any pursuit. The ability to launch attacks and retire was responsible for the long duration of many of their battles, which could last several days. When the Arabs invaded and conquered Spain in the seventh century and later in Gaul, Sicily and south Italy, they encountered Western armies and may have influenced their infantry tactics. Arab light cavalry would harass their opponents then, if the opportunity presented itself, the heavy cavalry might charge home. If the enemy were too strong, the cavalry withdrew to their infantry supports. The foot were formed into dense blocks with aisles for the cavalry to pass through. Each block comprised spearmen formed in ranks, kneeling and covered by their shields, with their spear butts wedged in the ground. Behind them were archers and javelinmen shooting overhead. The javelins served to back up the archery with a heavier missile that would damage armoured cavalry. The infantry were to stand firm and repulse their opponents' cavalry, who would then be hit in retreat by the Arab cavalry issuing out to the attack. When appropriate the Arab bowmen and javelin throwers could advance in skirmish order to protect the infantry from opposing missile-men.

The Arab kingdoms in Spain were closely connected to their co-religionists in the Maghreb across the Straits of Gibraltar. Under pressure from the resurgent Christians the Spanish Muslims invited Berber armies across to support them. In the late eleventh century this alliance led to an effective conquest of Andalusia by the Almoravides, austere Muslims from the Sahara. At the battle of Zallaca in 1086, the Almoravid units, all clad in black, conducted disciplined manoeuvres to the accompaniment of drums. Implementing their infantry in defensive blocks they were able to defeat the heavier horse of the Spanish and crusader knights.

Northern Europe

In northern Europe, outside the formal frontiers of the Roman Empire, cavalry were initially less important numerically, though socially the

Huscarl (mid 11th century)

The huscarl were an oath-sworn bodyguard of the Anglo-Danish aristocracy, which ruled England prior to the Norman Conquest of 1066. Although men of high status who rode to battle, huscarls dismounted to fight in the traditional Scandinavian manner. He wields a long-handled axe which could decapitate a horse at a blow, as the Bayeux Tapestry depicts. He has slung his kite-shaped shield, popular with both infantry and a cavalry of his era, on his back to allow him a double-handed grip for extra weight in the blow. Axemen such as these were usually paired with a spearman, who also wielded a shield to cover both of them, so making a dangerous offensive and defensive team. Archaeological investigation in the River Thames produced several examples of such axes, probably connected with the Danish siege of London in 1012. They are known as 'bearded' axes because they are asymmetric with the lower cutting edge being much longer, reminding observers of the long beards which the Vikings wore.

mounted warrior still enjoyed the most prestige. It was always accepted in the West that mounted warriors would dismount for battle if it was tactically advantageous. Thus at Mons Lactarius in 553, the Goths of Teias dismounted against the Byzantines and the *Strategikon* described the 'fair-haired races' as always ready to deploy on foot. Descending to ground level had the advantage of stiffening the infantry, who could see that their social superiors intended to stand and, if necessary, even die alongside them.

The infantry tradition was strong in England and Scandinavia. When Viking raiders arrived in England their first aim was to quickly capture horses in order to gain strategic mobility; however, they fought dismounted. In both France and England the Vikings used fortifications extensively, often at island sites such as Reading in the Thames from where they could raid and to which they could return with booty.

> *'The English are not skilled in jousting or in bearing arms on horseback. They carry axes and gisarmes; a man using an axe cannot protect himself, as he has to hold it in both hands if he wishes to strike great blows.'* – WACE, ROMAN DE ROU

In 871, King Ethelred of Wessex and his brother Alfred sought battle with a Danish force at Ashdown. The Danes were in two wings, one commanded by two 'kings', the other by 'many earls'. Alfred (the future King Alfred the Great) attacked without waiting for his brother. A reading of the poem *The Battle of Maldon* gives a good insight as to why. Both sides formed shield walls and they then exchanged missiles. 'Out flashed file-hardened point from fist, sharp-ground spears sprang forth, bows were busy, bucklers flinched.' As a phase of missile-throwing preceded the main clash, narrowing the gap might reduce casualties from thrown weapons. Although there is evidence that the English and Vikings formed dense bodies, Maldon describes a looser kind of warfare where the leaders and their immediate entourage sought each other out. The English were victorious at Ashdown, perhaps because Alfred, having engaged both Danish wings, held them until the king arrived with fresh troops, possibly on a flank of the melee. Casualties were heavy in this sort of warfare, and most participants were unarmoured apart from a shield. Also, with everyone dismounted, the pursuit, which the English maintained until dark, was particularly murderous.

The infantry of the Vikings and English appears in the sources as crude and brutal, relying more on heroism than art. Sometimes the sources, however, let slip a hint of greater sophistication. Many Vikings carried bows and used them from within the infantry line, perhaps as a back rank. Vikings were also capable of making a flank attack through woods and forming the *swynfylking* or boar's head formation, a densely packed wedge aimed at breaking the enemy's line. The Rus, who were slavicized Swedish Vikings, used bodies of archers to support their line of infantry spearmen at Dorostolon against the Byzantines, moving them out to the flanks to harass the Greek cavalry.

During this period the same troops were to fight on land, in naval battles, and to build and use effective field fortifications. In England both the Danes and the English *thegns* and *fyrd* used horses for strategic manoeuvre, and the Danes used their longships to retire and then appear elsewhere, penetrating deeply up rivers. The English (and the Carolingians in Gaul) responded with programmes of fortification.

In the Carolingian Empire four great challenges had to be faced: Vikings, Magyar raiders from Hungary, Muslim attacks from Spain and into France and Italy and endemic civil wars as the fissiparous tendencies of the Frankish ruling house combined with the unwieldy nature of the empire to make a united response to threats impossible. Few battles are remembered over 1000 years after they are fought, but an exception is the battle of Poitiers in 732, where Charles Martel turned back a Muslim raid that, had it been allowed to continue, might have led to the conquest of Gaul.

The Franks established themselves across the Muslim route back to Spain, in the angle of two rivers at Moussais la Battaille. Although he possessed both infantry and cavalry, Charles dismounted and thus stiffened his infantry. He also avoided his cavalry being drawn out in rash pursuit by the Arabs' feigned flight tactics. The Arab commander Abd'er Rahman attacked, at first exploiting his superior missile capability and then by assault. The men of the North stood firm in their battle line 'like a wall of ice'. After a day of desperate assaults the Arabs abandoned their tents and set off for home without their booty. We hear little of infantry in the Frankish Empire, but they certainly did exist, not least because of their role in siege warfare. They are hinted at in the size of the casualty list from the civil war battle at Fontenoy (845) and the description of formations as 'dense

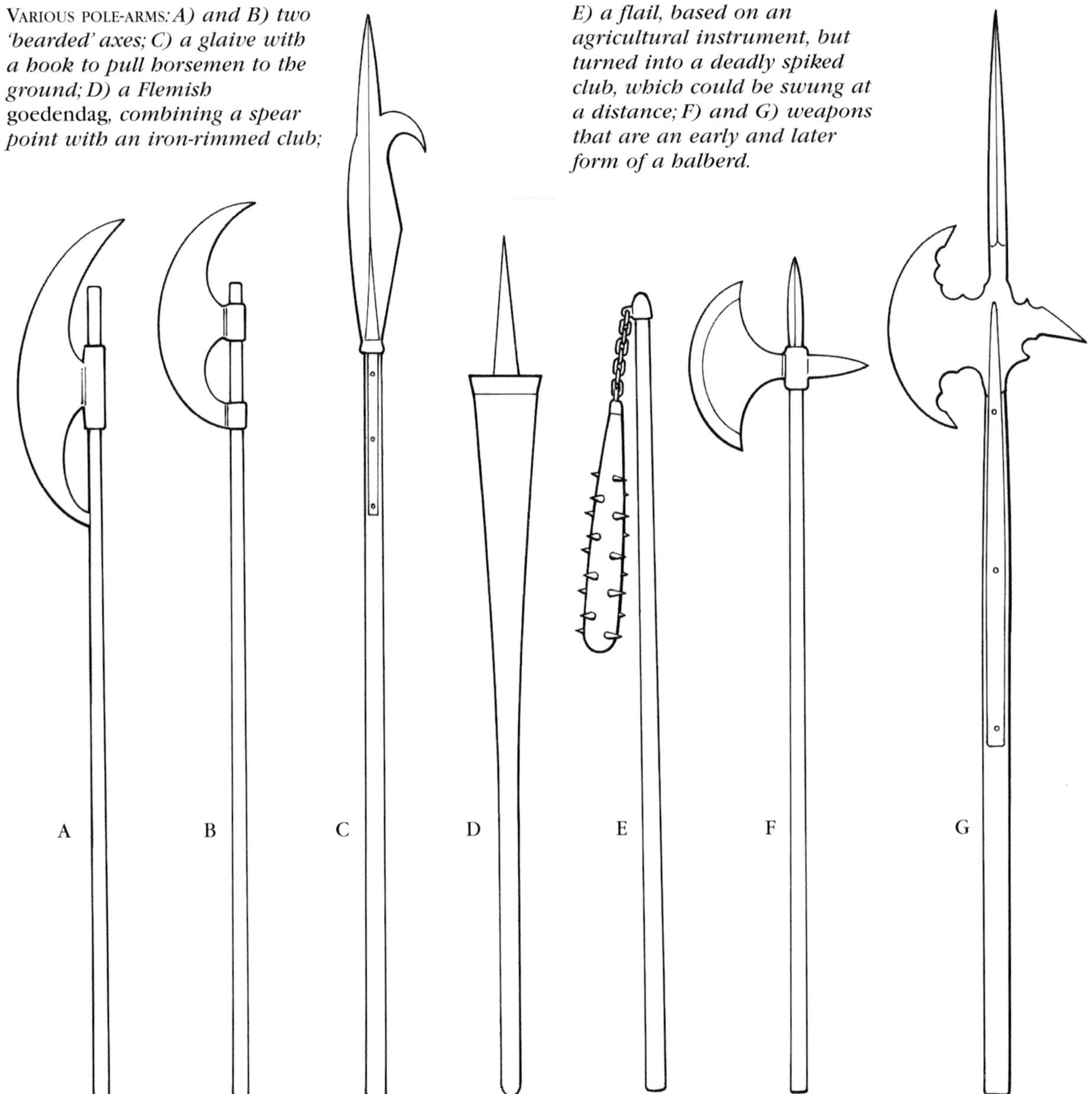

VARIOUS POLE-ARMS: *A) and B) two 'bearded' axes; C) a glaive with a hook to pull horsemen to the ground; D) a Flemish* goedendag, *combining a spear point with an iron-rimmed club; E) a flail, based on an agricultural instrument, but turned into a deadly spiked club, which could be swung at a distance; F) and G) weapons that are an early and later form of a halberd.*

phalanxes'. Saxon foot soldiers were also hired as mercenaries in 850.

At Montpensier in 892, King Odo divided his army into two, with infantry and archers in front and cavalry behind. This was a classic medieval deployment, with the infantry protecting the cavalry, who were more vulnerable to archery, until the cavalry could be released for the attack. Towards the year 1000, the best infantry were found in areas that were not effectively dominated by knightly cavalry: regions of mountain or marsh, the Celtic fringe and the towns where a spark of independence still burned.

Normans Versus Anglo-Saxons

The Battle of Hastings (1066) was once conceptualized as a struggle between the modern forces of the Normans, flexibly deploying archers, spearmen and knights, and the archaic Anglo-Saxons packed tight on 'Senlac' hill, with an armoured front rank backed by peasant levies throwing stones tied to sticks. Today this view has been revised. The English huscarls, mail-armoured, mercenary bodyguards of the king and earls, are seen as the best infantry in Europe. They were supported by armoured infantry raised by a system that levied one soldier from every five hides of land. Evidence from the poem of *The Battle of Maldon*, an Icelandic saga which describes the English victory at Stamford Bridge, and the Bayeux Tapestry, suggests that the infantry shield wall incorporated archers, and may have been supported by lighter-equipped and more mobile groups of spearmen. The battle line was then a complex unit with armoured spearmen bearing large shields at the front, and behind them men hefting two-handed Danish axes, and others with bundles of javelins. The archers were incorporated in the formation, probably delivering aimed shots at short range (which may be what the solitary archer on the Tapestry is intended to represent).

The English warriors commonly rode to battle and tethered their horses behind the line. At the Battle of Brunanburh (937), when the English defeated an alliance of the Norse and Scots, after they had achieved victory they remounted and pursued their beaten foes. Such mobility provided a great advantage over purely infantry armies which had no cavalry component – these could defeat, but not destroy, a beaten enemy if the enemy could not be encircled or trapped. Being mounted also gave the English considerable strategic versatility. In 1066, King Harold was able to march his army north to Stamford Bridge, defeat the Norwegians of Harald Hardraada and head south again to meet William's invasion, all in the space of one month.

The Anglo-Saxons must not be seen as tactically one-paced. For example, in 1063 Harold Godwinson and his brother Tostig campaigned in Wales. According to Gerald de Barry (writing c.1200), Harold kitted-out his huscarls in light leather armour, with light shields, to counter the guerrilla tactics of the Welsh. Tostig led the English fleet to transport this force to the seaward ends of the Welsh valleys. Unable to escape, the Welsh killed their own prince Gruffydd, bringing his head to Harold to symbolize their surrender.

At Hastings, against the dense English shield-wall, the Normans set out a three-line battle formation. First came the infantry, archers and spearmen (which are not shown on the Bayeux Tapestry, but are described in the eyewitness account of William of Poitiers). The Norman archers opened the action, then the spearmen assaulted the English line to prepare the way for the knights. When these tactics failed the Norman spearmen withdrew, probably forming defensive blocks around which the knights could rally after each attack. So determined was the English resistance that William's left flank broke in flight. This drew a group of defenders out of their lines in pursuit, but they were surrounded by the more mobile cavalry and cut down.

Duke William is said to have been inspired by this result to direct his knights to perform feigned flights, thinning the English lines still further. Harold's two brothers are recorded as being killed, possibly while trying to co-ordinate the pursuits. As the day-long battle drew towards evening, William instructed his archers to shoot high into the air. Tired men could no longer hold up their heavy shields to defend themselves and were hit in the face, like King Harold himself. Taking advantage of the resulting confusion, William launched his knights into the thinning enemy ranks and the king was cut down as his army dissolved around him.

Despite the result, the English defence had been well sited, with the flanks and rear protected by woods and the front by the slope that took the momentum out of the cavalry charge. That the struggle lasted 11 hours is a tribute to the English soldier's capacity for resistance. Had the Normans relied solely upon their cavalry the English might have won the battle. However, the Norman's advantage in having a truly balanced combined-arms force and the ability to use each part, including the knights, archers and spearmen, decided the day.

The Anglo-Normans

The conquest of England brought about a melding of the traditions of English infantry and Norman cavalry and archers, as three battles in Normandy show. In 1106, in the civil war battle at Tinchebrai, King Henry I and his brother Duke Robert of Normandy both dismounted their knights to stiffen the infantry. Henry, however, kept a flanking cavalry force, under his vassal Helias of Maine, at some distance from the battlefield. Once the lines were closely engaged, Helias led a flanking force to rout the Norman rebels.

In 1118 at Alençon, Fulk of Anjou made better use of his infantry. He deployed his spearmen and archers to hold off the Norman cavalry, then, when they retired, counter-attacked with his own cavalry. In 1124, at Bourg Théroulde, the royalist commander Odo Borleng formed a core of dismounted knights with wings of archers. Aumary of Montfort's rebel cavalry charged the Norman centre where the banners were, but they were shot down by the archers and repulsed by the main battle. This action could be considered to prefigure in miniature the Battle of Crécy, which was to take place two centuries later.

'The greater part of the English knights, then dismounting, became foot soldiers, a chosen body of whom, interspersed with the archers, were arranged in the front rank. The others mustered with the barons in the centre, near and around the Standard.'

– Richard of Hexham

Back in England a Scottish invasion was met by the bishop of Durham at Northallerton in 1138. The Scots formed up with several 'battles' (divisions) of spearmen, a small mounted force of knights and bodies of wild Galwegians, loose-order bands of enthusiastic warriors. The Anglo-Norman knights dismounted with their *fyrd* (English foot), thereby stiffening its resolve. The archers were interspersed between the knights, protected by them and perhaps retiring through the infantry ranks when the Scots charged. Being unarmoured, the Galwegians made an easy target. They charged, were shot up and then routed. The battle ended in disaster for the Scots.

These battles indicate the tactical flexibility of the Anglo-Normans. It is likely that the verbal transmission of experience and the survival of manuals such as those of Vegetius gave commanders an adequate framework to create varied dispositions. War was the métier of the upper classes; they travelled widely and had, in French, a common language. It would not have been exceptional for a noble in England to have met knights who had fought in France, Spain, southern Italy and Palestine against French, Arab, Byzantine and Turkish armies.

The Battle of Arsuf: 1191

On 8 September 1191, Richard the Lionheart, King of England and crusader, met the forces of Saladin in battle at Arsuf, a small port on the Syrian coast. In truth, this was the culmination of a fortnight of conflict as the crusaders had marched from the recently captured city of Acre. Their eventual goal was Jerusalem, to be reached by the road inland from Jaffa, but in order to achieve it they had to endure constant assaults by the Muslims who were determined that they should not reach it. Although the crusaders in general, and Richard in

A CRUSADER INFANTRY *formation of the 12th century illustrates how the spearmen brace their spears against the ground while sheltering behind shields. The slow-loading crossbowmen then have time to prepare their weapons to drive back any assault. They could even reload in relays, passing the bows forwards to whomever was best placed to shoot.*

particular, are popularly associated with daring cavalry exploits, the king well understood the vital importance of infantry. They provided both protection for the small number of knights and their valuable horses, set behind lines of shielded spearmen, and the ability to strike back against their attackers with bows and crossbows. Only when the enemy were disorganized or weakened by losses were Richard's knights unleashed in a devastating charge. This procedure was a terribly difficult tactic to master, and required the highest quality of generalship.

The warriors of the First Crusade (1096–1099), who arrived in the East a century before Arsuf, had to learn to manage movement through hostile terrain. Their armies were infantry-heavy, while their opponents could muster large numbers of mobile cavalry. Turkish horse-archers were especially dangerous to the Christian knights, as they could shoot down the horses and deprive the crusaders of their crucial weapon: the mounted charge. It is often assumed that all Muslim armies produced such soldiers but they were usually Turks, the Arab cavalry fighting more conventionally with the lance. Muslim rulers valued the horse-bow greatly, though, and recruited light, skirmishing horse-archers. They also created bodyguards of more heavily armed cavalry, known as mamluks, who more often used the bow at the halt, to soften up the enemy for a charge with lance and mace.

In order to counter this threat, crusader commanders had to use their infantry intelligently, in close combination with the cavalry. As a result they developed a formation for the 'fighting march'. This was essentially a box made up of

infantry with spears and missile weapons, drawn up around the cavalry and the baggage. The soldiers of the First Crusade had learnt to do this, perhaps from the Byzantines, and deployed the formation to especially good effect against the Fatimid Egyptians at Ascalon in 1099. Unfortunately, the skills were not passed on to the new arrivals from the West and had to be learnt the hard way. During the Second Crusade (1144-50) the Christians were almost destroyed due to this failing as they crossed Anatolia in 1147. In general, Christians in the Latin Kingdom of Jerusalem were competent in employing the tactic; but their defeat at the Battle of Hattin in 1187 led to Saladin's conquest of all but a few coastal redoubts.

On that occasion, King Guy had been attempting to reach the city of Tiberias on the Sea of Galilee, to raise Saladin's siege of the place. The Muslims, however, managed to separate the horse and foot in a waterless zone and then defeat them separately. This is what Saladin hoped to do against Richard's soldiers of the Third Crusade (1187-92).

'Those whom nature or fortune had made foot soldiers (for many nobles had lost or sold their equipment, and were marching among the crowd) were drawn up at the very rear to oppose with their bows the Turkish arrows.'

– ODO OF DEUIL, *LOUIS VII'S CRUSADE*

The March Begins

In mid-July 1191, King Richard finally engineered the surrender of Acre, a crucial bridgehead for re-supplying the crusader states with men and supplies from the West. All the time the crusaders had been besieging Acre, they had themselves been besieged by Saladin's army. After the city's fall he prevaricated so much about ransoming the Muslim prisoners that eventually, on 22 August, Richard had them executed. Two days later the march south commenced. Immediately, the rearguard, composed of French knights under Duke Hugh of Burgundy, straggled and was nearly cut off and surrounded by the Muslim attackers, but Richard was able to rush to their succour. As a result, from then on the Brother Knights of the Military Orders, the Templars and Hospitallers, were detailed to take it in turns to occupy the dangerous and responsible positions of the vanguard and rearguard. Being under monastic rules, and so used to discipline and taking orders (unlike their secular counterparts), they could be relied upon for this duty.

The main responsibility for defending the line of march fell on the infantry. Numbering some 10,000, they were divided into two wings, with between them the main body of the cavalry (2000 strong) and the baggage. Because the crusaders were marching southwards along the coast, their right flank was covered by the sea. Also, they could be supplied by the crusader fleet whenever the nature of the shoreline allowed it. Richard arranged for the two wings to take turns on a daily basis, one day enduring the constant Muslim assaults, the next marching in relative security along the shore. Saladin may have had as many as 30,000 men under his command, with a proportion of about 2:1 horse to foot. His infantry are described as being 'black', although they are also called Bedouins 'carrying bows and quivers and round shields'. It is possible that they may also have been Sudanese troops, frequently recruited by the rulers of Egypt, also for their archery skills.

Yet it was the horse-archers who most alarmed the crusaders. Ambroise, a minstrel in the crusader ranks, outlines the threat they posed: 'The Turks had one advantage that brought much harm to us. The Christians are heavily armed and the Saracens unarmed, but for a bow, club and a sword or metalled spear or knife. When they are chased after they have such horses – there are none better

RICHARD THE LIONHEART, *king of England, (1189-99), provided the leadership and tactical genius that kept the crusaders in tight formation on the march to Arsuf and led to the defeat of Saladin in battle.*

Battle of Arsuf

1191

The crusader force under the command of Richard the Lionheart attempted to march along the coast of Syria to the town of Arsuf. Leaving the protection of a wood, they had a march of 10km (6 miles) to achieve in a single day - tough, when considering they were under constant attack. In order to protect his troops from the archery of the Muslim cavalry, Richard drew them into a box-like formation. The knights with their precious horses were kept behind a barrier of infantry. Only the Military Orders, possessing excellent discipline, were exposed to risk. The Templars took the vanguard while the Hospitallers covered the rear. Under a burning sun and constant attack by the Muslim horse archers, the crusaders slowly crept towards their goal. Late in the day the Hospitallers' nerve cracked and they launched a charge against their persistent enemy. Richard was able to react swiftly enough to co-ordinate further charges and inflict a signal defeat on his great enemy.

SELJUK SULTANATE OF RUM
SYRIA
ARSUF
JAFFA
SALADIN'S EMIRATE

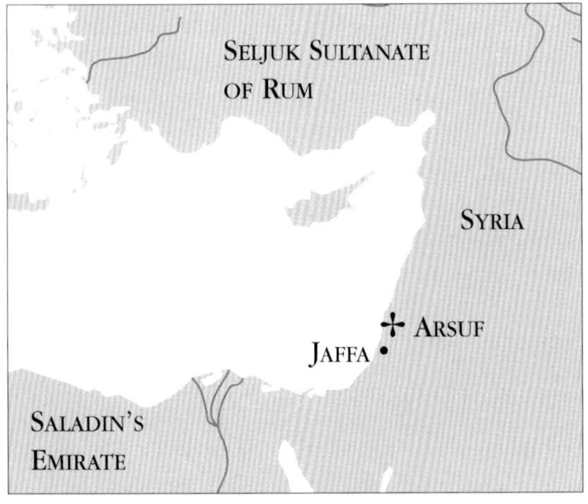

After capturing Acre, Richard the Lionheart advanced along the Syrian coast in order to strike inland to Jerusalem. However, he first had to defeat Saladin in battle.

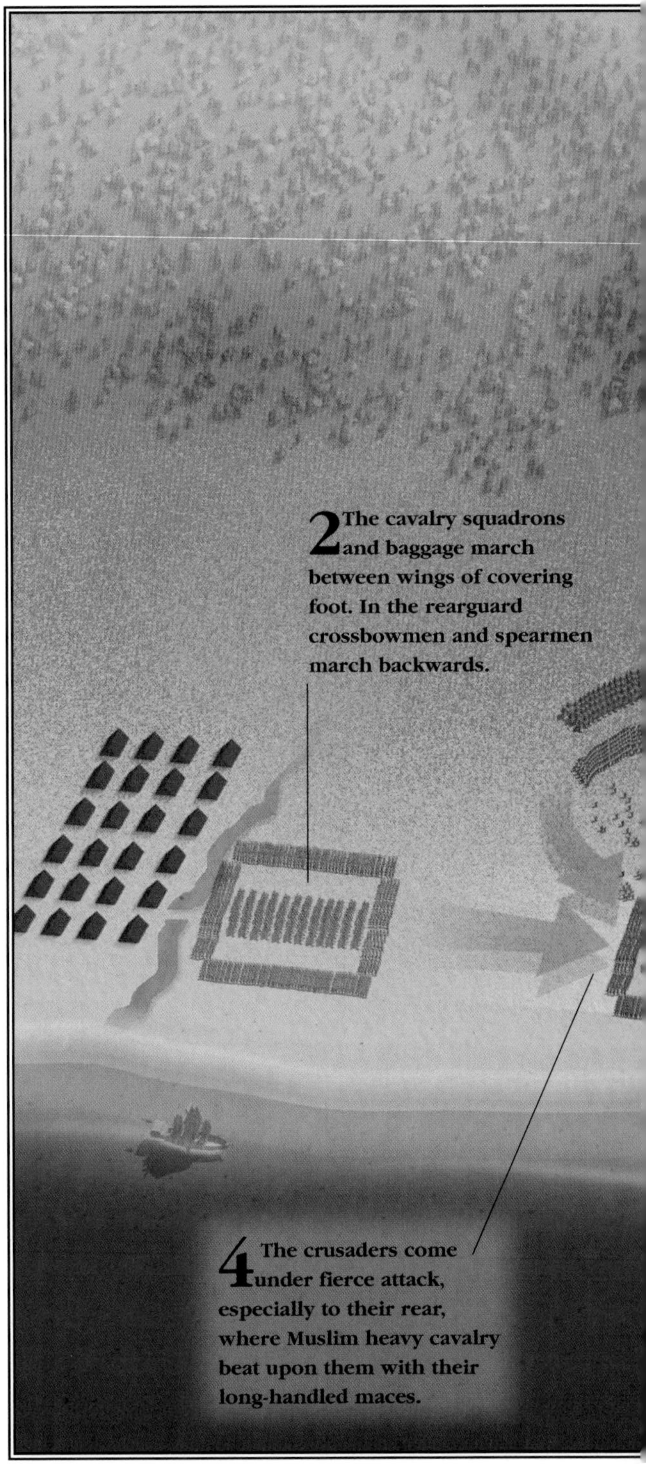

2 The cavalry squadrons and baggage march between wings of covering foot. In the rearguard crossbowmen and spearmen march backwards.
4 The crusaders come under fierce attack, especially to their rear, where Muslim heavy cavalry beat upon them with their long-handled maces.

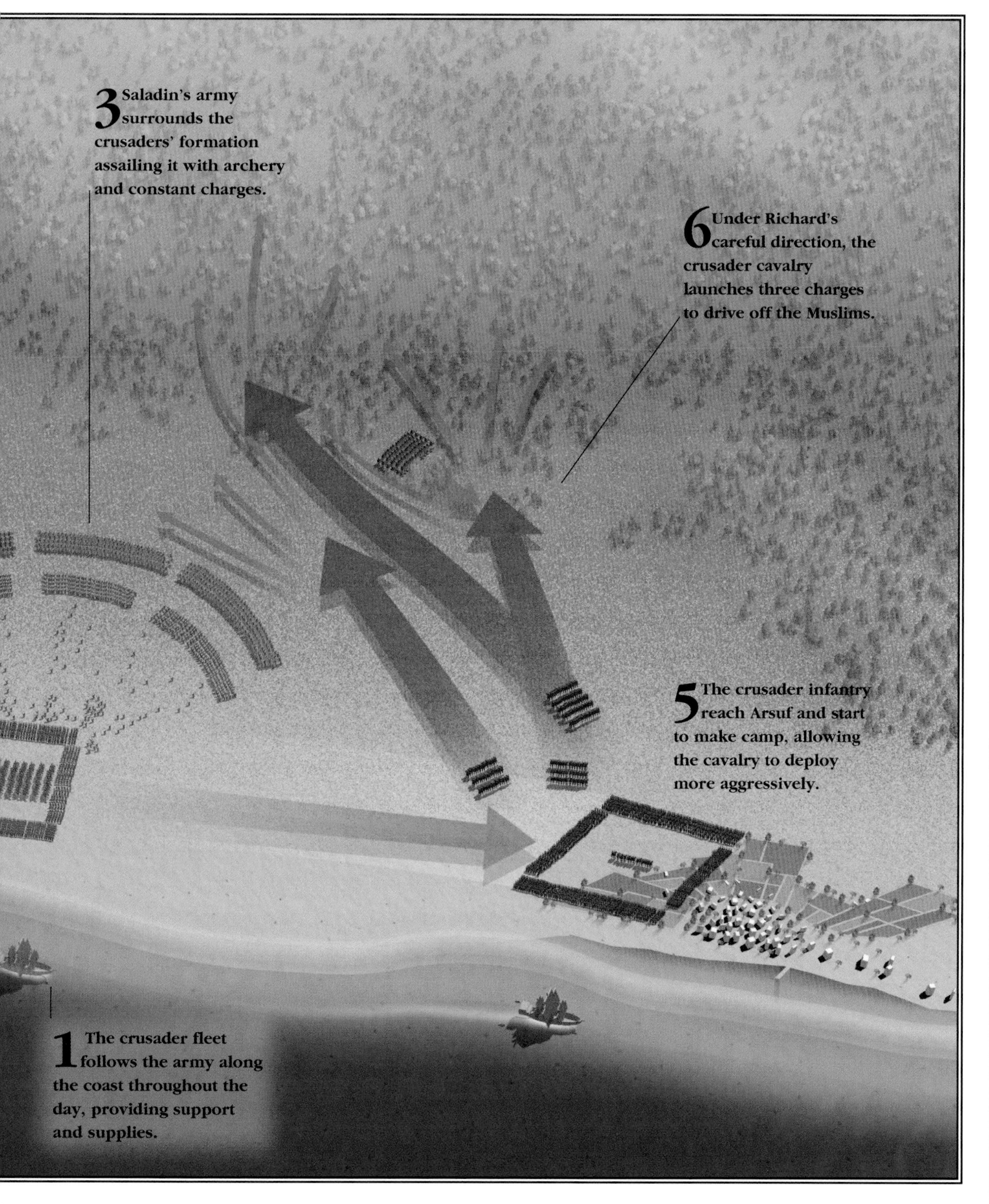
3 Saladin's army surrounds the crusaders' formation assailing it with archery and constant charges.
6 Under Richard's careful direction, the crusader cavalry launches three charges to drive off the Muslims.
5 The crusader infantry reach Arsuf and start to make camp, allowing the cavalry to deploy more aggressively.
1 The crusader fleet follows the army along the coast throughout the day, providing support and supplies.

anywhere in the world – they seem to fly like swallows. When the Turk is followed he cannot be reached. Then he is like a biting fly; when chased he flees; turn back and he pursues you.'

Crusader Foot Soldiers

The *Itinerarium,* another eyewitness account, describes the dangers posed by the Muslim missiles: 'keeping alongside us our army as it advanced, struggling to inflict what it could upon us, firing darts and arrows which flew very thickly, like rain. Alas! Many horses fell dead transfixed with missiles, many were gravely wounded and died much later! You would have seen such a great downpour of darts and arrows that where the army passed through you could not have found a space of four foot of ground without shafts stuck in it.'

In reply the crusader infantry offered dogged resistance: 'They fought with untiring bravery, turning to face the Turkish assault which threatened them from behind. So they walked backwards as if they were retreating, because otherwise they could not protect their backs adequately. In fact, because of the Turkish threat to the rear of the army they advanced with their faces turned back towards them all that day, marching back-to-front, fighting every step of the way.'

'The Frankish cavalry stand together and the infantry form a ring around them with large shields, like a wall. They march step-by-step towards our men, then let forth a pre-arranged cry and the infantry creates an opening for the cavalry to charge out.'

– Beha ad-Din, Life of Saladin

The Muslim commentators were equally impressed by the resilience of the crusader foot. Saladin's secretary, Beha ad-Din, who was also present during the fighting, tells that 'their infantry drawn up in front of the horsemen stood as firm as a wall, and every soldier wore a thick gambeson (padded jacket) and mail hauberks so thick and strong that our arrows had no effect. I saw soldiers with from one to ten arrows sticking in them, still trudging on in their ranks.'

The conditions of the march bore particularly cruelly upon the foot soldiers. The heat often became unbearable for men carrying heavy equipment for long hours. For this reason Richard allowed them to take plenty of rest days to recover from their exertions. It took the crusaders four days to arrive at Caïphas (Haifa) on the other side of the Bay of Acre, a bare 16km (10 miles). 'They stayed there for two days, preparing their equipment. There, they threw away what was of no use and kept what seemed useful. For the foot soldiers, the lesser men, had come with such difficulty, so burdened with food and arms for the battle that a number had to be left behind to die of heat and thirst.'

As the soldiers marched south, 'the army advanced along the sand, in order and at a slow pace for it was excessively hot and the day's journey was long and arduous, not a short one. The heat was so intolerable that some died of it; these were buried at once. There were many who could not go on, worn-out and exhausted, together with the sick and infirm, whom the king, in his wisdom, had carried in the galleys and small boats to the next stage.'

The crusaders pressed on towards Caesarea, which they reached on the last day of August. It still possessed powerful walls, but Muslim raiders had totally destroyed the town. There was nothing to be done but continue the advance, stopping at rivers along the way to provide for the men and horses, dehydrated by the day's march. A thick wood now lay between the crusaders and Arsuf, a march of 10km (6 miles) and itself a mere 16km (10 miles) from Jaffa. Richard was concerned that Muslims would set fire to the trees, making the advance more difficult still.

In fact, Saladin chose not to do this, probably because he had chosen the plain as suitable place to offer battle.

Crusader Dismounted Cavalryman (c.12th century)

Although the crusader cavalry had a vital role in dealing with their Muslim opponents, Turkish archery often deprived them of their mounts. This led to many knights and sergeants serving on foot. The figure shown here represents such an individual. He wears an open-faced helmet rather than a barrel-helm, which allows him to communicate more effectively. He has removed his spurs, which might cause him to stumble, and has cut down his lance to make it easier to handle. He retains his shield and sword, the latter being an important supplementary weapon. Dismounted cavalrymen played a crucial part in stiffening the resolve of their infantry and provided well-armoured protection for the missilemen. During the fighting around Damascus on the Second Crusade (1148) the chronicler William of Tyre describes the German practice of 'dismounting their knights in a crisis', which echoes their ancestors' behaviour in the armies of Julius Caesar and during the invasion period at the end of the Roman Empire.

The Battle

As the crusader army emerged from the forest, Richard took particular care of its formation. He arranged it in five 'battles': vanguard, centre and rearguard with two infantry wings. Not all the mounted squadrons are named, but we are told that the Templars led the way, followed by the Breton and Angevin contingent, King Guy of Jerusalem and his followers, the Normans and English guarding the 'Dragon Standard'. The Hospitallers brought up the rear.

The standard was of especial importance as it was mounted on a cart, flown from the top of a ship's mast. In a formation probably a mile long, and with the air filled with dust from the marchers and the Muslim attack, the standard allowed men to keep their bearings and to be assured that the army was still surviving the fiercest onslaughts.

Saladin launched continuous attacks throughout the day. A mass of cavalry swept down upon the crusader line of march, all in well-ordered squadrons. The constant din of trumpets, tambours and kettle-drums assailed the Christians with almost physical violence. The Muslim squadrons charged, wheeled away and returned to the attack, pressing ever closer on the defenders. Muslim infantry also closed in to skirmish with bows and javelins. The rain of their arrows darkened the sky. At times their armoured cavalry closed to hand-to-hand, beating upon the crusaders with their long-handled maces.

As always, the greatest pressure was on the rearguard, where the Hospitallers were suffering heavily, losing many horses. Their master sent to Richard on several occasions, asking for permission to charge and scatter the Muslims, but Richard forbade an attack. He was waiting until the enemy's horses were exhausted and he could catch them with his slower knights. Not until the signal for the charge was given – two trumpet blasts in the van, centre and rear of the army – were the crusaders to react. As the day wore on, the heat, dust and constant noise of the Muslim trumpets and drums, together with growing casualties, especially among the horses, began to erode the crusaders' patience. They had advanced possibly 3.2km (2 miles) in as many hours.

Although contemporary sources concentrate upon the actions of the leaders and of the knights, the social elite, the role of the infantry in protecting the cavalry and shooting back at the attackers was crucial.

The Hospitallers in the rearguard found themselves forced back upon the French squadrons in front of them, which threatened to disrupt the crusader formation. In addition, their master felt that he could no longer bear the dishonour of suffering without striking back. Together with another knight, Baldwin of Carew, he launched a charge. The rest of the Hospitallers and some French squadrons chased after them.

This rebellious action was not the disaster that it might have been, because it anticipated Richard's orders by only a short time. Either that or Richard reacted very quickly to the circumstances. As his vanguard reached the gardens and orchards that surrounded Arsuf, Beha al-Din reports: 'I myself saw their knights gather together in the middle of their infantry; they grasped their lances, shouted their war-cry like one man, the infantry opened out, and they rushed through in one great charge in all directions – some on our right wing, some on our left and some on our centre, till all was broken.'

The crusaders pursued the fleeing enemy for a mile. This was the most dangerous moment for them. They were separated from the supporting infantry, while Muslim tactics depended upon their superior ability to rally and return to the attack on knights riding blown horses and in disorder. Richard's discipline held, however. The English and the Normans with the Standard had advanced cautiously in reserve, so that the attacking squadrons were able to fall back and reform upon them. Arsuf is often described as if one charge decided the day; but this is not true. The crusaders charged twice more.

First they had to respond to the counter-attack led by Saladin's bodyguard of 700 cavalry, clad in the traditional yellow of Muslim household troops. After a fierce fight even these elite warriors were driven off. Meanwhile the crusader infantry had reached Arsuf and immediately began pitching tents. The camp provided a secure base from which to charge out. In response to the last attack on his rearguard,

Richard led a third charge and swept the enemy cavalry right back to the top of the wooded hills overlooking the plain.

His cavalry did not pursue further for fear of ambush. Crusader sources claim that they found 7000 enemy corpses on the battlefield, including 32 emirs. Despite this, the Muslims returned the very next day with harassing tactics. Yet, by careful combination of horse and foot, Richard had proved that he could not be denied his goal of capturing the town. Infantry are very often written out of accounts of medieval battles; but here they proved their worth for all to see.

Light Infantry

There were several different categories of medieval infantry, of which light infantry were critically important to tactical flexibility. Light infantry could be found in several different types.

Bidauts

'From Navarre and from Spain came the *bidauts*, armed with two javelins and a spear, as well as a *coutel* (large knife) at their belt; they wear no armour' (*Guiart*). The Pyrenean foothills of southern France were a natural source of light infantry, called *bidauts* or *cotereaux*. They were famous for their savagery and had a fearsome reputation for ravaging, which was considered a valid strategic option for a medieval army trying to bring an opponent to battle.

At Courtrai in 1302, javelin-armed *bidauts* began the battle by advancing with the French crossbowmen. Withdrawing as the knights charged home, the *bidauts* then re-appeared in support of their cavalry, now engaged with the Flemish infantry line, by throwing their javelins,

WELSH SOLDIERS WERE *recruited in large numbers in the 1280s by Edward I, king of England (1272–1308), after he had conquered Wales. From the north came spearmen, with archers coming from the south. The latter were the original longbowmen, who made English armies so feared in the 14th and 15th centuries.*

Almogavar Light Infantryman

The mountainous regions of Iberia produced a type of light javelinman capable of swift raids and withdrawals and also of fighting in the battle line. He looks lightly armoured, but this almogavar *from Catalonia, in eastern Spain, was a fearsome fighter. Armed with javelins and a knife-like butcher's cleaver, an* almogavar *could take on any infantry of his era. Recruited as mercenaries for the Byzantine Empire in 1302, within a few years they had carved out a state for themselves based on Athens. In 1311, they even defeated the chivalry of Frankish Greece by using marshy terrain, which rendered the knights' charge ineffective and left them floundering, at the mercy of their nimble opponents.*

The Catalan chronicler Ramon Muntaner describes an individual combat between a almogavar and a French knight during the Sicily campaign. As the horseman charged, the almogavar, showing immense bravery, stood his ground. He hurled his heavy javelin into the horse's chest, bringing down the knight, who was then at the mercy of the infantryman's butcher's blade.

stabbing at the enemy pikemen and no doubt rescuing individual knights in trouble.

Almogavars

The Muslim conquest of Spain stopped short of the Pyrenees, probably because hill country did not suit the Arabs' mobile style of warfare. The resurgence of the Christian states in the north led to the creation of a society on a permanent war footing: the towns provided militias of foot and horse, military orders of knights based in great castles and, in the kingdom of Aragon, the almogavars. The last were a breed of aggressive light infantry who were shepherds, bandits and raiders of the Muslim kingdoms by turn. The almogavars developed in the ninth and tenth centuries as the Christians pushed south into the depopulated border lands.

Almogavars wore an open-work iron helmet, a sleeveless sheepskin jacket, the *abarca* (a tunic) and light but tough sandals. They carried a short spear, the *azcona*, javelins that could pierce armour and a knife, the *colltell*, which has been reconstructed as a combination of knife and butcher's cleaver. It was very heavy and wide but had a sharp point. The almogavar relied upon his mobility to deal with armoured opponents, throwing his javelins, stabbing at the horses with the *azcona* and cleaving through armoured joints with the colltell. The Catalan chronicler Ramon Muntaner records that one man 'gave such a cut...to a French knight that the greave with the leg came off in one piece and besides it entered half a palm into the horse's flank.' As the enemy grew close they clashed their weapons together and chanted '*Aur! Aur! Desperta Ferra*!' (Listen! Listen! The iron awakes!).

In the 1280s, the crown of Aragon, frustrated by the growth of Castilian territory which reduced its own options for expansion in Iberia, attacked Angevin French Sicily. There the almogavars won a reputation against French knights who were surprised how deadly such lightly equipped adversaries 'wearing only shirts' could be.

At the conclusion of the Italian campaign of 1302, the Byzantine emperor, Andronikos II, hired them to fight against the Turks. The almogavars duly performed, being especially effective at fighting in towns. The Byzantines' failure to pay the 'Catalan Company' led to a rebellion in which the 8000 almogavars and their allies set up on their own and ravaged the empire.

'The almogavars hurled their javelins so it was the Devil's work they did, for at the first charge more than a hundred knights and horses of the French fell dead to the ground. Then they broke their lances short and disembowelled the horses.'

— *Muntaner*, Catalan Chronicle

In 1311, the Company fell out with another employer, the Frankish duke of Athens, which led to the Battle of Kephissos. The Athenian duke brought together a coalition of 6000 knights and 8000 foot soldiers. Outnumbered, the Catalan Company occupied a hill behind the valley of the River Kephissos, which they had previously dammed to convert their front into a marsh. The knights charged, but were disordered by the marsh, and failed to break the Catalans.

The almogavars then counter-attacked, their lightly armed footmen infiltrating the ranks of mired horses to massacre the heavily armoured riders. The wily Catalans had played to the arrogant weakness of the Franks who did not have the patience to use their missile-armed foot soldiers to weaken their enemy, but could only see before them a tempting target for the charge. The resultant surprise, brought about by the almogavars' sheer aggression, psychologically unbalanced their foes. This, however, was no 'infantry revolution', but simply the crafty response of highly professional mercenaries who had extensive experience facing off Arab cavalry in their homeland, the Turks in Anatolia and against similar knightly armies in Sicily.

The Frisians

The Frisians were a Teutonic people who occupied coast lands of north-west Europe. In their marshes and dunes they formed another 'frontier' society and were, suitably for their location, adept at naval warfare. According to Matthew Paris they were: 'armed with javelins which they call *gaveloches*, in the use of which they are very expert and with Danish axes and long spears. They wear linen jackets with light armour'. In the winter of 1256, a group of Frisians ambushed William of Holland and his household in marshland. William was in armour and his horse was wearing a mail caparison, so he crashed through the ice and was rendered completely helpless. His companions fled and the Frisians 'attacked him on all sides with their javelins. He offered his murderers an immense ransom for his life but these inhuman men, showing no mercy, cut him to pieces.'

Warfare between the infantry and the knights was frequently very bloody. The knights lived in the chivalric world where laws limited war and a beaten opponent might surrender and become a valuable asset for ransom. The infantry were of no such value, and war involving them frequently incurred high casualties, with no quarter given or taken in the massacre of the defeated.

> *'Above the front ranks, the wall of pikes and* goedendags *gleam in the sunlight. Whoever has seen the Flemings so deployed can say that they are animated by great pride. Their commanders continually repeat that they must keep the packed ranks tightly closed. They must not let anyone penetrate them.'*
>
> – *Guillaume Guiart, French chronicler*

Courtrai: 1302

The Flemish victory over the French at Courtrai in 1302 provides a good check list of the actions necessary for traditional medieval infantry to combat a knightly army.

1. Protect the rear. The Flemings were besieging Courtrai castle which contained a French garrison. When the French knights charged the Flemish battle line the garrison sortied-out, but were repulsed by the crossbows and spears of the men of Ypres. At other battles, such as Mons-en-Pévèle (1304), a garrisoned screen of wagons was placed to the rear to prevent the more mobile knights outflanking the Flemish line. When the Flemings advanced they formed 'crown' formations capable of halting and presenting an all-round defence like the Scottish schiltrons of spearmen.

2. Protect the flanks. At Courtrai, the marshy River Lys provided an anchor to the Flemish flanks so that they could not be turned.

3. Make the front difficult of access. The Groenig Brook and the Grote Beek, both swampy declivities, provided obstacles that slowed and disordered the knightly charge, so that they arrived at the Flemish line without the impetus necessary to break through.

4. Be uphill. From the brooks the land rises to the town, bestowing an advantage on foot soldiers combating knights.

5. Form a reserve. Jan van Renesse had a reserve body of men, possibly the dismounted knights of Zeeland, whom he was able to bring to the relief of the men of Bruges when they were being bodily pushed back, which was the crisis of the battle. The reserve would ideally include mounted troops who could follow up the defeated enemy, but the Flemings lacked sufficient knights to do this.

6. Provide a skirmish screen. This was to prevent the enemy thinning the ranks of the close-order infantry by missile assault. Robert of Artois sent his French crossbowmen forwards to weaken the Flemings. However, the Flemish crossbowmen were deployed in front of their spears and were able to keep the French at a distance until they had run out of ammunition.

7. Ensure good order. The Flemings fought in contingents by town and guild. Their clothing was uniform and each guild had its banner so each man knew his station, and they learnt a battle cry to distinguish friend from foe. The pikemen and *goedendag* men (the *goedendag* was a heavy two-handed club with a single spike at the point) knew how to work together. The pikemen rested the butts of their weapons on the ground to form a hedge the knights could not break; the *goedendag* man struck the knights and their mounts once they were halted.

8. Keep the line intact. Jan van Renesse advised: 'Do not let the enemy break through your ranks. Do not be frightened. Kill both horse and man. "Flanders, the Lion" is our battle cry.... Every man who penetrates into your ranks or breaks through them shall remain there dead'.

9. Dismount the leaders. The Flemish princes, Guy de Namur and Wilhelm van Jülich, both dismounted with their bodyguards and banners and took position in the front rank. Showing that the leaders could not run away (nor do a deal with the French to abandon the common soldiers) provided a crucial boost to morale and an addition to fighting power.

10. Stiffen morale. Before the battle the commanders made speeches to their troops with fighting instructions and a reminder of their cause. Soldiers were enjoined to kill any of their own side who broke ranks to loot the rich corpses of French knights, for that imperilled the good order and safety of all. Guy de Namur knighted more than 30 of the leaders of the common people, thus elevating the representatives of the artisan army. Before the battle all were confessed of their sins and ensured of a path to heaven, for if they died it was in a righteous cause.

11. Pursue rigorously. Despite being on foot, the Flemish commanders (who were mainly knights) sensed when the last French reserve had failed in its attack and ordered an immediate pursuit. The infantry hurled themselves at the downed knights, slaughtering them and preventing the French cavalry from reforming. They pushed on, routing any remaining opposition, seizing the French camp and plundering it. The Flemings named Courtrai the 'Battle of the Golden Spurs' because of the thousand symbols of knighthood they won.

SCOTTISH PIKEMEN AROUND *the year* 1300 *were armed very simply, with minimal armour often consisting of little more than a leather helmet and shield. Many would not even have had helmets. But when tightly packed together in* schiltron *formation, they proved capable defeating the English heavy cavalry charges.*

Bannockburn: 1314

When King Edward I came to the throne in 1272, he was already an experienced soldier, blooded on crusade in the Holy Land. He proved to be one of the greatest of England's warrior kings, conqueror of the Welsh and 'Hammer of the Scots'. Under his leadership English forces began to take on the shape which they would have for the next two centuries. Edward's experience in the Welsh wars (1277-83, 1294-95) convinced him of the value of archers, which he raised in great numbers from all over his kingdom. The human resources of England completely outmatched those of Scotland.

The English invasion of Scotland in 1296 could not be opposed, but then Edward was drawn off to fight the French. A minor Scottish nobleman, William Wallace, was elected Guardian of the Kingdom, raised troops and defeated the remaining English at Stirling Bridge (1297). This victory was achieved by what was effectively an ambush, as Wallace tempted the over-confident English cavalry across a narrow causeway and then overwhelmed them with his pikemen as they attempted to deploy. The limitations of Scottish tactics were exposed at Falkirk in 1298. The Scottish formations would have been recognizable to the Picts of half a millennium earlier: massed pikes with sword and targe men, and others carrying axes and bills.

The warriors were largely unarmoured, although the front-rank pikemen wore small round helmets and the cheapest form of armour, a padded tunic known as the 'jack'. They were also weak in cavalry. Edward mustered 3000 men-at-arms and 20,000 foot soldiers for the campaign. His cavalry drove off the Scottish horse allowing his missilemen - crossbowmen and archers - to shoot down the immobile schiltrons, shield-shaped formations of foot soldiers armed with spear and axe. As the Scottish forces began to falter, the English cavalry rode in to disperse them. The result was a massacre.

It began to look as if there was no way that the Scots could oppose the English in the field. The defeat of the French by the Flemings at Courtrai in 1302 deprived the Scots of outside support, prompting prominent noblemen such as Robert Bruce to offer their submission. In 1304, Edward took the strategically crucial castle at Stirling and the opposition appeared routed.

Robert Bruce, outlawed for murdering a rival to the throne, resorted to guerrilla warfare. Establishing his authority over the Scots in 1307 at Loudoun Hill (the same year as Edward died), he wore down the English by raids and capturing isolated castles. Edward II lacked his father's military talents. His invasion of 1310 achieved nothing due to Bruce's strategy of avoidance. By 1314, the situation was critical, as the Scots were besieging Stirling, and the king was obliged to relieve the castle.

In March 1314, Edward mustered 2500 cavalry and over 20,000 foot raised from Wales, the Midlands and the northern counties. It is likely that his infantry was considerably reduced in number by midsummer, the date by which he had pledged to relieve Stirling. This can be inferred from the previous campaigns of his father when, because the foot soldiers were not obliged to serve for long periods, they often could not be kept on campaign, even deserting in numbers inconceivable in a modern army. Also, many may have been raw troops. There was undoubtedly a core of good foot soldiers; for example the 3000 recruited in Wales including 1000 archers. In total, there were around 12,000 infantry, about half of whom were archers. In combination with over 2000 men-at-arms, this was still a formidable force. Opposing them, Robert Bruce could only muster a handful of heavy cavalry, some 300 light horse and up to 10,000 foot soldiers of the types already described. They also seem to have been weak in archers, which was a serious disability in the face of the massive English superiority in this arm. How was King Robert to avoid repeating the massacre at Falkirk, 16 years earlier?

He could not afford to allow Edward to relieve the castle, because this would seriously undermine his authority and hand the strategic initiative to the English. So he had to be inventive with the resources which he had to hand. A great advantage to the Scots proved to be the terrain which the English had to traverse to reach Stirling from the south. Known as 'the Carse', this was an area of boggy ground intersected by streams and with numbers of peaty pools. The only solid ground was

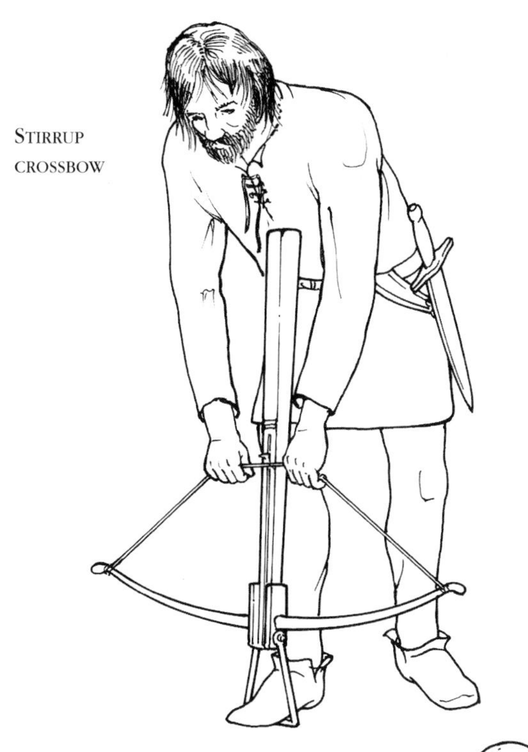

associated with the Roman road from Falkirk to Stirling. This crossed the Bannock Burn (stream) 5km (3 miles) south of the town. The terrain was further restricted by woods to either side of the road. If the English wished to avoid them then they had move to the right flank. Here the land was extremely marshy due to the tidal waters of the River Forth, although there was a route significantly known as the Dryfield Way which could be used to outflank the Scottish position.

The First Day

The Dryfield Way may not have been known to the English initially, for on 23 June their advance guard rode straight down the Roman road to ford the Bannock Burn. Here King Robert had taken the precaution of having potholes dug. These *pottis* were a foot in diameter and knee deep, containing a wooden stake and concealed from view. Such defences had been known since Roman times as

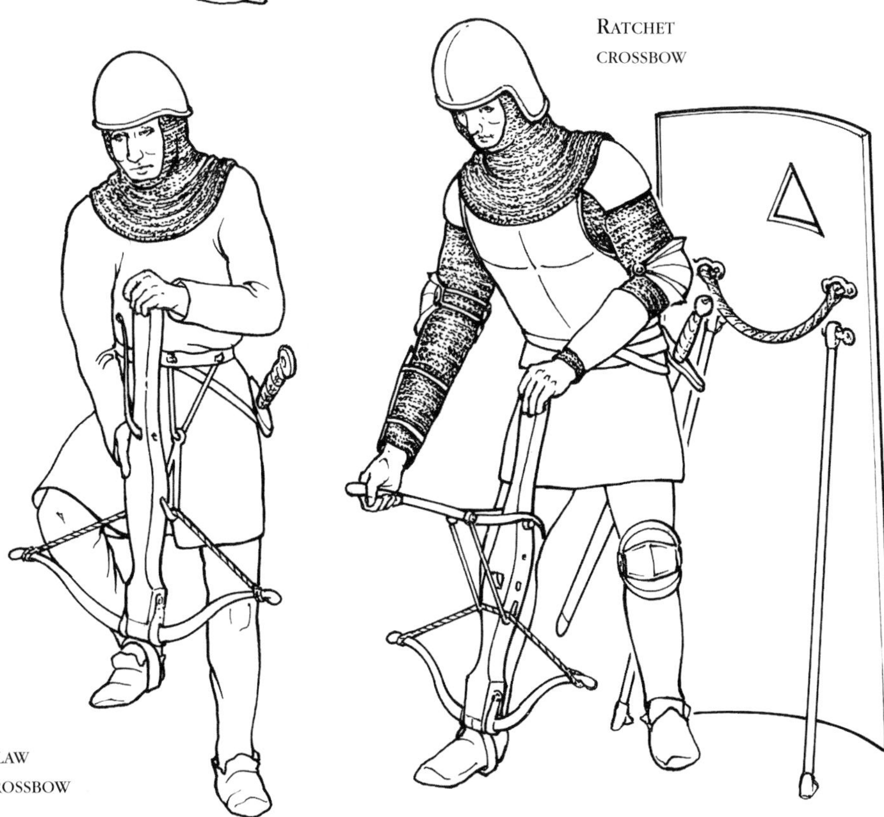

SPANNING THE CROSSBOW. *Top: c.1200. Hand-drawn bow, with the foot placed in the stirrup. Far left: c.1300. 'Claw' hanging from the belt makes the loading swifter and easier. Left: c.1500. Ratchet device allows the development of much more powerful steel bows with ranges of 400 metres (450 yards).*

Battle of Bannockburn

1314

The day before the beginning of the battle the Scots held the English attacks by defending the Bannock Burn creek and digging potholes to thwart the enemy cavalry. At night the English attempted a flank march, but on unsuitable terrain. Streams, marsh and a steep escarpment prevented the English forces from deploying their combination of heavily-armed and armoured knightly cavalry and foot archers to best effect. On the day of the main battle they were huddled in some confusion in a disadvantageous position, with their backs towards the Bannock Burn. This allowed King Robert to advance with his *schiltrons* of spearmen and swiftly crush them, before they had time to form into an effective formation. He also sent his small force of cavalry to destroy a potentially dangerous flanking movement by some English archers. King Edward's English could go neither forwards nor back and were overwhelmed, with many dead and captured.

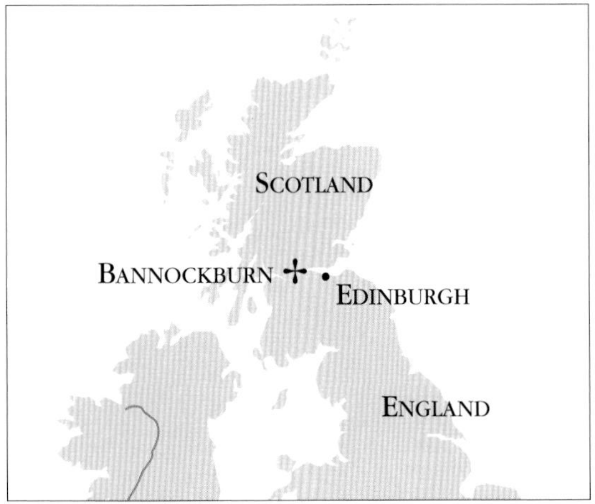

Bannockburn lies just to the south-west of Stirling Castle, a position which is strategically crucial in Scotland. The Battle of Bannockburn was fought over possession of the castle.

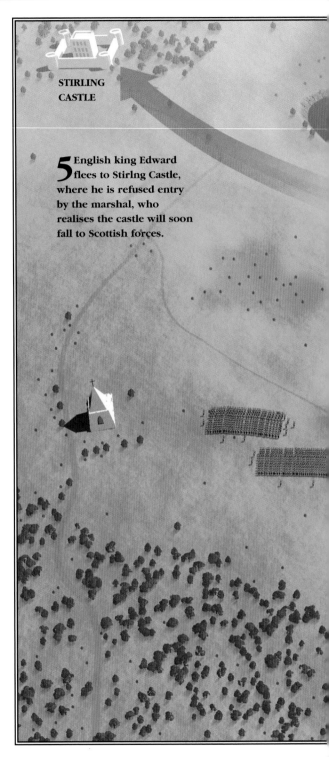

STIRLING CASTLE

5 English king Edward flees to Stirlng Castle, where he is refused entry by the marshal, who realises the castle will soon fall to Scottish forces.

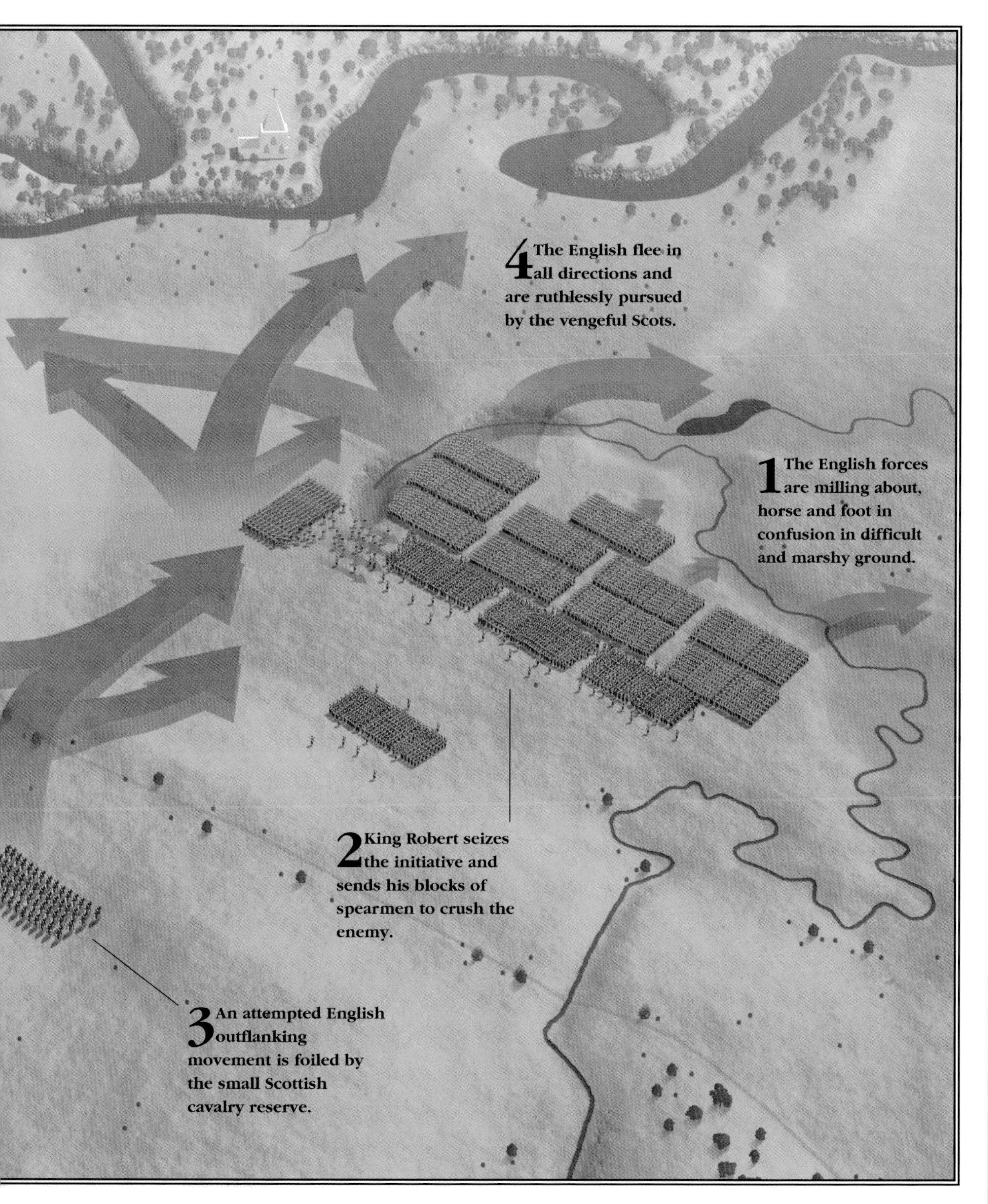
4 The English flee in all directions and are ruthlessly pursued by the vengeful Scots.
1 The English forces are milling about, horse and foot in confusion in difficult and marshy ground.
2 King Robert seizes the initiative and sends his blocks of spearmen to crush the enemy.
3 An attempted English outflanking movement is foiled by the small Scottish cavalry reserve.

'wolf-traps' and were deadly to cavalry. They were spread over the whole area of the 'open field beside the road, where he thought the English would have to go if they wanted to move...to the castle'. Unperturbed, the English cavalry rode to force the ford. Foremost was Henry de Bohun, who found himself engaged in a duel with the king himself.

This ended swiftly and to the Englishman's disadvantage. As he charged Robert with levelled lance, the king jinked his horse, ducked the blow and smashed his opponent with a battle-axe. Meanwhile, the Scots foot were running to take up defensive positions. The heroic actions of their leader must have served to bolster their morale. They too had a crucial role to play, though, for Sir Robert Clifford led 300 cavalry across the stream and on to the potholed plain beyond in an attempt to reach Stirling castle. The available Scottish foot, perhaps only 500-strong, drew up in schiltron to prevent this manoeuvre. The odds were considerably in the favour of the horsemen, but the steel-tipped row of pikes served to keep them at bay, and several notable knights were killed trying to break open the formation. Without the support of their archers, who were far behind with the main body of the English army, the cavalry were impotent against determined foot. The high morale of the Scots, no doubt boosted by King Robert's gallant exploit, prevented the English vanguard from achieving their objective cheaply. As night fell, King Edward and the bulk of his army reached the field, but it was too late to attempt further assaults.

That night was difficult for both armies. On the Scottish side, Robert, whose whole strategy had been built upon avoiding battle before then, had to decide whether to risk battle in open field. The English possessed superior numbers, better armoured troops and the deadly weapon of their archery, which had destroyed Wallace's army at Falkirk. Clearly, King Robert would be gambling everything he had won since his coronation, probably the entire Scottish army as well as his life, if he was to offer battle the next day.

The English, though, were in terrible disarray. They had force-marched over the last few days to meet the midsummer deadline at Stirling, and now found themselves with only a bog to set up camp in. Men and animals needed clean water, so the cavalry crossed the Bannock Burn to find it, while many of the infantry remained on the other side. It is possible that the English attempted some kind of manoeuvre around the Scots' left flank; but this may have been just the result of the army spreading out for the night. Crucially, the mounted men-at-arms seem to have become separated from their supporting infantry. Robert was made aware of the English disorder by a Scottish knight in English service, Sir Alexander Seton. He came over to the Scots and made it known that the English were tired, disorganized, dispirited and poorly led. Armed with this information, King Robert decided on a bold strategy. He would attack the following morning at first light.

'The English cavalry squadrons being thrown into confusion by the thrust of pikes upon the horse, began to flee. King Edward's bodyguard, observing this disaster, led him away from the field towards Stirling castle, although he was loathe to leave.'

– *Sir Thomas Gray,* Scalachronica

The Second Day

Dawn comes early in the summer in Scotland, so at just after 3AM the Scots began to move forward against the English, who were camped in uneven groupings around the Bannock Burn. The cavalry seem to have gathered in the Dryfield, north of the stream, while the bulk of the infantry were south and east of it in the bogs and marshes of the Carse of Balquiderock.

Indeed, it is uncertain whether the bulk of the fighting took place on the Stirling side of the

Bannock Burn, or on the far side. For the latter to have been the case it would have been necessary for the schiltrons to cross the stream and re-form on the far side. The truly remarkable event, in the eyes of contemporaries, was that foot soldiers dared attack fully-equipped knights and men-at-arms. According to Sir Thomas Grey, an English eyewitness of the battle (who had been captured in the first day's fighting):

'The Scots resolved to fight, and at sunrise marched out of the woods in three divisions of infantry. They directed their course boldly upon the English army, which had been under arms all night, with their horses bitted. The English mounted in great alarm, for they were not accustomed to dismount to fight on foot; whereas the Scots had a taken a lesson from the Flemings who before that at Courtrai defeated on foot the power of France. The Scots came on in line of schiltrons and attacked the English column, which were jammed together and could not operate against the enemy so direfully were their horses impaled upon the pikes. The troops in the English rear fell back upon the ditch of Bannock Burn, tumbling one over the other.'

As to the English archers, the *Lanercost Chronicle* records that they 'were thrown forward before the line and the Scottish archers engaged them, a few being killed and wounded on either side but the King of England's archers quickly put

KING ROBERT BRUCE'S *relationship with his peasant spearmen is captured in this Victorian engaving. Much less well armoured than their English opponents, they possessed the morale and the weaponry to overwhelm their enemy.*

the others to flight.' This success seems to have had little impact on the rest of the fighting. Although, Barbour's Bruce does assert that a number of English archers were able to shoot into the melee from the flanks and that 'they shot so fast that if their shooting had persisted it would have gone hard for the Scots'. Some sources suggest that the small force of Scottish cavalry, 350 men, may have been instrumental in charging and dispersing this threat.

For the main part, though, the English cavalry seems to have fought unsupported, allowing the Scots to repeat their success of the first day. On this occasion, though, the mounted men had nowhere to escape to as they were pinned on the banks of the stream and the marshy ground. The schiltrons advanced, probably in wedge formation, remorselessly, driving the knights before them. Another, possibly legendary, tale has the 'small folk' - the horse-boys and camp followers - appearing in the Scottish rear, convincing the English that reinforcements had arrived and encouraging more to flee. The Scots pressed so hard upon the English that they almost captured King Edward. Some grasped the caparison of his horse, but he lashed out with this mace and drove them away. His horse was killed, and his shield bearer, Sir Roger Northburgh, was brought down and captured. The king owed his safety to Giles d'Argentan, Earl of Pembroke, who escorted the royal entourage towards Stirling castle.

Then, unable to bear the shame of flight, d'Argentan returned to the fray, where he was killed. Edward was refused entry to Stirling by its castellan, Sir Philip Moubray, who rightly guessed that the castle would fall as a result of the battle, leaving the king in Scottish hands and liable to a huge ransom. So Edward scuttled from the scene of the disaster, his army wrecked. According to Barbour's Bruce, the Bannock Burn was so choked with bodies that it could be crossed dry-shod by the victorious Scots.

> *'The Scots did not flee, densely drawn up against English attack, under shining helmets and behind their shields, they withstood the arrows of the English at the beginning of the battle; but the first line of armed men were greeted with fatal blows.'*
>
> — *Geoffrey le Baker, Chronicler*

Robert Bruce's victory set a moral superiority over the English in warfare for the rest of his reign. He never risked a large encounter again, but did defeat English forces in battle in 1319 and 1322. On the latter occasion, Edward led a large force towards Edinburgh, but Robert pursued a scorched-earth policy, withdrawing before him. As a result the English army began to starve and was forced to withdraw southward. The Scots followed with a largely mounted raiding force. Catching up with the English rearguard in north Yorkshire, near Rievaulx Abbey at Old Byland, Robert dismounted his men and charged uphill. The English were caught off guard and routed. Once again Edward was nearly captured and lost his personal treasure.

Apart from this, Robert largely restricted his activities to raiding. In 1327 he humiliated the large force brought to Scotland by the teenage Edward III by avoiding battle and watching the English army fall apart for want of supplies in appalling weather conditions. Apparently, Robert's deathbed advice to his son, David, was to avoid battle with the English in the open field and stick to the 'small war' of raiding.

Unfortunately, neither the young prince nor his guardians heeded the advice. A revitalized English army under Edward III, combining archers and dismounted men-at-arms to maximum effect, inflicted a series of defeats upon the Scots in the 1330s. Finally, in 1346 at Neville's Cross, just outside Durham, King David himself was captured after a fruitless assault on the northern levies. The Scots proved unable to overcome the 'English System' for as long as it endured.

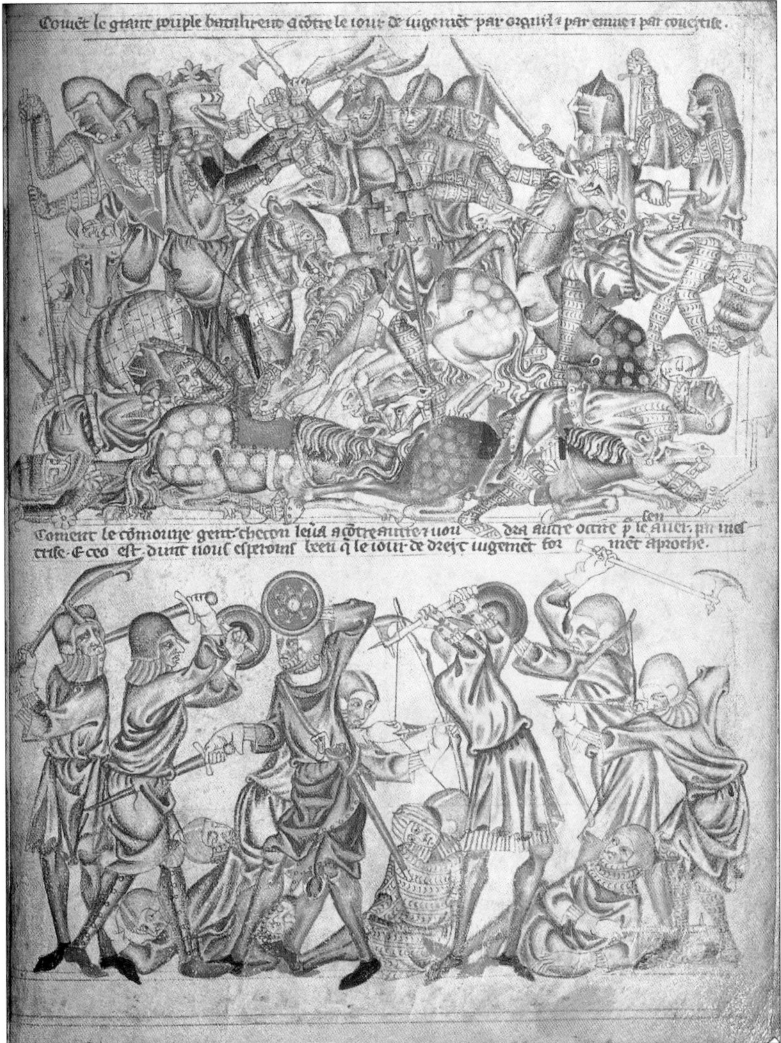

HOLKAM PICTURE BIBLE *(mid 14th c.) half-page entitled, 'How the lower classes fight'. As well as a range of swords and pole-arms, the archers' bows are accurately represented as thick and knotty staves.*

The Battle of Bannock Burn did prove, though, that an infantry army, well led, could overcome even the best opposition of its day. The message sent out by infantry victories of Courtrai and Bannock Burn was that the chivalric classes should not take their superiority in war for granted. Indeed, they were forced to turn to their own foot soldiers - the redoubtable longbowmen - to restore it.

Tactical Developments During the Hundred Years' War

Despite their signal defeat at Bannock Burn, the English continued to develop the use of archery in battle. Bannock Burn's outcome had shown that it was difficult to combine missile infantry with cavalry charges if the enemy acted aggressively. So, in the fourteenth century, archers were used in combination with dismounted men-at-arms. A series of encounters showed how the system was perfected. The first occasion was against the Scots in 1332. Claimant to the throne, Edward Baliol, leading a few hundred exiles, landed near Perth, where they were attacked by a much larger Scottish force. They defended a natural defile with archers on the flanks and their men-at-arms at the end, with a small force of cavalry in reserve. Over-confidently, the Scots advanced on foot, and after initial success from weight of numbers, found themselves hemmed in and overwhelmed by arrows. The result was a massacre. Several thousand of them died, including leading nobles.

In 1333, the English repeated the medicine at Halidon Hill. This was a much more significant and symbolic occasion, for the Scots had promised to raise the siege of Berwick by a certain day. King Edward III led several hundred men-at-arms and several thousand archers to a position on the hill a couple of miles north of the town. Again the Scots seem to have had superior numbers, but again they attacked on foot in clumsy masses, their schiltrons of pikemen supported by dismounted men-at-arms. The English were deployed in three divisions ('battles') with archers flanking the

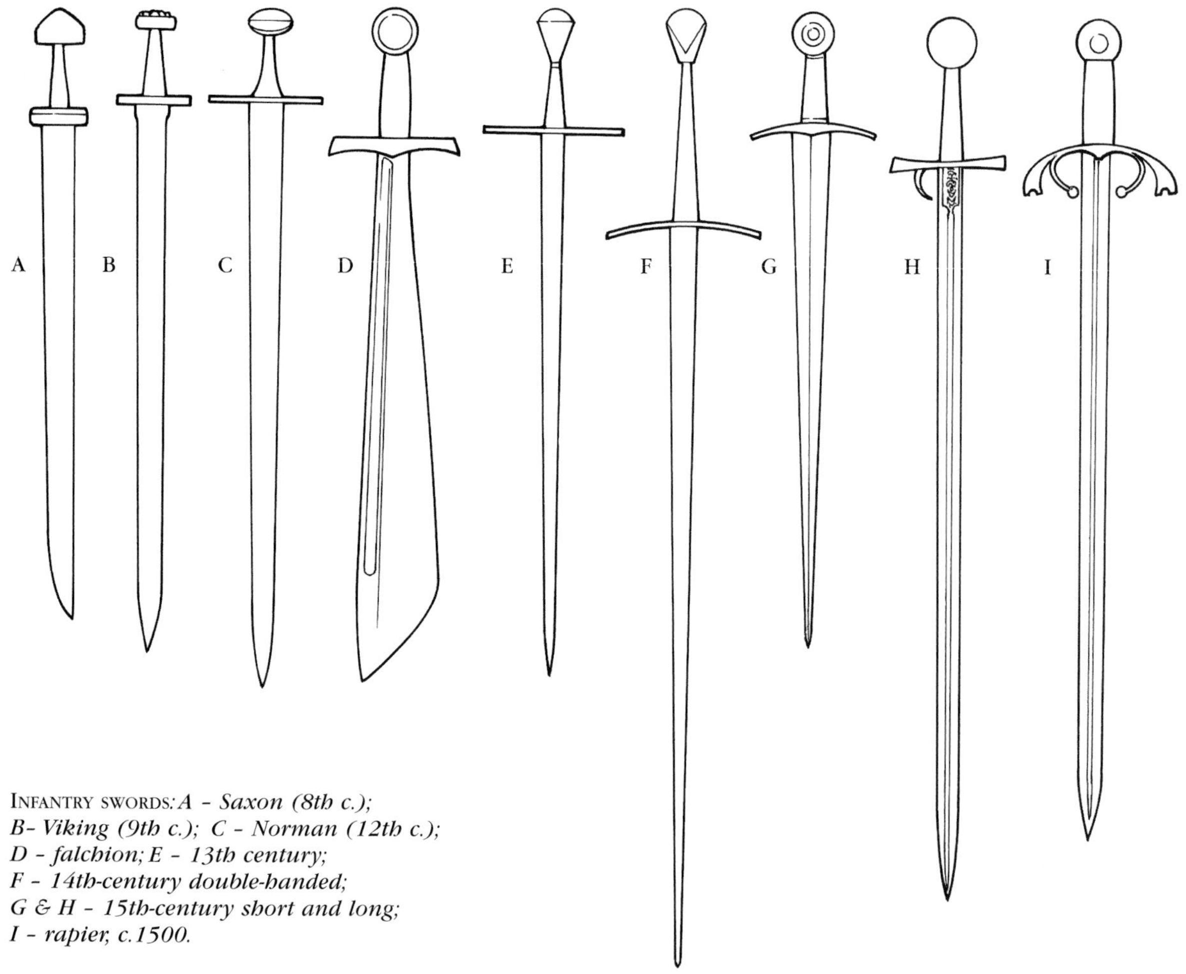

INFANTRY SWORDS: *A - Saxon (8th c.); B- Viking (9th c.); C - Norman (12th c.); D - falchion; E - 13th century; F - 14th-century double-handed; G & H - 15th-century short and long; I - rapier, c.1500.*

dismounted men-at-arms. The hill was steep and the ground boggy, which slowed the Scottish advance while the arrows fell as thick as 'dust in a sunbeam'. While their men-at-arms were fought to a standstill, the unarmoured men in the rear ranks suffered from the arrow storm. Eventually the lead division gave way, taking the other two with it and the English launched a bloody pursuit.

The outbreak of the Hundred Years' War (1338–1453) with France, meant that the 'English System' was exported to the continent. Edward III's Flanders campaigns were initially stalemated by the French refusing to offer battle. Involvement in the Breton civil war did produce a victory at Morlaix (1342), however. A small expeditionary force under the earl of Northampton took up a defensive position. It was protected by a ditch to the front and a wood to the rear. From this position the force managed to successfully hold off waves of cavalry charges.

The experience at Morlaix may have been crucial in the summer 1346, when Edward launched an invasion of Normandy. He actually advanced as far as Paris, before falling back northwards in the face of superior French forces. Crossing the Somme at its mouth, his force of 3000 men-at-arms and 10,000 archers was brought to bay at Crécy by King Philip VI with 12,000 cavalry, 6000 Genoese crossbowmen and large numbers of levied spearmen. Edward, with Northampton's advice, drew up his force on a hill, with his rear protected by woods and his wagon train. He dismounted his men-at-arms, forming three battles, with archers on the flanks. One source mentions digging potholes on the slopes in front of the position to bring down charging horses.

The French plan was to send in the mercenary crossbowmen to counter the English archers, but they were completely outshot. 'The English archers then advanced one step forward, and shot their arrows with such force and quickness, that it seemed as if it snowed...[they] continued shooting as vigorously and quickly as before; some of their arrows fell among the horsemen, who were sumptuously equipped, and killing and wounding many, made them caper and fall among the Genoese [crossbowmen], so that they were in such confusion that they could never rally again' (Froissart, Chronicles). The French chivalry, despising the Genoese, rode them down in their enthusiasm to get at the enemy. Yet they were unable to penetrate the English ranks; multiple charges proved fruitless.'The archers shot so fiercely that those on horseback suffered from these deadly barbed arrows: here, one horse was refusing to go forward, there, another leaping about as if maddened, here, was one bucking hideously, there, another turning its haunches to the enemy' (Jean le Bel). Even the French king suffered injuries as he lost 1500 of his knights on the field.The English success in battle was crucial because it enabled Edward to take Calais and establish a vital bridgehead in France.

In 1356, the Prince of Wales, Edward (the 'Black Prince') was conducting a *chevauchée* (plundering raid) in southern France, when he also found himself confronted by a large army under King John. Edward led about 3000 men-at-arms, 3000 archers and a 1000 Gascon *bidauts*, dismounting the lot in broken ground behind hedges and marshy land.

The French, probably three times as strong, with a preponderance of armoured men-at-arms, tried a new tactic. Picked knights on barded horses (protected by armour on head, chest and sometimes the rump) were launched down two roads into the English line; but it held. There followed several thousand dismounted men-at-arms under the Dauphin, and finally another mass under the king himself. Despite extreme pressure, the English held the hedge line, allowing Edward to remount some troops under his Gascon vassal the Captal de Buch, and swing them into the rear of the now stalled enemy. Caught between two forces, the French king and many of his troops were forced to surrender and were then held for costly ransoms.The 'English System' had delivered total victory, not to be matched until Agincourt in 1415.

> *'The archers of the English vanguard were safely positioned in the marsh; but they were of little use there. For the French cavalry were well protected by steel plates and leather bards, so that arrows either shattered or glanced off heavenward, falling on friend and foe alike.'*
>
> – Battle of Poitiers, Geoffrey le Baker, Chronicler

The intervening two generations saw the English effort falter in France, mainly because the French learnt to avoid battle, instead preferring to harass English *chevauchées* and win via a fortress strategy.Two battles fought in other theatres during this period offer important clues to our understanding of tactical developments, though. In 1385, at Aljubarrota in southern Portugal, an English expeditionary force defeated France's Castilian allies. Uniquely, the battlefield has been excavated and reveals the extensive field defences that had been created to foil cavalry charges.The left flank of the position was based around a church and a ditch dug to connect with a field of potholes.These were about 0.9 square metres (1 square foot) each and set 0.9m (3ft) apart in a V-shaped formation 182m

BATTLE OF POITIERS, *1356, from a late 15th-century illustrated version of Froissart's* Chronicles. *This was an immensely popular work that celebrated chivalric heroes and their deeds. Ironically, as with the Black Prince's victory, the infantry often played the major role.*

(600ft) wide by 91m (300ft) deep. This disposition enabled the archers to stand behind or among the pot-holes as they shot. Furthermore, the holes disrupted enemy formations and enabled the English to defeat attacks by men-at-arms on both horse and foot.

In 1396, a largely French and Burgundian crusade army encountered the Ottoman army at Nicopolis on the Danube (in modern Bulgaria). Despite the warnings of their Hungarian allies, the crusaders launched a cavalry charge at the Turkish light horse. This mobile screen then parted to reveal a field of stakes 'a bow-shot deep' full of Janissary bowmen. Halted by the stakes, and losing their horses to the archery, the knights dismounted.

Although they defeated the more lightly armed Janissaries, by the time they emerged from the staked area they were exhausted and were swiftly rounded up by the sultan's cavalry. For those that survived the resulting ransoms were enormous. One survivor was Marshal Boucicault, a French nobleman, who ironically was to encounter stakes again at Agincourt.

The 'English System'

By the 1420s, the 'English System' had been adopted by other armies. First were the Burgundians, allies until 1436. Then the French themselves developed a royal archer guard and Ordinance Companies in the 1440s. This imitation, combined with the development of field artillery, enabled them to beat the English at their own game. By the mid-fifteenth century, France and Burgundy were developing flexible armies combining the best from the English and Swiss traditions, with pikemen, archers and handgunners in their uniformed companies. England, in contrast, which fell into the generation of civil strife known as the Wars of the Roses (1455–1487), stuck to the old system.

The biggest battle, at Towton (1461), which won the throne for the Yorkist Edward I, was a slugging match between infantry blocks of dismounted men-at-arms and billmen. The only tactical variation was intelligent use of a following wind by Yorkist archers, who took a step back as the Lancastrians replied, to see the enemy's arrows fall short. Recent interpretations of Bosworth (1485), in which the pretender Henry Tudor defeated Richard III, stress the impact of the French component of Henry's force. Their tight and mobile formation of pikemen provided solidity to his line, although his victory probably owed most to the defection of the Stanley forces, leaving King Richard with no option except a desperate cavalry charge.

The English did not adopt the continental 'pike and shot' tactics until the middle of the sixteenth century onwards, although this need not be seen as stubborn backwardness. In 1513, at the Battle of the Spurs near Calais, Henry VIII was able to defeat Francis I of France by the use of flanking archers, much as his namesake had done a century earlier. The English System was superseded not because it was inefficient, but because as gunpowder

ALJUBARROTA, 1385. *This extremely rare archaeological example of a medieval battlefield is found in southern Portugal. The plan shows the left flank of an entrenched English position, with a ditch encircling a church as a strongpoint. The fan-shaped field of potholes was designed to protect the longbowmen and bring down enemy knights foolhardy enough to charge them.*

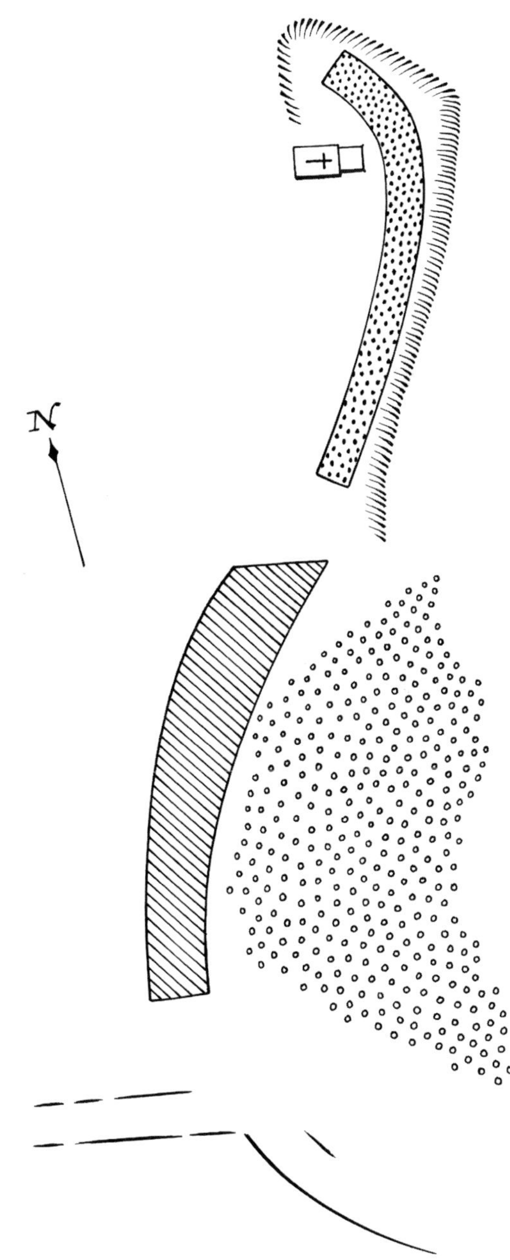

FRENCH CROSSBOWMEN *of the late 15th century are depicted in a 19th-century engraving based on a medieval manuscript. Here they demonstrate the importance of the large pavise, often carried by an accompanying pavisier, for the slow-loading missilemen.*

weapons became cheaper, lighter and more readily available, the archer, who took a lifetime to train, could be replaced by a weakling with a musket.

Battle of Agincourt: 1415

King Henry V of England invaded Normandy in the middle of August, 1415, to make good his claim to the crown of France. He brought with him an army of some 10,000 men, which was first employed besieging Harfleur in the mouth of the River Seine. The siege took almost two months to complete and Henry's army was devastated by disease in the process. The king decided to march across hostile territory to the English possession of Calais, with a much-reduced force. It was, by then, late in the campaigning season and the weather was foul. Henry took with him a week's supplies, yet, when he reached the River Somme on 13 October, he found it defended against him and impossible to cross. As a result, he was forced to lead his army inland and upstream for another week, until he managed to cross undetected near Peronne. He then struck out for Calais, but a large French army placed itself across his path some 50km (30 miles) short of his goal.

Henry led about 1000 knights and men-at-arms, together with some 5000 archers. The French had at least three times that number, with perhaps 10,000 men-at-arms (fully equipped in plate armour), capable of being used as cavalry. Furthermore, many of the horses were barded as part of the French plan to make it possible to charge the English archers without losing too many mounts to their shooting, and so neutralize Henry's most potent weapon. For the French had been trying to work out how to defeat the English System, combining the resilience of dismounted men-at-arms with the striking power of the archers, since their defeat at the battle of Crécy in 1346. They had not been notably successful, though. Dismounting their own knights at Poitiers (1356) had left them with clumsy and immobile formations and led to the capture of their king, John. One of his sons, the aged duke of Berry, had already advised the commanders of 1415, who were military officials of the royal household, not to take the king on campaign with them against the English, since 'it were better to lose a battle than the king and the battle'. In fact, King Charles VI was already disqualified by virtue of his recurrent bouts of madness. Nonetheless, the pessimistic point was well made.

The French Plan

D'Albret, the constable, and Boucicault, the marshal of France, had devised a plan to overcome the English combination of arms. Their plan was only discovered in 1981 in a fire-damaged manuscript in the British Library. It was designed for the vanguard of the French army, some 6000 strong, should it need to face Henry's similarly sized army in battle. The vanguard's role on the campaign had been to shadow the English force as it marched out from Harfleur. The French had crossed the Somme before Henry and sought to join up with the main body, probably near Bapaume.

The plan envisaged dismounting the bulk of the men-at-arms and positioning them in formation with ordinary infantry on either flank. In front of this foot battle, also on the wings, were to be placed the missilemen - bows and crossbows - with their aim to counter the English shooting. Further out, on one flank 1000 mounted men-at-arms, under the command of the 'master of crossbows', were supported by half the valets of the army (another 1000, perhaps), mounted on their masters' horses. (A valet was a lightly armed member of the knight's military household). On the other flank 200 mounted men-at-arms were supported by the rest of the valets. The intention was for the larger force to charge forward directly against the archers, while the smaller one rode around behind the other enemy flank to attack the camp and catch the English line from behind. With small, well-disciplined forces, led by the experienced officers of the Household, it is possible that it could have worked. Unfortunately for the French, three important factors militated against its success.

'First the archers began with all their might to shoot volleys of arrows against the French. Most were without armour, dressed in their doublets, their hose loose around their knees, axes and swords hanging from their belts. Many were barefooted and without headgear.'

– Enguerrand de Monstrelet, Chronicler

The first was that Henry discovered the plan and was able to make his own plans in order to thwart it. According to the report of an eyewitness of the battle, one of Henry's chaplains who wrote *The Deeds of Henry V* (effectively a diary of the campaign): 'As a result of information divulged by some prisoners, a rumour went round the army that enemy commanders had assigned certain bodies of knights, many hundreds strong and mounted on barded horses, to break the formation and resistance of our archers when they engaged us in battle. The King, therefore, ordered that every archer, throughout the army, was to prepare for himself a stake or staff, either square or round, but six feet long, of sufficient thickness and sharpened at both ends. And he commanded that whenever the French approached to give battle and break their ranks with such bodies of horsemen, all the archers were to drive their stakes in front of them in a line and some behind them and in between the positions of the front rank, one being driven into the ground pointing towards themselves, the other end pointing towards the enemy at waist-height. So that the cavalry, when their charge had brought them close and in sight of the stakes, would either withdraw in great fear or, reckless of their own safety, run the risk of having both horses and riders impaled.'

Battle of Agincourt

1415

The French army took up a blocking position on the road to Calais, Henry's destination, outnumbering the English by at least 3:1. However, the over-confident French commanders were unable to deploy their superior numbers on a narrow battlefield. Henry seized the initiative and advanced his small force into bow range. His dismounted men-at-arms formed a solid core to his force. The more vulnerable archers were protected against enemy cavalry by the wooden stakes, forming a deep zone of obstacles. The French cavalry charges failed to make an impact and instead disrupted their own dismounted men as they fled. Those in the main body, wounded by arrows, dazed and confused, made little impression on the English. Even the lightly-armed archers swarmed over them and took them prisoner. The battle was effectively over in an hour, but late French counter-attacks forced Henry to order prisoners to be killed to prevent them rejoining the fray. A massacre ensued and the English were totally victorious.

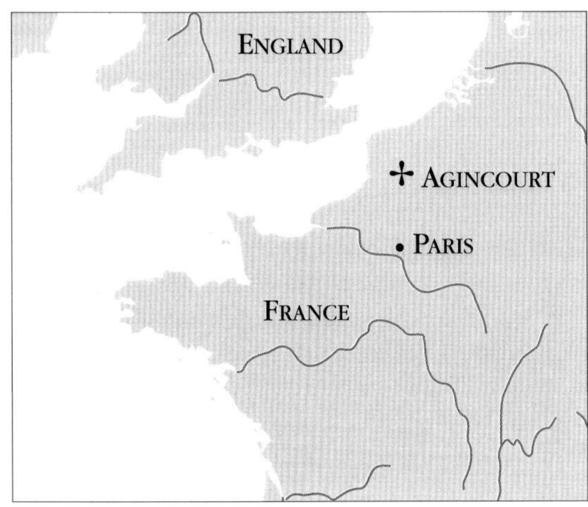

Agincourt lay on the Calais road 50 km (32 miles) south of the town. The battle was fought in a narrow gap between two woods, which still survive to this day.

6 The French mounted reserve launches a last futile charge, but is repulsed. Many French prisoners are executed in the confusion.

2 Flanking French cavalry units launch charges on the English archers, but are repelled by arrows and the stakes.

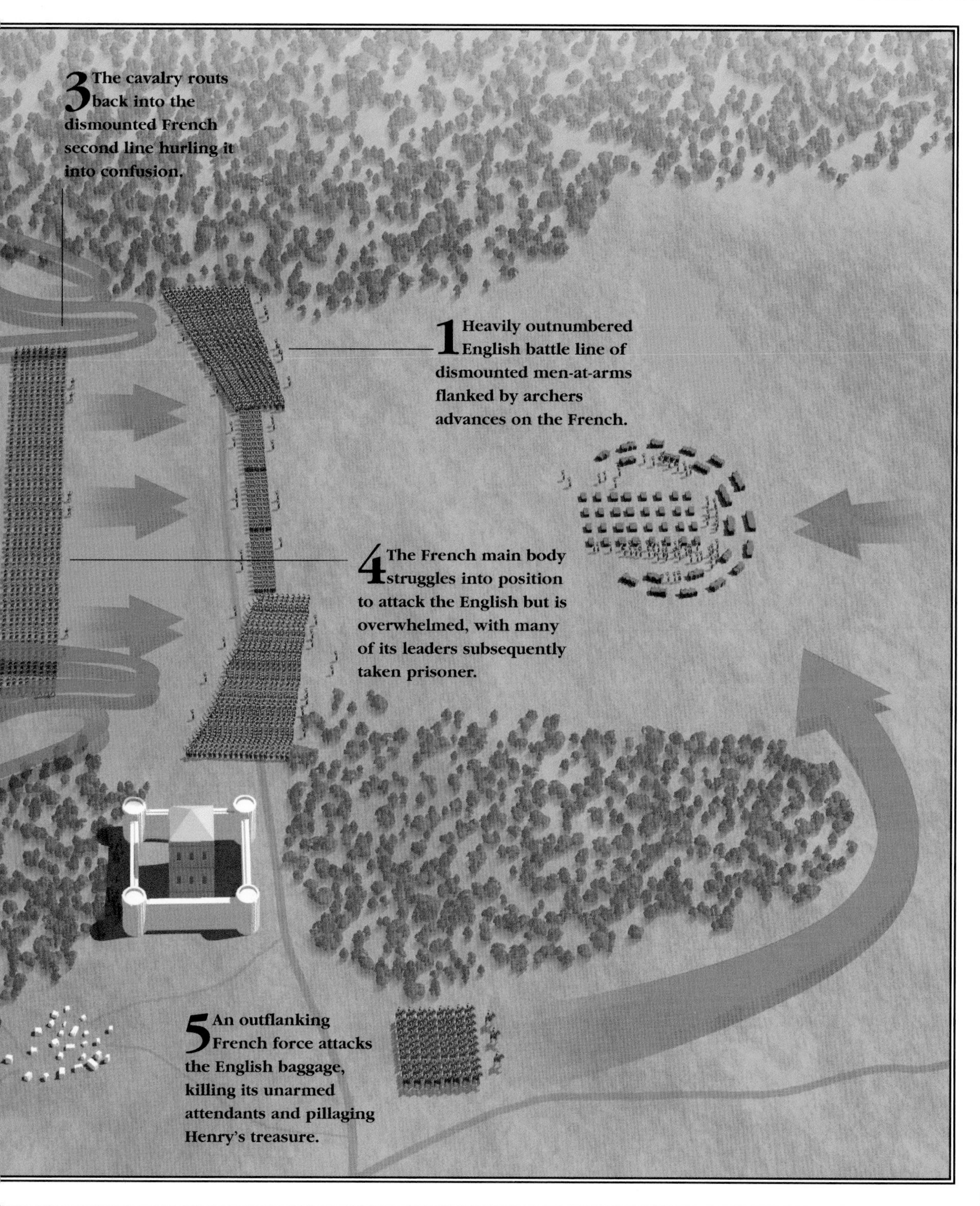
3 The cavalry routs back into the dismounted French second line hurling it into confusion.
1 Heavily outnumbered English battle line of dismounted men-at-arms flanked by archers advances on the French.
4 The French main body struggles into position to attack the English but is overwhelmed, with many of its leaders subsequently taken prisoner.
5 An outflanking French force attacks the English baggage, killing its unarmed attendants and pillaging Henry's treasure.

It must be stressed that the preparation of man-portable stakes was an innovation which can be credited personally to Henry V. It was believed at one time that he learnt the technique from the duke of York, from the disastrous Nicopolis campaign of 1396 against the Turks.

This evidence, however, comes from a pro-Yorkist source more than fifty years later at the time of the Wars of the Roses, when stakes were regularly used by archers. Since the duke was not actually on the Nicopolis Crusade, it is more likely that Henry read of how the Turkish Janissaries had used stakes to protect themselves from the crusader cavalry charge. Ironically, his source was probably the memoirs of Marshal Boucicault, which had given an account of the events. In this way the veteran French marshal was to find his own experience turned against him in another crucial battle. The French army that confronted Henry at Agincourt was much larger than Boucicault had originally envisaged.

> *The Confederates attacked with great force, cutting, thrusting and shooting the Austrian knights. The enemy suffered great loss from the men of the Forest Cantons, particularly the nobles who did not want to yield and wished they had foot troops with them....*
>
> – SEMPACH, GEBHARD DRACHER, CONSTANCE CHRONICLE

French accounts of the battle include those of several eyewitnesses, and the numbers which they give are terrifying to consider in the light of Henry's small force. The French first line consisted of some 6000 dismounted men-at-arms. It was intended that they should be supported by 4000 archers and crossbowmen, with two cavalry forces on either flank (somewhat like the original plan): 1600 on the left and 800 on the right. In the second line there stood up to 6000 more dismounted men-at-arms, with about 8000 cavalry in the rear. Even if these numbers are exaggerated, the English were still massively outnumbered.

Yet the second factor against the French helped to even out the odds. The field of Agincourt was extremely disadvantageous to the French. First of all, it was very narrow, no more than 900m (3000ft) wide between the villages of Agincourt and Tramecourt. Both villages were surrounded by thick woods, which effectively funnelled the huge French forces into an area too cramped for their proper deployment. In addition, the October storms had soaked the ploughed land that lay between the two armies, making it little more than a bog. The ground condition made it difficult for the cavalry to get up any impetus in a charge, and turned the local clay into the same kind of Somme mud rediscovered by the armies of 1914–18. Eyewitnesses describe the heavily armed dismounted knights sinking up to their knees in the gluey soil.

Finally, the French command structure, which had been small and coherent in the vanguard force, was now disorganized. When the French forces had combined, the honour of command fell to the most noble in the French army, such as the dukes of Alençon and Orleans who were inexperienced and over-confident. To such callow warriors it seemed inconceivable that King Henry would not just surrender in the face of such odds. So Marshal Boucicault's carefully constructed plan was not properly put into effect at all.

English Dispositions

Henry, meanwhile, had deployed his small force in the traditional manner. What this was exactly has occasioned no little debate by historians over the last two hundred years. The current orthodoxy, established by a debate in the *English Historical Review* in the 1890s, is that the dismounted men-at-arms formed three battles, each with a forward projecting flank of archers. Where these projections met they created a hollow V- or

wedge-shaped formation. Indeed, the chaplain's account of Agincourt speaks of a wedge-shaped deployment, using the Latin word *cuneus* to describe it. This led to A.H. Burne, the great British military historian of the Hundred Years' War, confidently to depict Agincourt, and indeed Crécy and other battles in which the English System was utilized, in this manner. To support his argument, Burne drew upon the chronicle of Froissart who describes the English army in 1346 as formed up in a *herse*. The derivation of the word suggests something spiky or projecting. However, Froissart also uses the term to describe the Janissary archers' deployment at Nicopolis, when they

BATTLE OF AGINCOURT *from a late 15th-century manuscript. This illustration shows both the muddy, ploughed fields and the woods, which played such an important part in the English victory.*

were scattered among a field of stakes, with no supporting heavy infantry. In fact, it is more likely that the word *herse* should be understood to mean in the shape of a harrow. This agricultural instrument was used to level the ground after ploughing and featured tines that were set off against one another so as to till the most ground. Actually, this is what the chaplain describes when he speaks of the archers driving 'their stakes in

English at Agincourt: Dismounted Man-at-Arms and Archer

The English men-at-arms (a term which embraced knights, squires and some non-noble warriors) were always prepared to dismount to fight alongside the archers, who were their social inferiors. These longbowmen usually deployed on the flanks or in broken ground to give them protection against more heavily-armed opponents should it come to hand-to-hand fighting. At Agincourt, King Henry V ordered that every archer should cut himself a stake to provide portable protection against cavalry charges. This worked to great effect in defeating the French. The miserable state of the English army, starving and living on filthy water, is shown the archer's need to let down his breeches, due to diarrhoea.

front of them in a line and some behind them and in between the positions of the front rank'.

So rather than imagining a palisade of stakes projecting a hollow wedge, what the archers deployed was a field of stakes, among which they could move at will relatively securely from enemy cavalry. As to the supposed *cuneus* formation, the word can also mean small units of men, and indeed is used so by the chaplain to describe cavalry squadrons in the rearguard of the French army. It is likely, therefore, that the English archers formed up on the flanks of the army, leaving dismounted the men-at-arms in the centre. Indeed there were so few of them that they formed one body rather than three battles, although they retained three places where the commanders of each battle stood, flying the banners of their commanders. King Henry V, under the Cross of Saint George, stood in the very centre of his small army.

The Battle

Remarkably, the French did not attack, a fact probably due to their over-confidence and confused command structure. So Henry took the initiative, and in about the middle of the morning advanced to the narrowest point of the field, within a bowshot's range. Here his archers drove in their stakes, then opened a 'galling fire' on the enemy, encouraging rash manoeuvre. This is exactly what happened. The cavalry wings began to move, but they suffered from four serious disadvantages. First, they were badly undermanned; instead of the intended numbers, they had mustered only around 150 each because the ill-disciplined knights had not formed up properly.

Second, the restricted terrain meant that they were unable to outflank the English archers. Third, the muddy ground blunted their speed, so they had to endure flights of arrows.

Those brave enough to charge onto the stakes had their horses impaled and were even catapulted out of the saddle to lie defenceless at the archers' feet, where they were promptly dispatched. Only in a section of the field where the ground was so soft that the stakes fell down did they make any impact. Most of the cavalry had no option but to wheel about and hurtle back to escape the arrow storm. As a result they cannoned into the dismounted men-at-arms advancing on foot. The result was chaos.

Nor were the French missilemen utilized, but rather pushed behind the vanguard that they should have been supporting. The attacks on foot were disorganized, swept by archery, blunted by the mud (with the resultant exhaustion of the men-at-arms) and repulsed by the relatively fresh English men-at-arms.

Although the second division of men-at-arms managed to push the English back a little way, and Henry suffered a blow to his helmet, which lopped off florets of his golden crown, the French were beaten. Many lords were killed or captured in the melee. To cap it all, the English archers proved nimble, deadly opponents in the boggy ground, even swinging the leaden mallets that they had used for driving the stakes in to the ground.

Seeing the defeat of the main body, the majority

'Mad Margaret'. *This 15th-century Flemish cannon epitomizes the development gunpowder artillery. A siege piece, it was made of long bars of iron bound around with hoops of the same material in an attempt to make a perfect seal for the explosive power of the charge.*

of the French third division ran away, leaving only one last charge under de Fauquemberg to help precipitate a massacre. A flank attack by the local lord, Isembert d'Azincourt, compounded the crime. This is usually dismissed as a group of local peasants, plundering the English baggage and murdering the grooms; but it may have been the last desperate attempt to put the French plan into action. Whatever the case, it made the situation worse for the French nobles trapped in the centre of the field.

Fearing that his small force would be utterly overwhelmed, and that prisoners might take up arms again, Henry ordered the killing of the prisoners. His knights refused to do this and so he had to order a detachment of 200 archers to undertake the job. This brutal necessity ended the day. Despite their best efforts the French proved incapable of outwitting the English System. It took them a generation, and a complete overhaul of their military system, before they could begin to even the odds and eventually expel the English from France.

'The Burgundians shot from behind their palisades with large, heavy cannon. They had a deadly effect against the Confederates in their formation.... I saw a few horsemen who were shot in two; their upper body was blown away and their legs remained in the saddle.'

– Peter Etterlin, Siege of Mürten

The Swiss: Apprenticeship

Switzerland is in the heart of Europe, but, owing to its mountainous nature, it is effectively a frontier district. In the mediaeval period the Swiss were of interest to surrounding powers because it was through their steep valleys that passes ran linking the German Empire to Italy. As traffic increased and became worth taxing and controlling, a conflict developed between the independently minded Swiss and the Austrian Habsburgs. In 1291, the three Forest Cantons of Uri, Schwyz and Unterwalden signed a covenant for self-defence.

In 1315, a dispute between the mountaineers and a Habsburg-protected monastery provided the pretext for war. Leopold of Austria led an army of some 1000 horse and over 2000 foot soldiers into the mountains. The Swiss, armed with polearms and crossbows, blocked his route at Mortgarten. When the Austrian column halted, about 1000 Swiss appeared in ambush from the wooded slopes on the flank. They rolled down boulders and tree-trunks then charged the immobile horsemen, as the Austrian foot soldiers fled back down the road. This was an example of an extremely successful ambush and the combined Austrian force was effectively routed, but it cannot be used to justify an 'infantry revolution'.

Inspired by this victory, the lakeside cities of Lucerne and Bern joined the Swiss Confederation. This was a major accession of wealth and population and was seen as a challenge to the surrounding rulers. The disgruntled nobility of the rival city of Freibourg launched an attack on Bern. At Laupen in 1339, the Swiss decisively defeated their attackers. Initially, the men of the Forest Cantons were held by the knightly cavalry, but the Bernese crushed the Freibourg foot soldiers and then outflanked the enemy horse and destroyed them. Another Austrian attack was met at Sempach, in 1386. The Swiss, again mainly armed with halberds, occupied the high ground. This time the Austrian knights dismounted and attacked on foot. The better-armoured knights pressed back the Swiss and the banner of Lucerne was borne down. However, unbeknown to Leopold III, the Austrian leader, he was only fighting against one single division of the entire Swiss army. When the main body of the Swiss arrived on the flank, the Austrians were overrun, and Leopold was killed.

The Swiss now became aggressors, seeking to unite their territories to the mountain lands

Armoured Swiss Pikeman (c. 1475)

This figure represents a well-armed front-rank man from the period of the Burgundian Wars (1475–77). On his head he wears a sallet, while his body is protected both by mail and plate armour. Only the legs are lightly armoured to allow freedom of movement. Most of the men in a Swiss pike-block would be much more lightly equipped, those in the back ranks not even wearing helmets. Although the Swiss are traditionally associated with the pike, they mostly used the halberd until the middle of the fifteenth century. After a pyrrhic victory over Italian militia pikemen at Arbedo (1422) they adopted the weapon and transformed infantry tactics for two hundred years. Although largely redundant in the face of improved muskets by the 1640s, the pike was not finally given up until the 1670s when the bayonet began to be introduced.

bordering their cantons. An attack on the Duchy of Milan in 1422 led to the Battle of Arbedo. The Swiss engaged with only part of their army, 4000 men (one-third pikes, two-thirds halberdiers). When a charge of the heavy Italian cavalry died on the pikes, the experienced condottieri general Carmagnola reacted quickly. He outflanked the Swiss with crossbowmen, dismounted his men-at-arms and sent them in deep formation against the enemy. A heroic struggle ensued which the Swiss were losing until a body of Swiss foragers appeared on the Italians' flank. Assuming that the rest of the Swiss army was upon him, Carmagnola withdrew, although the lightly armed Swiss had suffered severe casualties. After this battle the Swiss greatly increased the proportion of pikes in their ranks, because the shorter halberd had allowed the knights to close and gain advantage from their better armour.

In 1444, the Swiss met a French army at St Jacob-en-Birs, now mainly as a force of pikemen. Hugely outnumbered, the Swiss crossed the River Birs, attacked the French centre, and then formed a schiltron-like formation with pikes levelled. The French then launched repeated cavalry charges, interspersed with bouts of missile fire from crossbows and archers. In the end the French won a Pyrrhic victory; the Swiss a moral one. The French had shown that to defeat the Swiss they had to be kept immobile and shot down; the Swiss had shown that they were fanatics who would not break whatever the casualties.

Tactically the Swiss had a limited repertoire. They had some crossbow-armed skirmishers and a few cavalry scouts, but they only had an effective mounted arm when allied with the duke of Lorraine. Their main strength lay in the blocks of pike, normally deployed in three battles: the *Vorhut* or vanguard, the main battle or *Gewalthut* and the rearguard, the *Nachut*. Each body was led by a committee of the leading men of the cantons of which it was composed.

The strategy was agreed before the battle in a highly democratic fashion and then carried out with immense bravery. Deployment in three bodies was quite conventional, but was extremely effective for the Swiss because they formed deep and wore only light armour. This enabled their columns to turn very quickly. They possessed a

A MOUNTED ARCHER *in Burgundian service, depicted in battle gear of c.1470 – note his long boots and spurs – is a wealthy mercenary. He wears an open-faced sallet (helmet), and a brigandine (made of small, riveted plates) to protect his torso.*

Knight and Crossbowman (c. 1480)

Those Continental armies that could recruit, train up or draw upon archers in the English manner, tended to rely on a combination of men-at-arms and crossbowmen to serve as the missile arm. Even the French got used to dismounting, from the era of Poitiers (1356) onwards, although it did little good in that they still lost most of the encounters in the open field. The slow-loading crossbowman was more effective in a siege, and he needed a large shield (pavise) to protect him while so doing. In any case both troop types were to find themselves increasingly rendered obsolete by the introduction of lighter, quicker-firing handguns from 1500 onwards.

ferocious discipline, which meant that when one column had defeated its enemy they could turn and help the others, as the Bernese did at Laupen.

The Army of Charles the Bold

Charles the Bold was duke of Burgundy from 1463. He had inherited a large but fragmented realm that he sought to unify and aggrandize. Charles' problem was that his possibilities for expansion were blocked by the French king and German emperor. He recruited an army of the best of everything. Italian condottieri provided heavy cavalry and infantry crossbows, handguns and pikes. He recruited English mounted longbowmen, the best in Europe (whereas the French king had to use inferior local imitation longbowmen), and pikemen from his Flemish

PIKEMEN AND HANDGUNNERS, C.1500. *This illustration comes from a late medieval manuscript depiction of the legendary exploits of the Persian king, Cyrus. He was believed to be a great military innovator, so it is fitting that the system of 'pike and shot' represented here was the shape of things to come.*

subjects. The artillery park counted well over 500 pieces. The troops were uniformed in blue and white with a red St Andrew's cross and bore systematized banners and pennons. Ordinances were published each year from 1471 prescribing the deployment of the army.

Charles' aim seems to have been the integration of the different arms, so that each could support the other. Thus pikemen were mixed with archers and supported by handgunners, and mounted archers were paraded with his cavalry to enable attacks to be shot-in. The artillery was to be deployed in fortified lines that were set at an angle to the expected attack to deliver flanking fire. This mimicked the successful French 'artillery camp' at Castillon in 1453, against which the assault of the dreaded English general Talbot had broken.

Unfortunately, the system was far too complex. Although the troops were well trained, there were too many elements that had to work together perfectly to deliver success. The pikes, being deployed thinly, proved unable to cope with the massive Swiss columns. In reality Charles was a 150 years ahead of his time because eventually, small pike battalions with sleeves of shot, artillery that could fire reasonably rapidly and cavalry that charged effectively would become a winning combination. But this was only to take place after the weapons systems had been developed and the discipline to use them perfected.

Burgundians Against the Swiss, 1476–77: Grandson, Mürten, Nancy

The crowning glory of Swiss achievement was the defeat, in three great battles, of the 'modern' army of Charles the Bold. In 1476, he took the Swiss-held town of Grandson, hanging the garrison. Rather than waiting to concentrate, the arriving Swiss vanguard arrived debouched from the forest and saw Charles' whole army awaiting them. Charles ordered two cavalry charges with his men-at-arms on plate-caparisoned horses to slow the Swiss advance. The Burgundian centre was then ordered to retire to deprive the Swiss of a target. Charles began deploying his innovative field artillery to smash the pike block, while surrounding them with his own pikes and longbowmen. During this complicated manoeuvring, the Swiss main battle and rearguard arrived on the field, the mass of pikemen cresting the slopes of the hill that had hidden their advance. Caught off balance, and perhaps misinterpreting the withdrawal of the centre, the Burgundian army took to its heels. Lacking cavalry the Swiss could not pursue.

Charles then recruited, trained and equipped a bigger army and set out to tempt the Swiss again. He sat down to besiege Mürten, en route for Bern, calculating that the Swiss would arrive to relieve the place. Charles sought to remedy the problem of halting them by building a fortification in front of his camp with palisades, liberally garnished with guns. The Swiss had 25,000 confederates and the support of several hundred well-armoured cavalry under their ally Réné of Lorraine. They judged their attack well, choosing a mealtime as the moment of assault. The defences were largely unmanned when the Swiss arrived before them, their flanks covered by the Lorrainer horse.

The guns could not fire and reload fast enough to stop them, and the garrison were too few to hold them as the pike blocks surged across the fortification and on into the camp. Here they met the Burgundians returning in some disorder and defeated each group in turn, crushing them against the lake that was at the rear of the camp. Again this was a triumph of simple tactics and élan over an apparently more sophisticated force.

Unwilling to give up, Charles now turned on Réné of Lorraine, besieging Nancy through the freezing winter of 1476–77 until a Swiss relief force arrived in January. With only 5000 men against 12,000 Lorrainers and 10,000 Swiss, Charles opted for defensive actions, with the River Meurthe on his left flank, a stream to the front and woods to his right. It was to no avail. The Swiss vanguard simply outflanked through the woods while the main battle and rearguard assaulted from the front. The Burgundians disintegrated and Charles was killed in the rout. The Swiss acquired a famous reputation throughout Europe for their

BURGUNDIAN FIELD GUN. *In 1467, Charles the Bold became duke of Burgundy and spent his enormous fortune on developing the military power of the state. He was particularly keen to improve the mobility of his gunpowder artillery and sponsored the development of the first true field pieces.*

apparent invincibility and the pikeman became the infantryman of choice. Flemish spearmen and the infantry of the German towns were upgraded in imitation, and the French even attempted to recruit pikes from the mountain valleys abutting the Swiss border. Swiss soldiers were undoubtedly the prime mercenaries at the end of the fifteenth century.

Contemporaries took the lesson that the inclusion of the social elites in the front ranks of the pike blocks, exposed to equal danger and unable to escape, gave the Swiss a moral advantage over other infantry. Once their opponents had adopted the pike, engagements became very bloody. In the Swabian War of 1499, the similarly armed Germans held the Swiss at bay, only Swiss determination winning them costly victories.

The Janissaries

From the middle of the fourteenth century the Ottoman Turks developed into a major European power, having conquered much of the Balkans and surrounded the city of Constantinople. Early Ottoman armies contained many infantry, but the social elite fought on horseback. Cavalry service was seen as the path to booty and a grant of land, leaving the infantry little more than an enthusiastic rabble.

This was a particular problem wherever there was difficult terrain or a siege, especially one that involved action against well-armoured and organized Europeans. The Turks may also have been impressed by the performance of the *almogavar* foot soldiers in Byzantine service. In 1330, Sultan Orkhan initiated the Janissaries (*yeni ceri* or 'new soldiers'), a corps of 1000 men raised from Christian prisoners of war who had the choice of conversion to Islam and military service, or slavery. Such recruitment still brought in too few soldiers, so from 1362 the Janissaries were raised by a levy (the *devshirme*) upon the children of Christian households under Turkish rule. This clever device provided manpower, utilized a section of the population that had hitherto been free from military service, and aided in the extinction of Christianity from the conquered lands.

The volunteer Muslim foot soldiers were used in action, such as at the siege of Constantinople in 1453, as fodder for mass attacks, to wear down the defenders and fill a ditch with bodies. The Janissaries provided a more solid, disciplined force and also wore combined mail and plate armour, although it was still much lighter than that of the

Europeans. They were armed with bows and crossbows for missile assault, and with spears, swords and axes for close combat. The Janissaries provided shock troops for the final assault on cities and a reliable foot guard for the sultan in the warren of streets that was Constantinople.

The Janissaries also manned fortresses around the Ottoman Empire, providing a useful element of central control and coercion. In open battle they were drawn up in the centre, stiffening the other infantry. At the Battle of Varna in 1444, the Janissaries were able to resist the charge of Hungarian knights, which implies a high proportion of pole-weapons in their formation as well as missile troops.

The Hussites

Although gunpowder weapons appear in Europe in the 1340s, they were mainly used in sieges. The earliest examples of the use of field artillery came from the industrial areas of Flanders and Bohemia. The Flemish developed the *ribaudequin*. This was a multi-barelled weapon with a line of small tubes on a wheeled cart, sometimes garnished with spikes to hold off attackers. The inventor of this early battery gun probably was looking to defend breaches, where the ability to blast an attacking wave with one volley would be important. Flemish inventiveness brought *ribaudequins* to field warfare at Beverhoutsfeld in 1382. Deploying this artillery enabled the Ghenters to hold their Brugeois enemy's attack while turning their flank with a body of infantry.

A religious war in Bohemia (Czech Republic) produced the first real combination of artillery and mobility. Jan Ziska, leader of the Hussites, was attacked at the siege of Nekmer in 1419. He formed a laager of his supply wagons and held off the attacking cavalry with cannon. Because the Hussites were mainly peasant infantry with no

BURGUNDIAN FALCON CANNON, *late 15th century. Under Charles the Bold's direction, wheeled, long-barrelled guns bought new standards of accuracy to field artillery.*

TURKISH JANISSARY CHARGING. *Founded in 1330, these Turkish slave-soldiers were essential to the military success of the Ottoman state and went on to become the model for discipline in the Western armies of the sixteenth century.*

tradition of pike warfare and few horsemen, the wagons proved an excellent way to foil the opposing knights. Ziska developed the laager idea into a wagon fort as a defensive bastion that resisted the attacks of the enemy until they retired, when the gate wagons would be rolled aside and the Hussite cavalry would emerge to pursue. Tactically the wagons stayed mainly on the defensive, forcing the enemy to come to them. Each wagon had a unit of 20 men that fought in and around it. They were mainly armed with fearsome military flails, halberds, crossbows and some handguns. The wagons contained *houfnice* light cannon and between the wagons were pavises which hid *tarasnice*, light artillery on a stand. The wagons were specially designed with loop-holed boards that could be raised to frustrate enemy archers and planks hanging beneath to prevent the enemy crawling under the cart. Because the waggoners could form the *tabor* (the wagon-laager), so quickly they could manoeuvre aggressively in front of the enemy. The Hussites cleared their own country of their Catholic enemy and then set about raiding and terrorizing the surrounding lands. Their neighbours soon copied them. Matthias Corvinus of Hungary hired a Hussite wagon force to provide a core to his army.

He used it against the Turks in 1444, so the Ottomans adopted the tactic too. The Hussite wagons were successful because the sheer number of guns deployed made them effective. In addition, the wagons denied an enemy charge impetus. Attackers had to endure the shooting from crossbowmen and handgunners crewing the wagons and, when they made contact, faced halberdiers and flailmen operating from an elevated position. If the enemy penetrated the *tabor* they were assaulted by the Hussite reserves and slaughtered with their backs to the wagons whose crews could also turn and fight them. The wagon fort was vulnerable to artillery itself, but it was not until the late fifteenth century that this was mobile enough to be brought up against the *tabor*.

Hussite tactics were not adopted in the West. In France, the Bureau brothers devised the artillery camp, an entrenchment full of guns of all sizes. This proved itself at Castillon, in 1453, the battle which saw the expulsion of the English from Aquitaine. The dukes of Burgundy were also great exponents of gunpowder weapons, although it was only in the 1470s that Charles the

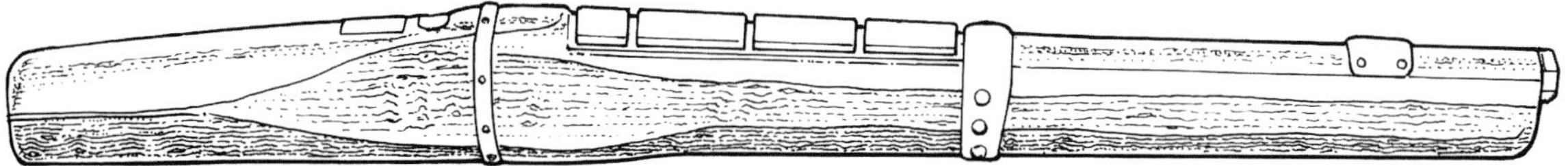

EARLY ARQUEBUS C.1500. *By this time handguns were becoming lighter, more portable and more accurate. At the Battle of Pavia in 1525, the Imperial* arquebusiers *proved their superiority over King Francis I or France's chivalric* gens d'armes *(knights).*

Bold had a substantial force of 'field guns'. Against conventional armies they were useful, because the new wheeled guns could be moved around and placed in different positions. However, the Swiss often moved too quickly for the cannon to be effective. Charles also inherited a force of handgunners. That he should have bothered to maintain large numbers of these indicates their effectiveness. Late medieval armourers had responded to the challenge of ever more powerful crossbows and massed longbows by producing a better design, resulting in a revival of knightly cavalry on armoured horses. However, the fluted armours and hardened steel that cleverly directed arrows and quarrels away were scant protection against handgunners. Intermingled or operating in front of dismounted men-at-arms and halberdiers, they were useful for sniping at enemy leaders and bringing down the armoured front ranks of pike formations. This also explains why handgunners were included in the mercenaries hired to participate in the Wars of the Roses. Despite all these developments, cannon and handguns do not seem to have exercised a decisive influence on the outcome of field battles until the sixteenth century.

HUSSITE WAR-WAGON. *The religiously-inspired Bohemian revolt (1417–35) produced a military genius in the form of Jan Zizka. He set up a laager using the war-wagons, filling the vehicles with all kinds of small gunpowder weaponry and supporting them with pole-arm men. This formation proved invincible to the traditional knightly armies sent against them.*

CHAPTER 2

MOUNTED WARFARE

Cavalry were the shock troops of the medieval age, used to demolish opposing infantry lines and secure final victory. As the period went on, however, new infantry weapons and tactics steadily stripped the mounted soldier of his martial supremacy.

It was once said: 'They are not well suited to infantry battles, but are nearly always on horseback, their horses being ill-shaped, but hardy; and sometimes they even sit upon them like women if they want to do anything more conveniently. There is not a person in the whole nation who cannot remain on his horse day and night. On horseback they buy and sell, they take their meat and drink, and there they recline on the narrow neck of their steed, and yield to sleep so deep as to indulge in every variety of dream. And

ALTHOUGH THE ARTIST *is attempting to interpret the description of the Battle of Crécy found in Jean Froissart's* Chroniques, *this illustration, from a mid 15th-century manuscript, portrays neither accurate battlefield geography or arms and armour. However, he does depict the arms and armour of his own time, with cavalry, infantry men-at-arms and archers dressed in full plate armour.*

when any deliberation is to take place on any weighty matter, they all hold their common council on horseback.... Sometimes, when provoked, they fight; and when they go into battle, they form in a solid body, and utter all kinds of terrific yells. They are very quick in their operations, of exceeding speed, and fond of surprising their enemies. With a view to this, they suddenly disperse, then reunite, and again, after having inflicted vast loss upon the enemy, scatter themselves over the whole plain in irregular formations: always avoiding the fort or an intrenchment.'

Unfortunately, this description of the Huns, written in the fourth century by Ammianus Marcellinus, has distorted the history of warfare in general and cavalry warfare in particular for several centuries. The Huns were a cavalry-dominant army, that is true, and they were accustomed to fight battles in which the cavalry force could overwhelm their enemies in the manner portrayed by Ammianus. However, the other Germanic tribes – the Visigoths, Ostrogoths, Vandals, Alans, Alemanni, Sueves, Burgundians, Lombards and Franks – who overran the Rhine and Danube borders of the Roman Empire beginning in the fourth century, fielded largely infantry armies with only small cavalries. Their victories can only rarely be attributed solely to their cavalry forces.

Yet Ammianus Marcellinus' description of the Huns does point out one important detail that should not be overlooked in analyzing 'barbarian' cavalry warfare at the beginning of the Middle Ages: the Germanic tribes used their cavalry differently than the Romans had, and they placed greater emphasis on their use of cavalry on campaign and in battle than did the Romans. For the Romans, the cavalry were mainly auxiliaries, furnished mostly by non-Roman units, while it was the infantry who were expected to undertake the primary battlefield fighting. The cavalries of barbarian armies, however, were to perform the principal manoeuvres on the battlefield, with the infantry following their lead and leadership. Barbarians therefore reversed the roles of the two types of forces.

'After gaining a victory, the general who pursues the enemy with a scattered and disorganized army gives away his victory to the foe.'

– *Emperor Maurice*, The Strategikon, *AD 600*

Barbarian Cavalry

It is also evident that the horse provided barbarian troops not only with a means of fighting, but also with a sign of social distinction and class. For most of the Germanic tribes, those who could afford horses and were trained in using them also provided military and political leadership. Thus began a cycle that perpetuated the dominance of cavalry warfare for the next 1200 years. Cavalries performed the primary strategic and tactical duties in medieval armies precisely because in them were found society's wealthy and titled. Their societal status and leadership also allowed them the money and time needed to train to be effective cavalry, completing the cycle.

More importantly, the cavalry were effective. In two of the earliest of their battles with the eastern Romans, Visigothic cavalry may even have decided the outcome. In 378 at Dibaltum, a cavalry force delivered the decisive blow on a force of Romans who had previously been successful at withstanding numerous infantry assaults. Even more impressive, in the midst of the battle fought at Adrianople, a few weeks later, the Visigothic cavalry struck the rear of a weakened Roman left flank, crushing it and folding it onto the rest of the line. This victory cost Emperor Valens his life and gave the Visigoths and other Germanic invaders freedom to campaign further in the Roman Empire. In neither conflict was the Visigothic cavalry larger than their infantry, but in deciding battles cavalry tactics found a legitimacy that would justify their continued use by Visigoths and other barbarian tribes.

Hun Horse Archer (c. 5–6th century)

The primary equipment of a Hun cavalry soldier was the bow, which he could fire effectively from his saddle at full gallop. A covered bow case was attached to his saddle, with a quiver of arrows slung over his back for easy retrieval. It is not known how many arrows would be contained in such a quiver. A sword, for use in close combat, was carried in a sheath belted onto the soldier's hip. Hun cavalry rode 'steppe ponies'. They were small horses, but were very strong and fast. Huns did not use stirrups, but this should not suggest an instability while riding on or fighting from horseback.

The Visigothic cavalry seems to have been well armed and armoured, what later historians would define as 'heavy cavalry'. The weapons used were spears/lances to thrust and long swords to slash down at enemy soldiers. Their wielders were supported only by their saddles to assist them in delivering the blows, fighting in a manner not changed since ancient times. The Huns used lighter cavalry, all carrying bows, with some also outfitted with spears and swords. They operated primarily as mounted archers who would not ride directly into opposing forces, but around them, firing as they passed. Claudian wrote a description of this manner of attack: 'Brisk, lithe, in loose array they first come on / Fly, turn, attack the foe who deems them gone.' There were infantry troops among the Hunnic armies, but they were few and seem to have initially been used entirely as auxiliaries. With the ascendancy of Attila in 433, more infantry began to be used by the Huns, provided frequently by allies and ruled peoples; his most famous defeat, at Chalons in 451, can even be described as an infantry-on-infantry battle. Still, cavalry almost always provided the central force in his armies and the mainstay of his campaign strategy and battlefield tactics.

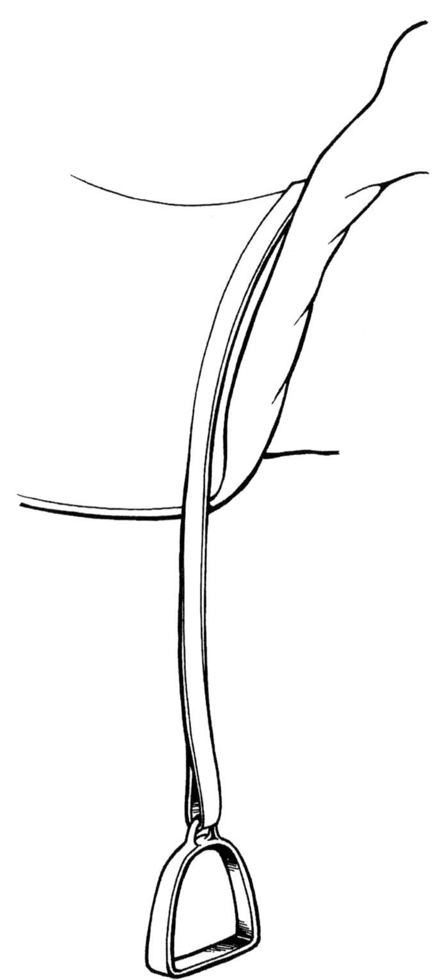

A SIMPLE TECHNOLOGICAL DEVICE, *the stirrup allowed medieval cavalry to couch their lances, thereby combining the impetus of the charging horse with that of the rider in delivering what became known as 'mounted shock combat'.*

Little is known about the horses that were ridden by the barbarian tribes in the early medieval wars. Few sources describe the mounts ridden by the heavier cavalry of the Visigoths, Ostrogoths, Vandals and others, although because the animals were required to carry horsemen wearing heavy armour it is generally believed that they were strong - indeed, speed may even have been sacrificed for strength. It is also assumed that these horses were smaller than more modern cavalry mounts, small enough to facilitate the thrusting of a javelin or swinging of a sword.

Hunnic Cavalry

More is written about Hunnic horses, which were reportedly light, short and fast. They could also go for long distances without tiring, although most Hun cavalry soldiers travelled with several horses during times of war, changing mounts frequently to preserve their horses' strength. The Hunnic military horses were most often mares, as their milk was often life-sustaining for the warrior on campaign, and mares were also easier to control than stallions. They may in fact have been the ancestors of the modern Mongolian horse, the mares of which stand 127cm (50in) high and can be milked four to five times a day, providing 2oz ($^1/_2$ pint) of milk each time.

The Franks, who crossed the northern Rhine River into the western Roman Empire later than their more southern and eastern counterparts, would eventually become the masters of western Europe. They also came later to cavalry warfare. Still, by the beginning of the sixth century they too had become accustomed to fighting on horseback – at least part of each Frankish army was cavalry. Composed in this way the Frankish army fought numerous campaigns and won numerous victories, although most of the time it seems that they used their cavalry solely as transportation and battlefield infantry support. For example, most of the fighting done by Clovis I (476–511), who united the Salarian and Ripurian Frankish tribes and began the Merovingian dynasty, was on foot, with his enemies also fighting as infantry. The Frankish cavalry travelled to the battlefield on horses and then dismounted to fight with the infantry, yet it is also clear that the early Merovingian cavalry could charge on horseback. Evidence of the nature of early cavalry warfare comes from Gregory of Tours, who tells the story of two soldiers, Dragolen and Guntram, who fought against each other:'[Dragolen] struck spurs to his horse and charged Guntrum at full speed. But his blow failed, for his spear broke, and his sword fell to the ground. Guntram...then, raising his lance struck Dragolen in the throat and unseated him. And as Dragolen was hanging from his horse, one of Guntram's friends thrust a lance into his side and gave him the finishing blow.'

The most famous Merovingian battle was undoubtedly that fought between Tours and Poitiers (and called by both names) in 732. In this battle the Franks faced a determined and, at least until this date, rarely defeated Muslim army, led by Abd ar Rachman al-Ghafiqi, which had crossed over the Pyrenees Mountains. Sources are meagre for this battle. Those that do exist – from both the Muslim and Frankish side – suggest that the Muslims, with Spaniards, Berbers, Moroccans and Arabs in their force, fought as a combined force of cavalry and infantry, as they were accustomed to, while the Merovingians, led by Charles Martel, fought solely as infantry.

Charles' infantry soldiers were very experienced, as they had fought in many previous campaigns, and this experience may have brought them victory at Poitiers. Their solid, tightly-packed line did not weaken no matter how many charges the Muslims made against it, nor whether cavalry or infantry made those charges (it was customary for the infantry to follow the cavalry into the attack, hitting their opponents' formations with great force once these were weakened by the cavalry charges). Eventually, Abd ar Rachman al-Ghafiqi was killed in one of these charges and, as night fell, his army left the field, although a burial party seemed to have returned to bury their leader where he fell. The tactic of standing solidly in an infantry line would always be successful against medieval cavalry, but it required an enormous amount of bravery, discipline and leadership. Few armies possessed such qualities.

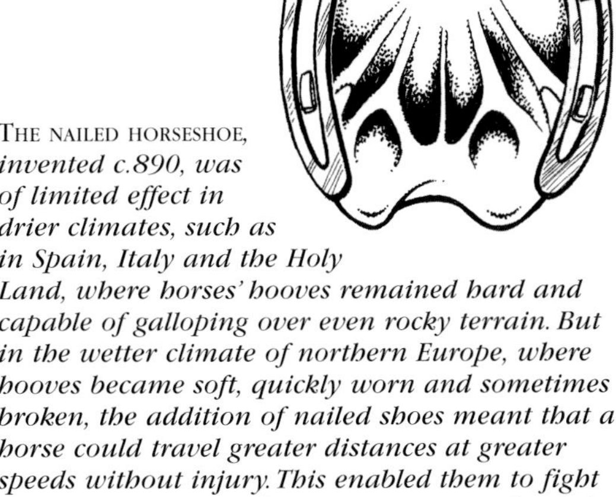

THE NAILED HORSESHOE, *invented c.890, was of limited effect in drier climates, such as in Spain, Italy and the Holy Land, where horses' hooves remained hard and capable of galloping over even rocky terrain. But in the wetter climate of northern Europe, where hooves became soft, quickly worn and sometimes broken, the addition of nailed shoes meant that a horse could travel greater distances at greater speeds without injury. This enabled them to fight battles at any time of year on any type of terrain.*

Technological Innovations

Despite the success of Charles' infantry at Poitiers, a short time after the battle he began to reorganize his army to provide more heavy cavalry, and to train them to provide an offensive impetus to match the defensive skill of his infantry. This reorganization continued throughout his reign and that of his son, Pippin II (the Short), who also founded the Carolingian dynasty.

The changes are not only seen in increased narrative accounts of heavy cavalry use, but also in the seizure of a large number of church lands by Charles Martel after the Battle of Poitiers, the Frankish mustering of the army from March to May when forage was more readily available to horses,

and the replacement of Saxon tribute payment in cattle to payment in horses. What prompted the tactical shift?

Historians once thought that even though the battle of Poitiers was won by Charles Martel, he was very impressed by his opponents' use of horses in the battle and thus became determined to reorganize his army to mirror it. That view seems to be countered by evidence that Muslim armies did not fight with large numbers of cavalry until the second half of the eighth century, perhaps responding to their encounters with the Frankish armies and not the other way around.

Another possibility is the innovation and proliferation of the stirrup. As theorized by Lynn White Jr in *Medieval Technology and Social Change* (Oxford, 1962), it was the adoption of this relatively small and simple technology - a rigid wood, rope or metal tread at the end of a strap descending from the saddle into which the horseman's foot would be placed - by the Franks that entirely transformed their organization and tactics, leading to an emphasis on the use of heavily armed and armoured cavalry. There is no doubt that the stirrup may be the most important invention for the military use of a horse. Before the introduction of the stirrup, the cavalry soldier was forced to stay on and direct his horse by pressing his knees into the horse's sides. As can be imagined, this limited both the horseman's ability to ride his steed and his capability of effectively wielding weapons while atop it.

The stirrup increased the cavalry soldier's stability, as well as adding new dimensions to his fighting tactics. Without stirrups, the rider's mount was little more than a mode of transportation, an immobile platform for thrusting down with spear or sword, or a mobile missile-launching pad. If he was to mount a charge in the customary fashion against an enemy, the force of his blow could just as likely unseat him from the steed as deliver the desired impact to his opponent. Despite their importance, stirrups were a relatively late invention. There was no ancient tradition of stirrups, and even though they were well known in China, India, Korea and Japan during the early Middle Ages, they seem not to have diffused to Europe or the Middle East until at least the seventh or even the early eighth century. It was at that time that the stirrup first appeared in Persia and from there was carried to other Muslim lands (although stirrups may also have first appeared among the Avars, who acquired them from other steppes peoples).

From the Middle East the stirrup spread almost immediately to Byzantium and then, either from the Byzantines or by direct diffusion, to the Franks. This evolution Lynn White seems to substantiate with archeological, linguistic, and, to a lesser extent, artistic evidence, all of which placed the use of the stirrup among the Franks in the early eighth century. At the same time, there was a change in weapons policy among the Franks that led them to discard their battle axes and barbed spears, both of which were only infantry weapons, and adopt longswords and heavier and longer wing-spears or lances, the most distinct feature of which was their prominent cross-piece that prohibited the impaling of an enemy so deeply that the weapon would be stuck. The horsed warrior would couch his lance under his arm during the charge, adding the momentum of the horse's movement to the lance's thrust, a tactic called 'mounted shock combat'.

As impressive as the stirrup was as an invention, and acknowledging its necessity to later medieval cavalry warfare, the idea that the adoption of the stirrup caused the Carolingian military reorganization has met with condemnation. Most critics speak of the insufficiency of evidence to prove White's prescribed role for the stirrup in the development of medieval cavalry. They suggest that archaeological remains, because of the meagreness in finds, difficulty in dating and the fact that it is impossible to use graves as evidence of Frankish customs, could not be conclusive substantiation for either the dating or the

THE BATTLE OF TOURS (POITIERS), *fought in 732, is depicted here in a highly romanticized 19th-century illustration. It shows the battle in which the Frankish general, Charles Martel, defeated a Muslim army, led by Abd ar Rachman al-Ghafiqi, thus turning back their invasion of Merovingian Francia from across the Pyrenees.*

significance of stirrups in early Carolingian military strategy. Artistic and linguistic sources are also suspect. At the same time, those who disagree with the stirrup thesis offer nothing to replace it in explaining the changes in Carolingian cavalry. Could it be simply a tactical decision made by Charles Martel without any outside influence? The answer may never be known.

What is known is that the stirrup, together with other technological innovations, changed the means of cavalry warfare, allowing for the 'mounted shock combat' to which White referred. These other innovations include the invention of the nailed horseshoe, c.890. This invention was of limited effect in drier climates, as in Spain, Italy and the Holy Land, where the horses' hooves remained hard and capable of galloping over even rocky terrain. In the wetter northern European lands, however, where hooves became soft, quickly worn and sometimes broken, the addition of nailed shoes meant that a horse could travel greater distances at greater speeds over even the most rocky terrains without injury. Battles could be fought at any time of year and over any type of terrain. Another invention that improved cavalry warfare was the saddle with high pommel and cantel, dated to the beginning of the twelfth century. Prior to this development, the saddle had been made of rigid flat leather. It replaced the ancient horse-blanket and riding cushions, but provided little more lateral stability. The saddle only prevented the rider from falling off of his horse, but did nothing to help him in combat. The addition of a high wrap-around cantel that sat against the rider's back prevented him from being thrown over the horse's rump. An equally high pommel protected the rider's genitals and lower stomach, as well as keeping him from being thrown over his horse's head. With these features the cavalry soldier was now able to use the full power of his horse to provide a mounted shock attack without being toppled from his steed.

Couching the Lance and Mounted Shock Combat

It would be a mistake to assume that, simply because ancient and early medieval cavalry did not have stirrups, they were unable to fight effectively. Cavalry warfare had existed for more than a millennium before the proliferation of stirrups in Europe, the Muslim world or East Asia. Those who fought on horseback must have been able to wield their weapons - spears, swords and bows - effectively, using their strong knees and legs to anchor their bodies to the horse. In a way, once stirrups became standard among cavalry soldiers, they also became a crutch, with those using them forgetting the older practices of wielding weapons from their stirrup-less mounts. Adding the other technological innovations mentioned above meant that eleventh- and twelfth-century cavalry could not have duplicated the abilities of their early medieval equivalents. In other words, a Norman horseman would not have been able to fight like a Visigothic or Hunnic cavalry soldier because the styles of fighting were so completely different. (On the other hand, the earlier medieval warriors might easily have been able to adapt to the newer technology.)

Of course, the stirrup did improve the ability of the cavalry to fight by adding the aspect of mounted shock combat, but did the couching of lances occur at the same time as the invention of the stirrup? If not, then when exactly did this tactic become adopted?

The answer to the first question is no; at least, there is no definitive evidence suggesting that the tactic and technology were concurrent. This has left historians trying to set a more precise date for the couching of lances and the adoption of mounted shock combat. For many centuries, it was assumed that the tactic was developed early in the Middle Ages, perhaps even as early as the Battle of Adrianople (378).

However, this view was countered effectively in 1951, when D.J.A. Ross, in an article entitled 'Plein sa hanste' (from *Medium Aevum* 20, pp.1–10), contended that the first couched lance descriptions could not be found before the composition of the early chansons de geste, which he dated to between 1050 and 1100. This thesis in turn was rebutted in 1962 by Lynn White, Jr, in the aforementioned Medieval Technology and Social Change. White claimed that mounted shock combat was known much earlier than the date which Ross had established, possibly as early as

Carolingian Lancer (c. 8th century)

No army since the fall of Rome was as large, strong or successful as that put together by Charlemagne. Although never as numerous as his infantry, Charlemagne built his forces around a core of heavy cavalry, whose strategic and tactical mobility and power gave the Carolingians victory in nearly every military engagement they fought. Among the most important equipment worn by the Carolingian horseman was his byrnie, a long chain or scale armour that covered the torso, reached below the hips and covered most of the arms. Helmets consisted of a cap encircled by a rather wide rim. Large round shields were also carried, although they were used almost exclusively when the cavalry soldier was dismounted. Wealthy Carolingian horsemen might also wear leg guards, greaves, armguards and gauntlets. Offensive weapons included lances or spears that could be couched or thrusted from the saddle, long swords and, sometimes, bows.

the eighth century, the same century that White believed saw the development of stirrups and the origin of the heavy-cavalry dominant army.

White's date for the origin of mounted shock combat, however, did not stand long without criticism. Within a year, Ross had defended his 1951 thesis using not only the chansons de geste but also the Bayeux Tapestry as evidence. This was echoed over the next two decades by a number of articles supporting him, all of which established the date of the introduction of mounted shock combat to some time between c.1050 and c.1150. In 1965, François Buttin used a copious number of original narrative sources to claim a mid twelfth-century date.

In 1980, David C. Nicolle affirmed an early twelfth-century date based on the influence of crusader-couched lance warfare on the Muslims. In 1985, Bernard S. Bachrach in 'Animals and Warfare in Early Medieval Europe' argued a twelfth-century date based upon the development of the high cantel and high pommel saddle. The same year, Victoria Cirlot used Catalan artistic, diplomatic and literary sources to set the date at c.1140 and in 1988 Jean Flori suggested a date of c.1100 based on Christian and Muslim narratives, epics and illustrated documents.

Whatever the original date may have been, it seems certain that, by the middle of the twelfth century, the couched lance had begun to dominate the battlefield, and that from then until the end of the Middle Ages, mounted shock combat was the primary, if not the only, use of the lance from horseback. It was also a tactic universally employed throughout western Europe, as is clearly seen in the large number of artistic sources from all western kingdoms that depict the cavalry lance held in a couched position.

Contemporary chronicles report that the lance was the principal offensive weapon of the crusaders in the Holy Land, where the first attack was always a mounted shock combat charge. In England, the 1181 Assize of Arms decreed by Henry II specifies only the lance as a required weapon for horsemen in battle. A similar requirement was ordered of all cavalry soldiers in Florence in 1260, and Spain, Germany and France also practised the battlefield use of mounted shock combat.

Byzantine Cavalry

Another important question about cavalry in the Middle Ages is: when did these forces become the dominant arm of their respective medieval armies? The eastern Roman Empire had witnessed the earliest attacks of the Visigoths and the Huns, with their respective cavalry forces. It was this region, having evolved into the Byzantine Empire at the dissolution of the western Roman Empire, that responded quickly to these military threats by adopting horsed units that could effectively oppose either heavy cavalry, as they had met in the Visigoths, or light cavalry and mounted archers, as they had seen with the Huns.

By the reign of Emperor Justinian (527–65), an almost complete transformation of military organization had taken place. Procopius, the prolific but not entirely supportive Byzantine chronicler, reports that cavalry in the Byzantine army, especially victorious under the leadership of the generals Belisarius and Narses, was already dominant. There were three types of Byzantine cavalry: heavily armed and armoured; more lightly armoured, largely skirmishing troops; and horsed archers. There were also mercenary horsemen, especially some Hunnic cavalry drawn from the steppes and eastern Europe.

All of these units were significant, but it was perhaps the mounted archers who were the most impressive. They were possibly inspired by what had been seen in facing the Huns a century earlier. Procopius reports that these soldiers were especially skilful, capable of shooting their bows with great accuracy from either side of their horses at full gallop. They could also fire across the rear of their horses in order to protect themselves and their companions in case of retreat, and their arrows had more penetrative power than those launched by either the Huns or their frequent enemy, the Persians. The Byzantine mounted archers were also better armoured than their enemies, with torso and leg armour (greaves reaching above their knees) and a shield mounted on the shoulder that was used to protect the neck and face when firing weapons. Finally, in close fighting they could become light cavalry, also carrying a sword.

The other impressive Byzantine force was the

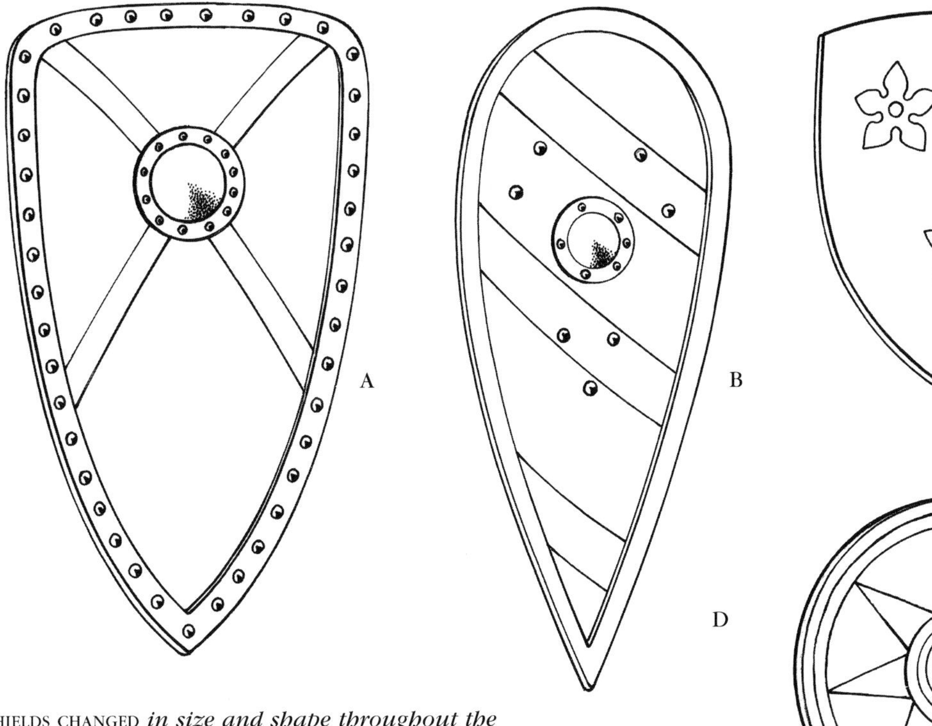

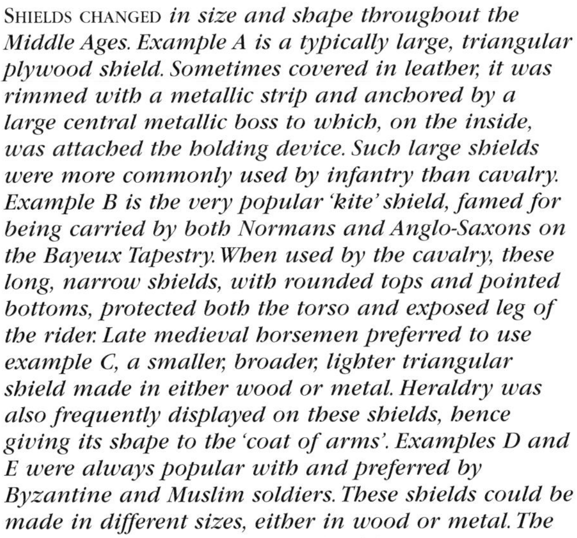

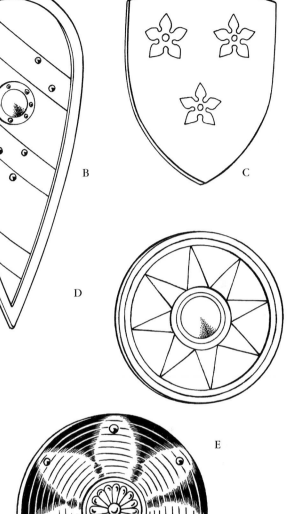

SHIELDS CHANGED *in size and shape throughout the Middle Ages. Example A is a typically large, triangular plywood shield. Sometimes covered in leather, it was rimmed with a metallic strip and anchored by a large central metallic boss to which, on the inside, was attached the holding device. Such large shields were more commonly used by infantry than cavalry. Example B is the very popular 'kite' shield, famed for being carried by both Normans and Anglo-Saxons on the Bayeux Tapestry. When used by the cavalry, these long, narrow shields, with rounded tops and pointed bottoms, protected both the torso and exposed leg of the rider. Late medieval horsemen preferred to use example C, a smaller, broader, lighter triangular shield made in either wood or metal. Heraldry was also frequently displayed on these shields, hence giving its shape to the 'coat of arms'. Examples D and E were always popular with and preferred by Byzantine and Muslim soldiers. These shields could be made in different sizes, either in wood or metal. The smallest are frequently called bucklers.*

heavy cavalry. Inspired by the ancient *cataphracti* whom their ancestors had faced in the Middle East, these Byzantine soldiers were armed with a bow in a bow case, a covered quiver holding 34 arrows, two lances and a sword. They were outfitted in long mail armour reaching to the ankle and including a coif, with a gorget to protect the throat and a plumed helmet. Their horses, too, were armoured, and when not being ridden in battle would be outfitted with all of the soldier's gear. Raised and paid for by private commanders in an effort to curry favour with the emperor, these troops were used by the Byzantines primarily to charge into infantry lines to cause disarray and confusion in preparation for an infantry assault. Needless to say, they were not known for their speed, charging more often at a trot than a gallop, the latter possible if only for a short distance.

The Byzantines bred their warhorses, setting up a large number of stud farms throughout the more secure and fertile agricultural regions of the empire. Efforts were also made to train these horses to accept the style of warfare practised by the different types of cavalry troops.

Of course, as with most other medieval armies, Byzantine cavalry were never more numerous than their infantry. Nor were their combined forces, numbering around 25,000 in general, more numerous than their opponent's forces. However, Justinian's armies were more often victorious than defeated. They pushed the Persians out of Asia Minor, marched across the Middle East, invaded Egypt, destroying the Vandal kingdom there and in North Africa, and then invaded Italy and destroyed the Ostrogoths. In each of these conquests, the Byzantines used their cavalry to take the advantage away from their more numerous enemies in battle. On campaign and at sieges, the cavalry would perform important foraging and reconnaissance duties.

Justinian's successor emperors, Maurice (585–602), Phocas (602–10) and Heraclius (610–41), continued his military policies and, for the most part, duplicated his successes. Italy was abandoned as too costly to hang on to, but campaigns against the Persians and a new enemy, the Avars, protected Byzantine Middle Eastern and Balkan lands and also added to Byzantine territory. War seemed constant, and this situation initiated the writing of several military manuals. The most famous of these is the *Strategikon*, attributed to Emperor Maurice, and dated either to the end of his reign or the beginning of that of Phocas. The manual is meant to instruct officers in the methods of fighting wars, and many of its suggestions are addressed to the operation of cavalry. In the text, the cavalry is the main unit of the Byzantine army, and it is clear that its author knows very well not only how to fight from horseback, but also how to train, take care of and protect cavalry horses.

'If you move rapidly, above all if the work of your scouts, your intelligence and your couriers is reliable, you can be certain of defeating a battalion with a detachment, an army with a battalion.'

– Anonymous Byzantine general

In facing the Persians and Avars, the Byzantines fought armies with their own dominant cavalries. Persian cavalry consisted largely of heavily armoured mounted bowmen, also armed with swords. Avar cavalry were similarly armoured, but also carried lances as well as swords and bows. Persians hoped to stay away from close combat and were clearly better trained as archers than swordsmen. Avars also preferred archery, generally at a greater distance than their Persian counterparts, but forced to fight in closer combat they seem to have been equally capable with lances and swords. There is also evidence showing that the Avars used stirrups and they may indeed have been the first European troops to do so.

Of these two enemies, the Byzantines were able to defeat the Persians more often and more completely, with Heraclius particularly successful in his campaigns and battles against them. Indeed, some historians credit these successful campaigns as the reason why a weakened Persian Empire was so easily overrun by Muslim forces later in the seventh century. Against the Persians, the Byzantines followed the strategy and tactics outlined in the *Strategikon*. These included diversionary tactics, ambushes, feigned flights, skirmishing, cutting off supply lines and even using caltrops to mine retreat routes. Such measures were meant to fatigue and demoralize the Persians, and it could not have been done without well-trained Byzantine horsemen.

Byzantine Heavy Cavalry (c. 10th Century)

Descendants of the ancient cataphracti, *the defining characteristic of these heavy Byzantine cavalrymen is that they, and their horses, were completely covered by armour. From contemporary artistic works it can be determined that these suits probably consisted of scale armour for the torso, a chain covering for the face, metal or hardened leather (*cuir bouilli*) bands for lower arm and leg protection, a helmet and small shield. The horses were equally well armoured, with barding made of metallic scales that covered the body and neck. A* chanfron, *made of similar material, protected the horse's head. Offensive weapons usually included both a lance and sword. The protection of the warrior provided by such defensive armaments is obvious. However, the added weight to the rider and horse so slowed the impetus of the Byzantine charge that it was often lost in encountering solidly formed infantry or lighter cavalry opponents.*

The Byzantines were less successful against the Avars, who ultimately came to control much of the Balkans and, in 626, even threatened Constantinople. Yet this relationship may have come more from a priority of pursuing warfare against the Persians than the Avars. However, there was some military contact, and the Byzantines seem to have profited from witnessing Avar cavalry warfare and adopted some of the strategies and tactics they observed.

Arab Horsemen

While early Byzantines fought well during the first three centuries of their empire's history, it seems that they, and in fact almost everyone else, were definitely not prepared for the horsed tactics of the Muslim Arab warriors who stormed across the Arabian peninsula and into Byzantine territory. These troops, originating as nomadic warriors who rode on horses or camels, were seemingly as accustomed to cavalry warfare as the Huns described by Ammianus Marcellinus above. Yet they should not be thought of as primitive desert-dwellers, fighting without advanced arms and armour or effective strategy and tactics. Indeed, while some undoubtedly fought as light horsemen or 'camelmen', it is known that other, more financially able, cavalry fought in heavy chain armour and helmets. Additionally, as far as effective strategy and tactics are concerned, the proof seems to come in their early military history. As cavalry-dominant armies, they were successful in piling up victory after victory against less religiously motivated enemies, including the once very powerful Persians, until they encountered the Byzantine Empire. Even then, the Byzantines were only able to stop Muslim military progress in Asia Minor, losing all of their Middle Eastern and North African lands in the process. Some historians also credit the Arab Muslim cavalry with introducing the Arabian horse to the cavalries of Europe. Others suggest that this breed was known to the Romans, and that, in fact, Byzantine cavalry horses were also Arabians.

For the next few centuries, the Byzantines took a largely defensive stance as they hunkered down behind fortified borders. Muslim Arabs and Egyptians continued to pose a threat to the east of the empire. The Avars, destroyed by Charlemagne in the eighth century, would cease to be a threat in the west, but they were quickly replaced by the Bulgars, Magyars and Russians. Byzantine emperors did occasionally attempt offensives against surrounding or Mediterranean lands,

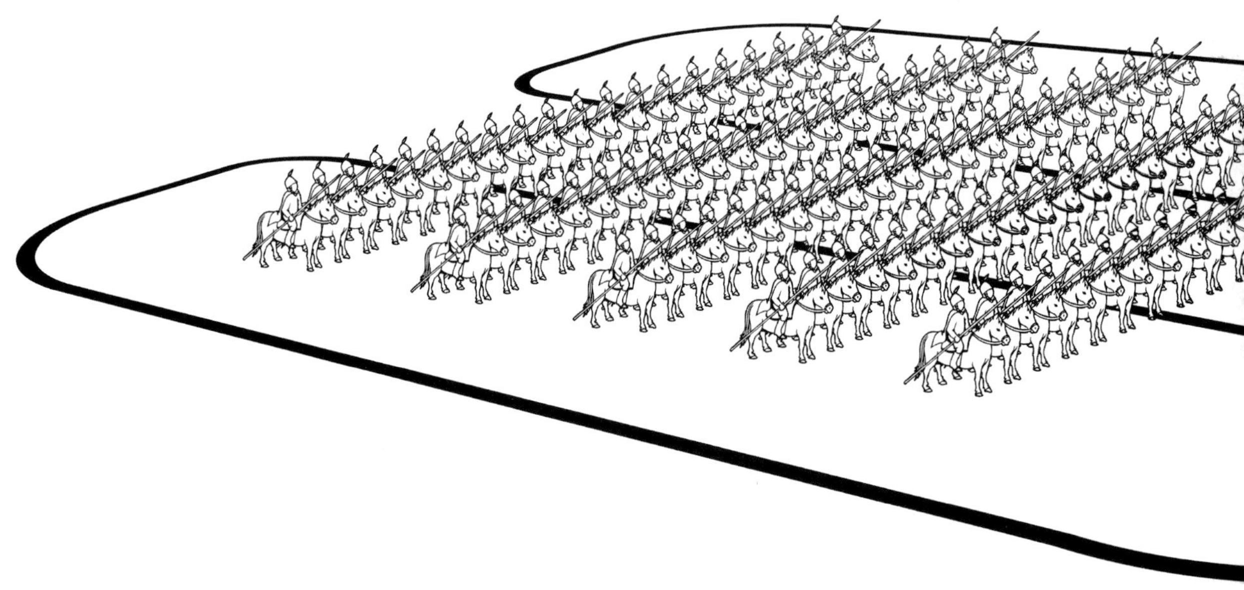

however, if successful, these were most often short-lived. Depending on the terrain of the conquests, the Byzantines continued to use their cavalry, although almost always in the role of support troops for the more numerous infantry.

Charlemagne and the Carolingians

On the evidence above, Charles Martel must undoubtedly be given credit for increasing the role and importance of cavalry in western European armies. Yet it was his grandson, Charlemagne, who must be recognized as the magnate who made cavalry a dominant arm of his military. Throughout his entire reign, 768–814, he fought wars. Indeed, according to Einhard, the Carolingian emperor's biographer, there was only a single year during his reign that no warfare was carried out by his armies. Through this activity, he conquered the Bretons, Avars, Lombards and Saxons, replacing their previous governments with his own rule. He also crossed the Pyrenees and attacked the Spanish Muslims by besieging and sacking Barcelona, and, to his later regret, by destroying the Basque-controlled town of Pamplona. (In revenge for this action, Charlemagne's baggage train, commanded by Roland, was ambushed and destroyed when returning from Spain, providing the basis for *The Song of Roland* later.) As a result of this warfare, Frankish lands more than doubled in size, and as a reward for defeating the Lombards in Italy, Charlemagne was crowned as the first Holy Roman Emperor.

Warfare was important for Charlemagne, so he continually endeavoured to improve his army, and many of these improvements were adapted for his cavalry. Charlemagne recognized very early in his reign that the defensive requirements of his large empire and his desire to conquer lands beyond its borders required a highly regulated professional army. To him, these requirements and desires necessitated a strict military organization and a cavalry-dominant force. They also demanded an army that was uniformly well armed and armoured, both offensively and defensively. The first extant law to state this policy was the *Capitulare Missorum* (a Carolingian law) of 792–3, which demanded that all benefice and office holders, titled 'nobles' in the Carolingian realm, possess full armour and shield as well as a horse and offensive weaponry. This law was followed in 802–3 by a capitulary again charging these horsemen to have their own helmets, shields and cuirasses, known to the Carolingians as 'byrnies'. Finally, in 805, the law was made even more specific In this capitulary, Charlemagne required anyone of his empire who held 12 *mansi* of land to have his own armour and to serve as a horseman in his army; if he failed in his duty, both his land and his armour would be taken from him. Infantry soldiers were not so well protected, although the Capitulary of Aachen, proclaimed in 802–03, did require them all to carry a shield.

Perhaps the most unique defensive armament of the Carolingian cavalry was the byrnie. To the

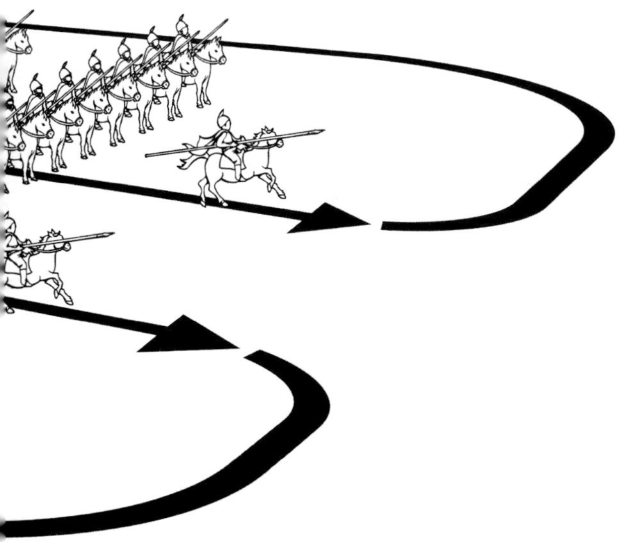

AN IDEAL CAVALRY *formation, much favoured by the Carolingian cavalry, consisted of several lines of cavalry (usually three or four) that all charged their opponents simultaneously. When a charge was stopped, generally by the solidarity of an enemy's defensive position, the cavalry would break off, wheel towards their flanks and regroup behind their other cavalry lines to be replaced by the next charging line. In this way an attritional effect could be achieved against a stationary enemy.*

Carolingian soldier, the byrnie was his most highly valued piece of armour, not only because of its cost, but also because no enemy he would meet on the battlefield would have one. Indeed, as early as 779 Charlemagne had forbidden the sale of this armour outside the realm. In 803, he added a declaration that soldiers were forbidden even to give it to a merchant, who might sell it to a potential enemy. It does appear, however, that some Frankish merchants still sold byrnies to Saracens, Bretons and Vikings.

There is some dispute among historians as to what exactly constituted the Carolingian byrnie. Relying, once again, only on artistic and some literary sources because of the lack of archaeological examples, some believe that it was a heavy leather jacket with metal scales sewn onto it. It was also quite long, reaching below the hips and covering most of the arms. Other historians claim instead that the Carolingian byrnie was nothing more than a coat of chain mail, but longer and perhaps heavier than traditional early medieval mail. Without more certain evidence, this dispute will continue. Leg guards and greaves also appeared during the Carolingian period, worn by the most wealthy of Charlemagne's horsemen. Emerging for the first time were arm-guards and gauntlets, later to be common armour for all cavalry. Charlemagne also forbade the sale of these armaments to foreigners.

Carolingian military policies remained dominant throughout the ninth and tenth centuries. The army continued to be primarily a well-armed cavalry-centric force with each soldier protected by a long byrnie (by now almost certainly chain mail), a segmented, wide-brimmed helmet and a large round shield made of wood and leather. Indeed, so influential were these Carolingian practices that they stimulated change in military tradition even beyond the borders of Charlemagne's empire. Carolingian-style armour developed into the standard defensive armament in Spain, Scandinavia, eastern Europe and England.

Charlemagne also established a standardized weapons policy for his troops. The principal weapon remained the spear, and it was to be carried by both infantry and cavalry troops. In 792–93, the *Capitulare Missorum* required the lance as a weapon for all horsemen. A similar command was echoed in capitularies decreed in 804 and 811. In addition, when a warhorse was owned, so too was a sword.

In fact in many narrative and literary sources the sword is reported to be the cavalry soldier's main weapon. Cavalry soldiers were also required to carry a dagger. Finally, there is evidence that some Carolingian cavalry operated as mounted archers, although whether they actually shot their bows from their horses, or dismounted to operate as infantry bowmen, cannot be determined from the sources.

The Charge

Historians have generally thought that Charlemagne's was the first western medieval army to use cavalry as its main force in battle. Their primary tactic was the charge, although one not yet effective in delivering a mounted shock attack. Should the charging horses come in contact with opposing lines of troops, most likely composed of

infantry, their riders would thrust down with their spears or slash down with their swords.

However, the point of the charge, here and later in the Middle Ages, may have been less to make contact with the enemy soldiers, than to cause those soldiers to flee in rout from the battlefield. Intimidation of poorer, less well-armoured infantry by wealthy, expensively clad cavalry was the key here. Should even part of the enemy line flee at the prospect of facing these heavy horsemen, the whole of the force would be weakened. The cavalry would then be able to ride through the holes left in their opponent's line, meeting little effective opposition. Subsequent charges would eventually cause the whole of the enemy army to flee, and victory would be won.

Recently, however, one historian of the Carolingian army, Bernard S. Bachrach, has suggested that this traditional view is not correct. Instead of delivering charges on the battlefield, Charlemagne's cavalry were used almost solely for 'search-and-destroy missions against small groups of relatively untrained enemies'. They also 'had a supporting role to play in siege warfare and for patrol duty as members of garrisons' (for publication details, see bibliography). In battle, this cavalry dismounted to fight.

Yet, these services provided by cavalry should not be seen as anything less important than that provided in the traditional description of Carolingian warfare above. Rather, such a role played by cavalry was vital to the entire, highly successful Carolingian military effort.

THE MOST FEARSOME *military tactic of the Middle Ages was perhaps the charging cavalry. At a time when the success of battle often depended more on forcing one's enemies to flee the battlefield than on actually killing them, it is no wonder that defeating such a charge depended on the discipline of much lower-class infantry troops and the leadership of their generals. The charges of Norman cavalry, such as those pictured above causing the flight of infantry opponents, accounted for many more victories than battles like the one fought at Hastings in 1066.*

Norman Cavalry

Because of the size of Charlemagne's territories and his prominence in warfare, Carolingian military tactics became widespread for the next few centuries. All European army forces became dominated by cavalry. To outfit all of these cavalries, a large number of horses had to be supplied. Although the Carolingians always demanded stallions as tribute, these never amounted to enough horses to supply their needs. By the end of the eighth century managed stud farms were established. The costs of warhorses made these extremely profitable businesses, and although they certainly had the support and protection of Charlemagne at the time they appear to have been largely private farms. They were owned and operated by influential local magnates and landowners, who controlled stables, pasture lands and the fields that supplied feed. More importantly, they also controlled breeding stocks. Before too long, it had become general practice to rotate both stallions and mares so that the stock did not become inbred.

It also seems that some experimentation was done by the breeders and stablemen of these horses, ultimately improving the strength and endurance of warhorses. In addition, they appear to have weeded out lesser steeds. Eventually, a stronger, heavier horse was bred. Known after the twelfth century as a destrier, this horse was selectively bred from Bactrian or Arabian stock through an intricate process over a long period of time, sometimes several years. Eventually this produced a horse 17 hands (173cm/68in) tall, while medieval horses had typically measured 12–13 hands (122–132cm/48–52in) in height. With strong bones and a strong, short back, it was an animal capable of carrying a heavily armoured soldier into a battle or a tournament (although rarely would a knight use the same horse for both).

Cavalry warfare continued, whenever necessary, between the eighth and eleventh centuries. 'Whenever necessary' because this was the age of invasions from the Vikings (throughout Europe) and Magyars (in eastern and central Europe), and sometimes defence against these forces did not

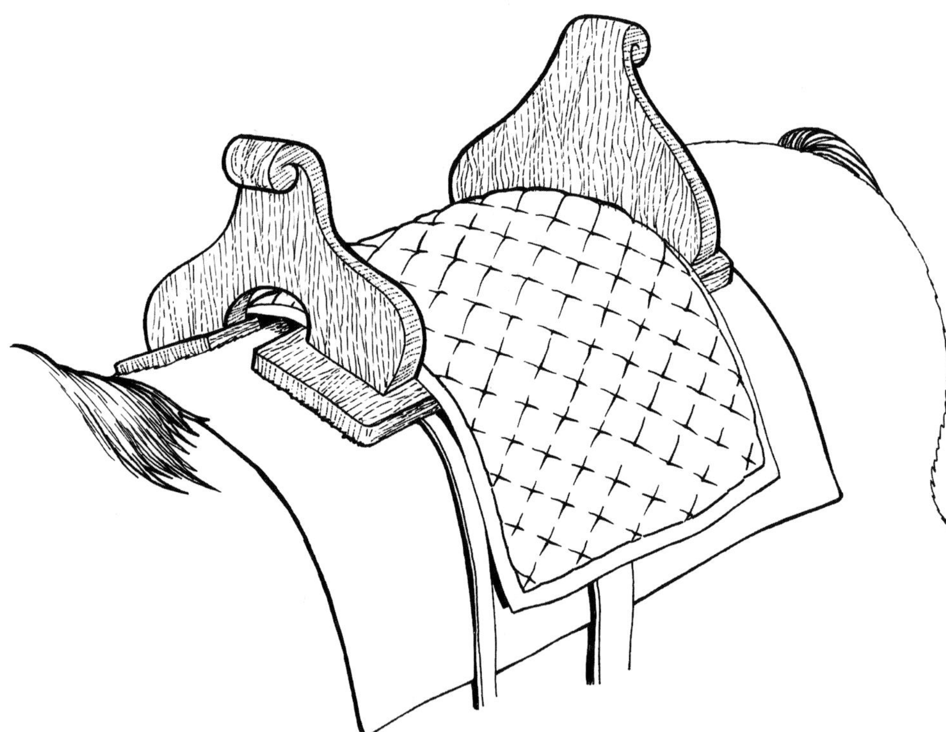

TECHNOLOGICAL IMPROVEMENTS *to the saddle, most notably the high cantel and pommel invented no later than the early 12th century, increased the stability of a cavalry soldier. A high cantel, sitting against the rider's back prevented him being thrown over the horse's rump. An equally high pommel protected the rider's genitals and lower stomach as well as preventing him being thrown over his horse's head.*

necessitate cavalries. Indeed, sometimes the defence did not necessitate any military action whatsoever, other than flight from the raiders to fortified locations. The Magyars rode horses, and the armies facing them, when this occurred, usually did so with forces dominated by cavalry. Ultimately, they decided the Magyars' fate when German cavalry forces gained victory against them at the Battle of Lech, fought in 955. The Vikings also rode horses, generally those they were able to steal or receive as bribes once they landed from their ships. Nevertheless, they seem to have used these mounts only for transportation and rarely fought on horseback; rarely, too, were they opposed on horseback.

Interestingly, perhaps the next important group in the history of medieval cavalry warfare were the the Normans, who were the descendants of the Vikings. Unlike their ancestors, they would use horses for much more than transportation. By virtue of their portrayal in the Bayeux Tapestry, historians have actually come to regard the Normans as the very symbols of cavalry warfare. Where and when the Normans acquired their cavalry abilities is not recorded in medieval sources, although it is almost certain that they developed them after their settlement in 911 in what would become Normandy. However, it cannot be determined whether they learned to fight on horseback from those among whom they settled and over whom they governed, or from one of the many armies they fought against between 911 and 1035. Certainly by the time of the ducal ascension of William the Conqueror (Norman leaders were known as dukes) in 1035, the Norman horseman had become well known and militarily respected throughout Europe.

William the Conqueror is naturally one of the most famous warlords of the Middle Ages, and his victorious generalship at the Battle of Hastings in 1066 certainly justifies his renown. This battle, however, was but one of several military adventures of his reign. Because William's ascension took place when he was quite young, and no doubt also because of his illegitimacy (although he had been recognized at birth by his father, Robert), there seems to have been many in his duchy who wished to strengthen their position and land-holdings at the expense of the young duke. Rebellions started early for William and continued sporadically at least until the early 1060s, as they were still being depicted in the Bayeux Tapestry's account of Harold Godwinson, Earl of Wessex, visiting the Duchy of Normandy. In the Tapestry's story, Harold is driven off course and falls into the hands of one of William's barons, Guy of Ponthieu, who despite holding the English nobleman, surrenders him to William at the duke's request. William, with Harold now in tow, then responds militarily to the rebellion of Conan of Brittany and successfully defeats him. William and his military entourage do all of this on horseback; no infantry appear in this part of the Bayeux Tapestry.

> *'Each horseman is to carry shield and spear, long sword and short sword, bow, quivers and arrows, and your carts are to contain implements of various kinds – axes and stone-cutting tools...trenching tools, iron spades and...implements which an army needs.'*
>
> – *Carolingian Muster Cartulary, 806*

Cavalry Army

One thing becomes quite clear: the army of William the Conqueror, although also containing infantry - spearmen, swordsmen and archers are all depicted in the Bayeux Tapestry - was dominated by cavalry. This is confirmed in the narratives that record the battle of Hastings. Yet William's was not the only eleventh-century Norman army so organized. Robert Guiscard's Norman invasion force of Sicily and southern Italy was also accomplished using a cavalry-dominant army, and he used his cavalry effectively in all

facets of his campaigns and against all enemies, Byzantines, Muslims, Germans, southern Italians and Sicilians. At the Battle of Civitate in 1053, the initial charge of Guiscard's cavalry, though outnumbered almost two to one by Pope Leo IX's army, caused most of the opposing infantry to flee from the battlefield and quickly defeated those remaining, thus fulfilling their customary role as battlefield warriors The Germans preferred to fight on foot, wrote William of Apulia, because they could not manoeuvre their horses as expertly as the Normans. Elsewhere in Sicily and southern Italy, they served as scouts and foragers for the army. In all of the battles of Normans, the cavalry charge prevailed as a central tactic. Sometimes these charges appear to be similar to those ascribed to the Carolingians and others prior to the Normans. Yet, as concluded above, the eleventh to twelfth century was also the period when lances began to be couched, and it seems likely that Norman cavalry started using this weapon application as well, although perhaps not as its sole cavalry warfare tactic. The Bayeux Tapestry portrays the Normans using both couched and thrusted lances.

That lances had begun to be couched, especially in cavalry-on-cavalry warfare, may explain the origins of the kite shield. The rest of the Norman cavalry body armour and helmets had not changed much from those of the Carolingian cavalry three centuries previously, especially in size. Yet the shield had changed considerably. The Carolingian shield, being round, did not protect the full body of the horseman, leaving almost his entire leg unprotected from enemy attack. At the same time, its large size made it unwieldy for a cavalry soldier to manoeuvre easily during battle. These problems were less significant when the horseman did not need to contend with an opponent couching his lance and thus driving forwards with the power of man and horse together. Any parts of the body, even those partially protected by greaves or other armour, would be susceptible to maiming blows from the couched lances. The problem was solved by making the shield narrower and kite-shaped. All of the cavalry shields depicted on the Bayeux Tapestry are long, narrow and kite-shaped, with rounded tops and pointed bottoms. They are all also shown covering the left legs, torsos and shoulders of their riders, facing the lances of opposing cavalry, couched across the bodies of the soldiers and horses.

The horse accompanied almost all of the soldiers who undertook the First Crusade. However, a study of the horses and the roles they played in this and other Crusades has yet to be written, leaving several unanswered questions. For example, it is uncertain how many horses travelled with the crusaders. How many of these were to be used for warfare and how many simply for

THE BAYEUX TAPESTRY, *perhaps the most famous artistic depiction of medieval warfare, shows William the Conqueror's campaign to gain the English throne. This scene portrays the attack of Norman cavalry against the Anglo-Saxon infantry shield wall at the Battle of Hastings. Note that while one or two cavalry lances are shown to be couched, most are thrust down on the infantry, indicating that at this time there was no single preferred position.*

transportation or cargo? Did many of the more wealthy cavalry initially bring several horses, including more than a single warhorse, as seems to have been traditional in continental campaigns of the same time? No doubt the horses numbered in the many thousands, and the problems associated with their feeding and cleansing, as well as the effect that the horses' waste produced on the health of the crusaders, were also numerous.

What is known is that most of these horses arrived in good health at Constantinople in 1096–1097, and that the warhorses among them carried crusader cavalry to their battlefield victories at Nicaea and Dorylaeum in 1097. It was also these knights who convinced Anna Comnena that they were 'irresistible' and that the knight could 'bore his way through the walls of Babylon'. The second historical certainty is that as the crusaders travelled across Asia Minor between Nicaea and Antioch, their horses began to die off, and to die off rather quickly, often for lack of fodder. Fulcher of Chartres writes that the situation had become so bad that 'sometimes even armed knights used oxen as mounts'. Still, the crusaders had some warhorses at Antioch and, having captured the town, they were able to respond to the siege of Kerbogha by charging out on these mounts into the surprised Seljuk Turkish relief force, defeating it. Raymond of Aguiliers concludes his account of the battle with 'the Lord laboured surprisingly well with men and horses...and those famished horses scarcely led from their scanty provender into battle by their masters, now pursued without difficulty the best and fleetest Turkish steeds'.

The success of the First Crusade allowed for the formation of several Crusade Kingdoms, all of which were populated with what became known as Resident Crusaders. Some Resident Crusaders even declared their devotion to the task of controlling the Holy Land by forming monastic military orders, the Knights Hospitallers and the Knights Templars being the most famous. Cavalry became as important to them in the Middle East as it would have had they been in Europe; the Templars even had instructions on how to deliver a cavalry charge written into their Monastic Rule.

Although illustrations of Templars frequently show two knights sharing one horse, their Rule indicates how many horses each knight was to possess: the knight commanders, four horses;

brother knights, three horses with an added one, if desired, for his squire; brother sergeants, one permanent horse with another, if the monastic house believed it to be necessary; five other brother sergeants with special duties, two permanent horses. As shipments from Europe could not be counted on to provide enough horses to fill all of these needs, they had to be acquired elsewhere. Some undoubtedly came from booty and ransom, and some from purchase. Others were farmed by these monastic military orders, with the farms breeding and training replacement mounts. Later crusaders most often brought their warhorses from Europe, transporting these across the sea in specially constructed naval horse transports, filled also with sufficient grain - generally hay and barley - and fresh water to satisfy the horses' needs.

Battle of Hastings: 14 October 1066

Perhaps because they happen so rarely in modern combat, modern military historians seem enamoured by the decisive military engagement. Medieval warfare in this regard compares with the modern: very few military engagements were actually decisive. The siege of Constantinople in 1453 was one - Byzantine before and Ottoman Turkish after. The only other decisive engagement of the Middle Ages may be the Battle of Hastings, fought between Duke William the Conqueror's invading Norman (and other northern French) troops and King Harold II Godwinson's Anglo-Saxon/Anglo-Scandinavian army. Although it would take him a while to conquer the rest of the island kingdom, William's victory in this battle essentially gave him decisive control over England, especially because not only the king, but also his two brothers, were slain in the conflict, leaving no one in the kingdom to dispute William's military claim to the crown.

The history of England in the half century prior to the Battle of Hastings is one of royal inheritance, confusion and upheaval. The eleventh century began with Ethelred II as the English king. Ethelred had been on the throne since 978 when, at the age of 10, he ascended as ruler after the murder of his half-brother, Edward II (the Martyr). Yet, his was never a very secure rule. Fraught with problems, in 1002 the king tried to shore up his weak control by marrying Emma, the daughter of Duke Richard I of Normandy, thus connecting his realm with that powerful duchy. However, this marriage alliance seems to have had little enduring impact on the security of Ethelred's kingship. In 1013 the Danish king, Swein Forkbeard, and his son, Cnut, attacked and conquered England. The following year, at the death of his father, Cnut succeeded to both the English and the Danish kingship, and in 1016 he married the recently deceased Ethelred's widow, Emma, once again establishing a marriage connection with Normandy.

Cnut ruled England strongly until 1035, but at his death the indeterminacy of inheritance threw the kingdom into a crisis. Cnut seems to have left no specific instructions as to his succession, and thus two men claimed the English throne. One, Harold I Harefoot, asserted his claim as a son of Cnut, albeit an illegitimate son by the king's mistress, Elfgifu. The other claimant, Harthacnut, was the legitimate son of Cnut, born to Emma. Harthacnut was ruling Denmark at the time of his father's death - Cnut had given him this kingdom to rule before he died while his half-brother was in England. His overseas presence gave the throne to Harold, at least initially, Harthacnut remained in Denmark. In 1039 or 1040, however, Harold died, and Harthacnut returned to England and ascended the throne. However, his reign, too, was short-lived, as he died in 1042.

Disputed Inheritance

With neither Harold nor Harthacnut having heirs of their own, the kingship passed to Ethelred's remaining son, Edward the Confessor, who had lived nearly his entire life in exile in Normandy. Still, Edward's inheritance of the kingdom was undisputed, even welcomed, as neither of Cnut's sons had proven popular in England. Furthermore, in entering his new kingdom, the unmarried Edward wed Edith, the only daughter of Godwin, the most powerful earl in England, also appointing two of her brothers to earldoms. The second of these, Harold, would succeed his father as Earl of Wessex in 1053, serving for the remaining years of Edward's reign as the chief counsellor to the king.

Norman Cavalryman (11th century)

During the 11th century, Norman horsemen dominated five military theatres: England, Northern France, Southern Italy, Sicily and the Holy Land. Their body armour, called a hauberk *by this time, was chain mail, made in one piece. Most* hauberks *reached to the knees and were divided down the front and back by slits that allowed for greater freedom of movement and comfort to a horseman. Some leaders and other more wealthy soldiers were also outfitted in mail leggings or* chausses. *Other defensive equipment included the kite shield and helmet. A long lance was the chief weapon of the Norman horseman, while a sword could be used for close-combat situations.*

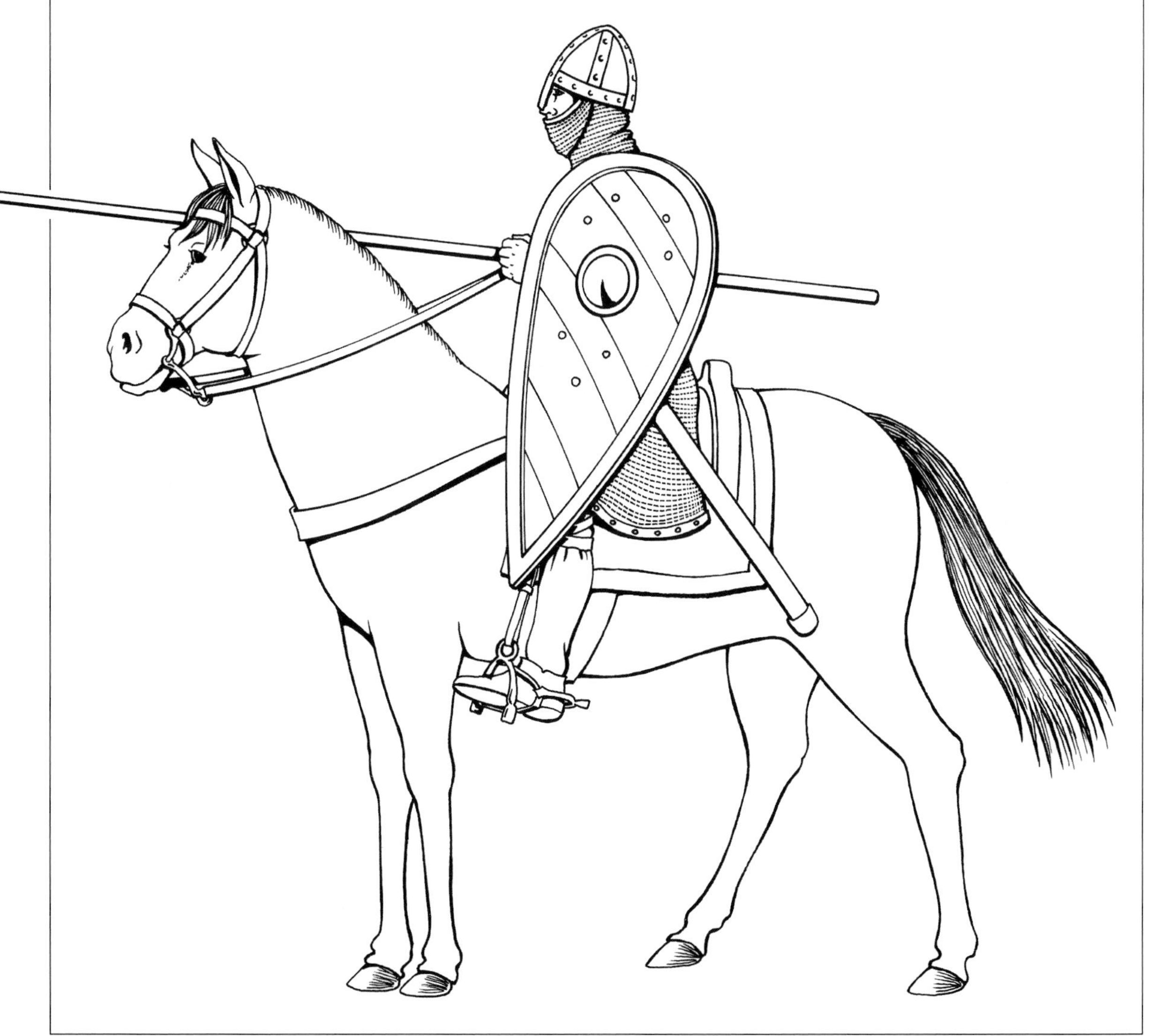

William the Conqueror had become duke of Normandy in 1035, also at a young age, 10, while his father Robert was away on pilgrimage to the Holy Land. Despite having been presented as his father's successor before Robert's departure, William, his illegitimate son, met with almost immediate rebellions among his nobles. These were put down rather quickly, initially by those barons who were loyal to William, with later ones put down by the duke himself. Consequently William began to show his military expertise, especially in waging cavalry warfare, although he proved also to be adept in laying sieges. By 1066, he was in control not only of his own duchy of Normandy, but of the county of Maine and parts of the counties of Brittany and Ponthieu as well.

Perhaps because of the necessity to secure his own continental holdings, William had little interaction with England before launching his conquest. Despite his kinship with Edward the Confessor, it seems only in 1052, during a period of exile for Earl Godwin and his family, that he actually visited the island.

It is then that most historians see the inheritance of the English throne being promised to William by Edward. However, when the Godwin family returned, and especially after their scion's death the following year, it was not William who became the obvious heir to the childless king's throne, but Harold.

The only other time that William's name comes up in connection with the history of pre-conquest England is in the 'visit' of Harold Godwinson to Normandy sometime in 1063–1064. Although disputed by some historians, as the visit is only recorded in Norman sources, Harold more than likely sailed to Normandy either by accident or as a means of discussing matters, undoubtedly the inheritance among them, with William. More importantly for the 1066 conquest, on this visit Harold was supposed to have sworn his allegiance to the Norman duke, to aid him in gaining the English kingdom when Edward died.

That Harold swore this oath with his hands placed on two holy relics did not seem to matter, however, when Edward the Confessor finally died on 5 January 1066. Nor did it matter to King Edward that he may have previously promised the throne to William. For, on his deathbed, he recognized his chief earl as his heir. In consequence, Harold Godwinson was crowned king of England the following day, and everyone in northern Europe immediately took notice.

'From their number [the Milanese] chose youths equipped with weapons, thoroughly trained in battles and swift on horseback; these youths toyed with the Emperor's darts, insulting the knights...and threatened with shields and spears, wounding some who were close by.'

– Arnulf of Milan, 1033

No fewer than three claimants to the English crown disputed Harold's crowning. One, Svein Estrithson, king of Denmark, decided not to press his claim, which he had through his kinship to Cnut. The other two, however, planned immediate conquest of England. William the Conqueror quickly began to gather soldiers, horses, provisions and ships. As soon as these were assembled, he planned to launch this fleet in an invasion across the English Channel from Normandy. The final claimant to the English throne was Harald Hardraada, king of Norway. His claim to the realm now under the control of Harold Godwinson was tenuous at best. Mostly, it appears that this bellicose Scandinavian king felt that England had been weakened by the ascendancy of Harold Godwinson to the throne, an attitude impressed upon the Norwegian king by Harold's estranged brother, Tostig Godwinson, who had fled to Norway after being outlawed in 1065 during a dispute with his own Northumbrian lieges, and was willing to accompany Harald and his Norwegian force on their attack of England.

Harald Hardraada and William the Conqueror were poised to launch their invasion fleets at the same time. Meanwhile, Harold Godwinson either thought that William was the greater of the two threats, or he may not have known of the Norwegian king's plans, or even Tostig's flight to him, although that seems highly unlikely. Whatever the reason, his army stood at least until 8 September prepared for William's invasion along the southern coast of England. Yet the Norman fleet was not the first to be launched. Because of poor weather, William had been unable to sail across the Channel. Harald, however, had not been so hindered, and in September 1066 he sailed first to the Orkney Islands and then to Scotland, where several allied troops joined his army, and finally landed along the northeastern coast of England down to the Humber River. In the middle of September, Harald then landed his fleet at Ricall and, on 20 September, marched towards York.

Standing at Fulford Gate in the way of his

WILLIAM THE CONQUEROR'S *campaign to gain the English throne is depicted here in the Bayeux Tapestry. In the top sequence, after being shipwrecked in northern France, the chief English earl, Harold Godwinson, is rescued from a Breton lord by William and his Norman cavalry. Thereafter the two join together in a campaign against one of William's rebellious lords. In the second panel, a grateful Harold promises to support William's claim by making an oath on two relics. He then returns by Norman ship to England. And in the third panel an ailing King Edward the Confessor dies. He is carried for burial to Westminster Abbey, whereupon Harold Godwinson, breaking his oath to the duke of Normandy, takes the English throne and thereby provokes William's conquest.*

march were two English earls, the brothers Morkere of Northumbria and Edwin of Mercia, with their armies. However, these proved no match for the invading Scandinavians, who quickly won the battle. Harald Hardraada proceeded to York, where he received the submission of the town, and then marched to Stamford Bridge where his troops rested, flushed with the achievement of victory and the knowledge that Harold Godwinson's army was nowhere close. This belief proved to be exaggerated confidence.

Although it is not known when Harold learnt of the invasion of the Norwegians, nor when he began his army's march to the north to counter their threat, there is no doubt that what he accomplished was an impressive feat, a swift march of his army to Tadcaster and then on to York, 305km (190 miles) north of London. The pace was 32–40km (20–25 miles) per day. On 24 September the English forces arrived in Tadcaster, and the next day they marched through York to Stamford Bridge. This advance completely surprised the Norwegian troops, many of whom were caught across the Derwent River away from their armour and their companions. The battle was swift, and the Norwegians quickly and decidedly lost. How this was done, however, remains something of a mystery. The tactics used by Harold at Stamford Bridge cannot be determined from contemporary sources, although several later Norwegian sagas report that the English king used cavalry charges to attack the Norwegian infantry lines, eventually causing their breaking into an ill-advised counter-charge. Both Harald Hardraada and Tostig Godwinson were among the slain.

Williams Lands

Two days after the battle of Stamford Bridge, as Harold Godwinson's soldiers were enjoying victory celebrations in York, William the Conqueror received his favourable weather and crossed the English Channel. His army landed on the southern coast of England, at Pevensey, facing no opposition. There they immediately erected a motte-and-bailey castle, the first of five such constructions that William would have built in the south of England before the Battle of Hastings. By constructing these fortifications, it is clear that William did not hope to fight a decisive battle against Harold Godwinson's forces. He merely looked to establish a beachhead, from which he could operate and to which later reinforcements might come to begin what the duke must have anticipated would be a lengthy conquest.

This was not to be the case, however. King Harold learnt of the Norman arrival a few days later, probably around 1 October. Repeating the speed of his earlier march, the king retraced his route, passing through London and marching on for another 80–96km (50–60 miles) to Hastings. Here he found terrain that he believed was favourable to a stand against the invading Normans. Choosing the high ground of Senlac Hill, he lined his troops some 600–800m (1968–2624ft) along the summit, or slightly below it, facing south towards the direction from which William would certainly come. It was a good tactic. His infantry, and possibly dismounted cavalry, were experienced warriors. Many of them had served with him in his victorious attacks on the Welsh in 1063 and every one of them had fought at the Battle of Stamford Bridge. They were also mostly well-armoured troops.

Dispositions

The wings of the English line were manned by the *fyrd*, a highly trained and skilled militia, adept with the spear and sword. In the centre were the king's *huscarls*, his most trusted and capable troops, armoured in lengthy chain coats and able to fight with all weapons, but especially feared for their use of the battle-axe, which they could swing either single- or two-handed. A few archers also seem to have been among the English forces, although their numbers were undoubtedly quite small, and some historians have speculated that neither they, nor any other lighter troops, who were without horse transportation, had reached Hastings from Stamford Bridge in any great numbers. Ultimately, this may have been a factor in the decisiveness of the battle.

William the Conqueror's army, while not entirely manned by cavalry, certainly was dominated by them. They, too, were quite experienced in warfare, with many of these horsemen having served the duke in his numerous

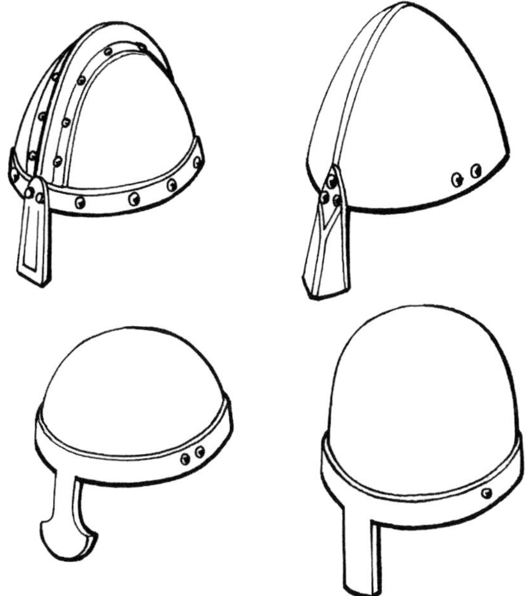

NORMAN-STYLE HELMETS, *derived from contemporary illustrations, were designed as a close-fitting conical crown with a somewhat pointed apex and a wide, flat, nasal guard descending over the nose and attached to the brim. Some appear to have been forged from a single piece of iron and hammered into the desired shape, while others were made of a segmented construction with a number of iron plates attached together.*

continental military adventures. Most were Normans, with others having been acquired from the counties of Boulogne and Flanders. Soldiers from the latter may also in fact have participated in their count's conflict with the Holy Roman Emperor, Henry III, in 1056. They must have been a superb cavalry force, and were probably the best in Europe at the time.

William's tactics though simple, were risky. His cavalry was to charge up the hill and against the line of English infantry. Hopefully, this charge would be successful in, at least, breaking the line, if not routing the soldiers altogether. If it failed, it would be repeated and repeated. Eventually, William figured, the English line would weaken and, once that happened, the Normans would have the day. There were also Norman archers and infantry at the Battle of Hastings, but their roles seem to have been limited.

What the duke of Normandy did not count on was the discipline of the English troops and the leadership of their general. No doubt he knew of their recent victory at Stamford Bridge, but perhaps he thought that that battle, together with the two long marches that they had made, would have exhausted their desire to fight. It seems unlikely that he had never faced a shield wall, the tactic of choice for most infantry lines fighting battles in the eleventh century. Shield walls were made by infantry soldiers overlapping their shields to construct a field fortification of their bodies. With spears reaching out from behind the shields, this structure was virtually impenetrable, so long as the infantry stayed in their defensive formation. That was the key. Should any break in the line occur, a charging horse with its rider slashing his sword or thrusting his lance down against the foot soldiers on each side of him would penetrate the line. Should there be no re-inforcement of the breach, the cavalry could use this opening to cause disorder of the infantry and defeat them.

The Battle

The battle was fought on and at the base of Senlac Hill on 14 October 1066. William the Conqueror divided his cavalry into three divisions, with most historians believing that these were ordered across a single front. In the centre were the Norman cavalry led by William himself, on his left were Breton cavalry, and on his right were a mixture of other mounted soldiers, called 'French' by most Norman chroniclers, but undoubtedly manned mostly by Flemish and Boulognese cavalry. In front of the cavalry lines were the Norman archers and infantry. These were to begin the battle with their own attacks on the English infantry, although these assaults turned out to be rather insubstantial. In fact, it is likely that William did not let his infantry pursue their attacks for long, as it was neither beneficial nor honourable to his cavalry to keep them out of the fray.

Thus the cavalry charges began not too long after the beginning of the battle. '[T]hose who were last became first', writes Norman eyewitness William of Poitiers, referring to the changes in the initial Norman formation. The Norman cavalry were not numerous. Contemporary sources claim

Battle of Hastings

1066

King Harold Godwinson positioned his English army in a solid formation on or slightly below the summit of Senlac Hill, near the town of Hastings. In the middle stood his huscarls, heavily armoured professional soldiers, with his fyrd, the kingdom's militia, positioned on their flanks. All Saxon soldiers fought on foot, forming a defensive 'shield-wall' by overlapping their shields with the soldiers next to them. William the Conqueror initiated the battle with an archery and infantry attack. But these troops quickly withdrew to allow for charges by the Norman cavalry. Several of these followed; through what became an extremely long battle, the English shield-wall stood firm. Only when the Norman cavalry performed a feigned retreat did the infantry line break and rush down the hill. William's horsemen turned and returned to the fight, defeating those who had pursued them. Harold tried vainly to regroup his troops, but was killed.

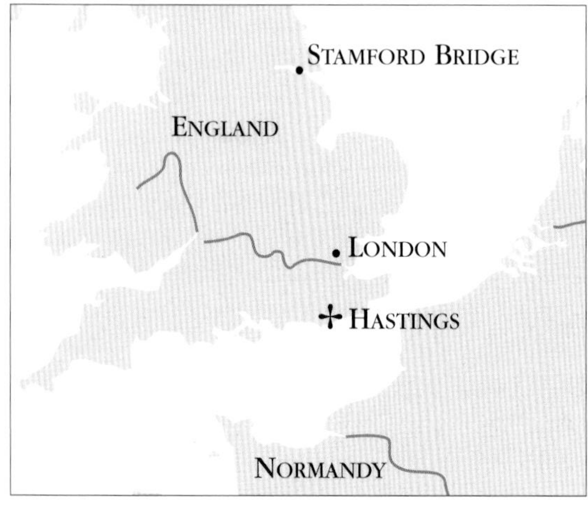

Landing on England's southern coast near Hastings, William quickly built five motte-and-bailey castles, establishing a foothold. Harold's march to counter this invasion met the invader at Senlac Hill.

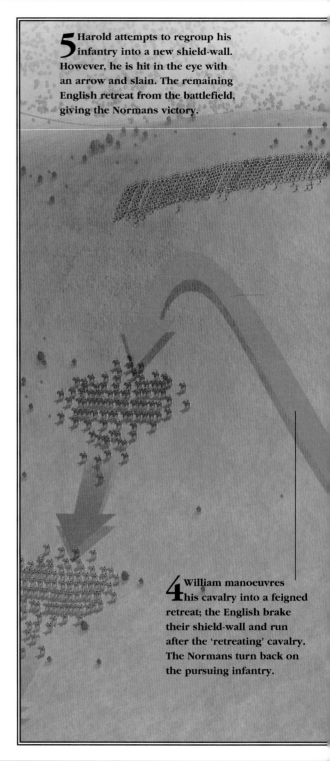

5 Harold attempts to regroup his infantry into a new shield-wall. However, he is hit in the eye with an arrow and slain. The remaining English retreat from the battlefield, giving the Normans victory.

4 William manoeuvres his cavalry into a feigned retreat; the English brake their shield-wall and run after the 'retreating' cavalry. The Normans turn back on the pursuing infantry.

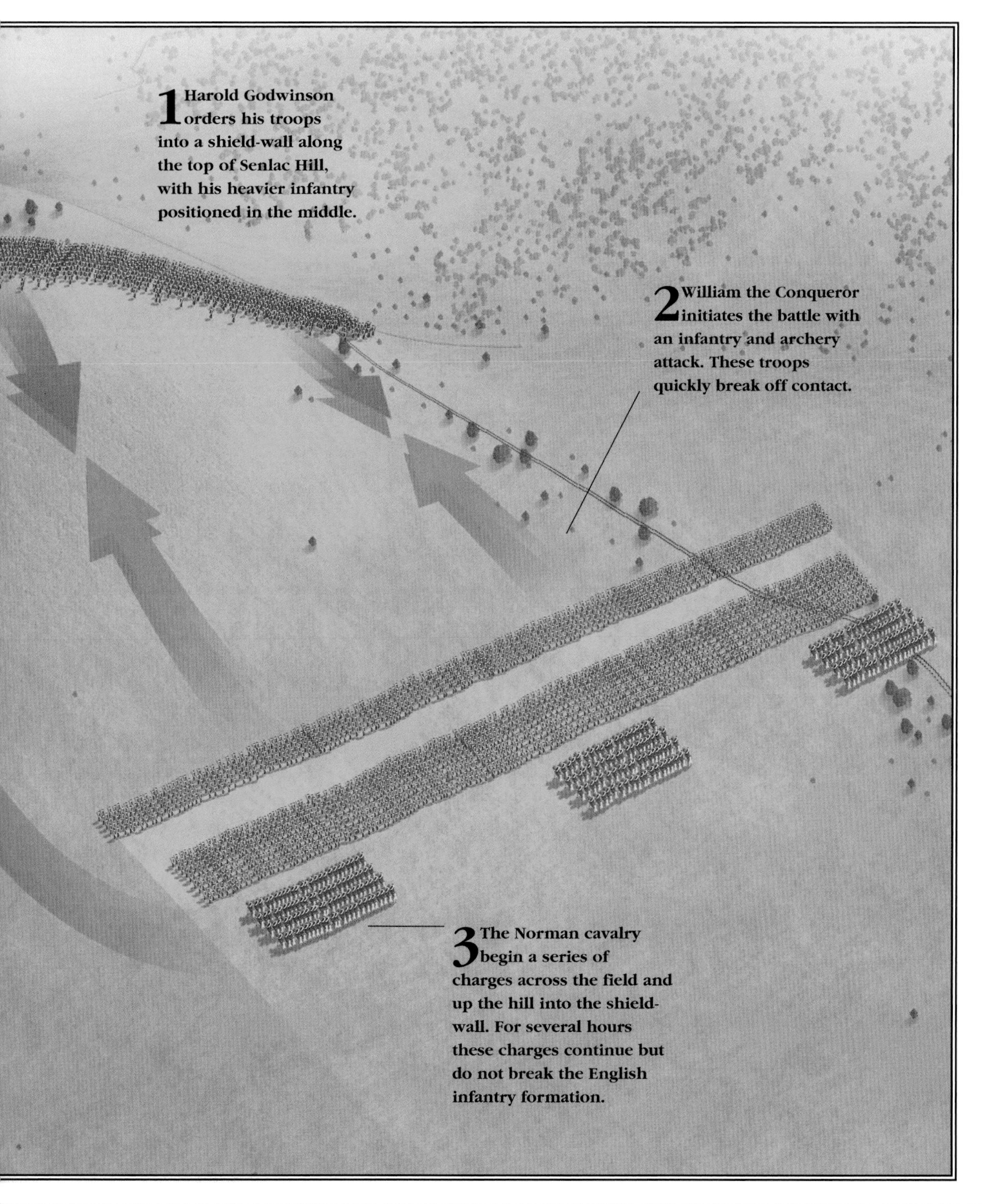
1 Harold Godwinson orders his troops into a shield-wall along the top of Senlac Hill, with his heavier infantry positioned in the middle.
2 William the Conqueror initiates the battle with an infantry and archery attack. These troops quickly break off contact.
3 The Norman cavalry begin a series of charges across the field and up the hill into the shield-wall. For several hours these charges continue but do not break the English infantry formation.

that they were far fewer than their infantry opponents. Still, they charged with a heroism few other warriors of the Middle Ages could equal, 'brave to the extreme' according to William of Malmesbury. Yet this charge was halted by the shield wall. So, too, was the next charge…and the next. Indeed, no one, contemporary or modern, agrees on just how many cavalry charges were made by the Normans that day. Each of them seems to have been stopped by the stubbornness of an extremely disciplined English infantry who stood solidly, not moving from their strong defensive position. William of Poitiers describes the scene: 'this was a strange kind of battle, one side with all the mobility and initiative, and the other just resisting as though rooted to the soil.'

It was also a long battle. Most such medieval engagements were decided in an hour or less, but not the Battle of Hastings. It went on and on; charge after charge was launched without breaking the infantry shield wall. Few casualties on either side seem to have occurred, with the horses stopping their assaults on the infantry before actually clashing with them. At one time, well into the battle, a rumour passed through the Norman cavalry that William had been slain. In an era before heraldry, such a mistake is certainly excusable, as most Norman horsemen would have looked alike, a fact confirmed by the Bayeux Tapestry. Also shown in the tapestry is that William quashed this rumour by doffing his helmet and showing his face, thereby preventing his cavalry from fleeing the battle.

The display of their leader still fighting among them seemed to re-energize the Norman cavalry enough, at least, to pull off one of the most difficult, but also very widely used, cavalry tactics: the feigned retreat. Recorded in Vegetius' *De Re Militari* (the military manual most widely read in the Middle Ages) as well as elsewhere, the feigned retreat demanded both skill and discipline, for a cavalry had to look as if they were running away from the battle, only to turn and charge again, in complete order and solidarity. Such a stunt could not be performed too early, and never more than once. Indeed, it is likely that should it not achieve

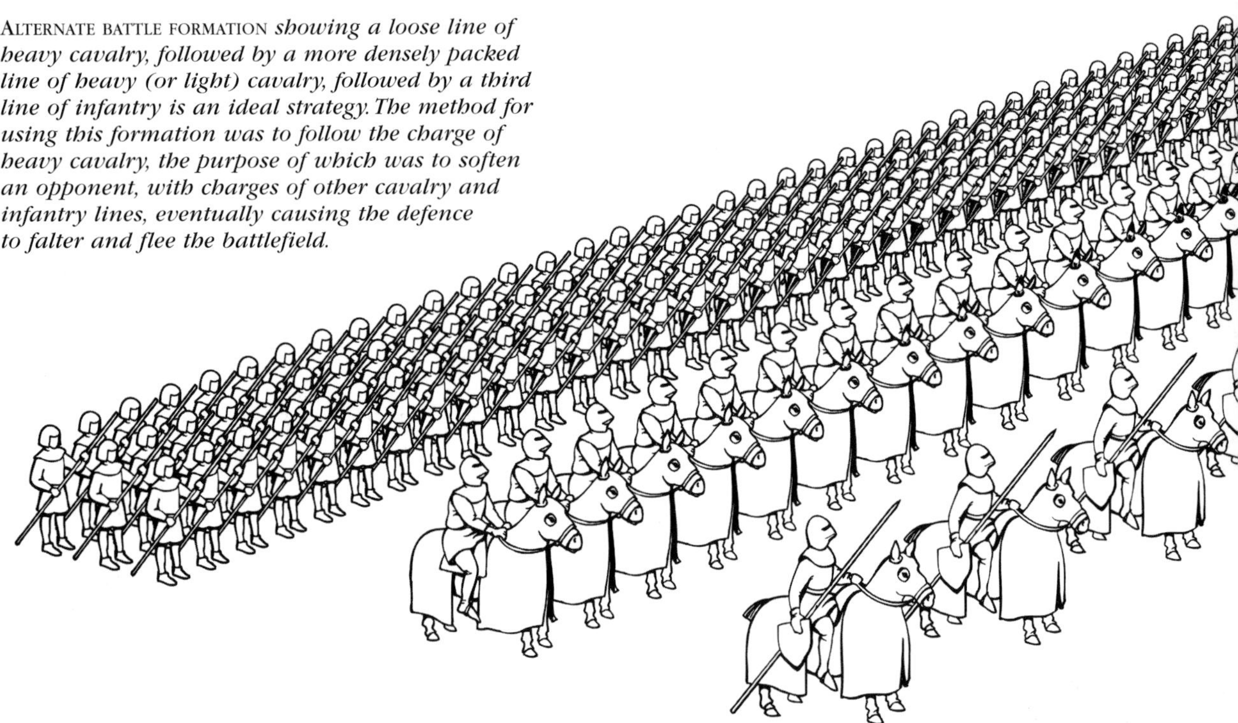

ALTERNATE BATTLE FORMATION *showing a loose line of heavy cavalry, followed by a more densely packed line of heavy (or light) cavalry, followed by a third line of infantry is an ideal strategy. The method for using this formation was to follow the charge of heavy cavalry, the purpose of which was to soften an opponent, with charges of other cavalry and infantry lines, eventually causing the defence to falter and flee the battlefield.*

its purpose, the breaking of the opposing line in celebratory pursuit, the battle would be over, with the cavalry retreating, this time earnestly, from the field. At Hastings, the feigned retreat worked well. Although several English soldiers remained in their lines, some broke and pursued the retreating Normans, only to realize too late that the cavalry had turned round and returned to the charge. Few of these English troops, who seem to have run down the hill after the Normans, could muster the speed or strength to return to their lines and were ridden down and slain. Among them seem to have been two of Harold's brothers, Gyrth and Leofwine, who had served as his lieutenants that day. If they had not been slain in the disordered pursuit down Senlac Hill, they were killed by Norman horsemen who now found the English shield wall weakened and penetrable.

The impetus of the battle had changed so quickly, that it was all Harold Godwinson could do to withdraw the soldiers who still remained with him and reform them in a much smaller line. However, this group proved to be too fatigued and disorganized to resist the Normans for long, although they did remain with their king until he was killed, most probably by an arrow that hit his face and pierced his eye. The last Anglo-Saxon/Anglo-Scandinavian 'English' army had been defeated, decisively it turned out. For although William still had to face opposition from Edwin and Morkere, who had stayed in the north after Stamford Bridge, this resistance proved to be rather meagre and easily defeated. William the Conqueror, still duke of Normandy and count of Maine, now added king of England to his list of titles, put on that throne by his cavalry at Hastings.

The Age of Chivalry and Tournaments

The period between the Viking invasions and the Hundred Years' War (1337–1453) has sometimes been described as the 'Age of the Horse'. The Normans and crusaders may stand out for the use of cavalry in their campaigns and battles, but they are only two of the many examples from the medieval period. All other European powers had adopted cavalry as their primary battlefield force by this time, including not only the lands of Byzantium, France, England, Italy and the Holy Roman Empire, but those on the frontiers as well, including Scandinavia, Scotland, Iberia, Hungary and the various Baltic and Balkan lands.

In the battles they fought, cavalry showed the confidence of their skill, wealth and, often, nobility. It was a confidence borne also by their numbers, the strength of their armour, the intensity of their training, the closeness of their formations and an accumulation of their victories. Ambroise, the poetic Norman chronicler, describes their military presence on the battlefield:

The most beautiful Christian warriors
That ever saw the people of earth.
They were serried in their ranks
As if they were people forged in iron.
The battle line was wide and strong
And could well sustain fierce attacks;
And the rearguard was so full
Of good knights that it was difficult
To see their heads, if not higher up;
It was not possible to throw a prune
Except on mailed and armoured men.

When formed into a tightly packed unit, called by different names throughout the Middle Ages – échelle, constabularium, bataille and conrois – the cavalry could charge with great force and fury. To stand against them, especially if not of the same wealth or status, took great courage, and few infantry soldiers of the High Middle Ages possessed it. Consequently, battles were often fought by cavalry against other cavalry. Dominant on the battlefield for so long, the infantry, for this moment in history, took a secondary role.

The discipline of this cavalry, and sometimes their training, was largely dependent on their leadership. To put it simply, during this 'Age of the Horse' a good leader most often led his horsed troops to victory, a bad leader most often to defeat. During the period of the domination of the cavalry over the battlefield, leadership was often determined by military obligation, and military obligation was based on what Philippe Contamine has termed 'the feudo-vassalic system'. He describes this as: 'Throughout the West, in tens of thousands, individuals, men and women, great and small, young and old, owed military service of various sorts to their lords for their fiefs' (*War in the Middle Ages*, p.77).

There was no uniformity in these obligations. Terms of feudo-vassalic responsibilities differed with nearly every contract made between lord and vassal. For example, in medieval Romania service was given until the age of 60, unless replaced by a suitable heir before then, with four months of the year spent in castle duty, four months spent in the field, and four months at home. In the Latin kingdom of Jerusalem, military service was for the entire year and until one died. Outside of these more embattled regions, however, feudo-vassalic military service was much shorter, usually being required only in defensive situations or when the

A TOURNAMENT SCENE *at the time of Charles V, who ruled France from 1364 to 1380, taken from the* Grandes Chroniques de Saint Denis. *Tournaments, which began taking place sometime in the 11th or 12th century, were initially meant to prepare a cavalryman for combat. In a tournament he could practice charging on horseback and couching his lance. Before long, however, they became sporting events, more spectacle than training ground.*

THE WEDGE FORMATION *consisted of battle lines made up of a number of deep wedges of cavalry, followed by infantry. The more heavily armed knights would lead the wedge, while the more lightly armed men-at-arms would form the centres. The idea was to slice into the ranks of the enemy and disrupt their formation, after which the infantry could follow up to provide the final blow.*

lord who was owed the obligation desired to go on campaign. Under a particularly bellicose leader, this might mean a military service which could last much of the year for many years in a row, while under a weaker, more peaceful leader, there was a likelihood of never being required to perform military duties. When called up, the medieval soldier was required to bring himself and his retinue and to pay for almost all of the arms, armour, horses and provisions needed to sustain them on their campaign or in their fortification. Ideally, this meant that no paid medieval army was needed. In reality, however, in order to fill out their numbers, most medieval military leaders were required to make promises of financial support or reimbursement for lost revenues or animals to those called into service.

Even this commitment did not always work. For example, in 1300, when Edward I called his already fatigued feudal levy to military service, only 40 knights and 366 sergeants responded. At times, kingdoms were also forced to supplement their forces with mercenaries.

Battle of Legnano: 29 May 1176

Even today the Alps provide a hindrance to their crossing by military forces. For medieval armies to cross the Alps, either into or out of Italy, narrow and precipitous passes needed to be traversed, with the journey long and arduous. The mountains, more than any strategy, army or weapon, protected Italy from numerous conquests. During the Middle Ages, despite being politically and legally part of the Holy Roman Empire, the Italian people always sought their own sovereignty, especially after the towns of northern and central Italy became more populous and more wealthy. This meant that they almost always opposed being ruled from north of the Alps.

Only if the Holy Roman Emperor could guarantee the security of his throne north of the Alps could he venture south to return his Italian subjects to his rule. This movement was a rare occurrence, as Germany frequently lacked any political security. When it did happen, though, the Italian towns were generally unwilling to surrender their self-governance without war.

Hence, many emperors fought in Italy in an effort to quell rebellions. Most often when these conflicts occurred, the Italians lost to the more professional, more experienced, more skilled, better led and better armed and armoured German soldiers. At times, however, they achieved victory. One of those battles was fought at Legnano on 29 May 1176 between the troops of Emperor Frederick Barbarossa and the soldiers and militia of Milan and other allied Italian towns.

By the time Frederick had been designated as the successor of Emperor Conrad III in 1152, he was already an experienced military commander. Indeed, it is undoubtedly the leadership he showed in 1146 in putting down the insurrection of Duke Conrad of Zähringen on behalf of Conrad that led to his being recognized as the successor, despite having no direct familial ties to the emperor. The same military leadership also allowed his unanimous election, a rarity in medieval German politics.

Frederick's Campaigns

Because of the solidarity of his control in Germany, in 1154 Frederick Barbarossa led his first campaign south of the Alps into Italy. It had been a long time since the Italians had faced a military threat from the north. Neither of Frederick's two predecessors, Lothair II and Conrad III, had been strong enough to pursue any more than a diplomatic connection with the inhabitants of Italy, leaving them, and especially those in the northern and central towns, in virtual independence. Yet it was not only allegiance to the Holy Roman Empire that had flagged during this period: the collection of taxes and other duties had almost completely ceased, while the passes through the Alps had become so filled with bands of thieves, that few traders, pilgrims, churchmen or other travellers could pass through without having to pay for protection.

Certainly Frederick wanted to change those situations in 1154, to clear up the lawlessness of the roads through the Alps, to collect the funds owed and to bring Italy back into union with the rest of the Holy Roman Empire. However, whether he felt that he could do that all at once is difficult to ascertain. If so, then his first expedition into Italy must be judged a failure, for although he was able to march his armies all the way to Rome, reaching there in the middle of 1155, he had not brought the rebellious forces in the north to heel, especially the Milanese and their allies. Nor could he even bring peace among the factions in Rome, although he did succeed in being crowned as Holy Roman Emperor by Pope Adrian IV, on 18 June, before returning to Germany.

That the town of Milan was at the head of the rebellion is not surprising when one realizes that its wealth derived largely from being in control of most of the Alpine passes. Anyone who wished to travel along those treacherous paths had to pass through Milan. This location meant that the town was almost always teeming with pilgrims and traders, who spent large amounts to hire housing, transportation, guides, protection and victuals from the town's merchants. Milan's wealth translated, as it often did elsewhere in the Middle Ages, into a desire for sovereignty.

Frequently, this meant being at odds with their German lords, with perhaps the most famous case before the reign of Frederick Barbarossa being the opposition of the town's leadership to Emperor Henry IV during the so-called Investiture Controversy. In addition, the Milanese seemed capable of influencing other towns in northern and central Italy to join their rebellions, even those that logic might have dictated would have been

Battle of Legnano

1176

After combining his personal cavalry force with other German cavalry at Como, Holy Roman Emperor Frederick I Barbarossa marched these forces toward the Italian town of Pavia, where he hoped to be reinforced. Although he tried to avoid the Milanese, their army surprised the Germans outside the town of Legnano. However, an initial skirmish gave Frederick the opportunity to form his troops into an unknown number of divisions; these faced four divisions of Milanese soldiers, cavalry supported by infantry. The Germans charged, causing the cavalry opposing them to flee. But the Milanese infantry did not follow, holding their positions against them. With their impetus lost, the Germans were attacked in the flank by those Milanese cavalry troops who, seeing the stand of their infantry, had been able to regroup. The Germans were soon routed, and victory fell to the Milanese.

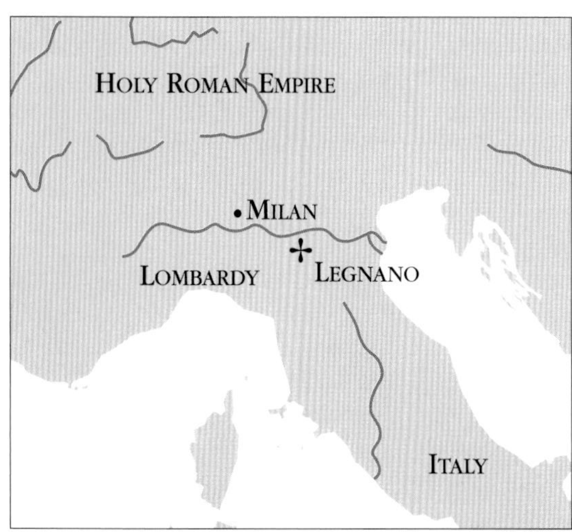

As a German army, led by the Emperor Frederick Barbarossa, marched from Como to Pavia, it was surprised by the Milanese army outside of the town of Legnano.

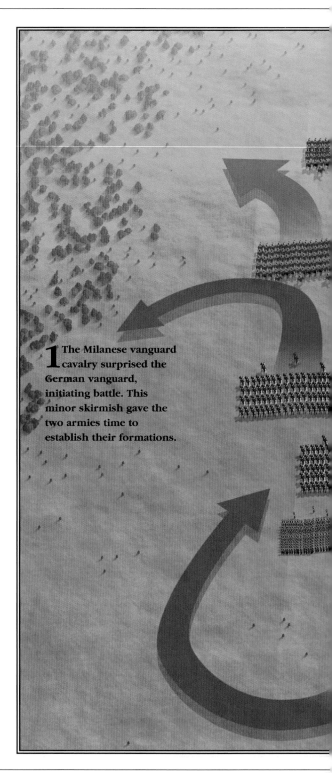

1 The Milanese vanguard cavalry surprised the German vanguard, initiating battle. This minor skirmish gave the two armies time to establish their formations.

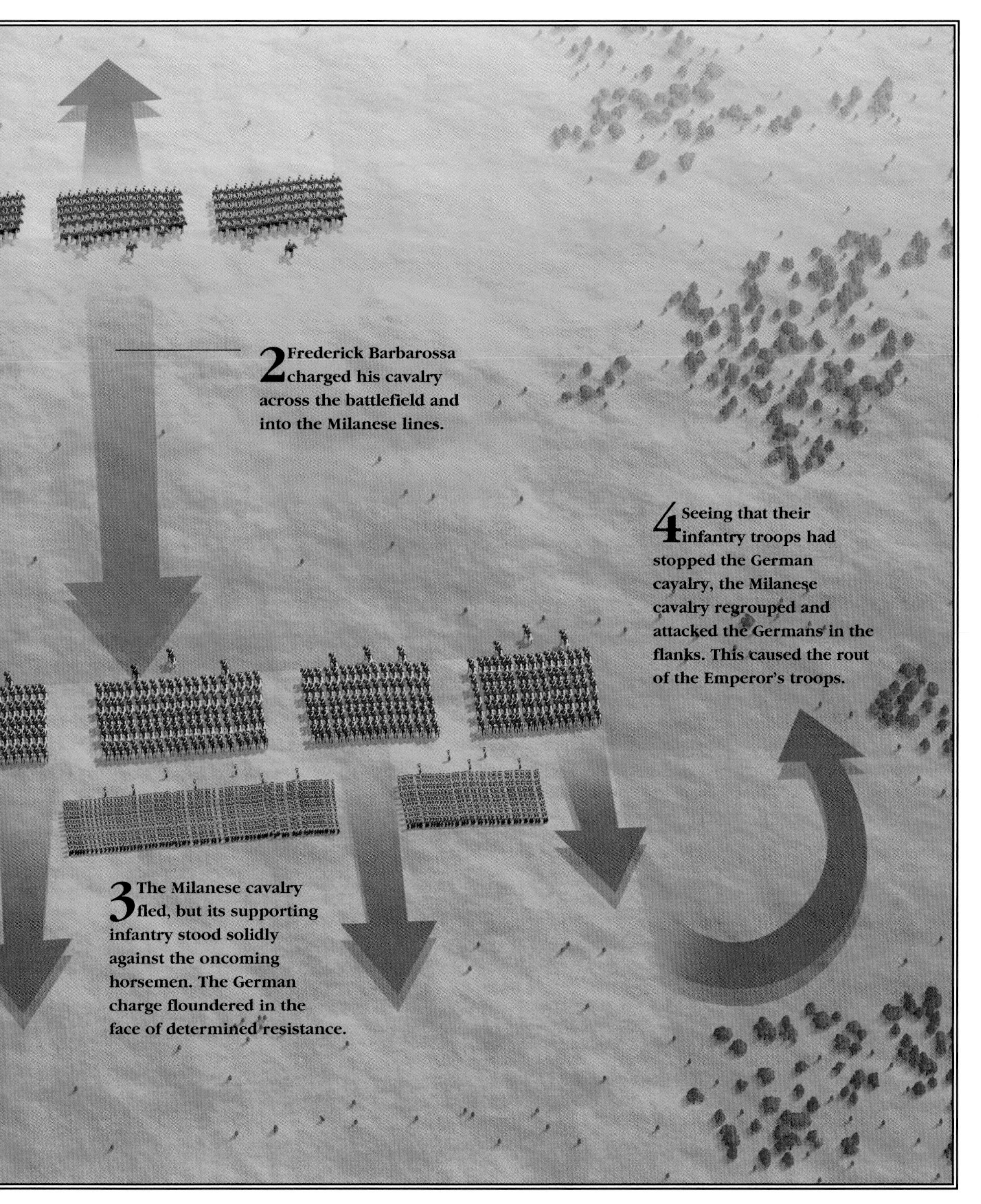
2 Frederick Barbarossa charged his cavalry across the battlefield and into the Milanese lines.
4 Seeing that their infantry troops had stopped the German cavalry, the Milanese cavalry regrouped and attacked the Germans in the flanks. This caused the rout of the Emperor's troops.
3 The Milanese cavalry fled, but its supporting infantry stood solidly against the oncoming horsemen. The German charge floundered in the face of determined resistance.

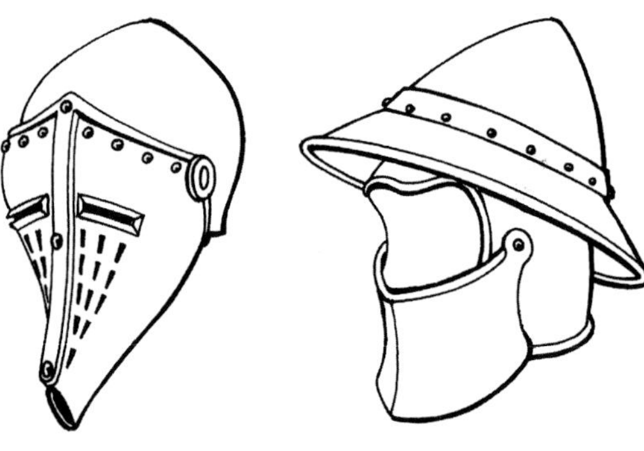

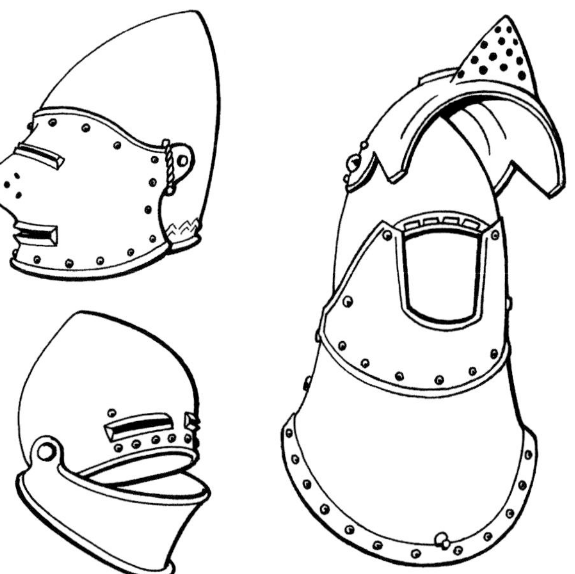

LATE MEDIEVAL HELMETS *varied in style with the wearer's preference. Descending from the earlier Great Helm, late medieval helmets, such as those illustrated here (taken from 19th-century drawings), generally fit more tightly to the face and neck. Still, some soldiers and leaders felt that they limited vision and communication too much. Therefore, they chose to raise their visors or fight without them.*

better off had they sided with Milan's opponents or, at least, remained neutral.

When Barbarossa returned north in 1155, having failed to secure Italy's subjugation, his German barons took this as a sign of weakness, and the recently crowned Holy Roman Emperor was faced with having to quell dissent among them, especially in the guise of Henry the Lion, duke of Saxony and, in 1156, also of Bavaria. Eventually through diplomatic sagacity as well as military power, Frederick was able to placate or defeat all adversaries, emerging in 1158 with an even stronger military presence in Germany and a renewed desire to return to Italy. His second campaign was far more successful than his first. Among his numerous early victories, the greatest undoubtedly was the capture of Milan, which fell on 7 September 1158 to Frederick's forces after a short siege. Other rebellious towns fell quickly into line. However, Italy would not stay quiescent for long. The death of Pope Adrian IV, whose support of Barbarossa had been wavering, forced Frederick to get involved in a prolonged fight over papal succession. This distraction brought further insurrection, with the emperor having to fight numerous engagements against almost all of the towns in northern Italy and Lombardy, including, again, Milan. It would not be until March 1162 that Milan would once more fall to German troops.

Still there was no peace south of the Alps. After only a very short stay in Germany, Frederick began his third expedition into Italy in 1163. On this occasion his army faced a new opponent, or rather a new alliance of old opponents, the Lombard League. The Lombard League was formed initially by Verona, Vicenza and Padua, with the later additions of Venice, Constantinople and Sicily. Milan, at least in the beginning, stayed out of the League, more out of fatigue than any disagreement with its anti-Imperial goals. Faced with the size and military power of this alliance, Frederick's 1163 campaign failed almost completely, as did another campaign, his fourth, in 1166. In this latter expedition, it was not only the Lombards who bedevilled the Germans, but also disease, in particular fever, which ravaged the invading troops, almost annihilating them.

Perhaps because of the setbacks of his last two Italian campaigns, Frederick Barbarossa did not march across the Alps again until 1174, drawn there to stop an alliance between the Lombard League and Pope Alexander III, who, although not a friend or supporter of the emperor's, to this time had remained neutral in more northern Italian affairs. It was during this campaign, in 1176, that Frederick fought and lost the Battle of Legnano.

The Battle

Unfortunately, the sources for the battle of Legnano are not sufficient to detail all the actions on the battlefield; certainly in comparison to narratives of other medieval battles, including Hastings, Bouvines and Nicopolis, the contemporary history of Legnano is meagre. Despite its importance to his Italian adventures, the always vocal chroniclers and biographers of Frederick Barbarossa are rather quiet about the battle, while the few local Italian histories are quite short. Nevertheless, there is enough evidence to determine the role played by the cavalry on both sides.

From 1174 to 1176 Frederick had journeyed around Italy, trying his best, but in vain, to defeat the Lombard League. Early in 1176, wishing to ratchet up the intensity of his campaign, the emperor had asked for German reinforcements to travel through the Alps, receiving, in response, additional troops from Swabia and the Rhineland. This force numbered around 2000 and was led by Philip, the archbishop of Cologne, Conrad, the bishop-elect of Worms, and Berthold, duke of Zähringen and nephew of the empress. It entered Italy from the Alps in April. The soldiers all appear to have been mounted troops–knights and sergeants, without any attendant infantry. This may have been because of the speed needed for travelling to meet Frederick's timetable, or perhaps the Germans were used to having infantry supplied by local allied Italians or mercenaries, or maybe Frederick Barbarossa felt that a reinforcing cavalry army was all that was required at the time. Unfortunately, not enough is known about Frederick's military organization or needs on his 1176 campaign to determine the reason for the lack of infantry among his troops. But the deficit cost him the battle.

The emperor added his own 500 cavalry to the force at Como in early May. That this was not his entire army in Italy at the time has led historians to assume that these 500 knights were only Frederick's bodyguard, to protect him on the journey to meet his reinforcements. They also assume that Frederick meant to join these troops to his other army in order to campaign more effectively against the Lombard League. However, as it appears that his main force was in Pavia, this assumes a move around Milan without arousing opposition. Should this be an accurate interpretation, then Frederick's strategy proved to be terribly short-sighted.

Of course, the Milanese knew of the German soldiers' presence, and without a doubt they also knew of the weakness of Frederick's forces, which were now split. Having fallen twice to the emperor, the Milanese also seem to have mustered all of their town's soldiers, as well as called in numerous allies in support of what they presumed would be another defence. German chroniclers number these troops at 12,000 cavalry, with an untold number of infantry, but these tallies are probably grossly exaggerated, the true number likely being only 2000 Milanese cavalry and perhaps no more than 500 infantry, the latter drawn mostly from Milan, Verona and Brescia. Also present with the army was the town's *carroccio*, a large ceremonial wagon that symbolized Milanese wealth and independence.

Judging that an attack of the divided German army would be to their benefit, the Milanese moved to intercept them. On 29 May, the two armies met outside Legnano. The battle began with an attack by the vanguard cavalry of the Milanese, numbering around 700, against the vanguard cavalry of the Germans, numbering significantly fewer, probably no more than 300. Frederick's troops seemed to have been surprised by this assault, evidently ignorant of the presence of the Milanese, who had effectively hidden their manoeuvres behind a forest, and were quickly routed. This engagement, however, had given the emperor time to establish his lines, which quickly took in their retreating vanguard and chased off those in pursuit of them.

The Milanese army then moved onto the battlefield and formed their own lines across from the German army. Contemporary sources report that the Milanese were ordered in four divisions, with the infantry and the *carroccio* behind these. What the German formation was is not recorded. It was to Frederick's benefit to take the offensive initiative, as his force was in unfriendly territory and could not count on relief, while he feared that his opponents' numbers would only increase if he delayed for too long. At the same time, the Annals of Cologne claims that the emperor counted 'it unworthy of his Imperial majesty to show his back to his enemies'. The German cavalry charged 'strongly', and their charge easily broke through the opposing lines of Milanese cavalry.

When they reached the infantry, which had held their ground despite the flight of their own cavalry – an important and incredibly courageous tactic – the impetus of the German cavalry charge was halted. 'With shields set close and pikes held firm', wrote Romuald, the archbishop of Salerno, the Italian infantry caused the German cavalry horses simply to stop, unable to penetrate the massed formation of infantry, and unwilling to ride onto their pikes. It was not a surprising result. It had happened before, at Hastings among other places, when cavalry troops charged against a tight formation of infantry, and it would happen again, often during the last two centuries of the Middle Ages. But it was rare in the twelfth century, a result that only came when the infantry were both motivated to stay in place and disciplined not to flee, even when they faced soldiers whose armour and warhorses displayed a wealth and power that was unattainable by almost all infantry troops.

The stand of the Milanese foot soldiers allowed a regrouping of their defeated, but not destroyed, cavalry. These troops repaid their infantry's stubborn bravery by returning to the battlefield and attacking the halted German cavalry's flank. Frederick's horsemen, frustrated by their inability to defeat infantry opposing them, were becoming very fatigued.

As such, they quickly broke off their attack of the Milanese infantry and tried to retreat to their former positions. This retreat was anything but orderly and, without their own infantry to rally behind, it quickly turned to rout. In the midst of this chaos, the emperor's banner was captured, and he had his horse killed from underneath him. Frederick barely escaped his own death, by a means not recorded, although for several days it had been believed that he had been killed at Legnano. Many others were captured, although the total numbers slain on the battlefield were not large, testimony to the protection offered by the chain armour worn by every German and Milanese cavalry soldier.

'. . . If you argue that the fury with which horses are driven to charge an enemy makes them consider a pike no more than a spur, I answer that even though a horse has begun to charge, he will slow down when he draws near the pikes . . . and will either stand still or wheel off . . .'

– *Machiavelli,* The Art of War, *1521*

Better than any other battle, Legnano displays the necessity of medieval armies to have both cavalry and infantry together on the battlefield. The fact that the Milanese army contained both infantry and cavalry, and that the infantry were able to withstand the assaults of the charging German cavalry, decided their victory. The fact that Frederick Barbarossa did not field an army with both cavalry and infantry, leaving no relief for his cavalry when they began to flee, decided his defeat.

Knighthood

During the eleventh and twelfth centuries, knighthood was instituted throughout Europe. Called *miles* in Latin, *chevalier* in France, *ritter* in the Holy Roman Empire, *caballero* in Spanish and knight in English, initially those who were so designated were nobles whose land, wealth, title and status distinguished them from ordinary soldiers. It is difficult to know exactly when the practice of making knights began or where it originated. No single document exists indicating how or why the first knights were made. More than likely, medieval knights were the result of evolution rather than revolution, meaning that they came to exist in the High and later Middle

Ages, not all at once, but over a long period of time.

Knights were, as the terms describing them often declared, cavalry. Before too long, however, more requirements were also placed on them. In other words, not all cavalry soldiers were knights. To be a knight meant that one had to earn the title through skill and action displayed in warfare or tournaments. Of course, wars were not waged often, and battles fought even less often. So cavalry practice had to be done elsewhere, and training accommodated by other means. The training began early in a boy's life, if he was a noble child. His teacher would be a knight himself, often a relative or close friend of the boy's father. The boy was trained in riding a horse, couching a lance, swinging a sword from his saddle and sometimes even throwing a javelin or spear from horseback. Instruction in mounted weaponry would be supplemented by equal training in weapons for

FRENCH KNIGHTS IN BATTLE, *from an illuminated initial found on a manuscript of* Lancelot of the Lake, *c.1330. Depicting a scene from the Arthurian romance, it accurately portrays the arms and armour of the period, including great helms, triangular shields and metal-plate leg and armguards. By the 14th century heraldry had also become prevalent and, as pictured, could appear on shields, banners and horse coverings.*

fighting on foot. Roger of Hoveden describes the knightly education, here in reference to the sons of King Henry II of England:

They strove to outdo the others in handling weapons. They realized that without practice the art of war did not come naturally when it was needed. No athlete can fight tenaciously who has never received any blows: he must see his blood flow and hear his teeth crack under the fist of his adversary, and when he is thrown to the ground he must fight on with all his might and not lose courage. The oftener he falls, the more determinedly he must spring to his feet again. Anyone who can do that can engage in battle confidently. Strength gained by practice is invaluable: a soul subject to terror has fleeting glory. He who is too weak to bear this burden, through no fault of his own, will be overcome by its weight, no matter how eagerly he may rush to the task. The price of sweat is well paid where the Temples of Victory stand.

The Tournament

One of the best places for the young knight or squire (a term describing a knight in training) to practise the art of cavalry warfare was the tournament. When and where the first tournament was held is unknown. Recent evidence has

MUSLIM SOLDIERS SET *upon a fallen crusader cavalryman. Once a horseman had been brought down from his horse, his opponents generally had the advantage. Either he could be taken hostage and ransomed, or, as is most likely in the case of this crusader from the Third Crusade, he would be killed by attacks through vulnerable openings in his armour, at the neck, armpit or groin.*

suggested that it might have been as early as the beginning of the eleventh century. By the early twelfth century they were certainly being held everywhere throughout Europe. They had also caught the imagination of many writers and artists, and this fascination would persist throughout the rest of the Middle Ages.

Early tournaments were mostly melees, where teams of cavalry participated in a mock battle ranging over a large field. Much of the fighting there seems to have been with swords and maces; the earliest tournaments may have been held before lances were couched (indeed, there may even be a connection between the development of the couched lance and the tournament). Eventually, the joust became more prominent than the melee and during the last couple of centuries in the medieval period melees nearly disappeared. In jousts, two riders divided by a barrier would approach each other with couched lances. Points were awarded for contact with an opponent's armour, shield (sometimes called the targe) and helmet. Rarely was a knight unhorsed, as that was thought to be too life-threatening, but should a lance shatter with audience-pleasing special effects, extra points might be gained.

Some knights made their names on the tournament circuit. Individuals, such as William Marshal and Ulrich von Liechtenstein, were renowned throughout Europe for their tournament skills, even having histories written about them (actually Ulrich von Liechtenstein wrote his own). Skilled knights could also make a living from jousting. Victors would 'win' their opponents' armour and horses, although these were always offered back to their owners for a ransom. There were also times when the Church and various governments tried to control tournaments, even prohibiting them. Rarely, though, did these bans last for long, as the urge to joust, and to celebrate the jousting, was simply too strong. Sometime after its origins, although how long has not been determined, knighthood also acquired its own code of conduct, called chivalry. The reasons for the existence of such a code of martial honour are also unknown. Was it instituted by the Church at the time of the Crusades as a means of regulating the actions of the warrior class? Or, was it something that came from within, from a class of knights who decided they needed a set of virtuous qualities or a rule of conduct to offset their bellicose activities and reputation?

While neither the origin nor the reasons for chivalry's existence are completely understood, the qualities that defined a chivalric knight are well known. John of Salisbury enumerated them in the twelfth century: '[a knight's role is] to defend the Church, to assail infidelity, to venerate the priesthood, to protect the poor from injuries, to pacify the province, to pour out their blood for their brothers...and, if need be, to lay down their lives.' They were also to honour women. Participation by womanhood in this code was to allow for this esteem and to support their knights with love and, on many occasions, with symbols of their support, such as a garter or sash.

Medieval chivalry was sustained not only by the brotherhood of knights, but by numerous works of art and literature. There were an extremely large number of tales of Arthur and his Knights of the Round Table written from the twelfth to the fifteenth century, reaching lands and languages that no comparable non-religious text or genre of text had before. In an age before printing, such a feat must be considered remarkable. It was also undoubtedly sustained by the frequent professional sporting events - tournaments - in which the knights often took part.

Development of Plate Armour

Some historians have proposed that tournaments led to changes in cavalry armour, especially the attachment of iron or steel plates to chain armour and the subsequent evolution to complete suits of plate armour. No doubt, those who frequently took part in melees and rode in jousts constantly sought stronger means of protecting themselves. However, most of the changes in armour seem to have come after the heyday of the tournament. Instead, the evolution to plate armour may have been prompted by technological and tactical changes in thirteenth- and fourteenth-century medieval warfare. Chain mail continued to be used by soldiers in the fourteenth century, but as high-powered crossbows and longbows were able to break the rings and penetrate the armour, new, more capable defence was needed. Ultimately, this need led to the development of plate armour, a change initiated in the thirteenth and early fourteenth centuries and one which lasted well into the sixteenth century.

Secure evidence for plate armour does not come until the early to mid-thirteenth century. Both artistic sources and written evidence mention the introduction of plate armour at this time. For example, one chronicler, Guillaume le Breton (d.1225), gives an account of a fight between Richard the Lionheart of England (at the time only count of Poitou) and William de Barres. Guillaume describes each combatant as wearing 'moulded iron plates' as extra protective garments under the chain-mail *hauberk*. The plate armour worn by Richard and William de Barres was most certainly not a primary but a secondary defensive armament. But it may well show the evolutionary process that produced the first plate armour, a process whereby the suit of armour was made in

EARLY MEDIEVAL ARMOUR *suits were most often made of chain links or metal scales. Chain armour (favoured in western Europe) consisted of thousands of round metal rings, the ring ends welded or riveted together. Chain coverings for the head, legs, feet, arms and hands later added extra protection for both cavalry and infantry soldiers. Scale armour (favoured in Byzantium) was made of a large number of metallic scales attached to each other by wire or leather laces and affixed to a linen textile undergarment by linen cord.*

CHAIN MAIL

SCALE MAIL

pieces of plate attached to the existing chain-mail or leather armour as added defensive protection. A manifesto written from German Emperor Frederick II to King Henry III of England in 1241 also mentions leather armour strengthened by iron plates sewn onto it. Artistic sources add evidence of metallic plates attached to other parts of the thirteenth-century armour-clad soldier.

By about 1350 chain mail specifically for torso protection was replaced by an independent breastplate. The breastplate was made from a solid metal piece fashioned to cover the chest, back and sides to the top of the diaphragm, with the rest of the torso - stomach, waist and hips - protected by a flexible horizontal coat of plate hoops (waist-lames) riveted to a fabric cover. By the end of the fourteenth century, the independent breastplate had become the primary piece of plate armour and was favoured by both cavalry and infantry soldiers. For the soldier on horseback, two features were added to the breastplate to make it even more popular. First, a hinged bracket was attached to the right side of the chest, and served to support a couched lance. Second, a V-shaped bar was riveted to the armour just below the neck and was designed to prevent an opponent's weapon sliding up along the slippery plate surface into the throat. These innovations were known as a lance-rest and a stop-rib respectively and became prominent features of the knight's breastplate throughout the fifteenth century.

By the end of the fourteenth century, armour protecting the limbs had also been fully developed, including: *cuisses* for the thighs; *poleyns* for the knees; *jambers* or *shynbalds* for the shins; *sabatons* for the feet; *gorgets* or *bevors* for throats and necks; *couters* for the elbows; *spaudlers* or *pauldrons* for the shoulders; *rerebraces* for the upper arms; *vambraces* for the lower arms; and gauntlets for the hands. A full suit of armour included all of these pieces together, with the addition of the helmet and, at least initially, the shield. This would disappear by the middle of the fifteenth century.

The weight of a suit of plate armour was immense. It has been estimated that a complete suit of plate armour for use on the battlefield weighed 23-28kg (50-62lb), while a suit of plate jousting armour, much heavier because of the definite geography and chronology of the tournament against the uncertainty of the battlefield, weighed 41-46kg (90-101lb). Still, despite the weight it was absolutely essential that everyone who could afford to do so should be outfitted with the finest plate armour and by the middle of the fifteenth century, all cavalry soldiers owned at least one suit. Defensibility with this armour was impressive, and failure to wear his armour could cost a cavalry soldier his life.

Battle of Bouvines: 27 July 1214

On 27 July 1214, a massive and violent battle was fought at the bridge of Bouvines, west of Tournai, in what was then the county of Flanders. To the participants in this battle, Bouvines seemed to be a worldwide conflict, for nearly every ruling magnate in northwestern Europe was directly involved, with the absent cheerleading of Pope Innocent III, the prince-bishop of Liège, Hugh of Pierrepoint and the king of England, John. Indeed, except for the battles of the Crusades, no medieval conflict can compare with Bouvines for its international scope and participation.

On one side fought Otto IV of Brunswick, the German emperor, together with his barons, the counts of Tecklemburg, Katzenellenboge and Dortmund, and their forces. Joining Otto was William, the earl of Salisbury, and half-brother to King John of England. William the Long Sword, as he was known, was there to command the troops sent from England, as well as being in charge of the substantial treasury donated by John to the allies. Ferrand of Portugal, the count of Flanders and Hainault, was also there with a large force of knights and foot, as were several rebellious nobles of France - Reginald of Dammartin, the count of Boulogne (an immensely powerful and influential leader) and Hugo, the baron of Boves. Also present at Bouvines was Willem, count of Holland, Hendrik I, duke of Brabant, the counts of Limburg and Lorraine and many other counts, dukes and nobles, 'bellicose men, expert in military matters' claims Roger of Wendover.

Opposing them was the king of France, Philip II, known to history as Philip Augustus, a cognomen given him by his biographer, Guillaume le Breton. The chronicler Clarius later would eulogize Philip as 'the most victorious king, who as a son of the Holy Mother Church stands as a defender and protector of Catholicism'. With Phillip, if not in body then certainly aiding him monetarily and morally, were the Pope and the prince-bishop of Liège, the latter of whom had sent troops to fight against the allies.

Dispositions

In all contemporary accounts, the Battle of Bouvines is a large encounter. Modern historians may not agree with the numbers of troops put forward in these early narratives. Some place each side at around 80,000 men, but they, too, suggest that it was a substantial medieval battle. Tallies of between 5000 and 20,000 for each army are suggested. Both armies were also dominated by large cavalry forces, with many knights among them. J.F. Verbruggen counts 1200 among the French force and 1500 among the allies. Their numbers, however, never exceeded those of the accompanying infantry, who at least for one army, the Flemings, seem to have totalled more than four times the number of cavalry. The allies' forces also outnumbered the French, although not by a large amount. Yet, as will be seen, this numerical superiority would not help them.

The day before the battle, Philip Augustus' army was in Tournai, about 20km (12 miles) east of Bouvines. There the king and his military leadership held a council of war, determining to march towards the allies and offer battle as soon as the opportunity presented itself. Early the next day, Sunday, the French left the town, intending to march to Lille. They were not seeking the enemy, nor were they running away from them. On the contrary, it appears that Philip, the experienced general, wanted to fight only on terrain that would be to his advantage.

The allies started the day of battle at Mortagne, only about 12km (7 miles) to the south-east of the French. According to the so-called Minstrel of Reims, it was only at Mortagne that the allied military leadership discovered the nearby presence of the French army, and that in hearing this news they rejoiced, as 'they believed that they had them in their net'. More confident in victory over the French king and his troops, the allies seemed only concerned with fighting them and not where this battle might take place or whether the terrain favoured one force over the other. There was little dissension amongst the leadership, and the allies lacked the wisdom of their more experienced opponent. Their march, on 27 July, was in pursuit of the French army.

Philip had placed a rearguard between himself and the allies. Their responsibility was to warn the king if his opponents were closing in on his army; they were also to skirmish with the pursuers, should the king need to separate himself further from his enemy. Instead of fleeing to Lille, however, Philip decided to stop on the other side of the bridge over the Marcq River at Bouvines, next to the Roman road on which they had been travelling. At the chapel in Bouvines, the king, 'fully armed', held mass with his barons. He then spoke with them, according to the Minstrel, and said: 'Lords, you are all my men and I am your Sire.... I have much loved you and brought you great honour and given you largely of what was mine. I have never wronged or failed you but I have always led you rightfully. For God's sake, I beg you all today to protect my body and my honour, and yours as well. And if you think that the crown would be better served by one of you, I agree to it and want it with good heart and good will.'

The French barons responded, 'Sire, for God's sake, we do not want any King but you. Ride bravely against your enemies, we are ready to die with you.' They then exited church and unfurled their banners, including the *oriflamme*, which was only to be unfurled against enemies whom the king thought of as heretics or rebels. Clearly, with the counts of Flanders and Boulogne, as well as other French nobles, among the allies, these were rebels. As Emperor Otto had been

THE BATTLE OF BOUVINES, *in 1214, was decided in favour of King Philip Augustus in one of the most important battles of the Middle Ages. There, the French king's armies fought against and defeated a coalition of forces from the Holy Roman Empire, England and rebellious French principalities. This highly romanticized engraving of Moreau du Tours, created in the 19th century, shows the obeisance to Phillip by the defeated soldiers.*

excommunicated by Pope Innocent III, and, as it was forbidden to side with an excommunicant, they were also heretics.

Why had Philip halted at Bouvines? The *Relatio Marchianensis de Pugna Bouvinis*, likely the earliest account of the battle and written by an eyewitness or taken from eyewitness accounts, reports that the French king, 'seeing that his adversaries were pursuing him terribly, like enraged dogs, and also bearing in mind that he could not retreat without too much dishonour, put his hope in the Lord and arranged his army into military echelons as is customary for those who are about to fight.'

Others suggest that it was more of a calculated strategy, that Philip realized the advantages that the terrain – a large, flat surface surrounded by river and marshes – offered him and set up his army in three large divisions there, cavalry and infantry in each division. Again, the Relatio Machianensis recounts: 'the knights and the auxiliaries, armed and arranged into ordered echelons, prepared in all haste for the battle. The horses' bridles were tightened by the auxiliaries. The armour shone in the splendour of the sun and it seemed that the light of day was doubled. The banners unfolded in the winds and offered themselves to the currents; they presented a delightful spectacle to the eyes.'

The allied army had been following behind the French at a very fast pace. Naturally the cavalry, and more particularly the Flemish and Hainaulter cavalry, led the rest. Their pace also quickened when they saw that the French army had stopped their own march. This stretched the allied army out for quite a distance; J.F. Verbruggen estimates that the length of allied march might have been as long as 10km (6 miles). The appropriate strategy at this point would have been for the Flemings in the allied vanguard to pull up their march and wait for the remainder of their army. This would allow the soldiers facing the French to realize their numerical superiority. Yet those in this lead group did not follow the cautious strategy. Before the whole army arrived, they formed their own units and marched onto the field of battle instead. A second division would join them before the battle began, but during the time it was fought other allied soldiers continued to arrive, some not reaching the field until the combat was mostly or even completely over.

'...the Champagne corps threatens the Flemings... With them are...the men sent by the Abbot of Saint-Médard, retainers famous on account of their great prowess.... Each of them, mounted on a horse, exulted in his armour and brandished his sword and lance; they were from the valley of Soissons which produces strong bodies.'

– Guillaume de Breton, at Bouvines

The allied left wing under the leadership of the count of Flanders, Ferrand of Portugal, filled mainly with Flemish and Hainaulter cavalry, faced a French right wing composed of heavy cavalry supported by lighter horsemen, led by the duke of Burgundy and count of Champagne. In the centre stood Emperor Otto, his German barons and their cavalry and infantry in almost equal numbers. They faced Philip Augustus, who also had both cavalry and infantry in his division. Finally, on the allies' right wing, Reginald of Dammartin and William Longsword led a force of their own soldiers and those whose services had been purchased by English monies. Although there was cavalry among this force, it seems to have been largely infantry, the numbers of which increased throughout the battle as other infantry soldiers of Low Countries arrived on the battlefield, this wing being closest to the road. They faced a French left wing composed of both cavalry and infantry and led by the counts of Ponthieu and Dreux, and the bishop of Beauvais, among others.

THE BATTLE OF POITIERS, *fought on 19 September 1356, was the second great battlefield defeat of the French by the English during the Hundred Years' War. Using a combination of longbow archers, infantry and dismounted cavalry, the English Black Prince led a force that withstood charges from both French cavalry and infantry to capture their opposing general, France's King Jean II. This defeat forced the French to agree to the Treaty of Brétigny, which ceded large amounts of land to the English. This 15th-century illustration commemorates the battle, but without arms and armour accuracy.*

The Battle

Battle began first between the allied left and French right wing in the form of simultaneous cavalry charges: horse versus horse, lances couched. 'The first French echelon attacked the Flemings with virility, breaking their echelons by nobly cutting across them, and penetrated their army through all impetuous and tenacious movement', writes the anonymous author of the *Relatio*. It was over quite quickly. 'The Flemings, seeing this and defeated in the space of an hour, turned their flanks and quickly took to flight', the *Relatio* continues. Again, French cavalry with more experience seem to have triumphed over their less-experienced counterparts. No infantry appear to have been involved in this combat.

While the cavalry-on-cavalry battle raged on his right, Phillip had delayed his attack. One can see in this decision the king's experience and expertise. He had ordered his infantry in front of his cavalry and, in such a formation, knew that a defensive posture was preferable to an offensive charge. Otto did not feel the same, however, at least not after his left wing had become engaged in fighting, as he charged into the French centre lines. Initially, this charge was successful in pushing back the French troops, the impetus even knocking the king from his horse. However, the French lines did not break or flee. Guillaume le Breton describes their recovery:

'While the French were fighting Otto and the Germans, German foot soldiers who had gone on ahead suddenly reached the king and, with lances and iron hooks, brought him to the ground. If the outstanding virtue of the special armour with which his body was enclosed had not protected him, they would have killed him on the spot. But a few of the knights who had remained with him, along with Galon of Montigny who repeatedly twirled the standard to call for help and Peter Tristan who of his own accord got off his steed and put himself in front of the blows so as to protect the king, destroyed and killed all those sergeants on foot. The king jumped up and mounted his horse more nimbly than anyone would have thought possible. After the king had remounted and the rabble who had brought him down had all been destroyed and killed, the king's battalion engaged Otto's echelon. Then began the marvellous fray, the slaying and slaughtering by both sides of men and horses as they were all fighting with wondrous virtue.'

Eventually, the German attack waned, with the French infantry, supported by the cavalry who were lined up as their reserve, pushing forwards and taking the advantage. Finally, Otto's own horse was wounded; turning away from the fight, it fled from the field, taking the emperor with him. The centre had also been won by the French.

It seems that about the same time as the centre forces clashed, so too did the final two divisions, on the allies' right and the French left. Again, it was the allies who charged, and, bolstered by

THE BATTLE OF SAN ROMANO, *fought in 1432 between Siena and Florence, was made famous in three paintings by Paolo Uccello, painted for the Medici family between 1435 and 1460. This panel celebrates the leadership of the victorious Florentine general, Niccolò da Tolentino. It also accurately portrays cavalry fighting in full plate armour, using lances and war hammers against similarly armed and armoured cavalry. One should also note the straight-legged riding style prevalent in many medieval paintings of cavalry warfare.*

French Knight (late 14th century)

The large amount of warfare taking place in 14th and 15th centuries (the last two centuries of the Middle Ages), led to some dramatic military technological changes. By c.1350 cavalry began wearing a more solid and independent breastplate made from a single piece of metal fashioned to cover the chest and sides. By the end of the century this had been joined to metallic plates covering the back, neck, legs, arms and feet, and was topped by a helmet that most often fitted tightly around the head and was equipped with a visor. Over this, the soldier usually wore a surcoat, which added no extra protection, but did serve heraldic purposes. The offensive weapons remained the same as earlier, a lance and sword, although in order to better face changes in armour, the former had increased in length and the latter had become shorter and stiffer, often with re-inforced, sharp points.

Battle of Bouvines

1214

Outside the town of Bouvines in northern France (near present-day Lille), French King Philip II Augustus decided to do battle against a combined force of German, English and rebellious French forces that were pursuing him. This was a crucial battle for Philip, since the allies threatened the very existence of the French throne. The allies, on reaching the battlefield, engaged French forces almost immediately, which were formed into three divisions. The battle was fought in intervals: the first a cavalry on cavalry battle between early arriving allied troops and the French right wing; the second between the two centre forces of both cavalry and infantry; and the third fought by French infantry and cavalry on the left wing against a largely infantry force arriving last on the battlefield. However, with allied troops still approaching Bouvines, the French defeated each of these contingents individually and won the battle.

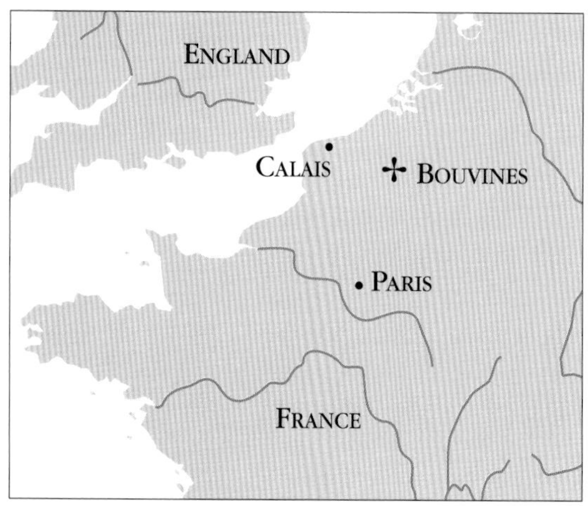

Philip Augustus, leading a large French army pursued by an equally large coalition of forces from the Holy Roman Empire, England, and rebellious French principalities, stopped and decided to do battle outside Bouvines.

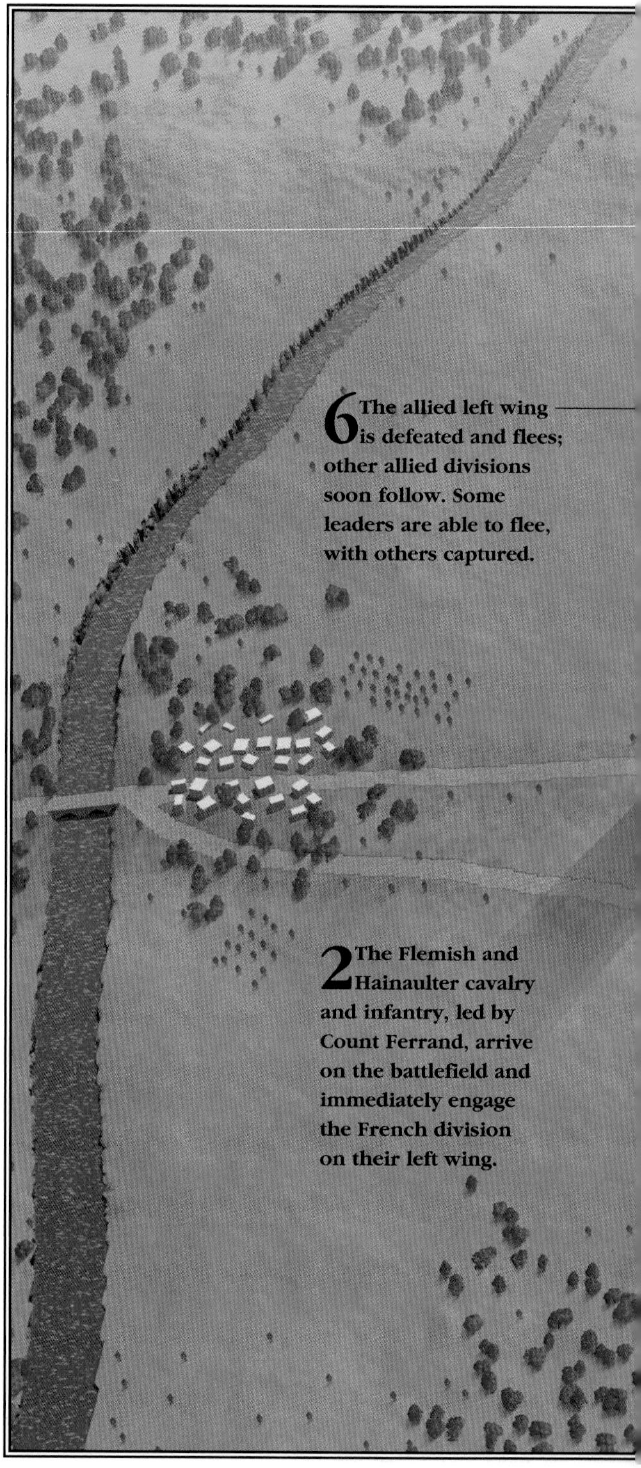

6 The allied left wing is defeated and flees; other allied divisions soon follow. Some leaders are able to flee, with others captured.

2 The Flemish and Hainaulter cavalry and infantry, led by Count Ferrand, arrive on the battlefield and immediately engage the French division on their left wing.

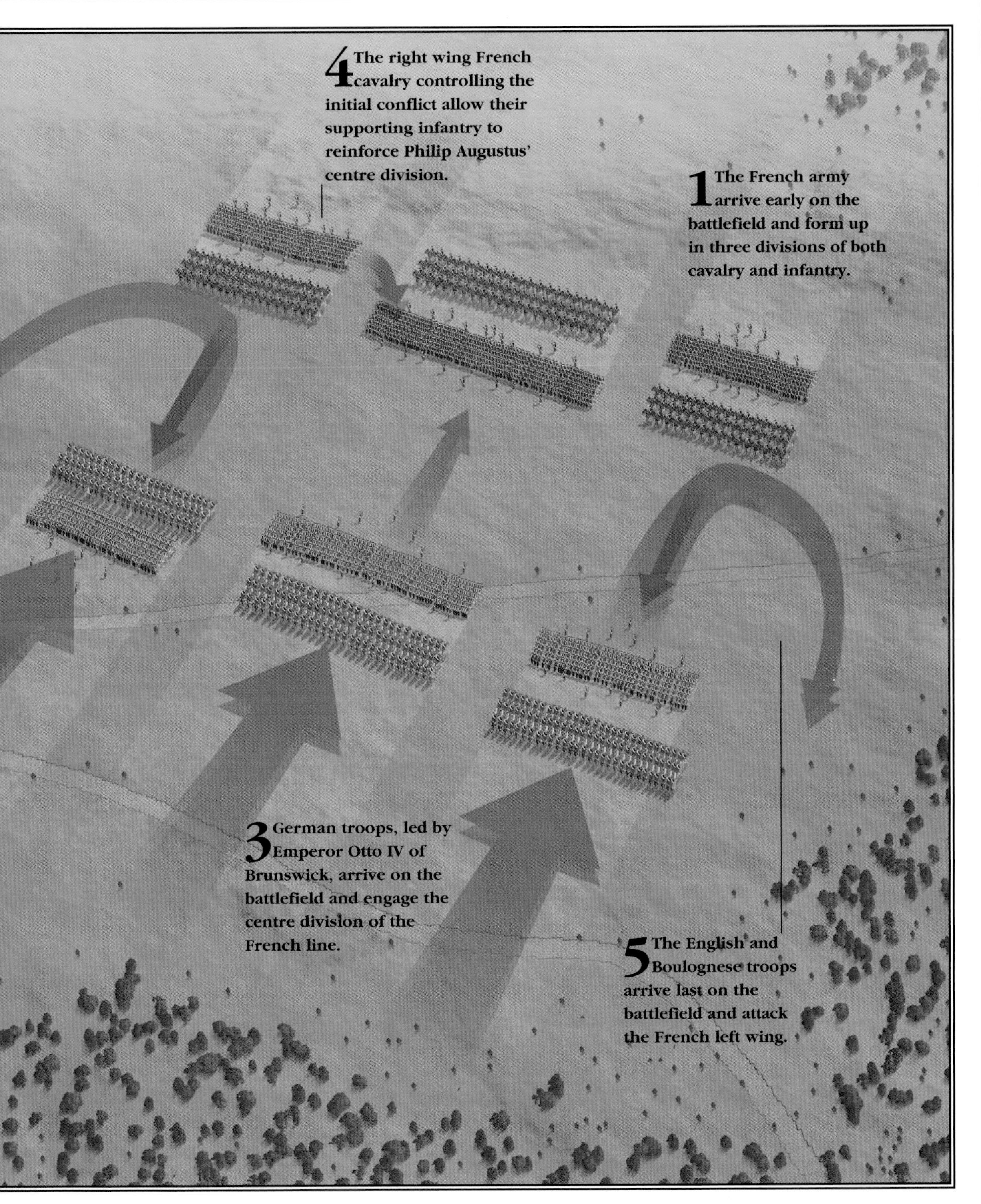
4 The right wing French cavalry controlling the initial conflict allow their supporting infantry to reinforce Philip Augustus' centre division.
1 The French army arrive early on the battlefield and form up in three divisions of both cavalry and infantry.
3 German troops, led by Emperor Otto IV of Brunswick, arrive on the battlefield and engage the centre division of the French line.
5 The English and Boulognese troops arrive last on the battlefield and attack the French left wing.

French Knight in Plate Armour (c. 1480)

By the middle of the 15th century, armour industries everywhere in Europe were producing excellent and very expensive suits of plate armour to outfit wealthy noble and aristocratic soldiers or jousters. Two styles of armour predominated: the Italian and the German, although Italian-style plate armour was not always made in Italy, nor was German-style plate armour always made in Germany. The pictured suit of armour, from the collections in the Musée de l'Armée, in Paris, is dated c.1480. Constructed in the Italian style, such armours were made principally for warfare, with heavier and sometimes more constricting protections being added for tournament use. The lack of a lance-rest here suggests that this armour was meant for infantry rather than cavalry use. The elongated sabatons *for the feet were added for fashion and could be detached when the wearer participated in combat.*

continually arriving infantry, they continued to battle, indeed long after the other two allied divisions had broken and run, according to contemporary sources. The fighting here was much more equal, causing Guillaume le Breton to write in admiration of the leaders there: 'Count Reginald of Boulogne who had been in the fray continually was still fighting so strongly that no one could vanquish or overcome him. He was using a new art of battle: he had set up a double row of well-armed foot soldiers pressed closely together in a circle in the manner of a wheel. There was only one entrance to the inside of this circle through which he went in when he wanted to catch his breath or was pushed too hard by his enemies. He did this several times.'

Eventually, as these French soldiers began to gain reinforcements from the other two victorious divisions, the only allies left on the field - a few cavalry with more infantry - began to fatigue and weaken. Yet only after the count of Boulogne's horse was killed beneath him, trapping him in the fall, did they finally end their combat. According to Guillaume le Breton, at this time only six knights remained by his side. The other allies, between 5000 and 20,000 in number, had fled the field or surrendered.

Surprisingly, despite the length of the battle and the number of participants actually involved in the fighting, only 169 allied and two French horsemen are reported to have been killed, suggesting the strength of the armour of their time. No figures for infantry deaths are recorded, but it is suggested that they, also well armoured, only lost a few men. Many more were captured and would see Philip's prisons. Among their number were five barons - Ferrand of Flanders, William of Salisbury, Reginald of Boulogne, Willem of Holland and the unnamed count of Tecklenburg - 25 other nobles and 139 knights. Only Emperor Otto IV of Brunswick, Hendrik of Brabant and Hugo of Boves managed to escape.

Decline of Cavalry Warfare

Another possible reason for the development of plate armour was that cavalry victories in battles began to decline, and the risk of death, especially at the hands of the 'lesser' infantry, began to increase. Therefore, greater protection was needed to preserve the lives of cavalry soldiers.

In spite of the importance placed on them by many military historians, early or high medieval battles were infrequent endeavours. Large medieval land battles were usually fought in desperation, and only when one power was invading or trying to stem an invasion (for example, Tours, Edington, the Dyle, Lechfeld, Stamford Bridge, Hastings, Manzikert, Northallerton, Arsuf and Falkirk) or when leading or encountering feudal rebellions (such as Cassel, the Elster, Brémule, Bourgthérolde, Lincoln, Legnano, Parma, Benevento, Tagliacozzo, Lewes, Evesham and Bouvines). On very rare occasions would a leader fight more than one large battle and then, it seems, only when their self-confidence overpowered their wisdom. As often as not, a leader flushed with victory in one battle - Harold Godwinson, Simon de Montfort and William Wallace - would meet defeat in a following engagement. Even the renowned warrior, Richard the Lionheart, was only involved in three pitched battles during his career, including all of those fought during the Third Crusade.

The reality was that for capturing land, the siege was almost always far more important and profitable for medieval leaders. A leader as astute as King Philip II (Augustus) fought only one major battle during his lengthy reign over France, the Battle of Bouvines in 1214, which in fact could be said to have profited him very little as far as actual land gains. Yet his sieges of notable fortifications and towns throughout Anjou, Normandy and Aquitaine brought him nearly all of the 'English' lands in France, save Gascony.

Battles were expensive, although not often in terms of deaths. As cavalry soldiers in medieval battles began to dictate what occurred in military engagements sometime after the rise of the Carolingians, although their numbers on the field never exceeded those of the infantry, deaths became less frequent. The ransoming of knights and other cavalry soldiers became more lucrative than killing them. At Bouvines, for example, fewer than 200 Allied and only two French knights were killed, despite perhaps as many as 40,000 fighting on both sides in the conflict. While at the Battle of

Brémule, Orderic Vitalis reported that although 'nine hundred knights were engaged, only three were killed', something which he attributes to the fact that 'Christian soldiers did not thirst for the blood of their brothers.' Other high medieval battles indicate a similar low casualty rate.

Large-scale Battles

All of these patterns of medieval warfare seemed to change in 1300. The number of large battles fought between then and 1550, already increasing during the latter half of the thirteenth century, would grow ever more numerous. Between 1302 and 1347, for example, no fewer than 19 major battles were fought in Europe, more than had been fought during the two previous centuries. Additionally, the fighters in these conflicts seem to have forgotten that they were fighting other Christian forces, as death rates increased noticeably, even among those soldiers who could bring the highest ransoms. At Courtrai in 1302 between 40 and 50 per cent of the French cavalry were killed; at Bannockburn in 1314, between 154 and 700 English nobles were killed; at Mons-en-Pévèle in 1304 both the French and the Flemings lost upwards of 4000 men each; at Neville's Cross in 1347, the lowest estimate of Scots killed is 2000; at Crécy in 1346, nine French princes, more than 1200 knights, and 15,000–16,000 others were slain; while at Kephissos in 1311, nearly the whole Athenian Frankish force disappeared.

ALTHOUGH MISSING ITS LEG *harnesses, this plate armour, dating from the end of the 15th century and currently located in Poland, shows a typical German-style armour for use in tournaments. The brackets added to the breast- and backplates are known as lance-rests and were meant to allow for the ease of couching the lance, while the more solidly attached, heavier helmet would better protect the head from the shock of a tournament lance hitting it.*

The high number of large battles would continue into the early modern period, as war after war began to be decided more on the battlefield than in sieges. Three battles, at Grandson, Murten and Nancy fought in 1476–77, decided the fate of the Swiss-Burgundian wars in favour of the Swiss, while the Wars of the Roses had no fewer than 15 major battles during its 32-year span. Finally, the wars between the Holy Roman Empire and France (and their allies), largely fought in Italy during the late fifteenth and early sixteenth centuries, are characterized more by their battlefield engagements than by any other military activity. (The engagements were at Seminara in 1494, Fornovo in 1495, Cerignola in 1503, Garigliano – two battles – in 1503, Agnadello in 1509, Ravenna in 1512, Novara in 1513, Marignano in 1515, Bicocca in 1522, Pavia in 1525, Landriano in 1529 and at Ceresole in 1544.) In all of these battles, too, high casualty rates were seen.

There could be several reasons for the increase in the numbers of battles at this time. The accelerated speed of sieges because of the proliferation of gunpowder weapons might have caused more frequent battles, except that innovations in fortification construction kept pace with the offensive technological advances. As a result, after only a brief time when sieges were

MAXIMILIAN OF AUSTRIA, *who ruled as king of the Romans from 1486 and Holy Roman Emperor from 1493 to 1519, was a great collector of armour and patron of tournaments and other chivalric displays and arts. He also participated in numerous jousts, fighting both on foot and on horse. In this contemporary illustration, Maximilian is shown unhorsing an opponent. Both are dressed in German-style plate armour with horses wearing chain barding.*

shortened considerably by gunfire, they returned to their traditional lengthy time commitment.

The most convincing reason for the increased numbers of battles between 1300 and 1550 might be that infantry had begun to dominate the battlefield. Although several battles during the Middle Ages had been fought using primarily infantry troops, and in some instances these troops had been victorious, the myth of cavalry superiority prevailed. This belief system would change in the early fourteenth century when Flemish, Scottish, Swiss, Frisian and Liégeois infantry soldiers all began to gain victories over largely cavalry-based French, English, Austrian and German armies.

Infantry Dominance

Battle-winning infantry tactics quickly evolved. The infantry would prepare the battlefield by digging ditches, constructing wagon-fortresses or flooding already marshy ground, so that their opponents had only one course of attack, the frontal assault. Next the infantry were ordered into a defensive formation in one or more solid lines to await a charge. When the charge did come, it quickly became disordered and confused. The impetus was lost, and the soldiers - cavalry or infantry - hit their target with little force. Horses and enemy infantry struggled to penetrate the defensive lines. Cavalry soldiers were pulled from their horses. Once on the ground they became vulnerable to attacks from their opponents' weapons. Lances, spears, swords, axes, *goedendags* and other short-range weapons proved effective against all targets, no matter who they were or how well they were armoured.

Once established, the new infantry tactics proved extremely effective against all opponents. When they were adopted by the English, which occurred at the Battle of Boroughbridge in 1322 and later at Dupplin Moor and Halidon Hill fought in 1332 and 1333 respectively, the English infantry added their own special weapon, the longbow, on their flanks to replace the need for ditches or woods to prohibit opposing flank attacks. The English subsequently won pivotal Hundred Years' War battles at Crécy, Poitiers, Najera, Aljubarotta,

ARISING IN THE 14TH CENTURY, *within 100 years the Ottoman Turks had begun to dominate the eastern Mediterranean. Relying primarily on infantry units, Ottoman cavalry were lighter than their western European counterparts and served mostly as support troops for the infantry. This cavalry included mounted archers as well as lancers, such as the Ottoman cavalryman shown here. Both archers and lancers were outfitted in the type of chain armour illustrated.*

Agincourt and Verneuil against much larger foes. Eventually, hand-held gunpowder weapons became prominent on the battlefields of continental Europe by the 1440s, replacing bow weapons, and they were tactically used in a similar way to the longbows, at least initially. Ultimately, the prominence of cavalry soldiers as main attack troops irrevocably declined. The democratization of death provided by the arrow and gunshot meant that the cavalry soldier who had little fear of his own battlefield demise before 1300 faced a greater likelihood of being killed in the years following that date. The cavalry warfare so dominant during the Middle Ages had essentially ended.

Battle of Nicopolis: 25 September 1396

The battle of Nicopolis, fought on 25 September 1396 on the plains south of the central Bulgarian city of that name, saw a truly diverse soldiery on the field that day. On one side, Bayezid I, sultan of the Ottoman Turks, led a force manned by troops from his homeland, Asia Minor, and from his and his predecessors' conquered and vassal peoples, namely Serbs, Bulgarians, Bosnians and Albanians. Added to these was the Turkish janissary corp, filled with young Christian tribute-children and prisoners of war, now converted to Islam and dedicated to the defeat of their old religious allies. The total Turkish number, estimated by contemporary chroniclers (mostly western writers) at more than 100,000, was probably closer to 15,000.

Opposing Bayezid was a force composed of allied troops from throughout western and central Europe. Called a crusade army by all contemporary western authors, it was composed of Hungarian, Wallachian, Transylvanian, Hospitaller, German, Burgundian, French and English soldiers. Fewer in number than the Turks, although closer to a total of 12,000 than to the 100,000 found in contemporary sources, it was controlled by the Franco-Burgundian cavalry troops and their leaders. This control became a problem, for the soldiers were foreigners to the region, and they refused to listen to the advice of those who lived closer to the enemy. In particular, the Franco-Burgundian generals were reluctant to listen to the recommendations of the Hungarian king, Sigismund I. (The generals were Phillip of Artois, the constable of France; Jean II le Meingre dit Boucicault, the marshal of France; Jean de Vienne, the admiral of France; Guillaume de la Trémoille, the marshal of Burgundy; Sir Enguerrand de Coucy VII; and the 23-year-old John the Fearless, whose succession to the throne of Burgundy gave him titular leadership over all of the Franco-Burgundian forces.) Their collected experience in military conflict, extremely impressive as it was, seemed more important to them than Sigismund's knowledge of and experience in fighting the Turks.

Nicopolis was the first battle where the Ottomans encountered a western European army. To this point, rivals of the Ottoman Turks had been either Byzantine armies or local, southeastern European militias. Of course, the Ottoman Turks were not an old political entity. In fact, they had existed for only about 100 years. Mythical origins aside - and these are numerous in later centuries - the Ottomans seem to have originated as a small, familial clan which under the initial leadership of Osman I (1280-1324) quickly expanded out from their local Asia Minor geography to conquer much of the eastern Mediterranean and southeastern European peoples. By 1396 they controlled most of Asia Minor and much of the Balkan peninsula. Among the casualties of these conquests was the once extensive Byzantine Empire. This had shrunk to little more than Constantinople and its neighbourhoods, with other states disappearing.

Western European powers began to worry about the Ottoman Turks from their earliest beginnings. The Ottoman speed of conquest and their European targets caused some, especially those of the papal court, to become frightened at the prospect of having to fight an Islamic enemy closer to their homelands than the Middle East or Spain. During the Hundred Years' War, however, neither the French or English monarchs were willing to make peace and redirect their bellicose activities towards the Ottomans. Meanwhile, the various German and Italian political leaders possessed neither the strength nor the inclination to fight a crusade against Islam. Only the Hungarians, primarily because of their proximity to the early Ottoman conflicts, began to prepare both an offensive and a defensive military response to the Turkish enemies.

In 1396, a 28-year truce was arranged in Paris in an attempt to halt the Hundred Years' War. It was dependent on the marriage of the English monarch, Richard II, who was still young, to Isabella, one of Charles VI's daughters, and a co-equal Anglo-French attendance on a crusade to the east against the Ottoman Turks. Initially, it was expected that both the kings of France and England would lead the crusade, but soon they had passed this responsibility onto their relatives, Louis, duke of Orléans, Philip the Good, count of Burgundy, and John of Gaunt, duke of Lancaster. Soon, however, they too had sidestepped this

Battle of Nicopolis

1396

Endeavouring to regain southeastern European lands (in the region of modern-day Bulgaria) recently lost to the Ottoman Turks, a coalition of western European and Hungarian 'crusaders', under the titular leadership of John the Fearless, heir to the throne of Burgundy, besieged the Turkish-held town of Nicopolis. In response, Emperor Bayezid I marched to the relief of the town. After refusing a tactical suggestion by Hungarian King Sigismund I, John chose to mount a cavalry charge against the Ottoman forces. Initially succeeding against a screen of lightly armed cavalry and infantry, this charge faltered after it could not penetrate the solid infantry formation arrayed behind a line of stakes. A second charge also failed. Crusader infantry forces not engaged fled from the battlefield, with many of the cavalry captured and put to death by the Turks. This battle put paid to the likelihood of the Christian kings stemming the tide of Ottoman gains in southeast Europe.

Attempting to raise the crusader siege of Nicopolis, Ottoman Turkish troops, led by Emperor Bayezid I, fought a battle against the Christian troops on the plains outside the town.

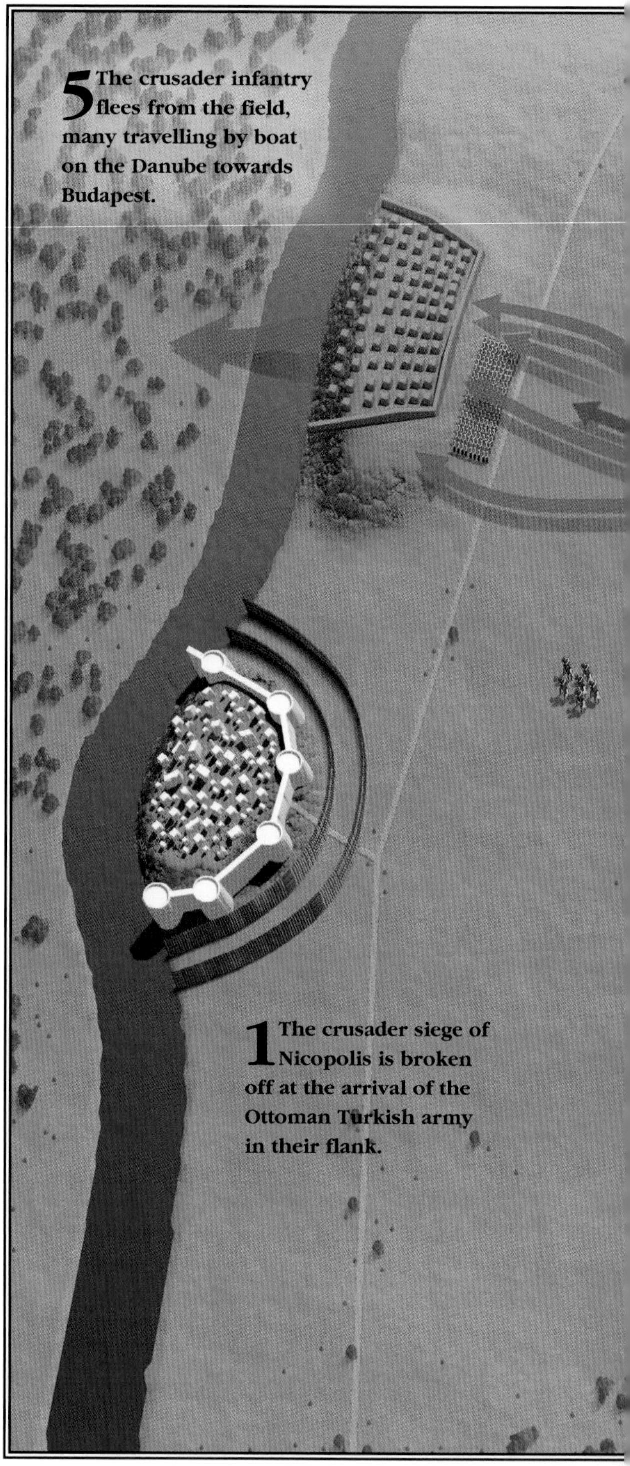

5 The crusader infantry flees from the field, many travelling by boat on the Danube towards Budapest.

1 The crusader siege of Nicopolis is broken off at the arrival of the Ottoman Turkish army in their flank.

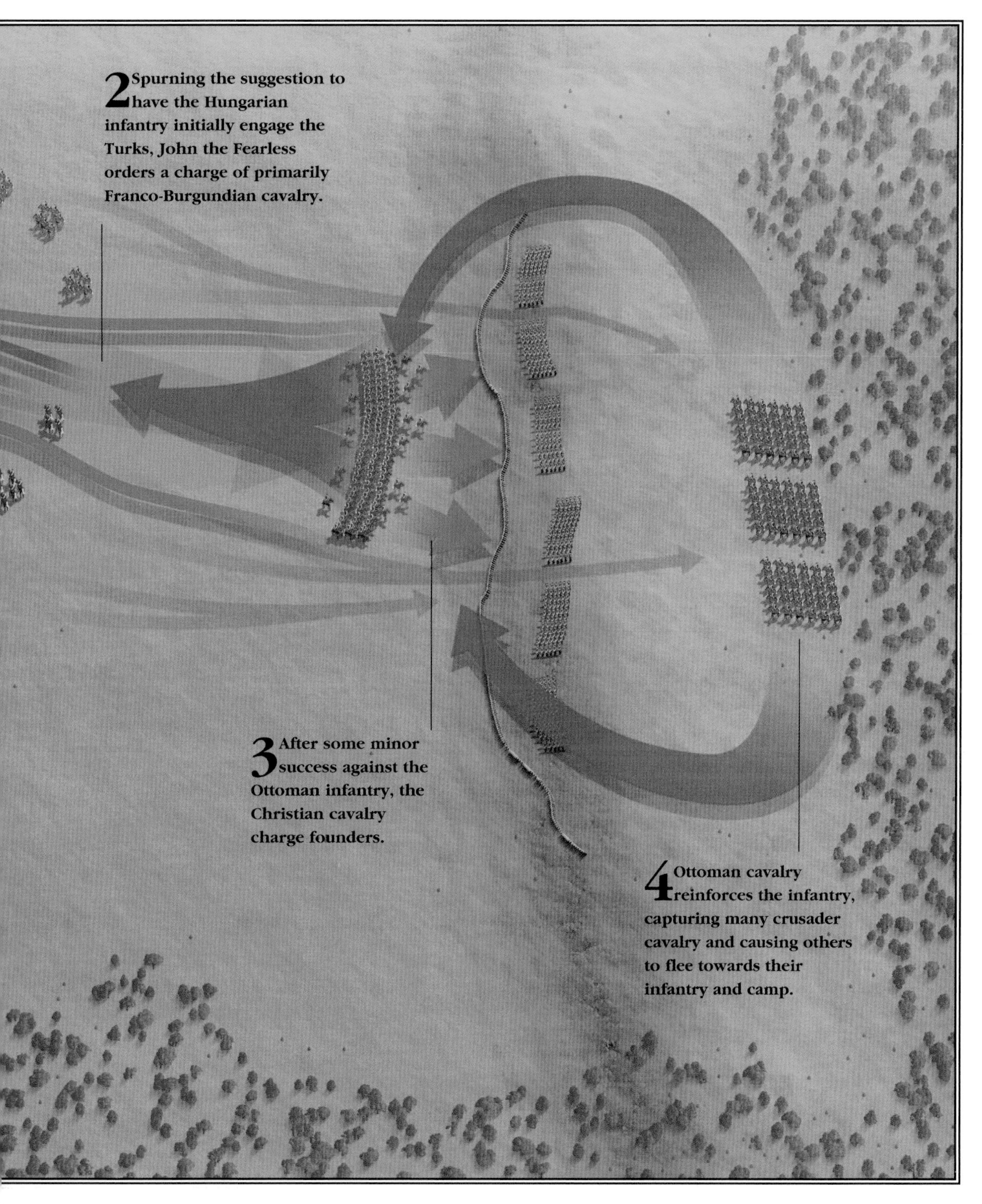
2 Spurning the suggestion to have the Hungarian infantry initially engage the Turks, John the Fearless orders a charge of primarily Franco-Burgundian cavalry.
3 After some minor success against the Ottoman infantry, the Christian cavalry charge founders.
4 Ottoman cavalry reinforces the infantry, capturing many crusader cavalry and causing others to flee towards their infantry and camp.

responsibility and leadership tasks fell to the young John the Fearless and his cadre of French military leaders.

The crusaders gathered at Dijon on 20 April 1396, from where they marched quickly and without difficulty throughout central Europe to Buda, in Hungary, arriving there at the end of June. There John the Fearless gathered his troops and those who had joined the crusade along the way. He also listened to those who had witnessed Ottoman warfare first-hand, and he discussed strategy and tactics with his generals and with Sigismund I, the king of Hungary. All, except for Sigismund, decided to march directly against the nearest Ottoman holdings, fortifications and towns which lay south of the Danube River, the king of Hungary counselling for a defensive posture, one where the crusaders would help him to defend his land against what he felt was an imminent Ottoman invasion. He was overruled by the other leaders.

'A great mourning began throughout the kingdom of France.... All our lords had solemn masses for the dead sung in their chapels for the good lords, knights and squires, and all the Christians who had died....'

– *Le livre des fais du Mareschal de Bouciquaut*

The Battle

Initial attacks against these fortified locations were quite successful. Vidin and Rahova (present-day Oryakhovitsa) surrendered after strong attacks from the crusading soldiers. However, news of these victories soon reached Bayezid, then attacking the remnants of Byzantium, and he moved quickly to counter the western armies' advance. He did this seemingly without the crusaders discovering his plans or knowing his progress. Indeed, it would not be until the day before the battle, and within only 6.4km (4 miles) of Nicopolis, that John the Fearless knew that the Ottomans were close by and were willing to fight against him. The crusaders, who had been besieging the town of Nicopolis before the arrival of Bayezid's army, broke off their siege and prepared for battle.

John the Fearless called a council of war. Sigismund recommended that his and the other central European troops, almost entirely infantry, should be in the vanguard, there to meet the irregular infantry of the Turks who stood in front of their own army. They would take a defensive stance and try to provoke the Ottoman army into a charge which would either be defeated at the contact of the two infantry forces or could be reinforced by the strong Franco-Burgundian cavalry ordered in the rear. This strategy the Franco-Burgundians refused to follow. Despite agreement with Sigismund by Enguerrand de Coucy, perhaps the most sage and experienced of the Franco-Burgundian leaders, Robert of Artois used his influence and constabulary office to counter the Hungarian king's proposal. This leader, in concert with most of the other crusader generals, believed that superiority on the battlefield lay in the heavy cavalry and the mounted shock charge.

With a flurry of pride and enthusiasm the Franco-Burgundian cavalry charged head-long into their Turkish opponents, infantry safely guarded behind a line of stakes. Initially, the force of this mounted shock charge brought success, breaking through the stakes and pushing the Turkish irregular infantry back. The Ottoman Turkish lines, however, did not break, and quickly reformed their organization and order in the lull before a second charge could be mounted. That second crusader attack achieved similar success, yet still the Turks did not flee. When a counter-attack came from Bayezid's regular troops, consisting of cavalry, infantry and archers the impetus of the crusader soldiers had been spent and, even though some German and Hungarian infantry troops rushed to re-inforce them, all were routed. Those who were still able, tried to retreat from the battlefield, but the Danube River blocked

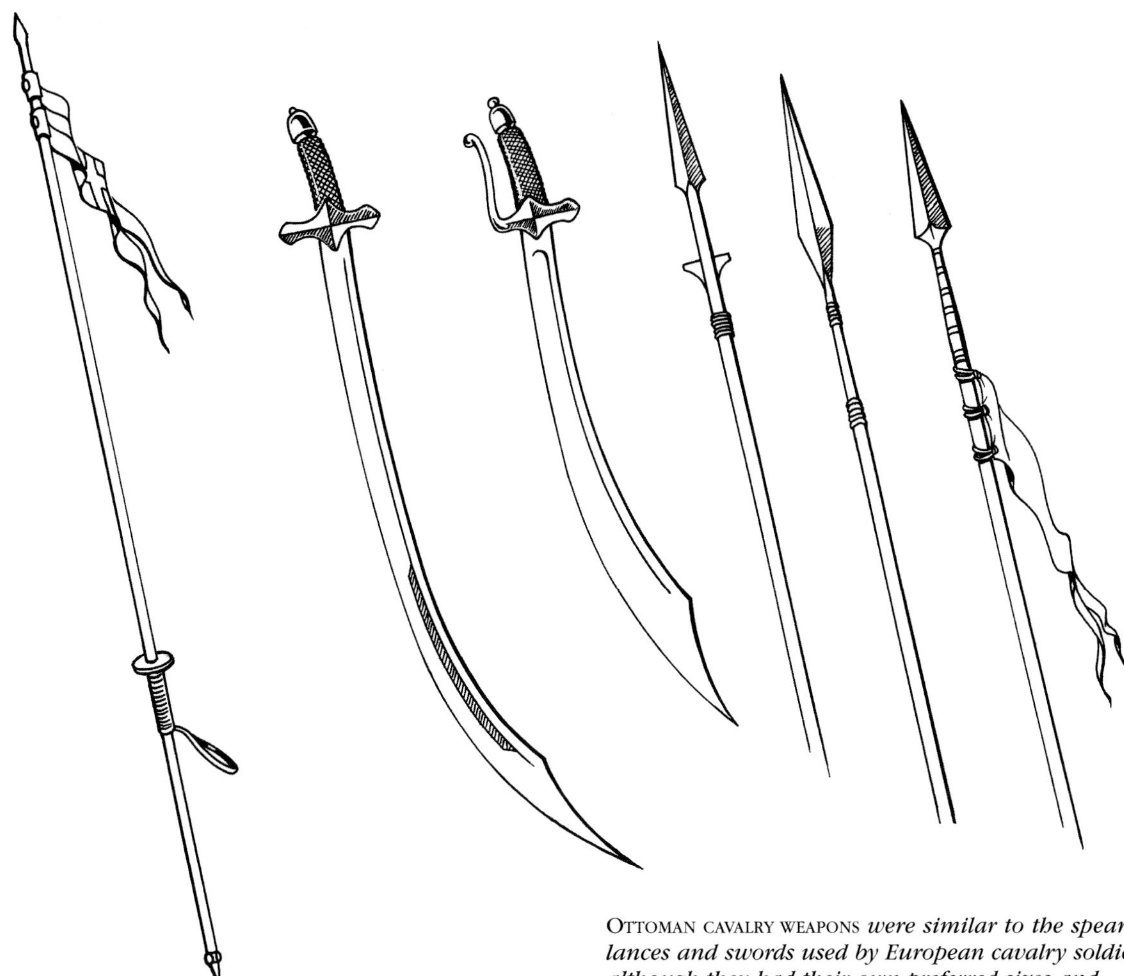

OTTOMAN CAVALRY WEAPONS *were similar to the spears, lances and swords used by European cavalry soldiers, although they had their own preferred sizes and styles. Most renowned of these was the Ottoman's sword or sabre, which was curved to give its user more of a slashing edge. But, as with European cavalry, the lance continued to be the weapon of choice for use in a charge and the sword for close combat.*

their path and few were actually able to leave the scene of what had in reality become a slaughterhouse.

Among those who were able to flee were the Walachians and Transylvanians. They had not been involved in the fight on that day. Instead, when the tide of battle turned against their allies they had refused to go to their fellow crusaders' aid. King Sigismund himself retreated to the Danube, boarded a boat and sailed to safety. The battle had lasted probably no more than an hour.

The effects of the Battle of Nicopolis were quickly felt. On the battlefield, Franco-Burgundian soldiers, used to the protection of ransom in western warfare, were instead hewed down without mercy. Only after the capture of John the Fearless were prisoners accepted, and even then several hundred more Christian troops were summarily executed at the sultan's order.

A mere 300, from a total of perhaps as many as 6000 who had been involved in the fighting, were eventually spared. Their ransom paid, an amount of more than 200,000 ducats, they returned home some nine months later. The Turks had also suffered huge losses, perhaps giving a reason for their blood-thirstiness, but they suffered far less than did the crusaders.

CHAPTER 3

COMMAND AND CONTROL

Medieval generals had limited technological resources with which to dominate the battlefield. Instead, they had to rely on tactical innovation and improvisation, especially when facing numerically superior forces.

During the medieval period, feudal Western Europe was assailed from all sides. In the north the Teutonic Order contended with pagan Prussians, Livonians and, later, Russians. From the north-west Vikings roamed not only the western seaboard, but wrought havoc as far inland as Paris and even reached Constantinople. Their voyages encompassed the great Russian waterways and the Mediterranean, virtually surrounding Europe. From the south the fanatic armies of Islam conquered Spain, Sicily and penetrated France to Poitiers, as well as eventually conquering Constantinople and

KNIGHTS CLAD IN *mail hack down unarmed Cathars during the Albigensian Crusade. This is a good illustration of the medieval riding style, despite the naive perspective. The leg is nearly straight to give stability for a downward cut. The saddle is much like an armchair to transmit the momentum of the rider and horse to the tip of the lance.*

Greece itself. From the east, Magyar and then Mongol hordes ravaged where they pleased, the latter only turning back when recalled. Later the Hussites evolved their own answer to the dominance of the western feudal knight.

The enemies assailing Europe were very different. They ranged from the ship-borne infantry armies of the Norsemen, through the balanced but lightly armoured infantry and cavalry armies of Islam, to the all-cavalry armies of the steppes and the armoured wagons of the Hussites. Those western generals who survived the onslaught did so by making the best use of the different types of troops at their disposal, exploiting their strengths against the enemy's weaknesses. Those who failed paid with their lives and the states they ruled were subsumed into the conquering power. In the hothouse of war, medieval generals were confronted with the same core problem as every general before and since: how to achieve unlimited aims with limited resources.

Tribes and Feudalism

The medieval period started with the gradual but irreversible decline of the Roman Empire. Beyond the borders of that already ancient empire, society and the armies it generated were mainly tribal in nature. Of these we have no contemporary record written by a participant but only that of outsiders, that is, their Roman neighbours. Later in the period we also have various ecclesiastical chronicles. Using these accounts, we can develop some understanding of tribal systems of war.

Medieval tribes were essentially informal and familial in formation. They extended from the nuclear family through the greater family into clans of several families. These clans were in turn connected by marriage to tribes of other clans. The dominant family leader would call on the members of the extended family to join in an attack or mutual defence, but by persuasion and bullying rather than coercion by law. Subsequently, obligation to join became the norm and leaders could impose a death sentence, a fine or land confiscation on those who failed to respond to a summons. The greater a family leader the more hearth troops he could support. In Saxon Germany, Jarls, anglicized as earls, could call upon the *fyrd* (known as the *Arriere-ban* in France) of able-bodied men to form a bigger army. The number thus summoned was based upon land held; one warrior was called from every parcel of land sufficient to support five families in Saxon England in the ninth century. Successful and charismatic leaders could raise bigger armies. Warriors could and did transfer to another tribe and a more successful leader. In later Saxon society transferring from one shire and earl to another had to be with the permission of the king and required a payment. They could also join the successful leader of a different clan or tribe, as happened under Chengis Khan, who certainly attracted warriors from other Asiatic tribes before uniting them under the Mongol standard.

THE ARCANE NORMAN *French of heraldry would describe the arms of King Edward III of England as Gules, three leopards* propre rampant. *In English, it becomes a red background with three leopards 'rampant' in their natural colours. Since the medieval artist who painted it had only a vague description of leopards to work from we finish up with this version of three rather fantastical lions.*

Leaders also drew about them bands of devoted followers, hearth troops (or *huscarls*), who depended entirely on the leader for their status and sustenance. They, in an ancient tradition of the heroic mode recorded by Caesar in his *De Bello Gallico* (Gallic Wars), might follow their leader to the grave if necessary. Individuals would bring the weapons they were brought up with, could afford and were accustomed to. This tended to produce an armed mob, though there were notable exceptions. Motivated by a common cause or simply greed, they fought for loot (there was no such thing as a soldier's wage) or glory or both.

'Such courage accounted for the extraordinary feats they had performed already. Only heroes could have made light of crossing a wide river, clambering up the steep banks and launching themselves on such a difficult position.'

– Julius Caesar

Tribal Structure

Tribal armies were generally terrifying in appearance, but unwieldy in use due to a primitive command structure. Subordinate leaders of decimal numbers were recorded for some peoples, leaders of ten or a hundred for example. This structure is typified by Saxon, Viking, Irish and Prussian armies. The tribal military system evolved into the leader expecting a number of warriors to appear based on the amount of land occupied by a family. The tribal leader himself would emerge through inheritance, or his own wit and charisma like Chengis Khan, who coalesced the Mongol tribes. He could also be elected by a council as king, like the Saxon monarchs.

The formal structures of the Roman Empire gradually collapsed as money, supplies, instructions, official appointments and reinforcements from Rome dried up. Post-Roman society had to fend for itself, the ultimate challenge for devolved government. But there was no clear instruction that 'you're on your own now', except in Britain, which did receive such an edict. Doubt, dithering and bickering followed and only the strongest leaders emerged, known by the late Roman title of *Duces* (from which we have the word 'duke'). These too formed their armies around bands of personal followers just like the tribal leaders.

Outstanding among these post-Roman leaders was undoubtedly Charlemagne. He inherited the Frankish kingdom, established by Childeric and fleshed out by Clovis, who adopted Catholic Christianity, and preserved from Arab conquest by Charles Martel. Charlemagne came to the throne in 768 and embarked on a 46-year reign extending his Frankish kingdom from Denmark to the Pyrenees, east to Rome and north again to Denmark, encompassing Switzerland, Bavaria and part of Austria. This was a feat not matched until Napoleon's conquests more than a thousand years later. Throughout his vast territory Charlemagne encouraged the notion of holding land in return for military service to the central authority – the king. He used this embryonic feudalism to extend his lands and multiply his armies. His role model was not lost on other rulers and feudalism spread like fungus on an old cheese, although varying in detail from region to region.

Royal and Religious Wars

Within medieval Europe, shifting marriage alliances and the inherited nature of power led to many conflicts large and small. Eleanor of Aquitaine altered the balance of power in Western Europe when she deserted her husband Louis VII of France and married Henry II of England. This brought her province of Aquitaine in the south-west of France under the English king's control. Her namesake of Castile brought her brother's disputed right to half of Gascony to the marriage bed of Edward I. These two marriages laid the foundation of the Hundred Years' War, triggered when Edward III stopped paying homage to the French monarch for these and other territories. The power-hungry Catholic Church was also a major force for conflict within Europe. It enforced its dominance by the sword against non-believers, dissenters, libertarians and political opponents alike in the Baltic Crusades, the Reconquista of Spain, the War of Castilian Succession and the Albigensian Crusade in the Pyrenees. Through a combination of royal intrigue and religious zeal, medieval Europe found itself in an almost perpetual state of conflict.

The Mongol Invasion of Europe: Leignitz 1241

A movie telling the story of Chengis Khan and the Mongols would seem like an impossible fantasy if it were not true. He was born named Temuchin, later adopting the name Chingis or Chengis when he became Great Khan of the Mongols. He had a hard but insignificant early life. He was forced to flee with his immediate family after his father had been killed by the tribe of a man he had killed earlier. From that inauspicious beginning he founded a dynasty with which he carved out the largest land empire ever seen, before or since.

The core of the Mongol army was the mounted warrior equipped with lance, bow and shield. He could be an unarmoured skirmisher or an armoured cavalryman capable of charging with the ferocity of any medieval knight. Mounted warriors could be supplemented by tribal levies of similarly equipped horsemen and a variety of specialist, often Chinese, soldiers. Two features, though, underline the uniqueness of the Mongol army, and both of them are key aspects of generalship: their ability to co-ordinate widely separated columns and, secondly, their ability to retain effective command during the heat and confusion of battle.

The Mongol invasion of Europe appeared to be a manifestation of the Devil to their enemies. To the medieval mind the emergence of a Mongol army from the limitless steppe was literally like a punishment from God (it certainly behaved like one, as we shall see). There was a higher Mongol plan of which the conquest of Europe was merely a part. Chengis died in 1227 and in 1229 Ogedei

CHARLEMAGNE AND HIS KNIGHTS *leaving Aix-la-Chapelle on pilgrimage to Santiago de Compostela. This was produced in the 12th century and so the details are those contemporary to the artist. We get another glimpse of the horse furniture of the time as well as the lance, the primary weapon of the knight.*

Mongol Heavy Cavalryman (13th century)

This Mongol warrior carries the standard of the Touman *(horde). He is different in every respect from his western counterpart. His principle tactic is to skirmish with his enemy wearing him down with archery before closing with his lance at the opportune moment. Not shown is the small round shield worn on his left fore arm. Among his equipment are spare bows and bowstrings. The bow is made from different materials glued together. Before stringing this takes a 'C' shape, pulled into its distinctive form by the tension of the string. This is so difficult you have to brace the lower end against your foot and use your whole body strength, arms, legs and stomach muscles to compress the bow sufficiently to hook the other end of the string on to the bow.*

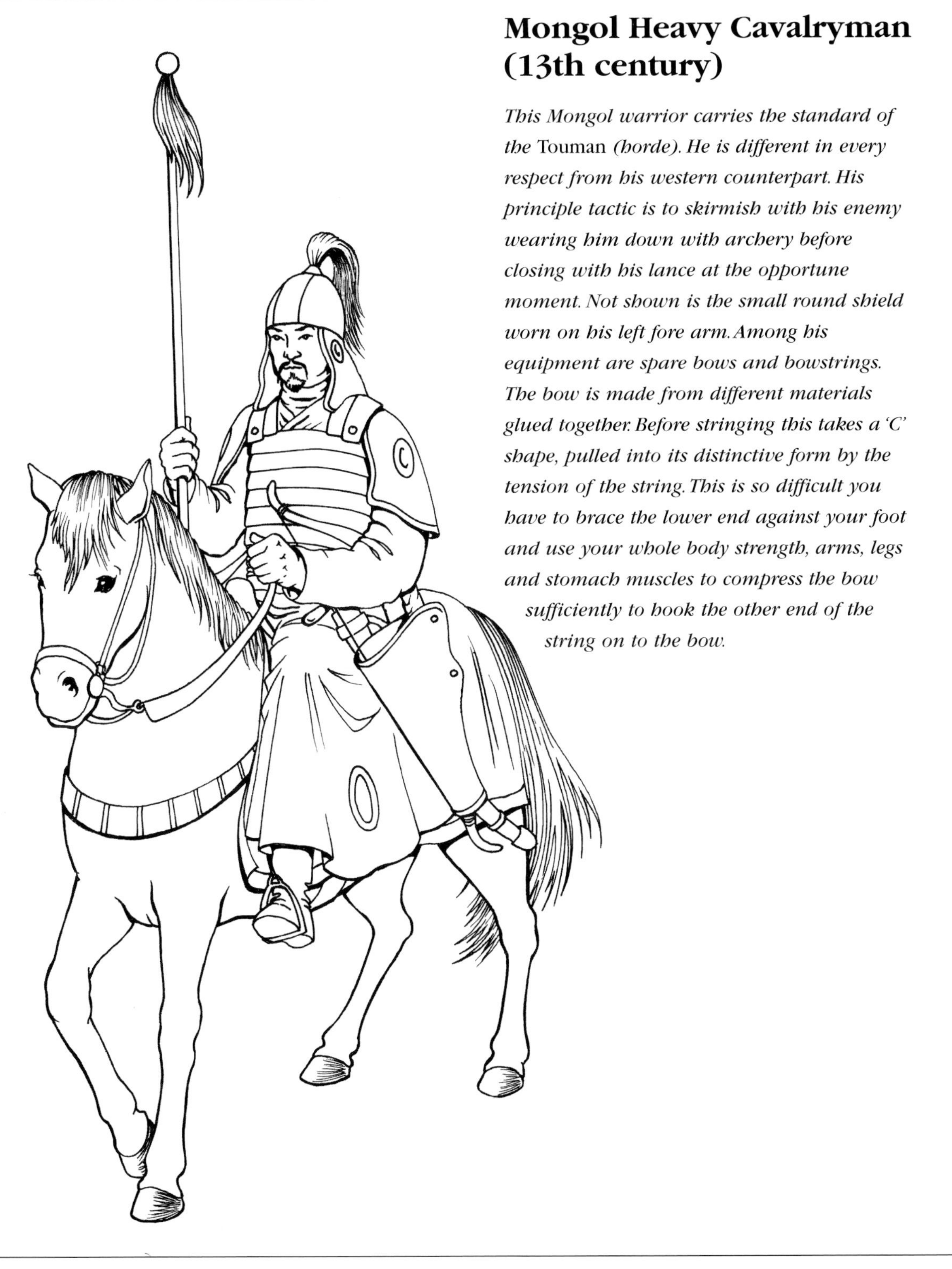

became the Great Khan. His father had already united the Mongol tribes and conquered the fabled Khwarizmian Empire of the central steppes. He had started the conquest of China, at that time split between the Chin and Sung dynasties. He is also responsible for founding the capital city of Karakorum. Ogedei summoned a conference of all the leading men in his empire.

The news emerged that Mongol armies were already reaching out to Georgia on the shores of the Black Sea. Ogedei announced he would continue the conquest of China. Batu, Chengis' grandson, was given Europe. He was also given some help: the pick of the experienced leaders and warriors to train and discipline the tribal levies conscripted from earlier conquests – 50,000 experienced Mongols, 20,000 conscripts plus Chinese and Persian specialists. This was enough to form seven *Toumans* of 10,000 men each. (The Mongol army was organized into *Arbans* of 10 men, *Jaguns* of 10 *Arbans, Minghans* of 10 *Jaguns* and *Toumans* of 10 *Minghans*.)

In Europe the old small-minded rivalries ensured there would be no united response. The Pope was at loggerheads with the Holy Roman Emperor, and neither could spare troops to support Bela IV, the king of Hungary who was in the frontline. His vassals were deeply divided and

THIS MONGOL HORSE ARCHER *rides a typical steppe pony. Capable of great endurance with a short but comfortable gait they were an essential part of the Mongol war machine. Note the absence of any breast band on the horse harness such as was required by the western knight.*

THIS VICTORIAN WOODCUT *portrays an inaccurate impression of the weaponry and equipment used by the Mongols or Hungarians. However, it does convey the kind of unholy scrum that must have ensued when the two sides met head on.*

his neighbours encouraged this disunity in the hope of taking some of his territory in due course. In the north the Polish state had fallen apart under a lax king who allowed too much power to devolve to his dukes. His heir was having a tough time reasserting his authority.

The Mongols planned a pincer movement on a grand scale. Nearly one-quarter of the army was sent north to draw out the Hungarian armies on to the southern Russian steppes. Lublin, Zawichos and Sandimir were taken. But the news spread so slowly the desired response never came. To the south the main army under Batu ravaged Wallachia on the northwestern shore of the Black Sea. Three passes through the Carpathian Mountains were forced, the rivers Danube and Tisza became corridors into the heartland and Batu closed on Pest faster than a snow-swollen river.

Bela, the Hungarian king, allowed the Cumans, who had been driven west by the Mongol steamroller, to settle in Hungary and began to fortify his border. As warnings of the inexorable Mongol advance increased, Bela summoned his army and what allies he could. They came, but they would not be led. The lords wanted the Cumans expelled, the border cracked, the barons bickered, the Mongol tide swelled. Three days after the news arrived at Buda, the Mongols were less than 30km (19 miles) away. The jealous Hungarian nobility assassinated the Cuman lords and their warriors rode off leaving a trail of destruction in their wake. Bela sat tight; his nobles could not leave while the Mongols were so close. In the north the Mongols probed right up to Krakow, then started to retreat.

Battle of Leignitz

1241

Although strategies might alter according to circumstances the traditional tactics of the western knight relied on a ferocious headlong charge into the heart of the enemy. At Leignitz the Mongols turned this to their advantage by tempting the first line to charge with their *Mangudai* - light cavalry that were trained in the feigned-flight tactic - which expected to lose but beat the Hungarian first division before withdrawing to the flanks of their heavy cavalry in the face of the Hungarian second division. Their charge was dissipated as faster horses outstripped slower ones and skirmishers from the flanks closed around the charging knights, shooting down some and causing further disruption. Only then did the Mongol heavy cavalry charge to the utter ruin of the enemy. Here they contrived a smoke screen to hide the fate of the knights. The infantry had no idea of their compatriots' progress until they routed back through the smoke. The surprise and dismay caused the infantry to rout as well.

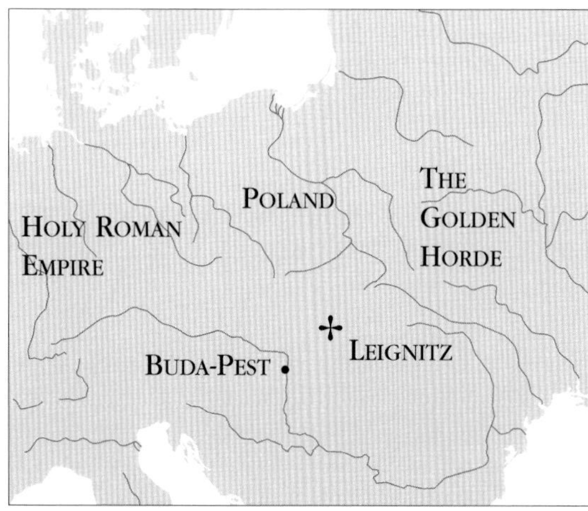

The Mongols succeeded in battle by degrading first the cohesion then the morale of their enemy. This was made easier by their reputation, which intimidated many foes before battle was joined.

2 **The Hungarian second division pursues the Mongol *Mangudai*.**

6 **The Hungarian infantry rout when the second division flees through smoke.**

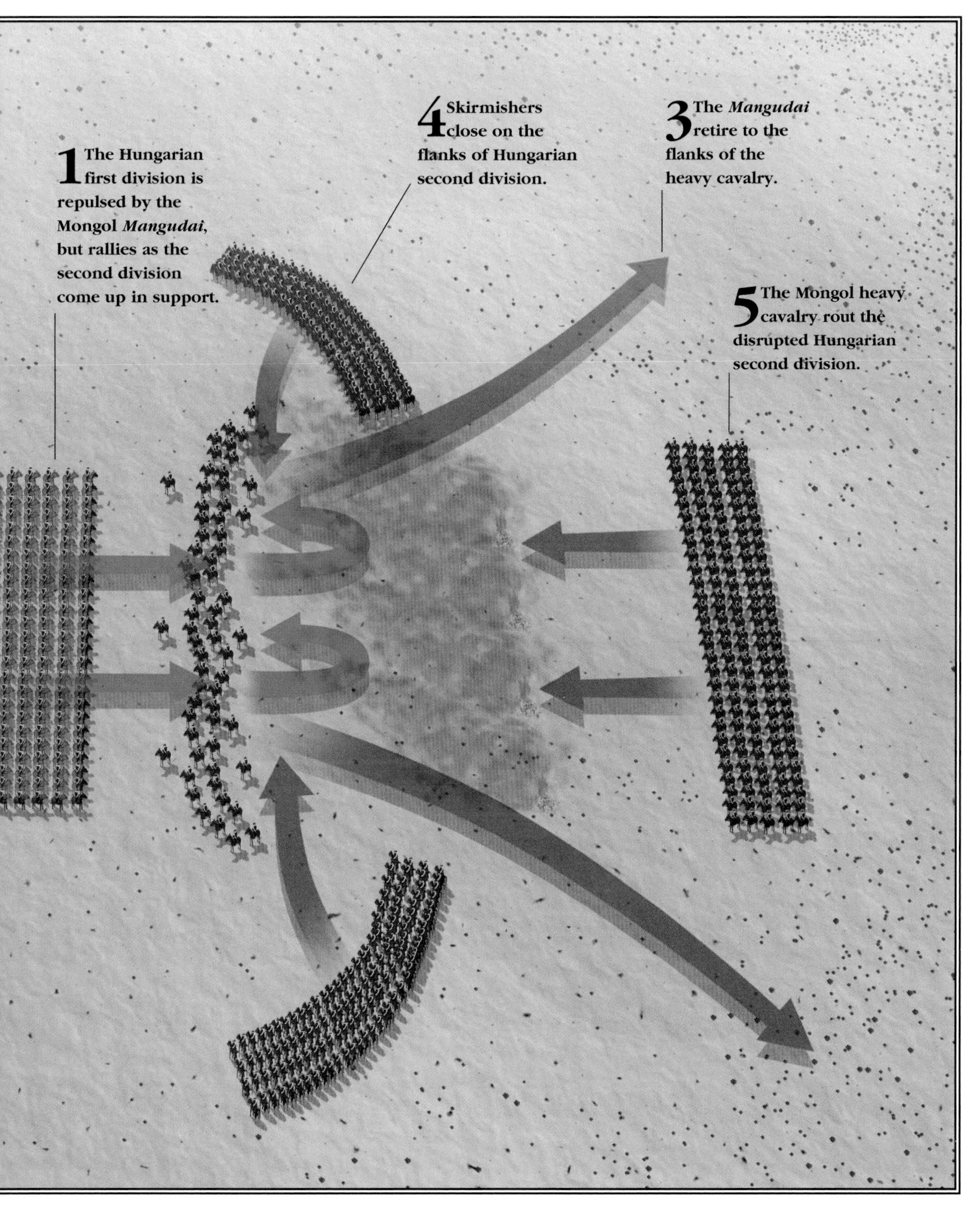
1 The Hungarian first division is repulsed by the Mongol *Mangudai*, but rallies as the second division come up in support.
4 Skirmishers close on the flanks of Hungarian second division.
3 The *Mangudai* retire to the flanks of the heavy cavalry.
5 The Mongol heavy cavalry rout the disrupted Hungarian second division.

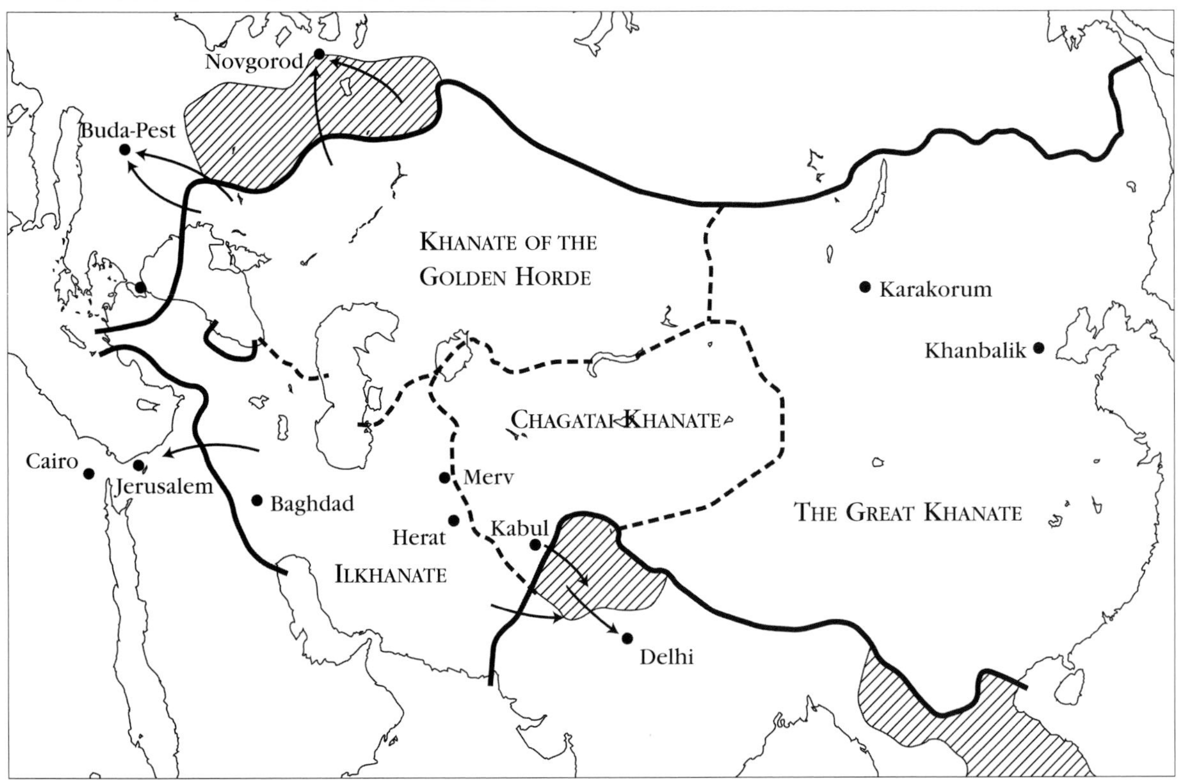

THE MONGOL EMPIRE IN 1300 *was the greatest land empire the world has ever seen. At its height, it stretched from Southeast Asia in the east to Poland in the west. Under the leadership of Genghis Khan's grandson, Batu, the Mongols first entered Europe in 1237, capturing the plains of western Russia in just a single winter.*

The Polish governor rode out in pursuit, and the Mongols accelerated their retreat to an apparent rout and abandoned their prisoners. The governor rode on to aid his father-in-law Bela of Hungary. The Mongol strategy had worked. About 39km (24 miles) from the haven of the city, the Poles died almost to a man under a storm of Mongol arrows. Breslau to the north of Krakow was the next target and as the Mongols were preparing to cross the River Oder and assault the city, their scouts brought in reports of a new army seeking to play mouse to their cat. Henry of Silesia had summoned the northern lords and awaited Wenceslas of Bohemia at Liegnitz. In a movement familiar to Napoleonic students, the Mongols prepared to strike from their central position at Henry before he could be reinforced by Wenceslas and his 50,000 men. The Bohemian was close, a day's march, but no more. Breslau was by-passed and battle joined on 9 April 1241.

Henry's army was mixed, encompassing the best and the worst. It consisted of militia and conscript infantry, feudal knights and sergeants, plus some knights from the Holy Orders – a few Knights Hospitaller and some Templars. But the fabled Teutonic Knights were also there under their landmeister. Total forces numbered about 20,000. The Silesian army formed in four great battles, all the infantry collected in one division, the Teutonic Knights in the centre with the other feudal contingents on either flank.

The Mongols deployed a *Mangudai* unit to their front centre. They were trained in the feigned-flight tactic. On their flanks were regular light cavalry capable of skirmishing with the bow or closing with the lance. To the rear of the *Mangudai* were the armoured heavy cavalry, just as capable of skirmishing as the lights, but also able to mount the full frontal charge. The Silesian light cavalry attacked the *Mangudai* first and were repulsed, but they rallied on the succeeding divisions and together they charged again. The Mongols to their front faked a rout and the Silesians rode on, deep into the heart of the Mongol horde. A smoke screen was started behind their charge to further isolate the knights. The Mongol flanks closed in, showering the knights with arrows. Then the heavy cavalry charged the depleted and tired Christians. One division drew up and attempted to rally back, but this just exposed their fellows and all, including the knights of the Holy Orders, were routed in turn. The infantry beyond the smoke screen knew nothing until they saw the routing knights and pursuing Mongols coming through the smoke and they too fled. The slaughter of the fleeing Silesians was immense. After the battle Wenceslas retired from whence he came and the Mongols swept back and forth along the valley of the Oder until the region was thoroughly depopulated.

Back at Buda in the south the same trick worked again. The Mongols started to retire; perhaps they thought the Hungarian host was too strong. Bela's nobles now wanted to fight an intimidated foe. He ordered all 100,000 of them out in pursuit.

The day after the battle of Liegnitz, another part of the Mongol army destroyed the city of Hermannstadt and the army of Transylvania 805km (500 miles) to the south. In the centre Batu also turned and faced the pursuing Hungarians and destroyed them at the battle of Mohi on 11 April. In three days the Mongols destroyed three armies, killing perhaps 150,000 warriors. Europe was wide open. Only the premature death of Ogedei recalled the Mongol hordes to settle the succession. Six separate columns of Mongols can be identified. Allowing Batu a double-strength force, and that each other column comprised a *Touman* of 10,000 men, that accounts for the 70,000 originally allotted for the invasion. We do not, regrettably, know how they coordinated their movements.

Military Resources

At the top of feudal society was the king. An inexperienced king, a queen or a juvenile could have a regent appointed by a ruling council. The active king or the regent could command the army in the field or appoint a marshal or constable. The army comprised lords of varying rank, their retinues and mercenaries. Feudalism added the authority of the state to the personality of the king. He could take away the estates and titles of knights who defaulted on their military obligations. Substantial fines were not unknown either.

The military resources available to a king's army were usually inherited. Very few generals were able to innovate and exploit new weapons or organizations to their full – life was just not long enough to do both. The means of production available in medieval society further limited the rate of change. As our period progressed technological change made very little impact on the ability of society to produce more arms and armour. Greater wealth and expanding population were the real driving forces of military change, however, while the fashion for more elaborate protection absorbed increasing amounts of time and resources.

Feudal retinues were obliged to serve their lord and through him the king for 40 days (this was thought to be the time elapsed between planting and harvest). At the end of that period they were free to return home. The 40-day system made a prolonged campaign very difficult and consequently mercenaries, paid by the king, were employed. These could be lords and those retainers whose feudal service had expired or captains of wandering bands of soldiers. The lord or captain agreed a contract to provide so many men, usually 200–400, whose skill was often specified, for so many days at a stipulated rate, or in return for the right to loot.

Peace treaties made these bands, or companies, redundant without any regard to their alternative employment. Faced by impending poverty many of them chose instead to continue their work, but for themselves. A mercenary company would capture and garrison a group of castles, then extort protection money from the surrounding area at will. When they were satisfied no more money was available they would move on to another area. The companies were sophisticated organizations. They included clerks, accountants and a man who divided up the booty and

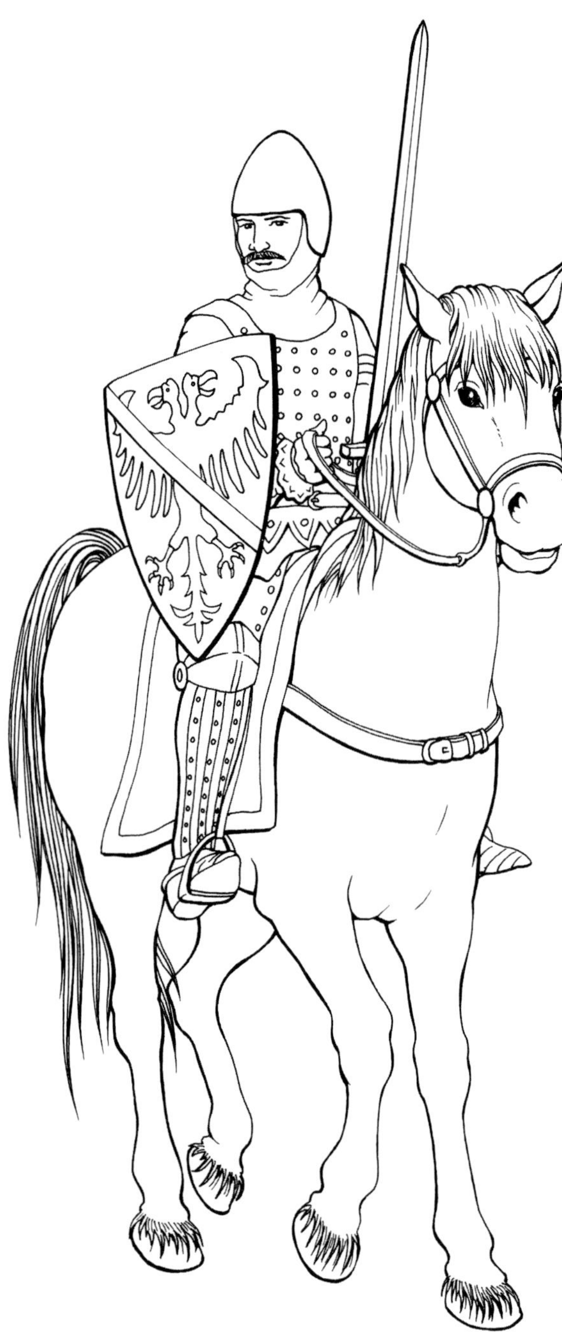

PHYSICALLY UNATTRACTIVE *as a youth, Bertrand du Guesclin grew up to be a strong, fearless warrior of considerable cunning. He bears the Breton double-headed eagle on his shield. From lowly beginnings he rose to be Constable of France.*

dispensed it according to a set ratio. Separate companies would merge for projects of a grander scale of their own. Some 16,000 men, for example, formed the Grand Company that ravaged the Rhone/Saone valley of southeastern France some time between 1360 and 1365. They could also be hired en masse for royal projects. Bertrand du Guesclin of Brittany was a low-born knight who later became, through his own bravery and ability, Constable both of Castile and France. He raised a company of more than 10,000 soldiers to help Henry oust Pedro the Cruel from Castile. They were made redundant, then the Black Prince, Edward Plantagenet (d.1376), the son of Edward III, who had previously commanded at Poitiers, hired them once again to recover Pedro's throne (see below).

As the Hundred Years' War ended and royal authority re-established itself, the Free Companies moved east, many operating in Italy where they came to be known as *condotierre* (after the contract signed between the captain of the company and the employing state). In addition, there was a tendency for lesser folk, armed peasants, to follow an army in the hope of making easy money from supplying its needs as well as plunder when the opportunity arose. Later called *ribauds* or *routiers* in Europe, they had no particular place in the chain of command and occasionally got in the way of their own side. However, they sometimes scored spectacular successes. For instance, they captured Beziers in the Albigensian Crusade (1209–55). They also evolved into mercenary bands.

Although taking a low profile in the chronicles, it is clear that ordinary townsfolk also played an increasing role in warfare. Particular trade guilds could be given the duty of maintaining and manning a part of the town wall. Collectively the town militia could also impose local law on miscreants, even when they were from the knightly classes. In three notable instances, in Scotland, the Netherlands and Switzerland, the common folk or militia formed the great bulk of the army, reducing feudal lords to a supporting role in the field. Exactly how many knights, spearmen or archers turned up ready to campaign could not be exactly predicted or controlled.

The king or marshall had to impose his will on this motley crew. This was not always an easy task, especially since the fastest way for advancement and riches was to gain the notice of the king and demonstrate your bravery or a particularly cunning plan. Add to that the proud nobility, raging about who had the right to lead ahead of whom, and you can see a weak king could be deafened by pleas from all sides.

Amalgamation of Power

The power and title of a king was hereditary through the male line. This was fine when there was an heir. When there was no heir at all the family tree of the deceased monarch had to be scoured to find the next most eligible candidates, distant cousins, for example. Frequently there might be more than one. The imported heir would usually bring his own estates, perhaps even a kingdom, into the melting pot. A further facet to the succession was the tendency of disputing parties to refer the inheritance to a higher lord. He might then adjudicate in a way that brought the territories within his own family's domain. Thus there was a distinct trend for the lands controlled by a particular family to increase. The post-Roman kingdoms of Northumbria, Mercia, Wessex and so on, evolved into England. France absorbed more than a dozen independent or semi-independent

MEDIEVAL CAMP LIFE *could be chaotic in the extreme. Nobles' servants competed for the most prestigious site for the tents of their masters and this bickering permeated the whole camp. All food had to be cooked on open wood fires, which created a tremendous amount of choking wood smoke.*

THIS FOOT SOLDIER *carries the banner of Castile and Leon. His shield is a distinctive shape thought to provide good protection while not impeding the movement of the left leg.*

counties, duchies and kingdoms to become the state we recognize today. In some parts of feudal Europe, however, Salic law (the laws of Salian Franks brought to Gaul in the fifth century) dictated that each male heir should get an equal portion of the estate. In this case the estates reduced in size until they were not economically viable. Principalities like Andorra, Luxembourg and Monaco only survived due to their insignificance.

The Albigensian Crusade: Muret 1213

The Languedoc region of France had shared the experiences of its neighbours: first the Romans who brought Christianity; then the Visigoths; the passage of the Vandals going south, followed by conquering Arabs going north; then liberation by Charlemagne going south with his Franks; and finally the arrival of feudalism. Through all this change the region retained some important characteristics. The language Oc survived, though it is barely spoken nowadays. A different interpretation of Christianity evolved – Catharism. Cathar society treated women as the equals of men and embraced the pleasures of song and dance (it is from this region that troubadours spread across Europe). The Cathars had no churches, only domestic meeting places where Good Men and Women preached to the faithful. Above them were deacons and bishops. The Good Men and Women rejected all materialism as unspiritual and therefore evil. They also condemned the established Catholic form of priesthood as being licentious, rapacious and materialistic.

For hundreds of years Catholic and Cathar tolerated each other, living in the same towns and villages. That tolerance started to crumble and dissent turned to criticism, then to dispute and, ultimately, intolerance. The Catholic archbishop wrote to the Pope about the situation. The Pope appointed a legate, who reported back to Rome that he had found an entrenched heresy. Next the Pope

THE ALBIGENSIAN CRUSADE (1209–55) *encompassed a massacre at Lavaur, depicted in this print of 1891. It shows the steep countryside in the Pyrenees and the desperate nature of the fighting. The artist has given both sides a cross as their symbol and has portrayed a pit representing hell waiting for the damned.*

Battle of Muret

1213

Having been distracted by an open gate and the prospect of a quick victory, King Pedro's besieging Aragonese army takes its ease almost in the shadow of the town walls. Suddenly, they perceive a column of cavalry moving swiftly south from an unguarded gate. Interest turns to alarm as the apparently fleeing column turns, splits into three and becomes an attacking formation. Two divisions launch themselves directly into the front of the surprised Aragonese and the third division is forgotten as the Aragonese forces focus on the immediate threat (a common occurrence in battle at close quarters). Reeling from the frontal hammer blow the disordered Aragonese fall back, disrupting the division behind. At just this point Simon de Montfort's third division of crusader cavalry appears from their right, shieldless flank, and slams into the king's reserve division. All three are routed by the decisive onslaught of a fraction of their own number.

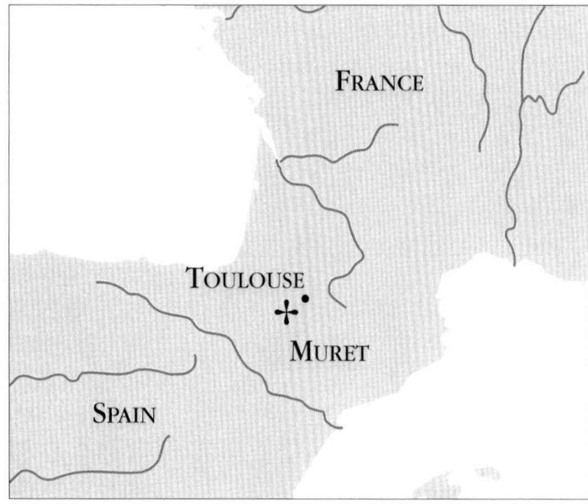

Transforming from God-fearing crusader to greedy baron in a few short months, Simon de Montfort tried to carve out his own fiefdom in the Pyrenees among the peace-loving Cathars.

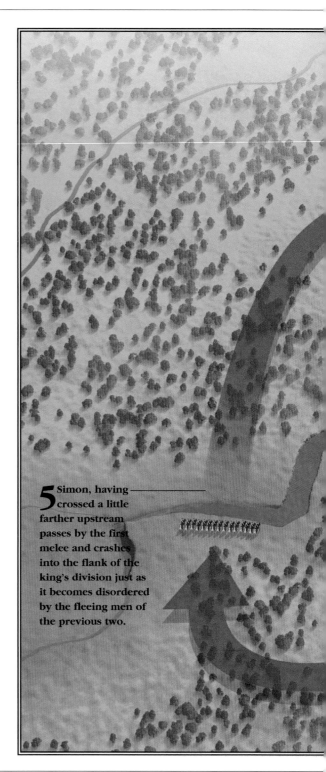

5 Simon, having crossed a little farther upstream passes by the first melee and crashes into the flank of the king's division just as it becomes disordered by the fleeing men of the previous two.

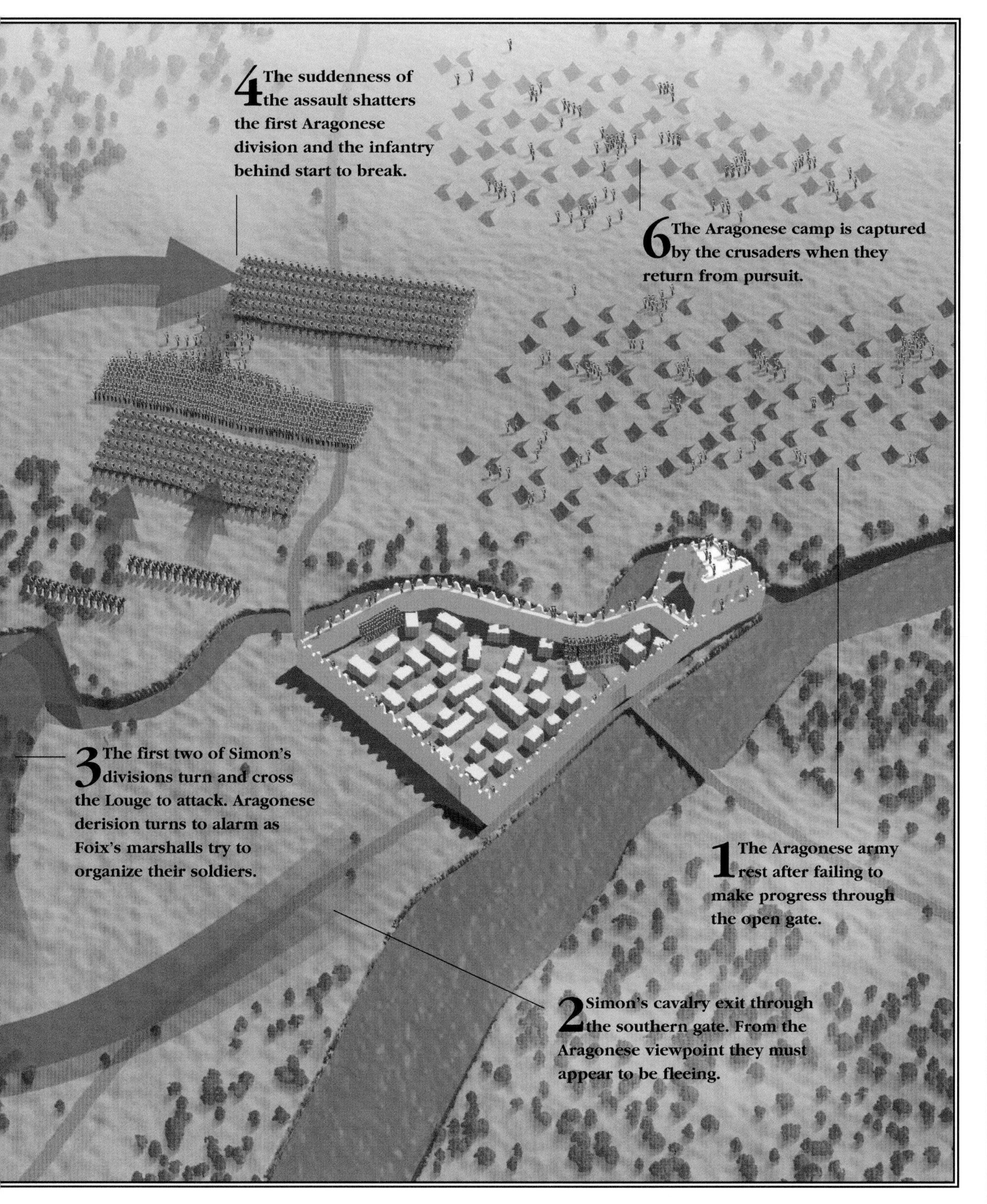
4 The suddenness of the assault shatters the first Aragonese division and the infantry behind start to break.
6 The Aragonese camp is captured by the crusaders when they return from pursuit.
3 The first two of Simon's divisions turn and cross the Louge to attack. Aragonese derision turns to alarm as Foix's marshalls try to organize their soldiers.
1 The Aragonese army rest after failing to make progress through the open gate.
2 Simon's cavalry exit through the southern gate. From the Aragonese viewpoint they must appear to be fleeing.

wrote to the local lord, Raymond IV, count of Toulouse, instructing him to act against the dissenters. He prevaricated and the Pope was exasperated. Catharism continued to spread. Eventually the Pope played his strongest card and declared a crusade against the heretics. An army assembled at Lyons on 24 June 1209, commanded by Arnaud Amaury, abbot of Citeaux, who was advised by Eudes III of Burgundy and Herve de Donzy of Nevers. They advanced to Valence, Montelimar fell, Beziers fell. Catholic and Cathar were slaughtered together. 'God will know his own', the abbot said.

Other towns fell to different columns. At Carcassone the heretics were allowed to go free, but the city was pillaged. When the 40 days were up the crusaders went home, almost. One minor lord was persuaded to stay. Simon de Montfort IV, father of the famous English rebel, agreed to remain and continue the fight.

> *'Techniques of information gathering and espionage never reached the same sophistication in medieval Europe as they did in the neighbouring civilizations of Byzantium and Islam.'*
>
> — *Nicolle*

Although, in the beginning, hundreds of Cathars were burnt as heretics, that persecution began to take second place to de Montfort's carving out his own fiefdom among the gorges and peaks of the Pyrenees. As the seasons turned he found he could keep conquering because although Raymond IV was in the field against him, with a much larger army, he continued to prevaricate and would not be brought to battle. The town of Muret was taken in September 1212 with the aid of another batch of 40-day men. At about the same time the fiefdoms of Lords Comminges and de Bearn were also attacked and absorbed into de Montfort's domain. This was a mistake – they were vassals of Pedro II, king of Aragon. To him they appealed for redress, after all Simon de Montfort was also a fellow vassal of the king, but he was setting himself up to be more powerful than his lord. Both sides, the abbot with Simon and the king of Aragon, lobbied the Pope in their cause. At an ecclesiastical council at Lavaur, Pedro was not allowed to speak, only to submit written argument and eventually the Pope sided with his own abbot. A showdown was inevitable. Pedro gave his protection to the people of Toulouse, revoked it for de Montfort and summoned his own host.

In September 1213 Pedro's forces arrived at Muret. Inside were 30 French knights and 700 infantry holding the town for de Montfort. Pedro's host included the men of Raymond IV, Lords Comminges and de Bearn. It was made up of between 2000 and 3000 mounted knights and sergeants plus an unknown but larger number of infantrymen. They camped to the north of the town above the small River Louge. The position was protected to the east by the Garonne and to the south by the Louge. It was, however, open to the west and north, and here Pedro's troops erected the stone-throwing engines with which they started to batter the walls on 11 September.

Meanwhile news of the attack had reached de Montfort at Fanjeaux 64km (40 miles) to the east. He had summoned his, much smaller, forces. Time being of the essence, they were cavalry only, consisting of 240 knights and 500 sergeants.

The resident defenders of Muret were too few to hold the walls of the town and the attackers swarmed in, just as de Montfort was seen arriving from the west. Whether by order or in panic the assaulting troops withdrew in haste. Better that than being caught in the rear by newly arrived knights. De Montfort entered the town unopposed. The next day negotiations were opened between de Montfort's bishops and the king of Aragon. During this brief lull, the northern Toulouse gate, nearest to the Aragonese army, was left open (some say by design, some by mistake). Either way Pedro could not ignore such a gift and ordered it rushed by the count of Foix's men who formed the Spanish vanguard, aided by some of Raymond IV's foot soldiers from the rearguard.

THE FIGURE WEARS *the armour appropriate to the Albigensian Crusade and bears the arms of Muret on his shield. The helmet obscures his face adding to the incipient menace of his appearance. Intimidating the enemy by your appearance has always been a useful weapon in the armoury of a soldier.*

The Spanish attempted to force their way in over the narrow Louge bridge, foot soldiers and cavalry together. A few got into the town, but were there outnumbered, surrounded and those few that couldn't escape were killed. The count ordered them to withdraw and eat before trying again. Meanwhile Simon had led his entire mounted force out of the Sales gate on the southern/western wall. He then organized them into three battles. The first two were to charge the front of the enemy, the third under his own command would sweep wide to the east and plunge onto the already engaged flank of the enemy. It was a bold plan. Each of his battles were but 250 strong. The Spanish vanguard easily matched that number on its own. But they had been distracted and at least some were taking lunch. Yet consider the time required to catch, saddle and bridle nearly 800 horses and arm the knights to ride them. This was surely no fortuitous series of coincidences. De Montfort's men must have been standing by ready to move on command.

The first battle exited the gate heading south on the Avenue des Pyrenees. De Montfort, echoing a stratagem from the Chinese Sun Tzu, placed all the banners of his host in this first division. The head of the column wheeled off the road to their right and moved out beyond the concealing walls. Time was of the essence. They executed a right turn, forming one deep line, and crossed the Louge to advance rapidly on the enemy. The second column followed, passing the rear of the first before performing its own right turn. So the two lines were then advancing on the first Spanish division in echelon. The Spaniards were mesmerized by the advancing knights with all their banners. Chaos reigned with dismounted lords calling for their squires and horses, those mounted struggling to find their position in the line. The impact of the advancing crusaders scattered the count of Foix's division like 'dust before the wind'. The infantry ran for the camp while the king's division struggled to maintain the line and was hit in turn by the pursuing horsemen. Simon, meanwhile, had stuck to his plan and now came in on the flank of the hapless men of Aragon. The king was killed in the melee and the rest fled, closely pursued by the desperate crusaders. Such was the disparity in numbers that de Montfort's men could not afford to deplete their own strength by taking prisoners for ransom and a great number were killed.

Co-ordinating the manoeuvres of Simon's two leading columns deserves some examination. Each would have been more than 500m (1640ft) long, assuming two abreast and allowing 4m (13ft) for each horse and space between it and the next. Turned into a line each would be only 307m (1007ft) long, 1.2m (4ft) for the frontage of each horse. The commander at the front would indicate the moment for the turn to be executed, but there was great potential for him to get it wrong. Turn the first column too early and the last man could still be in the city gate. Turn the second column early and it would overlap the rear of the first and some men would be ineffective. Turn it too late and the gap between lines would be too large, risking each being swamped by the enemy's superior numbers.

There are two ways an efficient turn could have been achieved (although we don't know which was used). Either the order to turn was given by the last man in the column as he reached the critical position or the commander used some mental calculation to register the distance covered. With modern infantry you can rely on counting a regular pace to judge these distances. Either way we must give credit to both de Montfort for his excellent plan and his subordinate commanders, Bouchard of Marly leading the first column and William d'Encontre leading the second, for its execution.

Planning

Where the modern commander is almost overwhelmed with radio reports from the front, advice from politicians at home, high-quality maps and satellite photographs, the medieval general dealt with very different sources of information. For a start, maps were rare and only registered the towns and probably rivers on a route rather than geographical features. Consequently maps were not reliable for planning troop movements or even determining location. Maps might, though, show the relative positions of different locations. To go from A to B the general needed to find someone who knew the way, as there were no street signs in the modern sense. Lord, priest, merchant or peasant, willing or not, all could be coerced into showing the route, and faced premature death if they were thought to be deceiving.

Once he knew the rough location of his foe, the medieval general could reasonably call a meeting of his household officers and council. From these meetings the king would decide where and when to attack and which lords could be summoned with their retinues. The custom was to announce, via heralds to senior nobility from whom the news trickled down the feudal ladder, the assembly of the host at a particular location on a particular date, perhaps several months in the future. From that date the feudal service began. So it was advantageous to start as close to the object of the campaign as was safe.

With the host assembled at the planned location, they would set out in order of precedence, as judged by the king's heralds. Each lord would have a war horse or two, a riding horse, squires, grooms and multiple servants, and probably more than one wagon with its own oxen and driver. The higher the social rank, the more paraphernalia was needed. By the time the lord was up, fed, dressed and mounted, his tent taken down and the process reversed at the end of the march, 16–24km (10–14 miles) in a day was as much as the army could be expected to move. Even when close to locating the enemy the general needed scouts, known as hobilars, to search them out. This was made easier if your foe invited attack by ravaging a particular area, when the smoke of burning buildings or campfires acted as a beacon. The co-ordination of separate columns, converging on a single goal, was almost beyond the ambition of medieval generals. It was only the Mongols were capable of achieving such a unified momement.

Closer to the foe, the army would be arranged in 'battles' or divisions. The first segregation was usually between cavalry and infantry. Moving at different speeds gave them a different function on the field. Cavalry might further be separated into the better-equipped knights and their sergeants though this was not rigidly adhered to. Infantry were often split between missile-armed divisions for long-range fighting and those troops armed with close-quarter weapons for melee fighting. Each group had to be led by a trusted, experienced lord of high rank. High-ranking aristocracy would not accept orders from lower-ranking lords.

Tactical Options

When faced with myriad foes and such limited resources, just what were the tactical options available to a medieval general? Along with the army he inherited there would have been some local military tradition. He would have known how his ancestors had combated a particular foe. He might also have had access to some of the Roman military texts like Frontinus' *Stratagems* and the works of Vegetius. In an age that largely relied on self-generated entertainment, much discussion of military matters can be taken for granted. The widely broadcast view that medieval armies deployed in three battles; vanguard, main and rearguard is too simplistic. Medieval generals formed as many battles or divisions as they saw fit.

The Norman king, Roger II of Sicily, organized his army into eight divisions to face a rebellious Apulian army formed into six divisions at the battle of Nocera, in 1132. The subsequent battle clearly demonstrates that tactical flexibility is useless without good deployment or battlefield control. Roger attempted to focus his whole army on attacking half the rebel host by deploying all eight divisions in a column facing the rebel right wing. It was a good plan. The first two divisions charged and were pushing the enemy back when the rebels wheeled their other three divisions onto the flank of Roger's winning pair, which were already engaged with the rest of the rebel army. In other words all of the rebel army was fighting one-quarter of the other side. The two engaged divisions were routed, carrying away the rest of

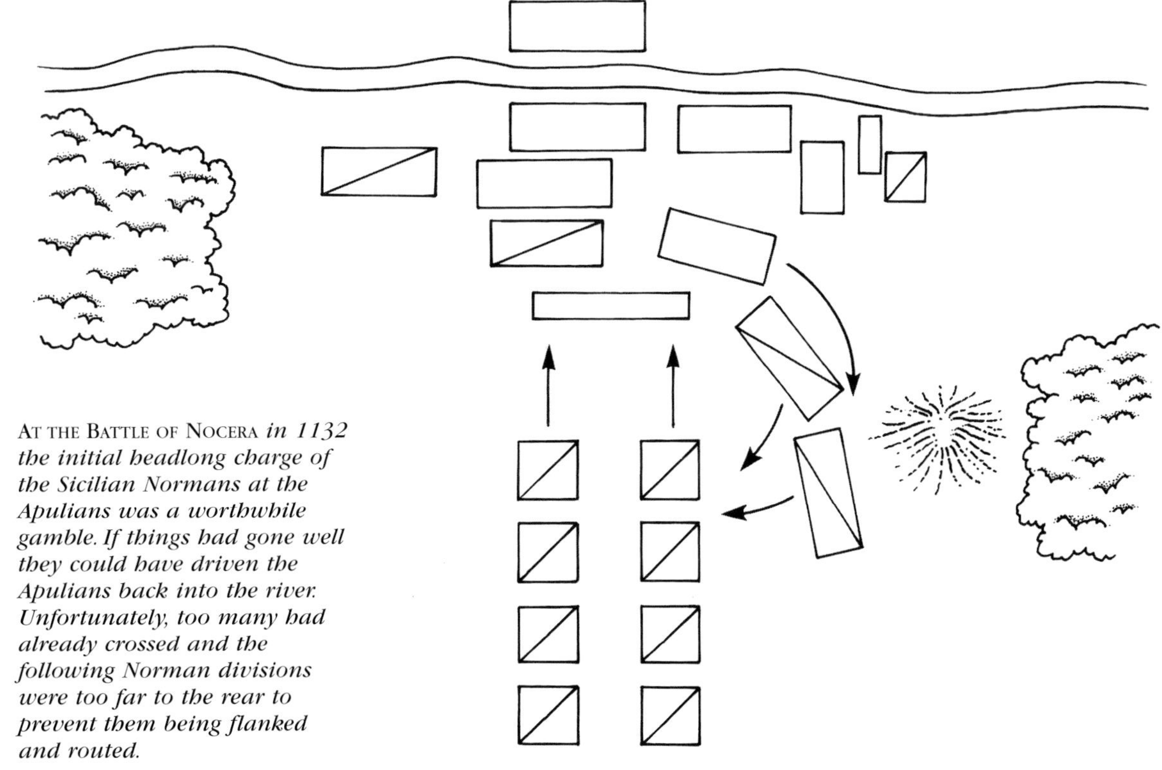

AT THE BATTLE OF NOCERA *in 1132 the initial headlong charge of the Sicilian Normans at the Apulians was a worthwhile gamble. If things had gone well they could have driven the Apulians back into the river. Unfortunately, too many had already crossed and the following Norman divisions were too far to the rear to prevent them being flanked and routed.*

Roger's army, which suffered enormously in the collapse. The instant of that wheeling movement by the rebels was the opportunity for the rest of Roger's army to attack while the enemy was manoeuvring. They were probably too far to the rear to do this or the rebels would not have dared to risk exposing their own flank.

Less complex plans were frequently more successful. The plainest of these has to be simply lining up and charging each other. Unfortunately, this clash of lines then became a simple test of which side was toughest. Against a hard and wily foe like the Mongols this was simply gift-wrapping the victory for them. It was far more sensible for a medieval general to utilize one or several of the following tactical options.

Ground of Choosing

By fighting on the ground known to him and of his choosing, a general opened a whole series of tactical options. English Edward III's choice of the battlefield at Crécy, an area he had previously hunted over, took advantage of a naturally occurring ha-ha with a 1m (3ft 3in) drop. Already distracted by English archery, approaching helmeted knights could not possiby have seen it. The French duly tumbled and fell over into the hidden drop and were slaughtered by the English archers and men-at-arms.

Hidden Ambush

Positioning troops in hidden ambush was another way a general could stack the odds in his favour. The surprise value of even a small force emerging unexpectedly from a vulnerable flank could have a catastrophic effect on an engaged army. Again, planning, timing and control, albeit remote, were vital for this kind of operation. This was one of the most popular tactics, but it worked time and again.

Return from Pursuit

One of the most difficult battlefield orders to execute is the return from pursuit. When troops have defeated the enemy they have been ordered

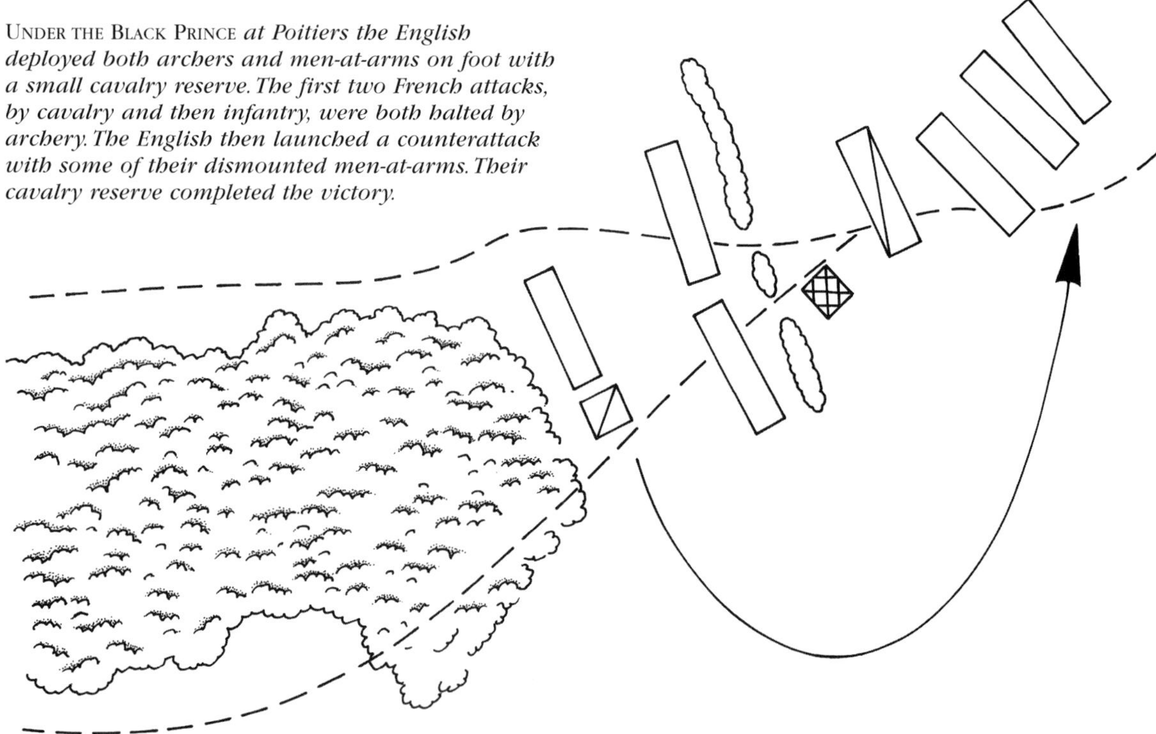

UNDER THE BLACK PRINCE *at Poitiers the English deployed both archers and men-at-arms on foot with a small cavalry reserve. The first two French attacks, by cavalry and then infantry, were both halted by archery. The English then launched a counterattack with some of their dismounted men-at-arms. Their cavalry reserve completed the victory.*

THE LONGBOW WAS *a tremendous weapon. The archers could loose a third arrow before the first struck. They often fought bare-footed to improve grip. It took regular practice to keep the strength needed to pull the bow. This was its flaw, though, as firearms, which were easier to use, became more widely available.*

to attack, it has always been a supreme test of the troops' discipline and the commander's abilities to persuade them to forego a vigorous and possibly profitable pursuit and return to order. Oliver Cromwell managed to impose such an order on his New Model Army when his Royalist enemy could not and even in the Napoleonic Wars British cavalry were notorious for being unable to do this.

Double Envelopment

Double envelopment can be a double-edged sword. A general may have surrounded the enemy, but if he has nowhere to run he has to stand and fight. Defeating him in such circumstances can be a costly affair. In August 1304, a French army attempting to suppress a revolt in the Netherlands came to battle with a militia army largely composed of spearmen. These were deployed between a village and a stream and had secured their rear with a triple line of defended wagons. Having been badly defeated by these spearmen two years earlier at Courtrai, the French were wary. First they attacked with crossbowmen, but these were countered by the rebels' crossbowmen. The French, whose cavalry were formed in 15 divisions, sent eight of these around to the rear of the position where they failed to penetrate the wagon line, while those to the front feinted against the spearmen during which there was some sporadic skirmishing. After a long day a truce was called for both sides to rest. However, the skirmishing continued with casualties to both sides. Both the French and Netherlanders claimed victory with slightly more casualties on the French side.

Feint Attack

Feint attack, withdrawal, counterattack has been used as a battle-winning strategy on the open steppes from earliest times. It requires planning before the battle, obedient warriors and good battlefield control to prevent the controlled retreat becoming an involuntary rout and to successfully implement the counterattack. William used it twice at Hastings and, surprisingly, the Mongols succumbed to it when fighting the *Mamlukes* at Ayn Jalut in 1260.

Turning a Flank

Turning a flank could have the same effect as a hidden ambush. The din of battle suppressed the ability to heed warnings - a general or enemy might not have noticed what else was going on until he was attacked from an unexpected direction. A Germanic army fighting in Italy under Otto II faced a Muslim army from North Africa fighting on behalf of the Byzantines. At the Battle of Cotrone in 982, the Germans charged the Muslim centre, killing their general and breaking the enemy to their front. They in turn were charged in the flank and their line collapsed, losing perhaps 10,000 killed and captured. Simon de Montfort combined this strategy with a surprise attack to spectacular effect at the Battle of Muret.

The War of Castilian Succession: Najera 1367

King Pedro the Cruel's possession of the throne of Castile was disputed by his illegitimate, but more popular, brother Henry. To complicate matters, Pedro's wife had recently and inexplicably died. She happened to be the sister-in-law of Charles V, the king of France.

Henry, already bankrolled by Aragon, now also secured French investment. Pope Urban V threw his weight behind Henry, citing the Jews and Muslims in Pedro's army, and promoted a crusade against Pedro. Unemployed mercenaries in France flocked to the prospect of pay and, in the name of the crusade, added white crosses to their armour, an early form of rebranding. Charles appointed Bertrand du Guesclin of Brittany to be commander. Although low-born he was a brave fighter and astute tactician. He took his army first to Avignon to be blessed by the Pope. Spiritually enriched, they then marched into Castile where events moved swiftly and bloodily. Towns were captured, Jews butchered, Henry was crowned and Pedro fled; dividend was issued. But Pedro wasn't finished yet. He, in turn secured the backing of Edward, the Black Prince of England (then in Aquitaine), plus the kings of Navarre and Majorca and renewed his bid for the throne. In the meantime the mercenaries were once more looking for hire, and the Black Prince was in need of an army. The market was flooded and the Prince hired only those he could afford. Augmented by the feudal vassals of Aquitaine, the mercenaries returned to negotiate a deal with their former employers.

Charles the Bad of Navarre charged both King Henry to block the Pyrenean passes and then the Black Prince to open them. He then hid in a castle, claiming captivity at the hands of a French knight, so he could no longer come to the aid of either.

King Henry had assembled his host at Santo Domingo da la Calzada. From this position he could advance north-east to Pamplona or move north to Miranda then north-east towards Vittoria. It was a good central position which would be difficult for the invaders to by-pass. It was far enough from the passes for him to move and intercept any such attempt as soon as the invasion route became clear. Once the Black Prince negotiated the passes his army encamped near Vittoria, the site of the famous English victory more than 400 years later. Henry moved his forces to Anastro, guarding the road which leads south-west from Navarre through Vittoria and Miranda to the capital of Castile, Burgos.

Now the different tactical traditions of the two armies began to show. The Spanish experience was of vast open plains, as well as crowded mountains, and fast, lightly armoured skirmishing cavalry. They had been fighting the Moors for over 600 years. The forces of the Black Prince and Pedro (here referred to as 'allied' forces) had learnt their trade in France, more densely populated and more intensively cultivated. Their scouts were more heavily armoured and used in far smaller groups and so the Prince sent out a mere 100 cavalry. Henry on the other hand had despatched 6000

men to harry the allied camp, which they did to great effect. These two forces met as Henry's men were returning. The allied troop dismounted, scattered their horses and formed a clump on top of a hill. From here they beat off the skirmishing cavalry, then several full charges from the Spanish heavies, before succumbing to an assault on foot from the French element of the party.

A RATHER ROMANTICIZED *print shows England's Black Prince persuading Pedro the Cruel to grant an amnesty to his illegitimate brother. Pedro is on the right foreground listening to an unidentified herald while the Black Prince stands bare-headed to the left. His arms are mirrored on the standard flying overhead. The figure to the right rear of Pedro represents one of the Holy Orders in his army.*

Neither army wanted to make the first move and for about a week each watched the other. The Black Prince was the first to break the impasse. He broke camp one night and led his army east and south through the Sierra Cantabria and crossed the Ebro at Logrono, which had stayed loyal to Pedro the Cruel. He had decisively turned Henry's position with a forced march of around 50km (31 miles) in two days. Henry followed as soon as he could, recrossing the Ebro at Haro and arriving at Najera while the Prince was at Navarette, 9km (6 miles) to the east on the road to Pamplona. This counter-manoeuvre continued to block the Prince's route to the capital.

Between the two armies was a large south-north stream just outside Najera and a wide open plain. It was ideal cavalry country. Henry chose to cross the stream and bring the Prince to battle. Du Guesclin's experience of fighting the English prompted the vanguard to advance on foot. Nearly 2000 strong they included French knights and squires, Castilian men-at-arms and some crossbowmen. The main battle was all mounted. In the centre and directly behind the vanguard was King Henry with 1500 knights. On each flank and slightly advanced were another 1000 mounted men-at-arms and a further 1000 genitors - lightly armoured cavalry used to skirmishing with javelins. These appear to have been supported with additional crossbowmen. Henry's third line was composed entirely of infantry, 20,000 strong.

The Black Prince also drew his army up in three lines, each of dismounted men-at-arms and a similar number of archers. The first line had about 3000 of each, almost half of which were mercenaries. The middle line was further divided into three groups, the centre commanded by the Prince with Pedro the Cruel's 4000 lancers. Each of the two flanking groups numbered about 4000, split equally between men-at-arms and archers. His third line, commanded by the king of Majorca, consisted of Gascons and the remaining mercenaries, perhaps 6000 men. In all perhaps 10,000 men-at-arms plus an unknown mix of English archers, feudal and mercenary crossbowmen, along with Gascon Bidowers, unarmoured infantry who fought with shield and javelins. These were huge armies for the time and reflect the glut of mercenaries available during this lull in the Hundred Years' War.

The two vanguards clashed, the impact forcing the Prince's men back 'a spear's length'. Then the

THE MUSLIMS INVADED *Spain in the 8th century and much colonization followed. Although the Christian Reconquista of Spain was successful Muslim enclaves remained with their own distinctive military traditions. These Muslim cavalry are less heavily armoured than their Christian counterparts and rely more on skirmishing than the full frontal charge.*

flanking cavalry attempted to close with the flanking divisions of the Prince. Here the English archers out-ranged the javelins of the Spanish *ginetes* (medium cavalry units originating from Andalucia) who were shot down in droves.

Both Castilian flanks fled the field. Clearly they had not paid due heed to the reports of Bertrand du Guesclin. They should have swept past on an encircling movement just beyond bow range. This would have forced numerous allied troops to turn and face, denying their use to the Black Prince as surely as attacking them at close quarters. On such a wide open plain there was no need for them to approach the English archers so closely.

Both allied flanking divisions now wheeled into the central melee and the Prince brought up his central division to reinforce the front. King Henry wasn't to be left out and repeatedly charged his cavalry, but could make no headway against the dismounted knights. The English archers were meanwhile shooting down the hapless Castilian infantry. The final *coup de grace* came with the king of Majorca slamming his third division into the left flank of the central melee. An encircling movement as described above could have pinned this third wave.

This was no mean feat for the king: to first recognize where he was needed when he had no vantage point to see from, then to wheel his unwieldy force first to his left around the scrum to his front, then to his right and into an existing melee. It can only have been achieved by the king leading with his standard and the rest following as best they could, rather than parade-ground manoeuvring in rigid lines. The Spanish crumbled and the flight began. Henry had no choice and he too fled to the rear. The French in his centre also had no choice; no horses and nowhere to run. They fought on until a full third had fallen and then du Guesclin offered his sword in surrender. The routed infantry were cut down in heaps and more drowned in the now-swollen stream. The Spanish lost about 7000, the Prince's and allied forces a mere four knights, 20 archers and 40 men-at-arms. As happens so often, winning the battle did not necessarily win the war. Henry remained at large and, although Pedro regained his throne, his allies and mercenaries returned from whence they came. Some 2000 nobility had been captured and therefore ransoms would eventually be forthcoming. Pedro, however, failed to meet his obligations and pay his mercenaries. Before a meeting of creditors could be arranged he was dead by the hand of his own brother.

Communication

Medieval scouts were lightly armed mounted warriors. They had to use their own horses - there was no equivalent to the Roman Imperial messenger service with regular fresh horses available to couriers. So, messages could take a long time to reach their destination. On the battlefield, horns and trumpets were used to boost morale, provide a rallying call and, perhaps, issue simple instructions. Later in our period drums also came into use, though probably for martial encouragement rather than communication. In the turmoil of battle a general in the forefront could only hope he was being followed. In the rear he relied on the sight of his banner moving to lead reserves to a crucial part of the battle line. Otherwise he would instruct a high- ranking noble from his own entourage to convey messages to those he wanted to direct.

Problems and Solutions

So, how well did medieval generalship rise to the challenges fate thrust before it? In the twenty-first century we are familiar with the arms race: one side develops a more powerful weapon, the other counters with more advanced armour and so on. In WWII the German tanks like the Tiger tank had slab-sided armour and powerful guns, but they were too few, too heavy and tended to stick in the mud. The Russians developed the T34 with sloping armour, which was a more effective use of the weight of metal, and broad tracks which had a lower ground pressure than a walking man.

So it was in the medieval period, except each side generally had to evolve strategies rather than technologies to counter the other. Typical offensive/defensive tactics are described below.

Sea-Borne Raiders

Navigating by a hand-held device that indicated latitude by sun shadow, the Vikings appeared from

Battle of Najera

1367

Spanish King Henry's central position allowed him to block the Black Prince's attempt to by-pass him and so forced the battle at Najera. However, Henry failed to make best use of the disparate troop types at his disposal. His skirmishing cavalry with crossbow support should have been used wide on the flanks to pull off the Prince's flank and reserve divisions, allowing du Guesclin's and King Henry's main infantry divisions to concentrate overwhelming numbers on the Prince. As it turned out, Henry's skirmishing cavalry were beaten by the English archers. Were they a deliberate sacrifice to let du Guesclin's men close unmolested with the English? We will never know. The Black Prince's death or capture could have significantly altered western European history. In a sequence of strategic manouevring that would have impressed Napoleon, both the Black Prince and King Henry demonstrated that medieval armies could march fast and decisively when well led.

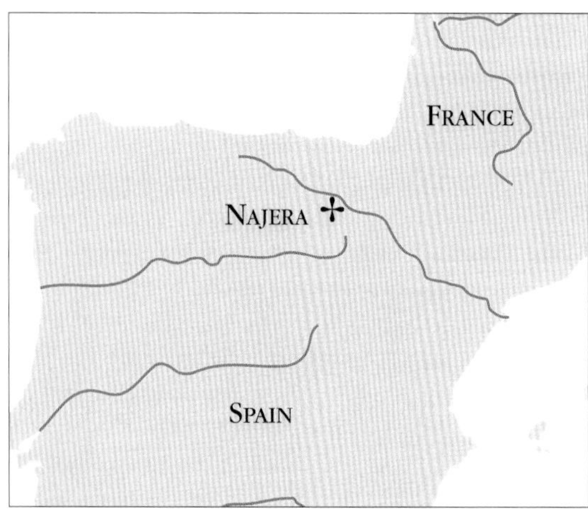

The final flanking attack is unusual since it assails the shielded side of the Spanish soldiers. But, it does separate King Henry from his lands away to the west.

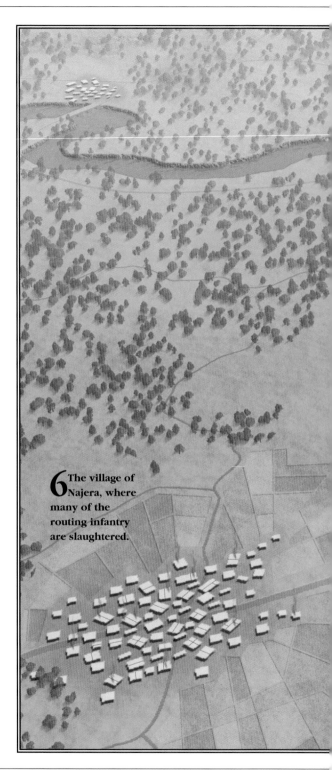

6 The village of Najera, where many of the routing infantry are slaughtered.

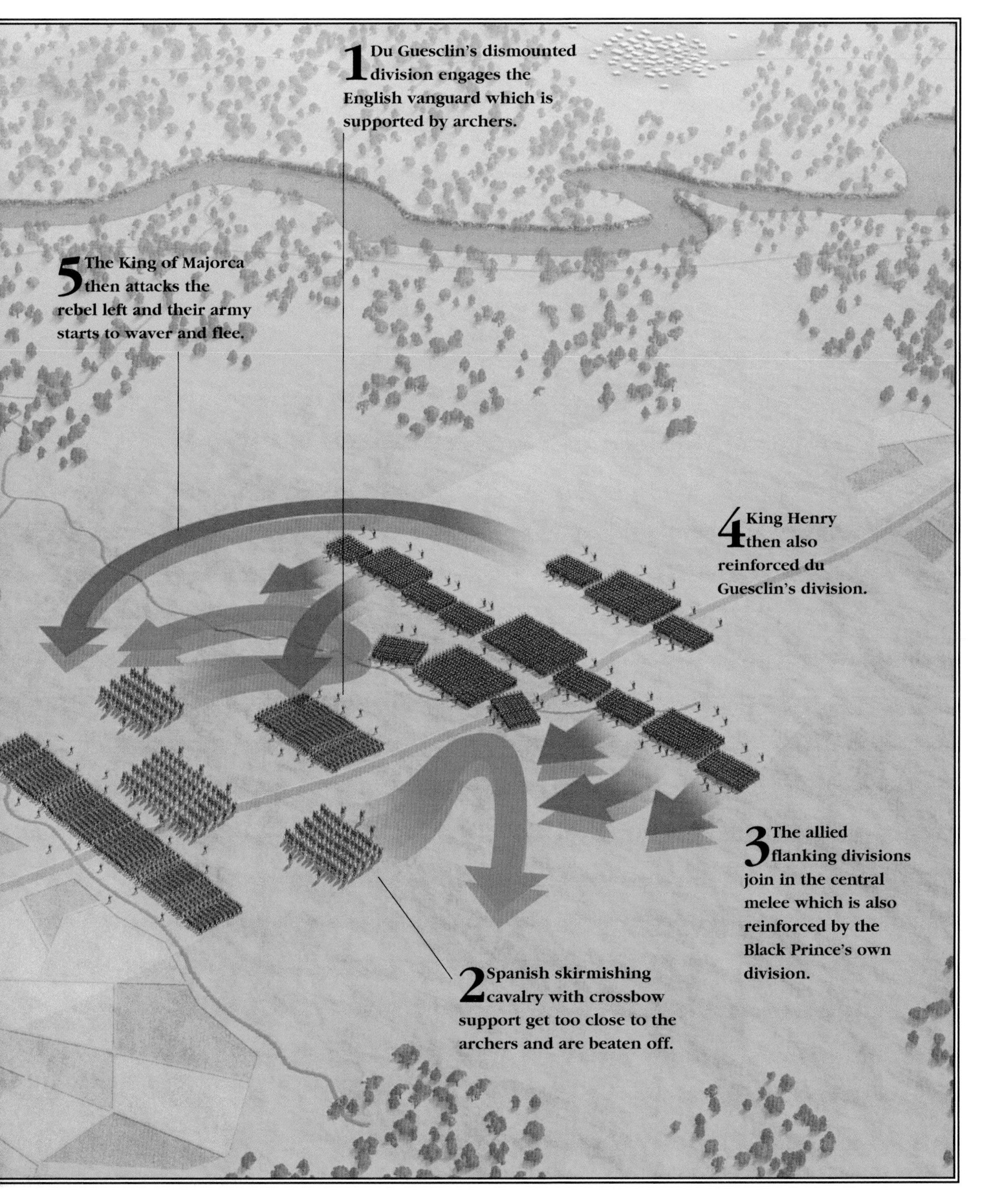
1 Du Guesclin's dismounted division engages the English vanguard which is supported by archers.
5 The King of Majorca then attacks the rebel left and their army starts to waver and flee.
4 King Henry then also reinforced du Guesclin's division.
3 The allied flanking divisions join in the central melee which is also reinforced by the Black Prince's own division.
2 Spanish skirmishing cavalry with crossbow support get too close to the archers and are beaten off.

the sea whenever and wherever they pleased. While holy men resorted to prayer, in Britain King Alfred the Great fortified key towns, devolved local defence to the earls and *fyrd* of each shire, and deployed the first navy to counter the unpredictable raids.

The navy could not intercept Viking raids very efficiently, but it did allow Alfred to block their line of retreat. The fortified towns restricted the movement of Vikings if they managed to land and the local defence provided a prompt response. Combined with major victories such as Ashdown in 871, Alfred ensured that the world's most widely spoken language is English and not Scandinavian.

Defeating the Shield-wall

The Normans faced the Saxons at Hastings in 1066. The latter held a very strong position, uphill and with secure flanks. The Normans resorted to feigned retreat and overhead archery to tease out and break the shield wall. In Italy, however, it was simply the terrifying ferocity of the charge that carried the day. Imagine standing in front of a fence at a major horse race as the horses thunder towards you. Add sharp, lowered lances and you begin to get the idea. At the Battle of Civitate in 1053, the first charge of the Norman knights routed the whole of a Papal army composed of Lombard cavalry and Swabian infantry.

The same tactic had worked against Byzantine troops, at Monte Maggiore in 1041, and again in Italy when 700 Norman knights supported by 1300 infantry launched an impetuous charge on a much larger force, which was deployed in two lines. The first line of Byzantines broke and carried the second away. (The Normans had been fighting as mercenaries for the Byzantines and were convinced that they hadn't been paid enough for their services, so they must have been extremely angry.)

'The warlord maintains his power through the threat of destruction and death.... To survive and succeed in the court of a warlord is to compete in an arena of perpetual terror. It takes an extraordinary person. Some are clever, some are tough, some are mad.'

— NEWARK

Facing the Lance

The Muslim armies of Spain were on the other side of the fence and had to contend with the crushing charge of the feudal knights. They resorted to placing large blocks of infantry in the path of the knights, showering the attackers with arrows and then enveloping them with lighter cavalry. At Alarcos in 1195, the Castilian cavalry of Alfonso VIII broke through the front line of Muslim infantry, but were then surrounded by more infantry from the second line and light cavalry from the flanks. The remainder of the front line then advanced on the Castilian infantry who were quickly routed. Here the boot was on the other foot – the knights with limited vision through their helmets being swamped with enemies on all sides. The Christian knights were swallowed up in the mass of infantry and very few of them managed to escape.

Retreat and Attack

Neither the technology of superior equipment, numerical advantage nor simple aggression was ever sufficient to dominate the medieval battlefield. Then as now, intelligent use of the difference between the two sides is what counted. The Magyars were basically horse archers, but they also carried javelins and lassoes. They had many similarities with the Huns of the earlier period, forming small loose groups rather than large formal units. They favoured ambushes and feigned retreat and counterattack strategies where their aim was to disrupt the enemy formation, decimate it with arrows and only close in to administer a *coup de grace.*

This tactical approach worked spectacularly

well at the Battle of Brenta in 899. A mere 5000 Magyars had been chased for about a week by a force of Lombard cavalry numbering three times their size. The Magyars crossed a river and camped, tried to negotiate, then mounted their fresh horses and attacked suddenly across the river while the Lombards were resting and eating. The Lombards were routed and then mercilessly pursued, most being killed in the process.

Every strength, however, has its weakness and the Magyars were defeated in turn at the Battle of Lechfield in 955, when their line of retreat was blocked by a force of 8000-9000 mounted Germans. They were forced into a frontal assault, which failed, although a small flanking movement managed to break the baggage guard and draw off another one of the eight German *legiones* present.

Walls on Wheels

Inspired by a combination of early nationalism and Taborite religious fervour, the people of Bohemia rebelled in 1420 against their overlord Sigismund, the king of Hungary and Holy Roman Emperor. He was able to field experienced, well-armed, but disunited, feudal levies against a host of ill-equipped and inexperienced townsfolk and peasants. The revolt was led by Jan Ziska, who had served in the Polish armies against the Teutonic Order. He devised a truly novel tactical formation which, in some ways, predicted future military tactics to this day: the impenetrable squares from which a counterattack could be launched.

The steppe nomads had become accustomed to circling their wagons to provide a defendable base which was not tied to a particular locality.

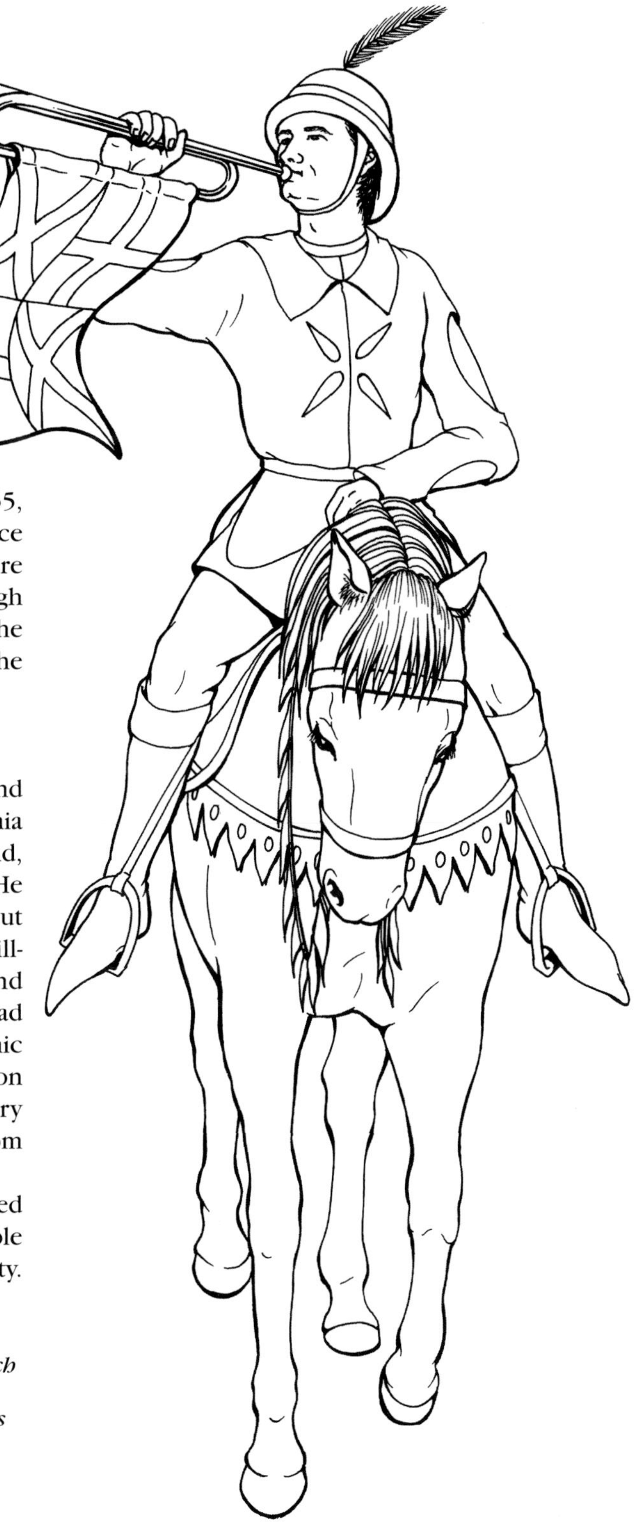

ENEMIES HAVE ALWAYS *needed to communicate with each other. This function, in the medieval period, was performed by the heralds. They also issued the king's proclamations to the army and kept the records of who was present with the army - nobles of course, not the peasants. These were called 'Rolls of Arms' and recorded names and coats of arms.*

Ziska adapted this idea and it evolved into armoured wagons from which the rebels could not be shifted, but from which they could sally out against a disorganized and disheartened foe. The sides of the wagons were heightened so a man could shelter behind them and they were loopholed so missilemen could fire from safety. They could be chained together or the gaps between wagons could be blocked with wheeled wooden walls. The wagon laager was placed in a strategic position, which the Hungarians then had to attack. Formed in two semi-circles, like a broken circle, one gap faced directly towards the enemy and the other directly away. This gap was protected by post and chain fencing - easy to erect or drop as the moment required. Each wagon had a crew, half of whom carried long-range weapons like crossbows and, later, primitive handguns. The other half used long-handled melee weapons, such as flails, halberds and pikes. The position of the wagon laager forced the Hungarians to attack. The missilemen ensured that they were disordered when they did so and the melee men made short, bloody work of those that reached the wagons.

The wagon fort had effectively nullified many of the mounted knight's advantages. His momentum counted for nought against a wagon, he was no longer higher than his infantry opponent and his lance was no longer than the crews' pikes. The wagon tactics were first used to the full at the battles of Luditz and Kuttenberg in 1421. As the long war of revolt progressed, small artillery pieces were added to the wagons, making them even more formidable, and the rebels started to use them aggressively, advancing the wagons towards the enemy in parallel lines. Eventually the feudal levies simply declined to assault the wagon forts. They had been effectively intimidated and beaten.

However, there is always a counter stroke. It was not the feudal lord who won the last battle of the war, but the divisions within the rebellion (one side

ATTACKING A HUSSITE *wagon laager presented a very difficult problem to the traditional medieval host as simple assaults proved ineffective. But the wagon fort required substantial open space and considerable time to set up, so it was vulnerable in difficult terrain and to sudden attacks.*

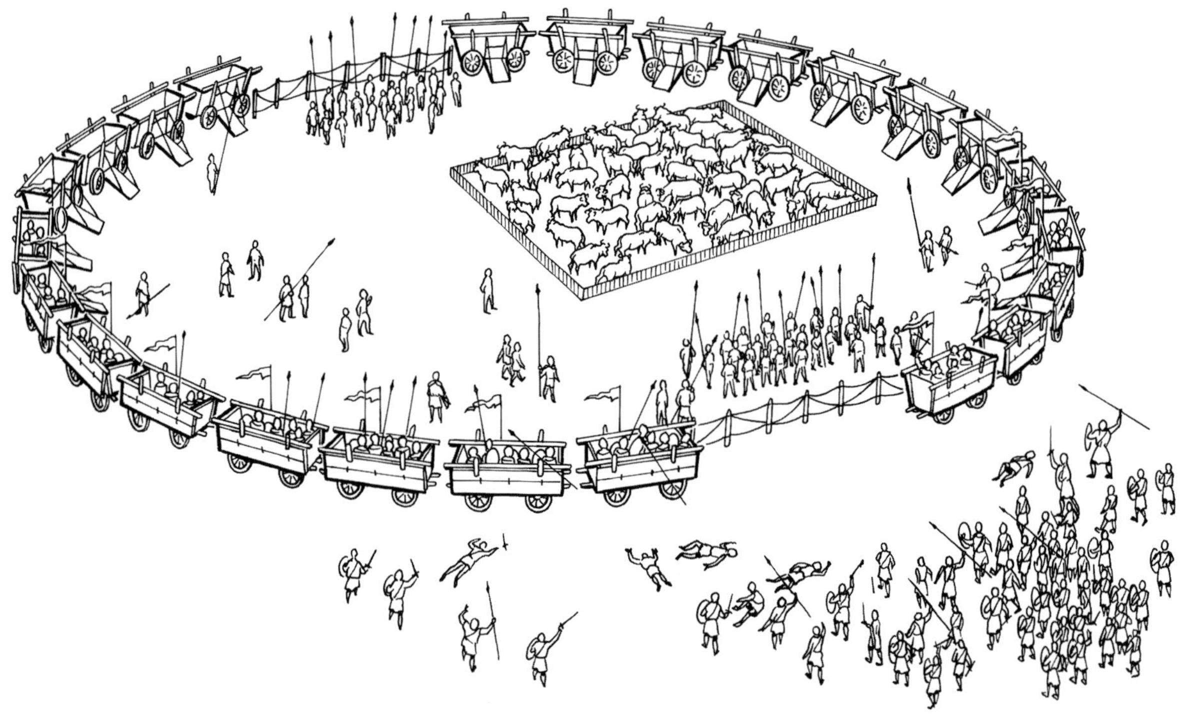

wanted to negotiate), that forced an internecine battle. At Lipan in 1434, the Taborite party of the rebellion were induced to sally forth from their wagon fort by their former allies the moderate party. They advanced too far and a force of cavalry swept around to their rear cutting them off from the wagons. Here, in the open, they were no match for their more numerous foes and were slaughtered.

Facing Weaponry

The French suffered massively at the hands of English archers during the early years of the Hundred Years' War. From French sources we know they deliberately tried to outflank the English longbowmen at Agincourt in 1415, and Verneuil in 1424. When they couldn't get that to work they resorted to sieges and roving bands of men-at-arms to try to pick off the English escorts of supply trains and foraging parties as at Patay (1429), Valmont (1416) and Clermont-en-Beauvoisis (1430).

Against the largely static massed spearmen of the Low Countries the French again tried to outflank them and then bring superior numbers of missilemen, including catapults, to the field to break up the enemy formations. The Burgundian armies of Charles the Bold failed to ever find a solution to the problem of massed Swiss pike, halberd and handgun-armed infantry. His losses against the Swiss at the three battles Grandson (1476), Morat (1476) and Nancy (1477) amounted to well over 20,000 men plus much expensive equipment.

The Hundred Years' War: Verneuil 1424

During the Hundred Years' War, which lasted for 120 years, both sides called in friends and allies to help. The English enlisted the Bretons, Burgundians, Gascons and Flemish, and the Welsh were also obliged to fight for them. The French also recruited Bretons, Bohemians, Flemish, Gascons, Genoese, German and Scots contingents. Some were obliged by their feudal oaths to fight, some fought for money, some through formal alliance. Much of the war involved fairly small-scale battles, raids really, designed simply for plunder or to capture a town or castle.

In 1423 the French secured Ivry on the banks of the River Eure as a base to raid into English territory. The following year the English under the Earl of Suffolk assembled a force to eliminate this base. The town fell but the garrison retired to the castle and were there besieged. As was customary in this period, the garrison agreed to surrender if not relieved by 15 August. The arrangement saved a great deal of effort and loss of life on both sides. Such was the importance to the French of this base that they mounted a huge operation to bring the required relief. Also part of the relief force was a large Scottish contingent supplied as part of the *auld alliance*. The commander of this force was the Scottish Earl Douglas.

Douglas' army arrived at Nonancourt south-west of Ivry. They were too late. On 14 August the English duke of Bedford accepted the surrender of the Ivry garrison and then retired with his army to Evereux, north-west of Ivry. The French held a council of war. The French commanders were wary, having received several hard defeats at the hands of the English, and were reluctant to force a battle over a town already lost. This made perfect sense. The English tended to win the major battles, so the French strategy was to wear them down through small actions. The Franco-Scottish [my insertion] alliance had not had a battle since Bauge three years earlier, which they had won, and the Scots were eager to repeat that success.

The plan was to occupy the town of Verneuil further upriver and southwards from their present position. This had the triple advantages of appearing to do something positive while taking them away from the main English army and providing some plunder for the troops and perhaps ransom money for the lords. Two of these objectives were met. There was no loot or ransom because the town opened its gates without a fight, (it was actually a fief of the duke of Alencon who was with the allied army). This move was followed by Suffolk with 1600 men. After all he didn't want to lose track of 14,000 enemy soldiers wandering around his borders.

Bedford set out to bring the French and Scots (here referred to as 'the allies') to account. Just to make sure, he politely invited Douglas to 'share a drink'. Douglas replied he had 'come to France to

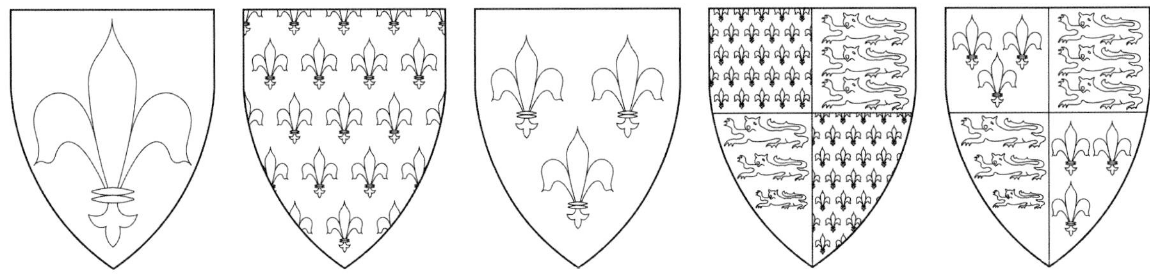

THE FUNDAMENTAL DIFFICULTY *with heraldry is illustrated here. As time passes and generations succeed each other the design needs to become more and more complicated. The final design here is quartered. The next shield could be subdivided not to eight parts but to sixteenths and after that to 256ths, rendering it impossible to read!*

seek him'. The allied plan echoed that used at Agincourt. Mounted troops on the flanks of the army would attempt to sweep around onto the flanks or rear of the English archers. At Agincourt the English had their flanks secured on difficult terrain. In front of Verneuil there was no such terrain. It was a good position. The allied army drew up in front of the moated and walled town. The Scottish contingent formed on the left of the allied line, each end of which was tipped with 600 cavalry, Lombards on the right, French on the left. They also had a significant but unknown number of archers. The other half of the army was mainly Spanish and Lombard mercenaries with a scattering of French soldiers.

To the rear of the English army was a large wood. If things went wrong the infantry could withdraw into the wood and it would hinder any mounted pursuit. The land between the wood and the town was clear, open and flat, a good position too for the English archers. The English army straddled the road from Damville with their baggage wagons in a rough circle and the horses tethered nose to tail three deep around the outside of the wagons.

About 2000 archers formed a reserve behind the right wing. The rest of the army consisted of approximately 6000 more archers and 2000 men-at-arms. These were formed into two divisions, men-at-arms in the centre, archers on the wings. The latter were also equipped with stakes to be emplaced when they got within range of the enemy.

The French advanced to attack, their archers and crossbowmen losing out to the more numerous English. The French cavalry charge caught the English archers before they got their stakes in place and routed about 500 of them. The Lombards on the other flank swept around the flank and pillaged the English baggage. Back in the centre the English men-at-arms counter-charged the French, who were then forced to fight within range of the awesome English bowmen. This support fire made the end inevitable and the French were routed back towards the town moat, pursued by the English. Bedford was able to rally his men and lead them back into the fray and the rear of the still battling Scots. They withstood this fresh onslaught, but when the English reserve archers, who had by then routed both the French and Lombard cavalry attacks, joined in against their right flank they too broke and fled. Over 7000 men from the allied army died with a further 200 prisoners captured for ransom. The English lost over 1000, which was a high figure. At Agincourt deaths were between 100 and 500.

We have to admire Bedford's power of command. The pursuing troops knew they had the chance of a fortune in ransom just in front of them, yet they turned to fight the still-potent Scots to whom due credit must also be given. Facing the English men-at-arms with close archery support was hard enough. To then contend with another enemy to their rear without succumbing amply demonstrates their tenacious fighting spirit.

Discipline

In a modern army the will of the senior officer is enforced by the established hierarchy; everyone knows whom they must obey. This system is backed up by a clear, formal procedure and range of punishments, enforcing obedience to orders. Medieval military discipline needed to fulfil the same requirements. As in normal life, civil jurisdiction competed with ecclesiastical law, depending upon the crime. Civil justice was meted out by a lord of superior ranking. Punishments included forfeiture of titles, lands or castles and imprisonment for lords and knights, with branding, maiming and execution for the lower orders. Ecclesiastical retribution included a variety of ad hoc penances, including flagellation, ex-communication (for individuals, whole towns or communities) and immolation.

On campaigns the judgmental process would necessarily have been shortened, but both civil and religious processes are recorded.There seems to have been little attempt to apprehend deserting individuals.This is presumably because there were too few spare personnel available to try to catch them and most crimes were of a pillaging or desecrating nature. Once the 40 days of service were up, a king's or marshall's troops were free to leave if they so desired and if they could not be persuaded to stay.

It was when there were real options to desert that true leadership kept everyone together. The tribal forces from around the periphery of Europe relied far more on the charismatic leadership of an individual to raise a force and hold it in the field through periods of inactivity and when events were going badly. Within a tribal society, a threat to the shared culture, appeal to traditions and reliance upon religion could generate huge support. (Religion meant a great deal to the medieval

THIS FRENCH KNIGHT *bears the Oriflame, the sacred silk standard of France. The Oriflame's divine inspiration prompted more ferocious and heroic actions from the French soldiery, especially at the Battle of Bouvines, where French king Philip Augustus defeated an allied force in 1214.*

Battle of Verneuil

1424

The English have followed a centuries-old foreign policy of supporting the weaker European country in any conflict to maintain a balance of power that would ensure belligerent forces were unable to contemplate an invasion of the British Isles. Equally, continental powers from Spain to Sweden have sought to limit this interference by supporting Irish and Scottish rebellions. The *auld alliance* between Scotland and France forms part of this pattern, though France supported the pact less wholeheartedly than the Scots. Nevertheless French policy has been successful at different periods, tying down men and materials in England as well as requiring troops on the continent to be hurried back to defend the English homeland. The Allies battle plan echoed that used at Agincourt, with the cavalry attempting to sweep round and attack the flanks of the vulnerable infantry. As it turned out, the awesome power of the English longbowmen turned the battle decisively.

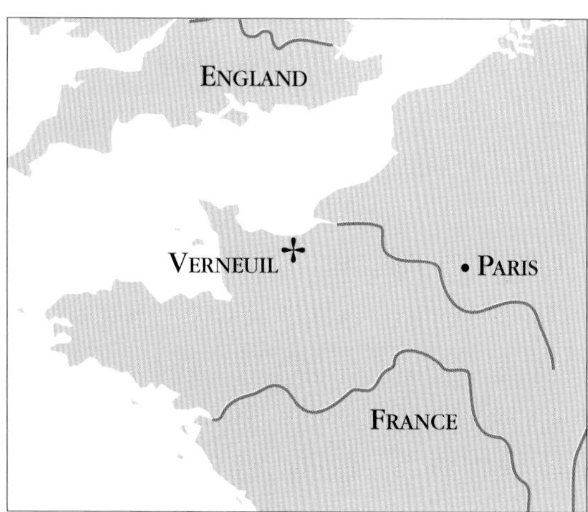

The Hundred Years' War was so protracted borders became quite clearly established. The river Eure formed one such boundary and saw considerable skirmishing.

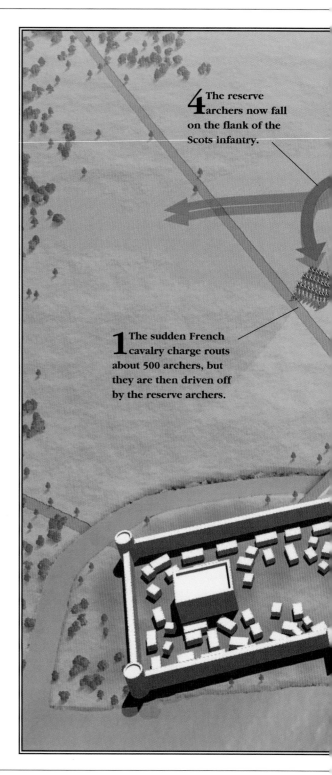

4 The reserve archers now fall on the flank of the Scots infantry.

1 The sudden French cavalry charge routs about 500 archers, but they are then driven off by the reserve archers.

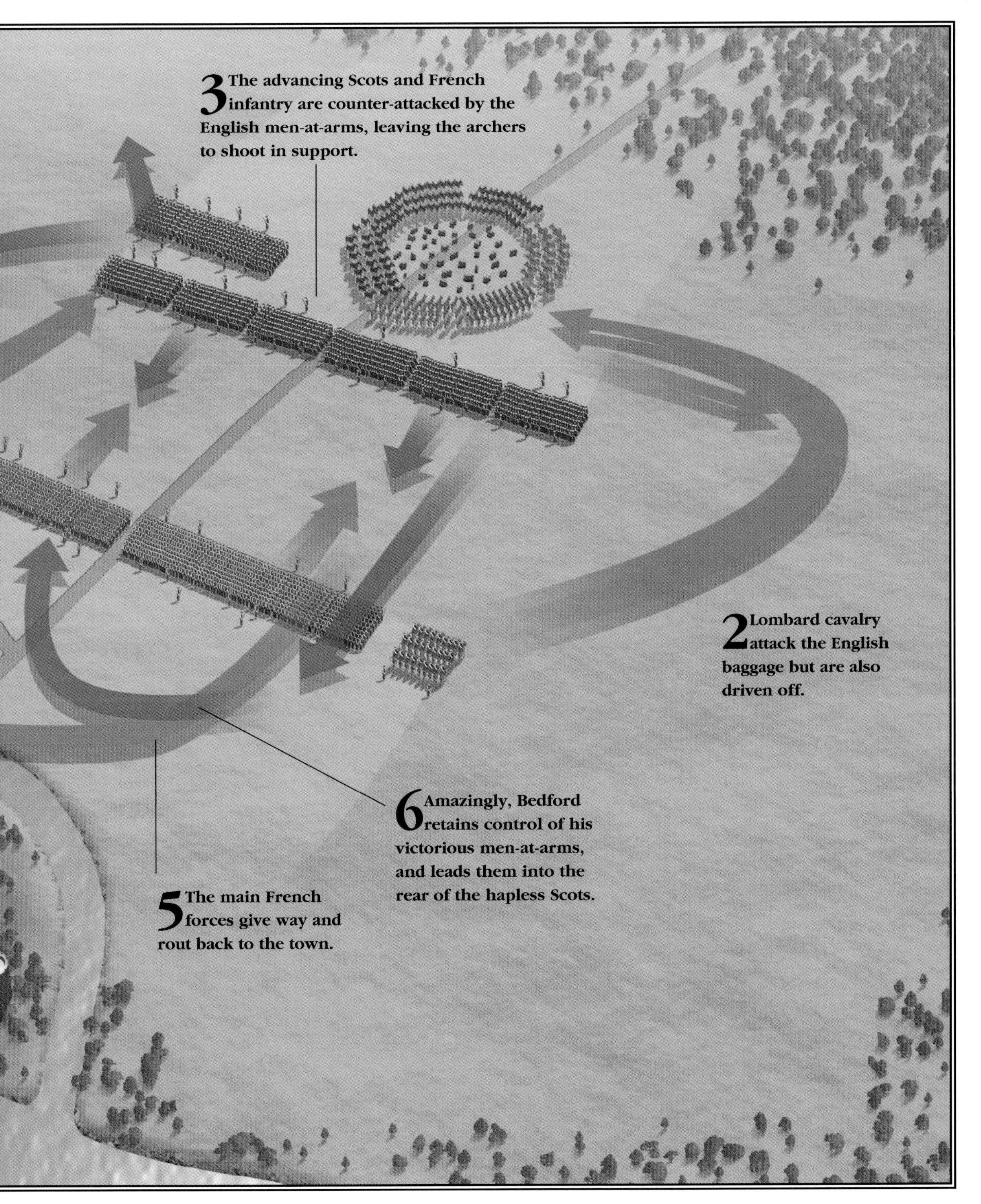
3 The advancing Scots and French infantry are counter-attacked by the English men-at-arms, leaving the archers to shoot in support.
2 Lombard cavalry attack the English baggage but are also driven off.
6 Amazingly, Bedford retains control of his victorious men-at-arms, and leads them into the rear of the hapless Scots.
5 The main French forces give way and rout back to the town.

mind and the thought that your actions would guarantee a place in the heaven of your choice bolstered morale enormously.) The pagan tribes facing the Teutonic knights could raise more than 40,000 warriors.

Motivation

The reasons why men fought also had an influence on the way they fought and across such a broad spread of techniques we can identify some over-riding motivations. The mobility of the raiding armies of the Vikings and Magyars allowed them the option of not fighting if they didn't think they would win. The Magyars plundered eastern Europe with ease, collecting what they wanted and escaping to safety. It was only when the Germans blocked them at Lechfield that they were brought to book. The Vikings came in the back door, terrified the locals, loaded their ships and disappeared back out to sea. Occasionally the raided population would put up a fight. The Vikings would often respond by inflicting horrible mutilations, making the next raid easier through pre-emptive fear. Spreading terror was just a sensible tactic to secure the aim of leaving alive with the loot they had captured.

The proud knight with his expensive armour and horses was forced by his lofty social position

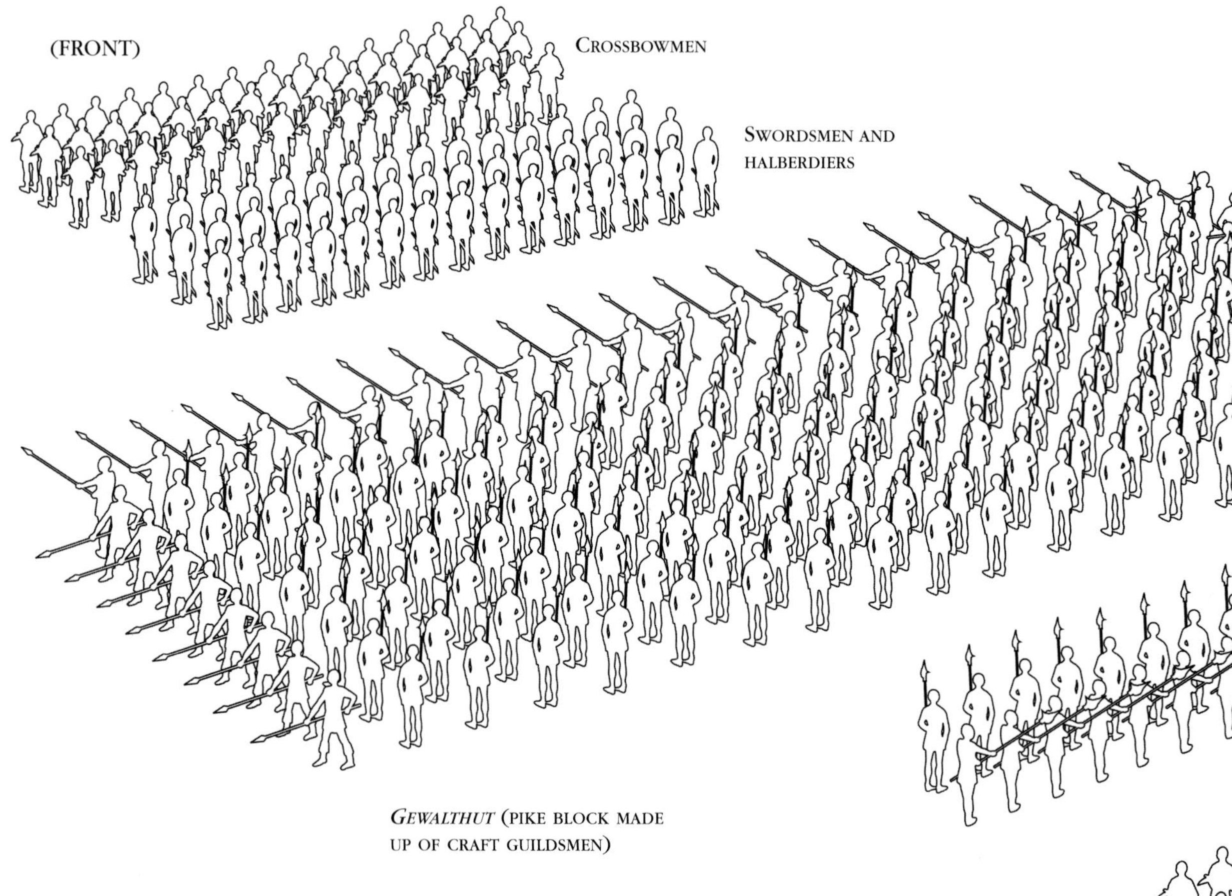

to fight. If he didn't he might lose his lands and his life. If he fought well he could gain money from ransoms and lands from his king. He was willing to fight even against seemingly impossible odds. That he managed sometimes to win in such circumstances is a tribute to his bravery or foolishness depending on your point of view. The medieval knight had a dreadful need of money and it made more sense to capture and ransom other knights than to kill them. When fighting for the church on a crusade, the goods and chattels he left at home were protected by a Papal edict and he gained remission of sins committed before and after the crusade. Even when enlisted to do the work of the church he sometimes succumbed to the money motive (Simon de Montfort, being an notable example), but so did the church, becoming fat on the sale of prayers and relics.

The people's armies of Switzerland, Flanders and Scotland fought to preserve their independence against the egos and avarice of their neighbours. They had to stand and fight, for a man on foot cannot outrun a man on horseback. But they were not armies of conquest; Scotland's attempt on Ireland under the command of Edward Bruce, brother of Robert, came to grief at the Battle of Faughart (1318). Although they might have been forced to behave aggressively, they were essentially defensive and spearmen might be good against cavalry, but they had no answer against massed archery.

We can see a distinct trend from all these battles. It is apparent that an arrow, whether fired from a longbow, crossbow or even from horseback, had the capability to knock an enemy out of action at a considerable distance. The archer that loosed that shot could then fire another and another, maiming foe after foe before the other side came close enough for hand-to-hand combat. Here we see the advantage of fighting at a distance. However, training an archer to be proficient took years to build up the muscles and stamina to pull back the bowstring, as well as practice at hitting the target.

Despite official edicts compelling practice at the archery butts in England, and her imitators in Scotland, Gascony and even France, it was always difficult to get enough trained men. Thus when soldiers found it easier to learn how to use the new handguns properly, the guns quickly became popular. As both manufacturing and product technology improved, firearms became more and more widespread in the Early Modern period.

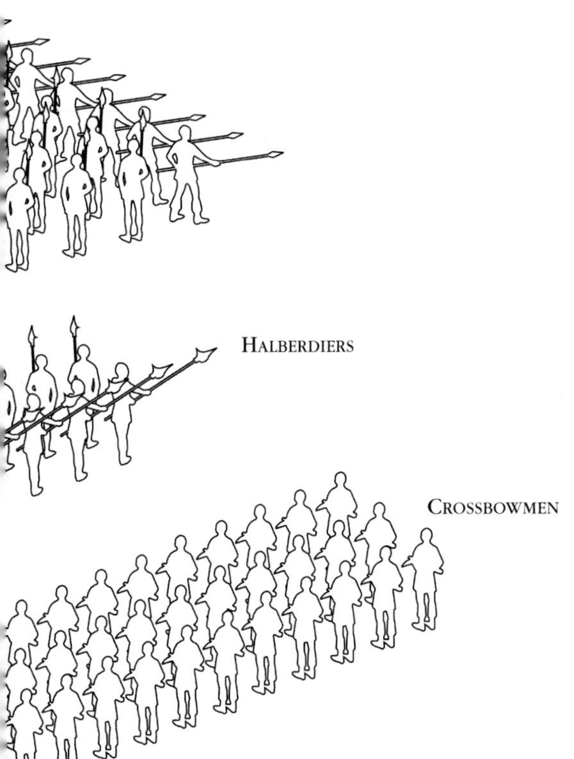

A SWISS PIKE BLOCK *is shown here with supporting troops. Although the Swiss relied enormously on pikemen they also needed other troops to ensure the pikemen could be delivered safely to the heart of the enemy, and to protect their flanks. The crossbowmen and hand-gunners can counter the enemy's missile troops long enough for the pike block to close. The halberd, a fearsome two-handed weapon with a long reach, was ideal for hitting cavalry in the flank while they were preoccupied in getting through a hedgehog of pike points to attack the men wielding them. While the pikes pinned the enemy, the halberdiers delivered the fatal blow.*

CHAPTER 4

SIEGE TECHNIQUES

Medieval siege warfare moved in a permanent motion between improvements in defensive fortifications and improvements in attacking methods – the one constantly inspiring the other.

In the world of medieval siege warfare, there were often long periods with little notable change. No one needed to make much effort to improve defences if the existing ones worked. Only the appearance of some innovative siege technique or weapon could inspire a major change in fortification. The most immediate cause of change was usually some new weapon that could bring down walls. Then the defenders had to endeavour to create either a stronger system of walls or some counter against the weapon.

In the early Middle Ages there were few new weapons. Men used those developed in ancient times, and it is even probable that the medieval

BY THE END *of the Middle Ages cannons had become the major weapon for sieges. Cannons of huge size could now be made. The effort required in transporting these large cannons made them impracticable for general use on mobile campaigns or battles but they were ideal for siege warfare.*

weapons were at first inferior to their ancient predecessors, since standards of manufacture may have declined. It is difficult to know the facts for certain, since evidence is rarely full. Today we see detailed plans of ancient weapons, but rarely are they based on plans surviving from ancient times – they are modern interpretations. Rather more is known of later medieval weapons, since there are both more illustrations surviving from the period, and some reasonably technical contemporary plans. Another problem here is that there is a considerable amount of literary evidence with many descriptions of sieges, some in detail. The writers, however, were rarely men who knew much about technical detail. They were usually monks, and most lacked any real experience of actual warfare. Thus the use of terms for weapons is often lax and one can not often be certain what engine is referred to by a particular term. For example, 'mangonel', might mean any one of several throwing or hurling weapons.

Ancient Siege Warfare

An examination of ancient siege warfare shows that the medieval pattern was nothing new. Sometimes historians write as though change in the ancient world was rapid in comparison to slow and rare change in the Middle Ages. This viewpoint is misleading. Modern historians of ancient times generally cover several thousand years against the mere 1000 with which we are concerned. In other words, medieval change was slow, but probably more rapid than had occurred in previous ages.

Nevertheless, we agree that the general nature of medieval siege warfare was established by the ancients. Early fortifications date from at least 3000 BC and early evidence for siege methods is found in illustrations of wheeled ladders to mount walls, dating from c.2000 BC. From c.1800 BC one finds representations of familiar siege weapons such as battering rams and wheeled towers (belfries). In the Middle East the Hittites and Assyrians made improvements in defence, including the construction of siege camps, mounds from which to mount an attack, moats, wall-towers, citadels and raised entrances to fortifications. We also find evidence for military mining, drawbridges and the making of ramps for deploying rams against walls.

Syracuse played an important role in spreading siege warfare techniques, especially under Dionysius I (405–367 BC), who learned much from

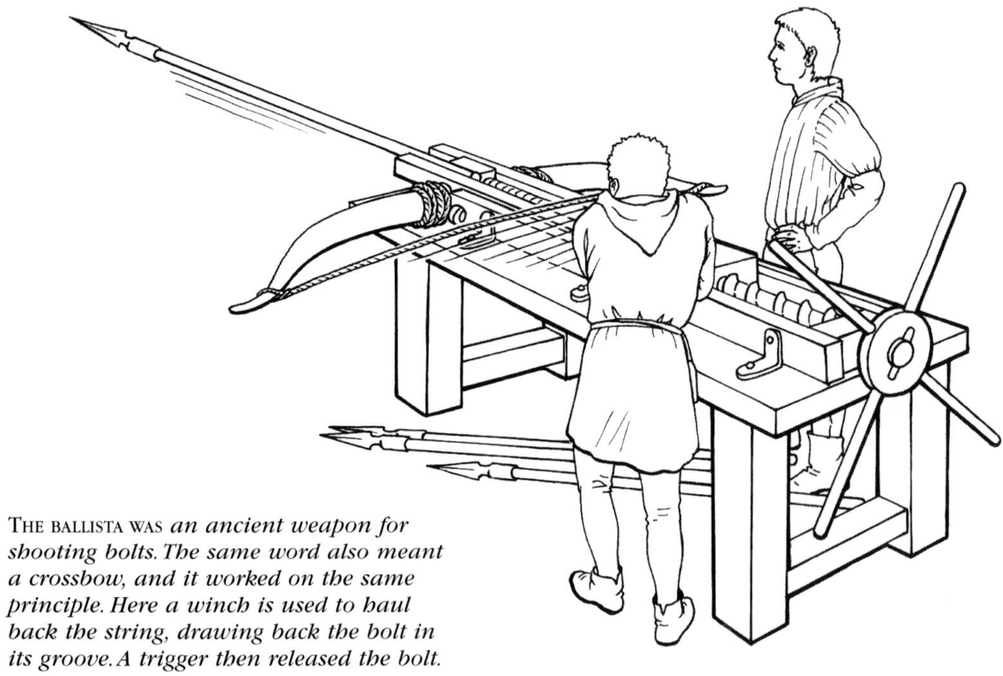

THE BALLISTA WAS *an ancient weapon for shooting bolts. The same word also meant a crossbow, and it worked on the same principle. Here a winch is used to haul back the string, drawing back the bolt in its groove. A trigger then released the bolt.*

the Phoenicians transferring Middle Eastern techniques westwards. Syracuse in turn taught methods to the Greek states. Stone defences became common. Syracuse attracted inventive engineers and developed improved siege weapons, such as new catapults including the *gastraphetes* (a type of crossbow), and the *oxybeles,* an engine that shot bolts. Syracuse also produced stone-throwing engines. Carthage, an enemy of Syracuse, was later credited with inventing the covered and wheeled ram.

Alexander the Great's father, Philip II of Macedon (359–336 BC), also used the talents of military engineers. His weapons used torsion provided by twisted ropes made from animal hair, later animal sinew, to give the impulsion for hurling. He used covered mobile ladders, mobile towers and covered rams. He also possessed the 'tortoise', a wheeled cover to protect men approaching walls for mining or filling ditches.

In the siege of Rhodes (305–4 BC), the Greeks employed wheeled towers, one of which was 43m (141ft) high, had iron plates to cover it, several storeys holding engines, and was moved by a capstan. After the siege the sale of the iron plates raised enough cash for building and erecting the Colossus of Rhodes (in the form of a pillar bearing the sun god Helios) in the harbour.

The early history of siege warfare is an account of one civilization borrowing from another – the Hittites from the Assyrians, the Greeks from the Phoenicians, and so on. The last major borrowing in ancient times was by the Romans from the Greeks. Roman methods were the first major development of siege warfare in western Europe and influenced all medieval European warfare. They proved significant in the conquest of the West, as in the case of Julius Caesar's siege of Alesia in Gaul in 52 BC. He showed typical Roman thoroughness, building a line of camps and forts to surround the Gauls under Vercingetorix. It was a key moment in the conquest of Gaul. Vercingetorix was captured, imprisoned, displayed at a triumph and several years later ritually strangled.

The Romans had benefit of a range of siege engines, including *ballistae* and stone-throwers, catapults, moving towers, mobile ladders and covered rams. In some cases the Romans improved on earlier weapons, as with the type of *oxybeles* known as the *scorpio,* or the throwing machine known as the *onager* (or wild ass) because of its kick-back (it was an important forerunner of various medieval weapons). The Romans developed a large *ballista* with a strong frontal frame, allowing heavier stones to be hurled accurately. They used a range of methods that became common in the Middle Ages, such as constructing ramps for engines, or mining under walls. Many Roman improvements seem 'medieval', such as structures with moats, drawbridges, fortified gates and even portcullises. Ancient and Roman siege techniques led directly into medieval methods of siege warfare.

Early Medieval Europe

Early medieval Europe was frequently at war, and the period was a time of invasions and instability. The Roman Empire collapsed, but did not disappear. It influenced the new military units appearing in the West. In eastern Europe the Roman Empire simply continued as the Byzantine Empire, which would survive until 1453, virtually the end of the Middle Ages.

Byzantium continued to refine its methods of warfare. One of the major developments of the early Middle Ages was the Byzantine invention of Greek Fire. This was said to have been invented by a Syrian engineer Kallinikos, who deserted to the Byzantines. It was such an effective weapon that its composition was a closely guarded secret, so secret that we are still not sure what the ingredients were. The main component was certainly naptha, and Greek Fire probably contained petroleum, resin and saltpetre. It was used in liquid form and the Byzantines made tubular 'cannons' through which it was shot against the enemy. At first it was mainly used at sea. It exploded into fire on impact and was deadly against the wooden ships of the seventh century onwards. Its first recorded use was at the battle of Cyzicus in AD 672. It played a major role in defying the early medieval besiegers of Constantinople – Arabs, Rus and others. Later it was used on land and versions of it came into the hands of the Arabs and later of western crusaders. It would play a major part in later siege warfare.

We have already seen how siege methods were borrowed from a people under attack or in contact with a more advanced civilization – be it Assyrian, Hittite, Phoenician or Greek. Now the 'barbarian' peoples invading Europe soon picked up Roman methods. They needed to capture towns defended by walls, increasingly built of stone. They needed defences that could hold out against sophisticated Roman techniques and weapons. Historians have often underestimated the barbarian's ability to learn from their enemy. Indeed to call these peoples 'barbarian' is itself a surrender to Roman views of their enemy. The Byzantine attitude to their enemies was similarly condescending and hostile. The barbarians of Europe were simply groups who came into conflict with Roman civilization. Many of them benefited from that civilization before overwhelming it. So far as conduct went, the Romans could be quite as barbaric as their opponents – the Byzantine Pergamon cut open pregnant women and boiled their foetuses in a pot. The barbarians learned from Roman culture as well as from their military methods.

The early medieval period was certainly a time of political instability, but it was not entirely one of crude barbarism. The barbarians were often employed in Roman armies or were allied with Roman forces, frequently living alongside the Romans. As the Roman Empire collapsed in the West, Roman civilization did not just disappear. The new peoples settled in Roman cities and often used Roman methods of government, Roman titles, Roman roads, even the Roman language. Many languages of modern Europe are directly descended from Latin. It should be no surprise that barbarian military leaders used Roman siege methods and weapons, as Attila the Hun used battering rams in the siege of Orléans. No doubt the story by Theophylact about Busas the traitor was one example of a common practice. The Byzantine Busas, captured by the Avars, sought to arrange his own ransom but was foiled by his wife's lover who did not want him released. In revenge Busas showed the Avars how to make a throwing engine for sieges.

Roman buildings were naturally constructed to protect the new masters and Roman stone buildings, earth ramparts and walls soon sheltered Franks, Goths, Visigoths or Saxons. In many cases new repairs were carried out. Most of the capitals of the new barbarian states were former Roman towns. Nor was Roman writing lost. Roman architects had put down their ideas in writing and these went on to become the textbooks for medieval architects.

THE RAM WAS *basically a log swung from a frame by ropes. A metal head gave it increased effect when swung against a wall. A covering of hides gave protection against attack, especially by fire.*

HOARDING OR BRATTICE-WORK *was a structure built of wood over the top of a wall. It had a dual purpose, firstly allowing defenders to drop objects such as oil and missiles straight on to the heads of attackers, and secondly protecting the defenders while they went about their business. When later built in stone this was called machicolation.*

The invading peoples used a wide range of siege weapons and methods. Leudegisel, the Frankish count of the stables for King Guntram, was described by Gregory of Tours making 'new machines' to besiege St-Bertrand-de-Comminges in 585. He made wagons fitted with battering rams that had wattle covers to protect the men operating the ram as they approached the wall. The Franks had hurling engines, mobile towers, scaling ladders and inflammable materials for throwing. Some historians have argued that the barbarians lacked the weapons and techniques to take well-protected towns, but the evidence is against them – towns were attacked and taken. In Britain, one of the first actions of the Saxons was to attack and capture Pevensey. Its powerful Roman walls still stand to remind us of their strength. Gildas wrote that all the major British towns were laid low by the repeated battering of enemy rams.

Roman Inspiration

Medieval military leaders often referred to ancient Roman literary sources for advice on tactics and weaponry. The greatest contribution was that of Vegetius (c.385–450), whose work was frequently copied and used. He gave, for example, detailed advice on how to carry out offensive mining and the use of catapults and throwing engines. The works of Vitruvius were also particularly influential. He wrote at the time of the Emperor Augustus (ruled 27 BC–AD 14) that his skills as a writer were a consolation for his plain looks. One of his recommendations, which would be taken up later, was that round towers gave better protection than square ones against rams and mining. He also recommended projecting towers in fortifications (see illustration), so that defenders could deal with attackers near the walls. Early medieval Dijon, as described by Bishop Gregory of Tours, seems to have followed his ideas. It had 30 fortified gates, walls 9m (30ft) high and 4.5m (15ft) thick, plus no fewer than 33 projecting towers. Gregory gives a long account of the events of his age, including many sieges, though they are rarely described in detail. He makes it clear that Roman fortifications were respected and frequently used in the sixth century AD.

The Vikings and the Siege of Paris

By the ninth century the barbarian nations had settled across Europe and in so doing had changed its political pattern. Now there were kingdoms of the Franks, the Goths, the Saxons, the Lombards and so on. Each king sought independence and possessed his own troops. In the east the Byzantine Empire withstood an onslaught from Avars, Persians, Arabs and Rus. The Franks came closest to reviving the Roman Empire in the West. The Frankish Merovingian kings gradually expanded their territories.

The Merovingians were replaced in the eighth century by a family from their own leading administrators, or mayors of the palace. This was the family of Charles Martel and his son, Pepin the Short, who seized the crown. We know them as the Carolingians. Their greatest king was Charles the Great or Charlemagne (*Carolus Magnus*). He conquered much of western Europe, excluding Britain and most of Spain. His empire was, however, short-lived. It lacked unity. His attempts to hold it together with centrally appointed administrators, the *missi dominici,* eventually failed. His son and successor, Louis the Pious, was an able man who did his best to keep the empire together. In the end, however, the efforts failed. In 843 the sons of Louis the Pious agreed a division of the empire into three - the west under Charles the Bald (West Francia, later France), the east under Louis the German (East Francia, later Germany), and the centre under the oldest son Lothar (Lotharingia or Lorraine). The central kingdom did not survive and subsquently broke into parts. Some of these parts were absorbed into the remaining two kingdoms.

A BELFRY WAS *a mobile tower. Here, as used by the Vikings against Paris, it is being pushed up to the wall. It contained several floors to hold attackers. Animal hides were often used to protect the wooden tower from fire.*

One of the reasons that the Carolingian Empire struggled was that it came under attack from a new wave of outside peoples - notably the Saracens from the south, the Magyars from the east and the Vikings from the north. By 885 the west was under Charles the Fat, the son of Louis the German, who briefly seemed to be reconstructing the empire under his rule. In fact West Francia was disintegrating and the defence against the Vikings had fallen into the hands of lesser men. The most effective of these was the family of Robert the Strong who was made count of Anjou in 861 by Charles the Bald. He commanded Neustria for that king and was made *missus* for Maine, Anjou and Tours. From 863-66 he won three crucial victories against the Vikings. In 865 Charles replaced Robert by his own son, Louis the Stammerer, giving Robert a position in Burgundy, but in the end was forced to restore Robert, who was called marquis of the Breton March. In 866 Robert the Strong met his death at the Battle of Brissarthe against the Vikings under Hasting.

Robert was killed, but the Vikings were defeated. Nevertheless, the Viking threat continued and attacks were made along virtually every major river. Towns were taken and sacked. The Vikings arrived in ever greater numbers and began to settle at various points along the French coast, mainly around river mouths. One base was the island of Oiselle in the Seine near Rouen. It is probable that the camps they built contributed to the development of medieval castles. They were defences of relatively small size, usually with earth bank ramparts and surrounding ditches or moats.

Robert the Strong's son Odo was a minor at the time of his father's death. When he reached his majority he partly recovered his father's position and was named Count of Paris. He held that office during the greatest test of the city against the Vikings. The Seine was one of the most attractive routes for the Northmen, who had attacked Paris several times before. In 845 they had demanded and received 7000 pounds in silver as a tribute to leave. Paris was sacked in 857 and attacked again in 861 and 865. The Vikings took advantage of the disunity after the death of Louis III in 882 to sack Rouen in 885 and move on to mount a major siege of Paris.

'They put their belfries into action facing the tower. Our men prepared heavy lumps of wood with iron embedded with which to shatter the Danish engines'.

– Abbo of Fleury, Chronicler

The Siege of Paris: 885–86

The siege of Paris was an important political event. The city was saved and, more important in the long run, its chief saviour was Robert the Strong's son, Count Odo. Appeal was made to the emperor, Charles the Fat, but no help appeared for a year. The siege played a big part in bringing Odo to prominence and eventually to the throne as the first Capetian monarch (888–98).

It was also an interesting siege that was described in detail – a rare thing for early medieval sieges. Furthermore, the account was by an eye-witness who was in the city (the 'queen' of cities to him) during the events he recounted. The author was Abbo, then a young monk at St-Germain-des-Prés, an abbey outside the fortified city on the left bank. Abbo's work was written only a decade after the events. It is not perhaps a perfect account for modern historians. It was written in verse and at times seems to exaggerate and embroider. Abbo's own abbot did not think much of it and modern historians have criticised the Latin – but it remains a vital piece of evidence.

In 885 the Vikings moved up the Seine once more to Paris. They came on 24 November in 700 ships led by Siegfried. There were new fortifications facing them, on the Seine bridges and in the city. The city consisted of dwellings on two islands in the Seine – now called the Île-de-la-Cité and the Île-St-Louis – and a defended ancient region on the left bank. There were houses and abbeys on both banks, but the islands were the city's heart and had recently had their defences updated (though not completed). The islands are still the centre of modern Paris, holding such buildings as Notre-Dame, the Sainte-Chapelle and the Conciergerie. It is not difficult to stand on one of the modern bridges or by the river and visualize the early medieval city.

The layout of the city meant that the Vikings could only pass further along the Seine by getting past the fortified bridges and would only be safe if they could take Paris by siege. The main defender of the region for many years had been Hugh the Abbot, but he had become ill and took no part in the defence of Paris in 885. He died the following year. The bishop of Paris, Gozlin of St-Denis, did take part in the defence. He shared authority in the city with Odo, Count of Paris. However, Gozlin also died in 886, and the burden of defence fell on Count Odo, the son of Robert the Strong.

First the Vikings tried to destroy the tower that defended the bridge leading from the Île-de-la-Cité to the right bank of the Seine. If successful they could sail their ships through. The tower stood on the mainland, preventing access to the bridge and the main city island. It was a recent addition to the defences, only begun in 870, but it had not been completed through the negligence of the citizens. The Vikings left their ships and attacked the tower from land. They failed to break in. During the night the Franks repaired the damage and even managed to add an extra storey to the tower.

Siege of Paris

885

The marauding Vikings approached Paris by sailing up the River Seine with 700 ships, sacking the town of Rouen on the way. Paris refused to let them through. The main city was on its island with fortified bridges to either bank. The Vikings first attacked the tower defending the bridge on the right bank. They attacked using engines and belfries, fire and mines, but failed to break in. They built a camp with the intention of starving the city into submission. However, they did not have enough men to surround the city completely, and so the defenders' supply lines remained open. They made one major attempt by storm, attacking from both land directions and from the river at the same time. This also failed. After some months the Plague hit the defenders. The city's bishop died but its count, Odo, fought on. A relief force sent by Charles the Fat was repelled and lost its leader but persuaded the Vikings to come to agreement. They were allowed to go on to continue their campaign in Burgundy but Paris was never entered.

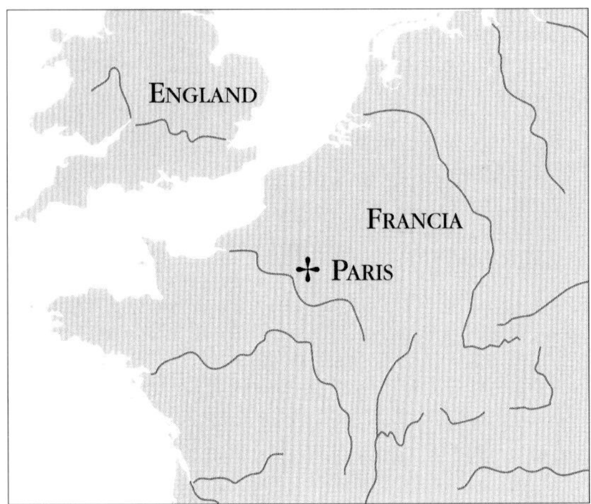

Paris was the key city defending the Seine from Viking approach into Francia. Its bridges, built by the Carolingian rulers, were aimed at preventing the Vikings from going on up the river.

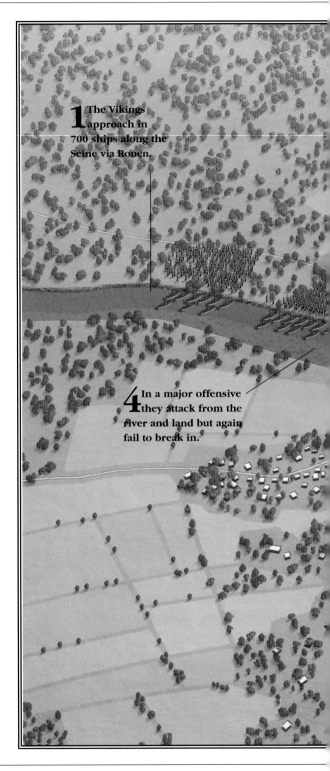

1 **The Vikings approach in 700 ships along the Seine via Rouen.**

4 **In a major offensive they attack from the river and land but again fail to break in.**

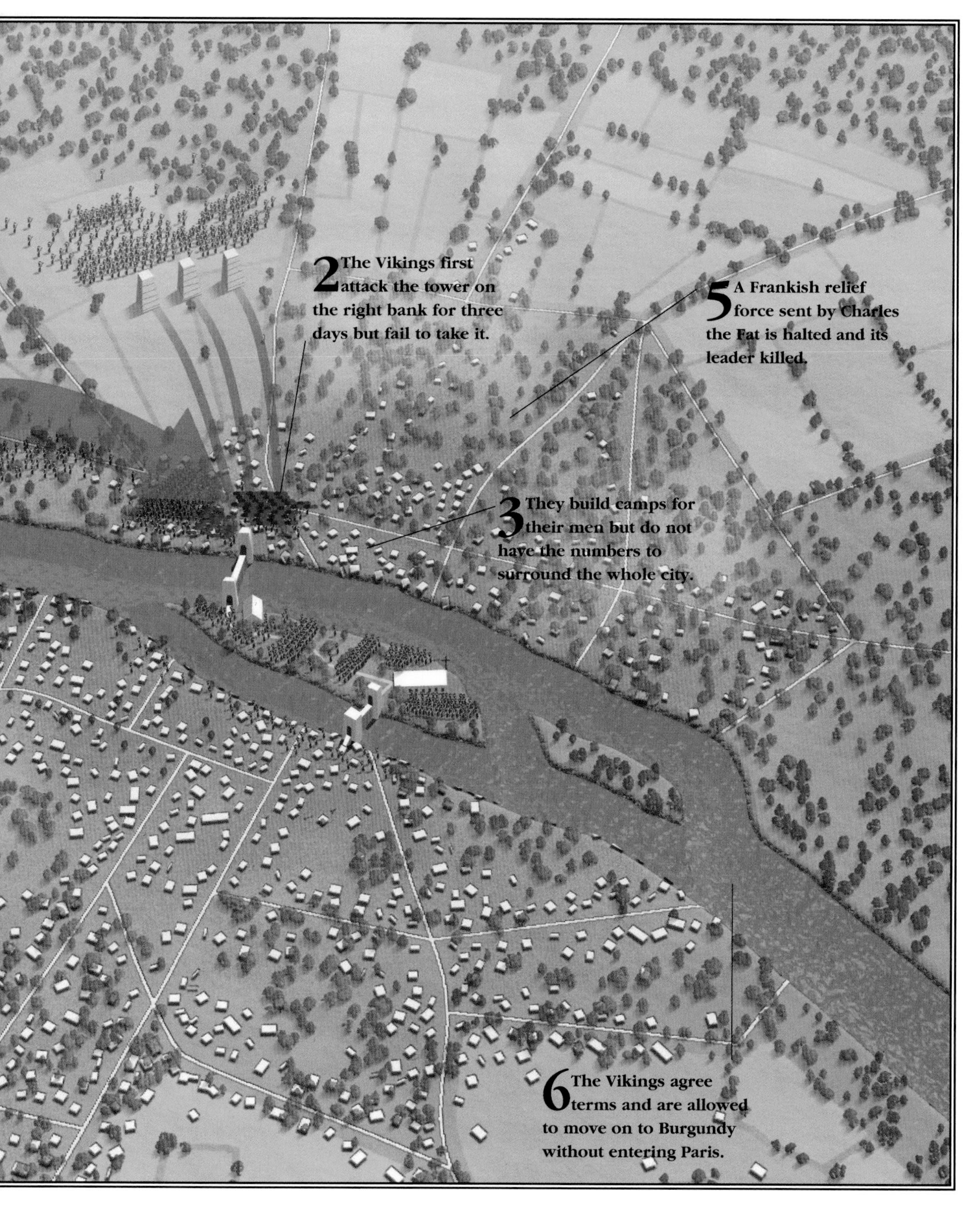
2 The Vikings first attack the tower on the right bank for three days but fail to take it.
5 A Frankish relief force sent by Charles the Fat is halted and its leader killed.
3 They build camps for their men but do not have the numbers to surround the whole city.
6 The Vikings agree terms and are allowed to move on to Burgundy without entering Paris.

At dawn the Vikings returned to the attack. They produced siege engines (*ballistae*) to shoot bolts at the defenders, and used picks to try and destroy the wall of the tower. The West at this time may not have possessed Greek Fire, but it did have inflammable materials. The defenders poured down a heated liquid mix of hot wax and pitch onto the heads of the Vikings. The defenders had powerful spear catapults and one bolt transfixed seven Vikings like a human kebab. A joker among the Franks suggested they should be hauled off to the kitchens. According to Abbo the tower was defended by 200 men while the Vikings had a force of 40,000 men - we may doubt the size of the latter. It is clear that from the beginning the Vikings possessed the usual array of siege weapons. We hear not only of the catapults and siege mining, but also of stone-throwing engines.

For three days the Vikings kept up a constant attack on the tower. They tried fire against the gate until smoke enveloped all the combatants. The defenders made a successful sortie and the Vikings decided to draw off from the tower to try a new approach. They now built a camp on the right bank and constructed new engines, including hurling machines that threw not only stones but also lead grenades.

The Vikings tried a new all-out attack with three land forces as well as ships. On land they formed a tortoise of shields over their heads to attack the wall and to try to fill the ditch. A belfry that the Vikings had built was wheeled up to the wall with archers inside. The Vikings built mounds to the height of the walls to use as ramps for attack engines. One engine was used against the tower, one against the gate and one from the height we now know as Montmartre. The defenders themselves brought up engines to face the attacks. Sorties captured two Viking belfries, but at one point the attackers did break through the wall. Count Odo had to fight hand to hand on the walls until the enemy was repulsed. It is clear that the Viking force was not enormous since they did not have enough men to surround the whole city.

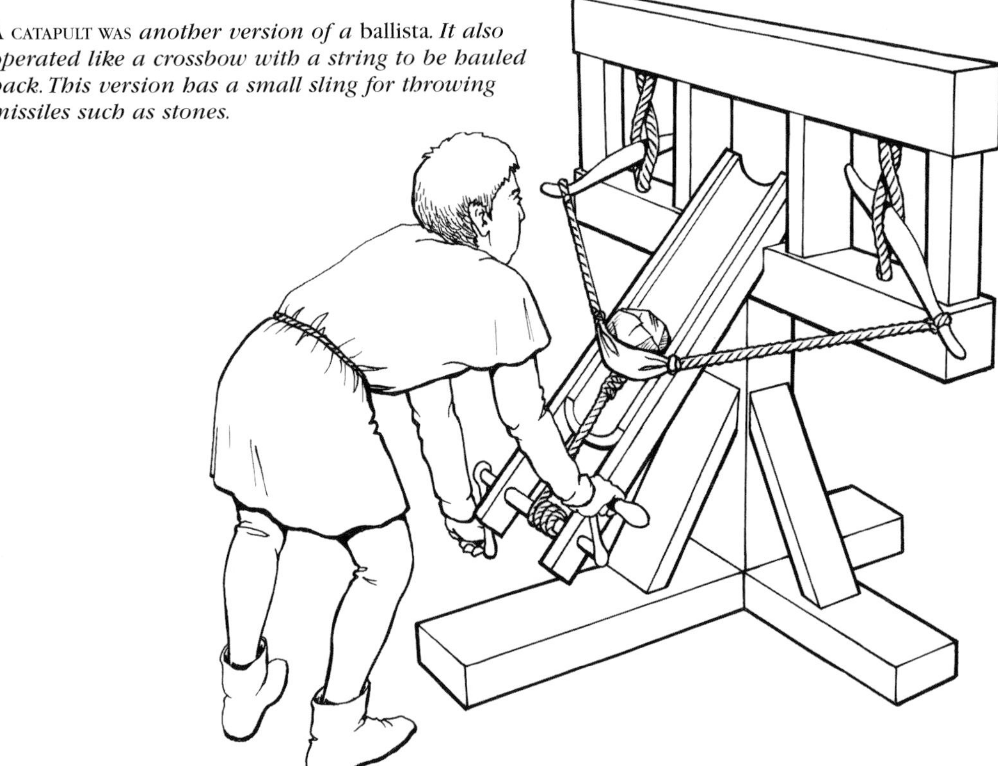

A CATAPULT WAS *another version of a* ballista. *It also operated like a crossbow with a string to be hauled back. This version has a small sling for throwing missiles such as stones.*

SIEGE OPERATIONS DEPICTED *in 19th-century illustrations of crusaders attacking. One notes a) the floors of the belfry, and the ram at lower level; b) a type of bore with posts to fix in the wall and a central swinging spike; c) defensive efforts against ramming such as mats hanging from the wall and the sow (mouse/weasel) or covered shed on wheels to protect the attackers attempting to mine the wall.*

The defenders then suffered from plague, which killed Bishop Gozlin. They did, however, have hopes of relief. Charles the Fat, who had become emperor in 881, promised aid. He sent Henry Duke of the Saxons, who fell when his horse stumbled into a Viking ditch. He was captured and killed. Charles the Fat then marched and a victory was won outside the gates of the city.

The siege was brought to an end by agreement in 886. Charles the Fat made terms that included payment of a tribute and he allowed the Vikings to move on to Burgundy. Count Odo and the Parisians refused to let the Vikings pass through Paris on the Seine and they had to drag their boats overland before continuing. Probably the chief consequence of the siege was the enhanced reputation of Count Odo. After the death of Charles the Fat, Odo was elected as king of the West Franks in 888.

Paris was saved largely by the determination of its citizens, who held firm, repaired the damage to the defences and made regular sorties behind bearers carrying saffron-coloured banners. The main focus of the conflict was the fortified bridge from the island to the right bank, preventing Viking progress down the Seine. Although the defences were not complete, the height of the tower gave the citizens a sufficient advantage over the attacking Vikings.

The Emergence of Castles

Perhaps the first truly original development to affect siege warfare in the Middle Ages was the appearance of a different kind of fortification. Of course there had long been walled cities and forts. The Romans had put the emphasis on fortified camps when on campaign. Castles obviously owed a debt to previous fortifications, but they also differed in vital ways. They were important strongholds and became the target of many medieval sieges. Castles were often more successfully defended than the longer length of city walls. Defended citadels within cities were not new either, but they now became castles.

One function of the castle, and perhaps the basic one, was to protect the great. Castles were the residences of lords - of kings, dukes, counts and castellans. They housed the lord, his family and his household, plus his bodyguard, warband or personal military force, and they reflected the change in society from one governed by a centralised public authority to one with more localized controls that occurred from about the ninth century. The actual origin of the castle is uncertain, partly because there was a development from earlier fortifications and the change was gradual rather than sudden. A major defining point of a castle was its size. Defending as it did a small group around a lord it need not be enormous. It was in one sense a fortified house. Given its small size it could then be defended with the best materials and by the best means available - with large ditches, strong, high and thick walls, with entry made as hard as possible for attackers.

> *'The castle is basically a fortified residence, a residential fortress. It is this duality…which goes far to distinguish the castle from other known types of fortress'.*
>
> *R. Allen Brown, Historian*

Most knowledge that we do have about early castles comes from archaeological rather than literary evidence. This is because the terms used for a castle were often the terms used for older fortifications too. There is no doubt that our views will alter as more structures are discovered and examined. Langeais in the Loire Valley used to be thought the oldest European castle (995). Then, not far away, Doué-la-Fontaine was excavated from 1967 onwards and proved to be older still (950).

These first two castles were built in stone but they were rivalled at about the same time by earthwork castles. These too came to be defended residences. They were cheaper and quicker to build than the stone castles and therefore useful for erecting during a campaign, or as the residence of a less wealthy lord. During the period of early castle building there would be more of these earthwork castles than the stone ones. The common type was the motte-and-bailey castle, consisting of a higher mound (the motte) on which was usually built a wooden tower for the keep, and a lower and larger mound (the bailey). Both mounds were normally protected by a surrounding ditch, rampart and palisade. A wooden bridge often connected the two parts. The bailey was generally used for various buildings giving support to the lord - for stabling, storage and so on. The keep on the motte was the residence for the lord and his close family, servants and troops.

The origin of the motte-and-bailey castle is even harder to pin down than that of the stone castle. One early site that has been excavated is that at the Hüsterknupp near Frimmersdorf in Germany. It seems to have begun life in the tenth century as a fortified farmhouse with a defended enclosure. Later a mound of earth was added within the enclosure and a timber keep was built upon the mound, making it into a motte-and-bailey castle. However, this site was relatively late in becoming a castle.

The earliest known earthwork castles seem to be found in northwestern Europe, in Flanders and France. They seem to have appeared first during the period of the Viking invasions and the most likely explanation of their origin is from a combination of Viking and Frankish fortifications, probably army camps rather than residences but turning into the latter as conditions became more stable. The Vikings certainly built many earthwork defences for their army camps. Areas that suffered considerably from Viking raids, such as Flanders, Normandy and Brittany, are the regions that saw the early earthwork castles. When William the Conqueror invaded Brittany he had to besiege a number of motte-and-bailey castles. The Bayeux Tapestry pictures them at Rennes, Dinan and Dol - all with earthwork defences and a timber keep.

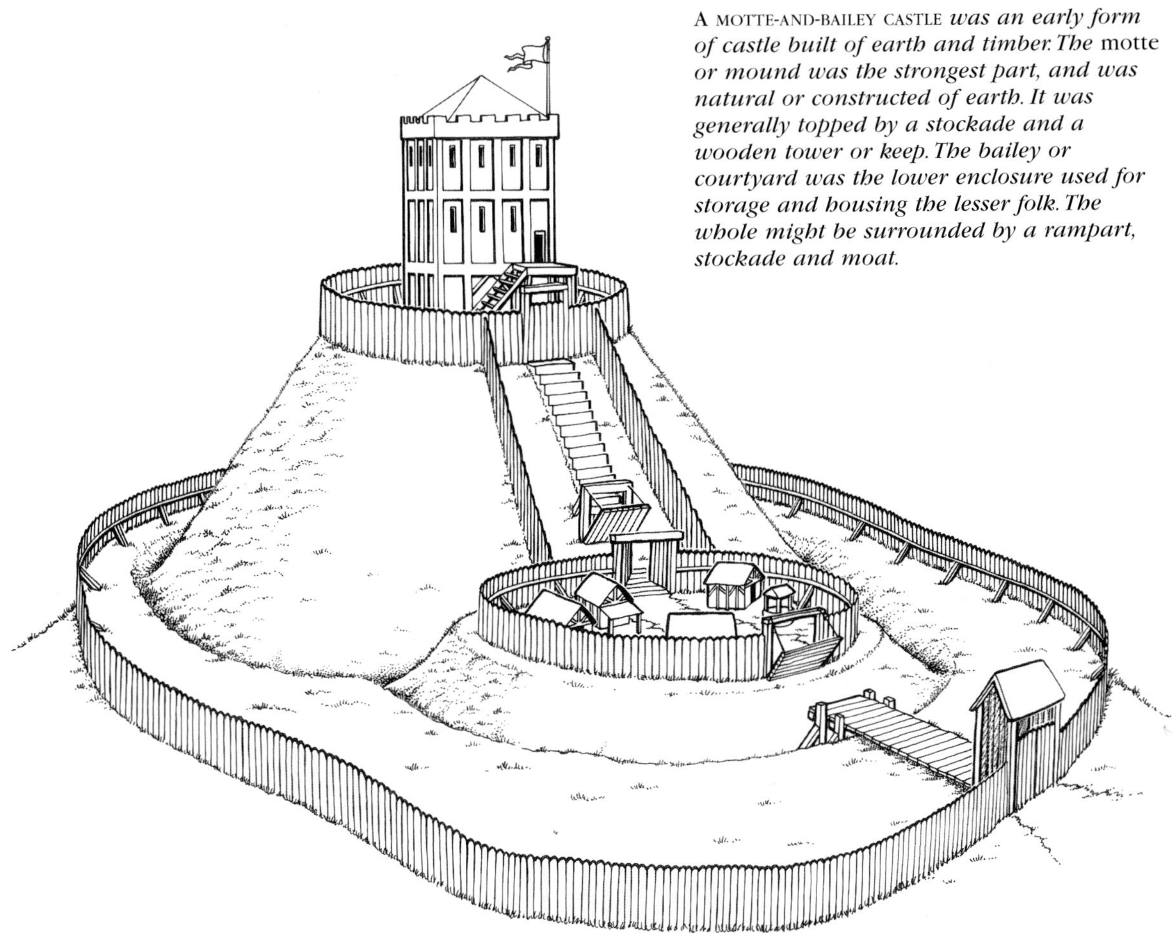

A MOTTE-AND-BAILEY CASTLE *was an early form of castle built of earth and timber. The* motte *or mound was the strongest part, and was natural or constructed of earth. It was generally topped by a stockade and a wooden tower or keep. The bailey or courtyard was the lower enclosure used for storage and housing the lesser folk. The whole might be surrounded by a rampart, stockade and moat.*

The tapestry also shows a motte-and-bailey castle at Bayeux itself. When the Normans invaded England in the mid eleventh century they built a whole series of motte-and-bailey castles in the course of their campaigns. Later, with more stability and more time, most of these earthwork castles (such as that at Hastings) were rebuilt in stone.

By the eleventh century it had become common in the West for lords to build castles for themselves, either in stone or earth or both. William the Conqueror began two great stone castles in England, at London and Rochester, as well as a host of earthwork castles. The Normans were also, at about the same time, building their castles in conquered southern Italy and Sicily. It had taken time, but western Europe had achieved a revolution in military defence. Now it was time to reconsider methods of attack as the castle, rather than the town, became the primary focus of sieges. Even in towns it was usually the castle acting as the citadel that provided the final defence. Frequently we find a town being entered but the castle remaining defiant.

Western Europe was becoming more stable by the twelfth century. The kings were gaining in authority and keeping better control of their magnates. The same could be said for dukes and counts over their castellans. Lesser men were finding it more difficult to rival the wealth and power of the kings, and the growing wealth of the great increased their security. They could build the best castles and produce the most effective siege trains. By the twelfth century new castles were generally built in stone.

IN LATER MEDIEVAL *castles built in stone it was common to have more than one surrounding wall - making a concentric castle. Rounded rather than square towers became common, as did projecting towers to cover the wall.*

To this date castles and their towers had commonly been rectangular. Now came a revolution with the introduction of rounded towers (or re-introduction - the Romans had used such features). This development partly came from a reading of Roman works like those of Vitruvius. It also partly came from the Crusades and contact with Middle Eastern and Byzantine architecture. Being round clearly made it more difficult to mine or destroy towers, since there were no corners to aim at. Many earlier castles, if still in use, were now rebuilt. It meant that attackers needed to seek new methods of attack if these stronger fortifications were to be overcome.

Classic Early Castles

The fortifications at Doué-la-Fontaine and Langeais in France are often held up as the earliest examples of medieval castles. The castle of Doué-la-Fontaine was found at the site known as La Motte. It appears first to have been a residence of the count of Blois, built as a stone hall in c.900, that was fired and then rebuilt as a donjon or keep by Count Theobald in c.950. The ground floor entrance was blocked off and a forebuilding and upper storey were added. Earth was piled around the foot of the keep to make a slope with the result that access to the wall was difficult - a type of motte. We call it a castle but clearly it was no more than the adaptation and improvement of an existing strong residence. As for the castle of Langeais, it is in the Touraine between the rivers Loire and Roumer. It was built by one of the greatest early castle builders, Fulk Nerra, Count of Anjou, and was finished by 995 when it was besieged by Odo I, Count of Blois. It was built upon an earth mound in the form of a rectangular stone keep. A later château was constructed nearby and the ruins of the old keep may now be seen at the foot of the gardens of the house. In form it differs little from the many rectangular keeps built during the next century in France and England.

The Siege of Montreuil-Bellay: 1149–51

Our second siege chosen for closer investigation is that of Montreuil-Bellay. This was a prolonged three-year siege from 1149-51. It was, in political terms, not a major event. It was caused by the rebellion of a lesser lord, Gerard Berlai, against the count of Anjou, Geoffrey V le Bel (the Handsome). Geoffrey V married Henry I of England's daughter, the Empress Matilda, and was the father of Henry Plantagenet, soon to become King Henry II of England.

Anjou had steadily grown as a power from a mere Carolingian viscountcy to one of the major principalities in France. Geoffrey needed to display his authority by dealing with the rebel Gerard even though the latter had shut himself in one of the most imposing castles of its time. We are not sure what the mid-twelfth-century castle looked like, because it was destroyed after being taken and later a new castle was rebuilt on the site. This later building may still be seen, in its late medieval white stone with romantic-looking rounded towers. What is clear is the difficulty of taking any fortification on the site - a high rock overlooking a mighty natural chasm called the Valley of the Jews. That chasm had to be crossed to approach the castle entrance. It stood by the River Thouet just south of Saumur. The original castle had been built by the great castle builder, a previous count of Anjou, Fulk Nerra.

The siege was described in detail by a near-contemporary source, a biography of Geoffrey V called *The Life of Duke Geoffrey*. It was written by a monk at Marmoutier, an abbey that came within the area of Geoffrey's power. John described the castle as it then was, with double walls and a keep 'rising to the stars', and he wrote detailed descriptions of the siege.

Geoffrey V brought his army to besiege the site. He fortified a siege camp to protect his stores. We are told that stone was used, so his works were clearly solid, probably in the form of a counter castle. Geoffrey also began to construct siege towers. Every effort was made to break the defence, but all failed. A long attempt to starve out the defenders began, and lasted for nearly three years. In order to cross the chasm Geoffrey finally ordered people attending the nearby fair at Saumur to come to Montreuil-Bellay and then to carry rocks and rubbish to the edge of the chasm and drop their burden in until the gap could be bridged.

MINING A WALL *was an ancient and common way of passing it. The idea was to tunnel under the wall, supporting the roof of the tunnel with props. When complete the props were fired and the tunnel collapsed, bringing down the wall with it. The attackers at ground level could then get in.*

Siege of Montreuil-Bellay

1149-51

Montreuil-Bellay was a castle held by Gerard Berlai who rebelled against his lord, Geoffrey V, count of Anjou, in 1149. The castle had a high keep 'rising to the stars'. It was protected on one side by the river, on the other by a deep natural chasm that acted like a ditch. As the local ruler with plenty of supplies and support, Geoffrey settled in for a long siege. His first major attempt to break in meant bringing all the people from the nearby fair at Saumur. They were ordered to drop stones and earth in the ditch and fill it. Then Geoffrey could advance his engines and belfries towards the castle. His final effort was to load throwing engines with vases containing Greek Fire. These were hurled at the castle and set fire to the gates and houses inside, causing havoc. Geoffrey broke in and captured the castle, bringing the three-year sige to an end.

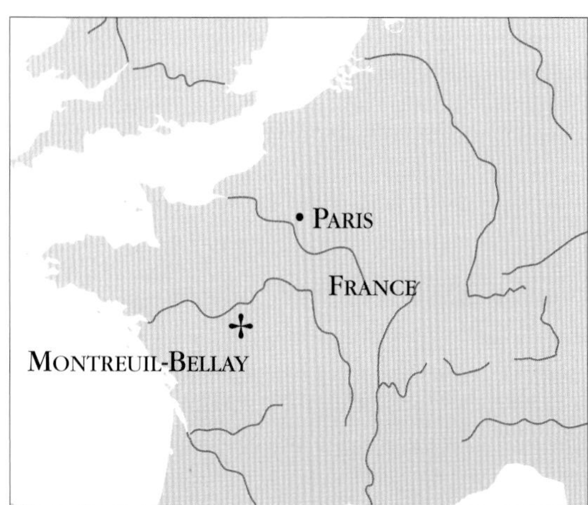

Montreuil-Bellay stood beside the River Thouet, a tributary of the Loire. It was to the south of Saumur, cut off on the land side by the chasm called the Valley of the Jews. The castle had originally been built by Fulk Nerra.

1 Geoffrey V approached the rebel Gerard Berlai in his castle at Montreuil-Bellay in 1149 from the direction of Doué.

5 With the wooden buildings burning, Geoffrey's forces broke in and captured the castle.

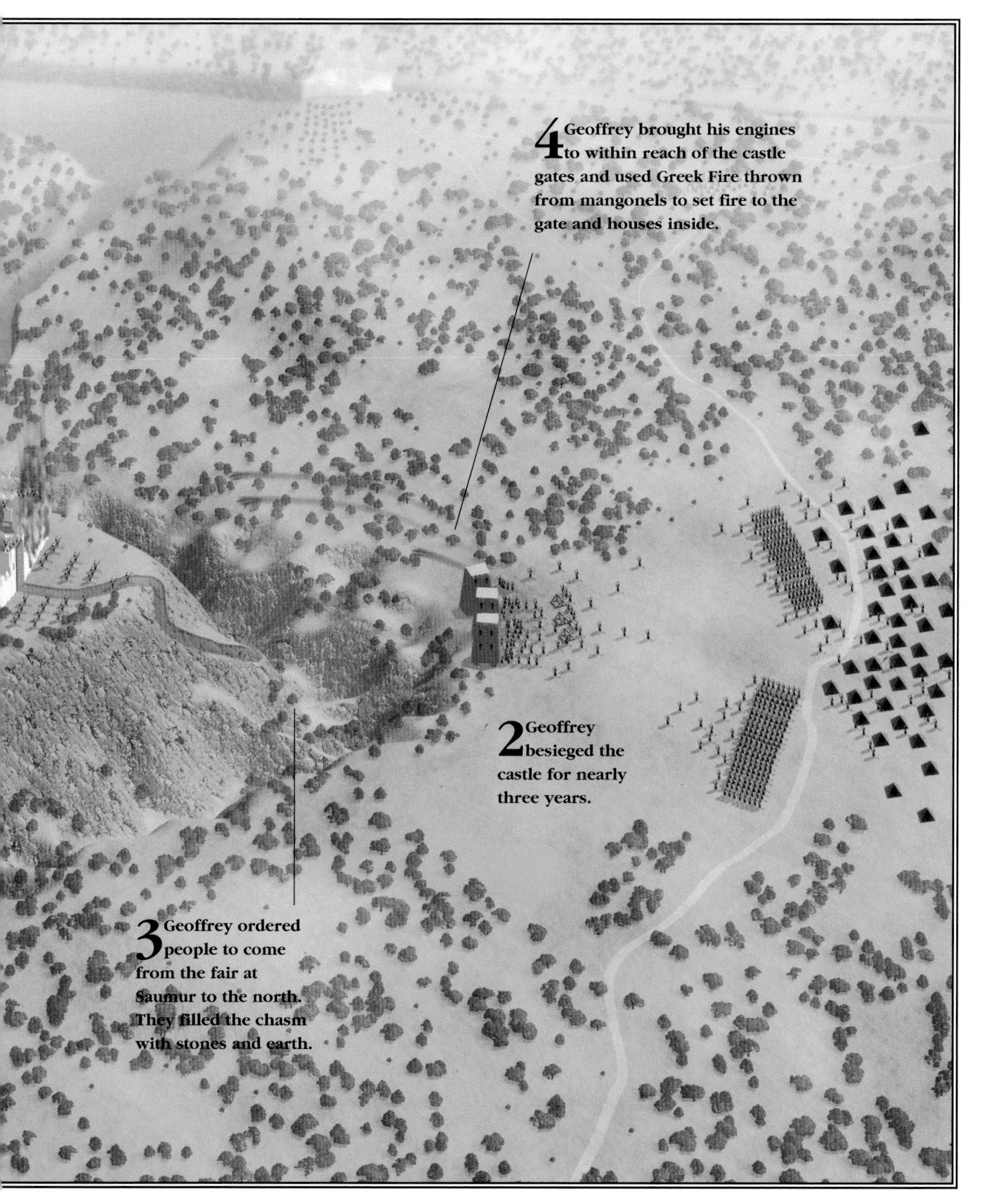
4 Geoffrey brought his engines to within reach of the castle gates and used Greek Fire thrown from mangonels to set fire to the gate and houses inside.
2 Geoffrey besieged the castle for nearly three years.
3 Geoffrey ordered people to come from the fair at Saumur to the north. They filled the chasm with stones and earth.

A THROWING ENGINE, *called a mangonel, worked by the torsion from twisted ropes. The spoon-like arm was hauled back and secured. The spoon was loaded with a rock or other missile. When released the arm sprang up, struck the bar and hurled the missile.*

At last it became possible to push a belfry over the filled gap and approach close enough to the castle to operate. Archers were placed within the belfries and shot a hail of arrows against the defenders. It was now that Geoffrey attempted a master-stroke, a sign of his brilliance as a commander and his willingness to innovate. The idea probably came from the fact that his family had long had a connection with the Holy Land and the Crusades. His father, Fulk the Young, had gone to the Holy Land and become king of Jerusalem, leaving his son to act as count of Anjou. Geoffrey had picked up knowledge of that ancient Byzantine weapon, Greek Fire. We also find in his household, named in charters, men called Robert de Greco, Archaloio and Halope - suggesting a possible Greek link. At any rate, by some means Geoffrey had gained possession of a quantity of the secret liquid. There is no earlier evidence of Greek Fire being used in western Europe, though it would be again afterwards - for example, by Richard the Lionheart (Geoffrey's grandson).

A belfry wheeled towards the castle was used as a shelter from which to hurl the Greek Fire from throwing engines. John of Marmoutier described the effect. 'It rose up in balls of flame and turned the whole castle into a blaze' - and it worked. The attackers now broke into the castle and the defenders, harried by archers, retreated to the keep for a last stand. The two sides agreed a one-day truce to allow the dead on both sides to be buried and the wounded to be treated.

The truce soon expired and fighting resumed. The count brought in his stone-throwing engines. The wall was breached but repaired. For inspiration Geoffrey V turned to his books. We find him now deep into his copy of the Roman writer Vegetius Renatus' *De Re Militari* (Concerning Military Matters). A number of monks from Marmoutier (our author John's abbey, perhaps including our author himself) were present. One of them, whom John calls only by his initial 'G', is described as 'a man of authority, of good reputation and better life, sharp in mind and a learned man of letters'. The man might be William (Gulielmus) of Conches, who we know spent time at Geoffrey's court and dedicated works to him. 'G' picked up the copy of Vegetius and began to read from it. He found a passage about how a tower that had been damaged and repaired might be captured. Geoffrey V listened thoughtfully and said, 'Stay with me tomorrow, dear brother, and what you find in your reading, you shall see put into practice'. Interestingly it was Vegetius (who lived before Greek Fire had been invented) who wrote about the use of inflammable materials and how they could be implemented against timber used to repair defences.

Now Geoffrey decided to use Greek Fire again against the keep. He ordered up an iron jar, strengthened with bands of iron. He called for it to be filled with the Greek Fire ingredients - his recipe included cannabis and nut oil. The jar was sealed with a strip of iron and firmly locked. Then the jar was placed in a heated furnace until the whole jar glowed and the oil inside was bubbling. Water was thrown over the chain fixed to the jar in order to cool it and then the jar was attached to a throwing engine. While still red hot the jar was hurled against the enemy defences where they had been repaired with timber.

The Greek Fire flowed out on impact and the timber flared up so much that not only the defences, but three buildings within, went up in flames. Gerard Berlai surrendered and Montreuil-Bellay was in Geoffrey's hands. He proceeded to demolish the castle, leaving only a part in ruins to remind all of his authority. Gerard was imprisoned until later released by King Louis VII of France.

A ROUND TOWER *under construction. From c.1200 round towers replaced square ones. Round towers without corners were less vulnerable to throwing weapons and to mining.*

Rounded Towers and Stronger Castles

The twelfth and thirteenth centuries saw further improvements in defences. The first major change was the introduction of rounded towers, as corner towers for the enclosure, as intermittent towers in the wall and for keeps. We have suggested already that this might be partly a result of interest in ancient Roman architecture, following the advice of Vegetius. The Crusades had also brought a close knowledge of Middle Eastern architecture, both Byzantine and Saracen. An excellent example of change in the period is found at Rochester Castle, besieged by King John against the barons in 1215. During the siege John mined the keep and one of its rectangular corner turrets was brought down. When the castle was rebuilt this rectangular tower was rebuilt as a rounded corner -though the other corner towers kept their old form.

Probably the earliest of the new round-towered castles in the West came from the work of Philip II Augustus, king of France (1180–1223). Recent archaeological work makes this suggestion even more plausible. Rounded towers were used at a number of twelfth-century castles, including Farcheville at La Ferté-Alais, Châteaufort, the Tour Guinette at Étampes and Neauphle-le-Château at Yvelines. Dourdan was another Philip Augustus castle with round towers. Several of these date from at least the mid twelfth century.

We now also know much more than we did about Philip II's great castle in Paris, the Louvre.

The Louvre became a royal palace and various later alterations were made. In modern times it has, of course, become a famous museum. The old castle seemed to have been destroyed, but modern archaeological work has now revealed an amazing survival of the lower parts of the original castle. These have been cleared and may be viewed underneath the Louvre museum.

Much of the great circuit of the outer wall may be seen with its massive rounded towers, and inside this circuit the equally impressive walls of a round keep. It looks in almost pristine condition.

KRAK DES CHEVELIERS *in Syria is one of the greatest crusader castles and was built on a mountain spur. The count of Tripoli passed it to the Hospitallers in 1142. It had to be repaired after earthquake damage and became a concentric castle with rounded towers.*

Crusader Castles

From the late eleventh century knights from western Europe carried out regular attacks on the Holy Land. Many of the invaders settled there and established forts for their own protection. Some of the sites, such as Beaufort and Krak des Chevaliers, were very impressive. The style of the castles was heavily influenced by Saracen and Byzantine fortifications. Some experts think that the move towards emphasizing the outer wall derived from crusader practice. Rectangular castles with corner towers and no central keep were common in the Holy Land. Belvoir was of this type, but had a double outer wall – a probable influence on concentric castle development in western Europe.

The Siege of Château-Gaillard: 1203–04

Much the same influences as affected French architecture were playing on the English kings of

the age. Richard the Lionheart, like Philip II, had been on crusade. He built his famous castle of Château-Gaillard at Les Andelys on the Seine. It stood on a great cliff over the river facing French territory, a magnificent site. Its name means 'the cheeky castle' because it was like a rude gesture to the French king over the river. The castle was built very rapidly for such a major stone structure – between 1196 and 1198. It covered a small, triangular plateau. There was only one feasible approach and that was strengthened by a series of ditches. The castle's wards had three major enclosures. These had to be taken in turn in order to get to the keep in the final section. The height increased from the outer to the inner wards, so that defenders could have advantage over attackers at each stage.

The outer bailey of the castle was protected by a ditch. A large gully separated the outer bailey from the middle bailey. Within the third and inner bailey, the keep was round with a massive *en bec* base, with a sloped base shaped like a beak to give added strength against mining. It had a massive appearance, unusually protected by joined semi-circular towers around the great rounded keep. The only way into the last bailey was via a narrow bridge of natural stone across a gully.

In 1203 Château-Gaillard was held by King John of England, Richard the Lionheart's younger brother. Roger de Lacy commanded the garrison for the king. Philip II Augustus, King of France came to take the castle as part of his campaign to defeat the Plantagenets and regain lands in western France. The siege of this powerfully defended castle was the key to the whole campaign. With its fall came the collapse of the Angevin position, the loss of Normandy and of much else besides.

The Seine was an obvious route into Normandy for Philip Augustus and Château-Gaillard an essential target. Philip invaded Normandy in 1203, arriving before the great castle in August. He had already taken a number of castles around his main target, thus isolating it from easy aid. The castle was part of a complex of fortifications at Les Andelys. The island there held a fortified palace. Bridges joined it to the land on either side, while a fortified ditch blocked access from the river. The castle itself was on the height overlooking the island.

Philip broke through the fortified ditch. He built a bridge of boats to cross the river, since the garrison had destroyed the existing bridge. He constructed towers on boats to float on the river, both to defend his bridge of boats and to attack the castle. John did attempt to send a relief army, divided into land and river forces. It acted on wrong information, however, so that the two attacks did not coincide – the tide delayed the river force. The land force led by William the Marshal and the mercenary captain, Lupescar, made a night attack. It was held off and many were killed, 'like sheep by a wolf' (William the Breton, *Phillipide*).

> *'We saw among them [the poor ejected from Château-Gaillard] the deplorable sight of a man who carried the skin of a dog and when told to throw it away said, "I will not part from the skin that has kept me alive".'* – WILLIAM THE BRETON

The river force, when it did arrive, received the full attention of all the defenders. The English had managed to damage the temporary bridge, but it was repaired by torchlight before the boats arrived at dawn. The French manned the towers and the bridge against the English fleet. Weights were dropped on the ships and arrows shot at their crews. One large beam was aimed well enough to sink two ships. The attack failed and the fleet drew off. Two of Philip Augustus' soldiers, the Le Noir brothers, captured two ships and went in pursuit.

The French could again concentrate on taking the castle. A swimmer called Galbert strapped vases containing Greek Fire to his body. He climbed the palisade defending the island and caused an explosion with his vases that went off 'like Mount Etna'. The timber caught fire, as did houses inside, and the island was then captured. The French now controlled the whole complex outside the castle and hope of relief had dwindled. Philip improved the defences around his own camp. New huts were built of wood and straw for the attackers. A covered way was built to protect the French movements. Hills were levelled off to be used as platforms for throwing engines.

Roger de Lacy found his stores diminishing. He sent out non-combatants. The first few were allowed through the French lines, but then Philip's attitude hardened and several hundred people found themselves trapped between the two sides. All they had to live on was grass and whatever scraps they could find. A chicken dropped from the walls of the castle was seized by the desperate people and completely consumed - beak, claws, feathers and all. One unfortunate pregnant woman gave birth in no-man's land. The people began to make desperate cries and pleas for help. Philip finally relented. He ordered that food should be given and they should be allowed through his lines. One of the men was holding the skin of a dog and would not let it go because he said the dog was all that had kept him alive. He did finally give it up in return for bread.

A French writer claimed that King John, rather than come to the aid of his castle, had promised to 'stay in a safe place' with his dog. In fact, in September, John did raid into Brittany, hoping to divert Philip from the siege. The French king was not impressed and stayed resolutely put. John abandoned his efforts and took ship from Barfleur on 5 December. He never went back to Normandy.

Philip II brought up new supplies for his troops. New belfries were constructed. In February 1204 the outer bailey of the castle was attacked with engines and mined while the king, helmeted and in armour, shouted encouragement. The French ladders were not long enough to reach the top of the walls, but men swarmed up them and cut footholds in the stonework of the upper part to get over and in.

Now only two baileys remained. The French found an interesting route into the middle bailey. John had built a house there in 1202 and it had a *garderobe* (toilet) with a chute downwards. Up this unpleasant tunnel the French climbed. At the top, one Pierre Bogis climbed on a friend's shoulder and was able to enter the cellar of a chapel. He then let down a rope for his comrades. They broke through the door of the building by using fire. The garrison was now awake to the threat as the fire spread and with it confusion. The French managed to open the gate into the middle bailey, let down the drawbridge to it, and their troops poured in. The middle bailey was a ruin of ashes. Those defenders who were able now retreated to the last bailey within the great keep.

The great keep looked imposing. It was arguably the strongest of its time. There was, however, one major weakness - not apparent at first, but spotted by the attackers. The only entrance was by a bridge of solid, natural rock. It was not easy to cross directly and could be defended, but it could not be removed. The attackers realized that they could shelter behind it while mining the wall. This was the way the French broke through the final barrier. On 6 March 1204 the last 20 knights and 120 men-at-arms inside Château-Gaillard surrendered.

Angevin Normandy quickly collapsed and was conquered by Philip Augustus. Rouen was taken and the French pushed through to the coast. Much of the rest of Angevin France collapsed and fell under Philip's power - Anjou, Maine, Touraine and part of Poitou. Brittany now recognized Philip. The English, however, held on to their more southerly territories including Gascony. The siege had been one of the most decisive in European history. It also contributed to discontent with John in England, where the barons would bring the king to the humiliation of accepting Magna Carta.

Siege Weapons of the Central Middle Ages

By the central Middle Ages siege craft was about to be transformed by two major developments: first the improvement of defence with the concentric castle, and second the improvement of attack with two major new weapons.

The constant need in sieges was to break into a castle or town, to destroy, get over or penetrate the outer walls. One group of weapons or aids was primarily aimed at crossing walls. The simplest was the ladder used for scaling. Ladders often had to be of considerable size, and were most commonly

SCALING WALLS USING *ladders was an ancient method, still used here in the fourteenth century. Medieval ladders commonly had hooks to grip the top of the wall. Escalade was the most direct and also the most dangerous way of assaulting a castle. The action consisted of the attacking forces moving forward from their lines to the base of the wall where they set the ladders against the wall, and then scaled them to engage the defenders in hand-to-hand combat. All the while they were being harassed by defenders trying to push the ladders away, throwing missiles and loosing arrows and bolts at them.*

Siege of Château-Gaillard

1203-04

Philip II Augustus, king of France, invaded and conquered Normandy from King John of England. In August 1203 he besieged the key fortress of Château-Gaillard, which had been built by Richard the Lionheart a few years before. It could only be approached by land at the point of the outer bailey. The defence was led by Roger de Lacy. John sent a relief force that tried to enter the castle with a combined land and sea approach. The attacks failed to coincide and were held off. John then abandoned the castle to its fate. The French fought their way into the three consecutive baileys by gradual stages. The outer bailey was mined in February 1204. The middle bailey was entered secretly through a *garderobe* (toilet) chute. The inner bailey was mined using cover from the natural rock bridge to it. The castle surrendered on 8 March 1204. Within a year Philip held all of Normandy.

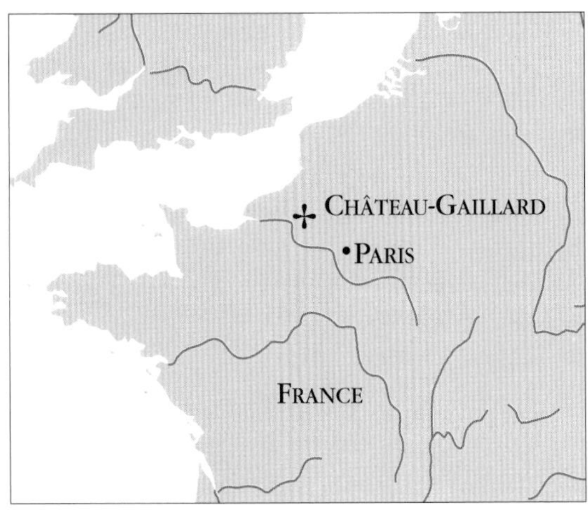

Château-Gaillard stood on the frontier between Normandy, then held by the king of England, and the territory of the French king. It lay to the east of Rouen on a magnificent rocky site above the confluence of the Seine and the Gambon.

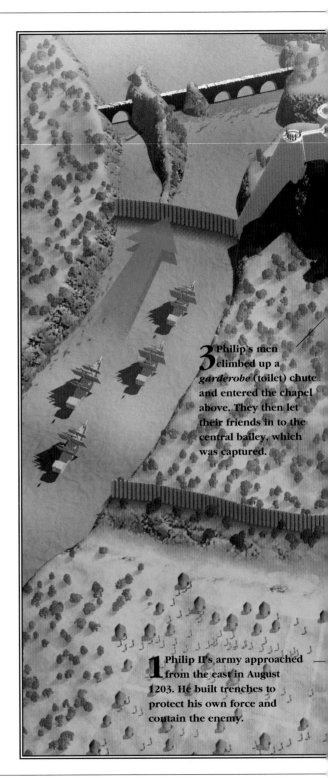

3 **Philip's men climbed up a *garderobe* (toilet) chute and entered the chapel above. They then let their friends in to the central bailey, which was captured.**

1 **Philip II's army approached from the east in August 1203. He built trenches to protect his own force and contain the enemy.**

4 A moat surrounded the inner bailey, crossed by a natural rock bridge. Using the bridge as cover the French took the inner bailey. The forces of King John surrendered on 8 March 1204.
2 In February 1204 Philip managed to break into the outer bailey by mining.

made of wood, but hemp rope ladders were also used. Sometimes hooks or claws were placed at the top end of the ladder to grip the wall. Another improvement was to place a ladder inside a covered tunnel to protect the climbers. Ladders were also placed on a lifting machine to raise them to the wall, and were sometimes used from belfries – they could be employed as bridges from a belfry, or sometimes from a ship against sea or river walls. Ladders were often used in large numbers so that many men could climb at once. In the siege of Jerusalem by the crusaders every two knights were told to produce one ladder. Ladders were also useful for climbing in secretly, during night infiltrations for instance, in order to break in and perhaps open the gates from the inside.

For breaching walls directly various engines were produced to hit or pick at the wall surface. The battering ram was an ancient weapon. Sometimes it had simply been a log carried by men to batter at a wall or gate. An improvisation in the period was to dismantle the mast from a ship and use it as a ram, but the medieval ram was usually more sophisticated. A metal head was common, giving greater battering power. The ram was usually placed on a trolley with wheels to make it easier to move against the wall, and was normally hung from a frame on ropes or chains so that it could be swung into action. It became common to construct a roof over the trolley to give added protection to the ram and its users. The bore was a similar engine except that it had a pointed head to pick at the wall between the stones.

The other common way to pass or destroy a wall was to go under it by mining. The Romans had used this method. The normal idea was to dig out a tunnel under the wall and undermine its foundations. This foundation might be held up on wooden props until the mine was complete. The props would then be set on fire and, when they collapsed, the wall would be brought down. King John did this at Rochester, using the fat from 40 pigs to improve the flammability of the props. Sometimes the aim of the miners was simply to build a tunnel to allow for entry into the town or castle.

Mobile huts called 'cats' were often made to cover the approach of the miners when they began work, but secret digging at night was a good idea in order to escape detection. At Toulouse in 1218 a large cat covered some 550 men. Mining was a dangerous operation and the miners were often killed in falls, sometimes engineered by the enemy making counter mines.

Missile Throwers

Probably the most frequently used weapons in sieges were various types of throwing and hurling machines. These may be roughly divided into two groups, those that acted by tension comparable to the action of a bow, and those that worked by torsion, usually through twisted ropes bending back an arm that could be released to hurl an object. These engines varied considerably in size and power. Some were meant primarily to shoot at individuals, others to knock down walls. There is a serious problem in identifying engines from written sources, which were mainly in Latin and produced by clerics who were not military experts. They knew the Roman use of the words but were often unclear about the nature of the weapon or engine concerned. Thus we cannot be certain that the use of a particular term, say *'ballista'* or 'mangonel', means a particular weapon every time. Illustrations, especially in manuscripts, do give some assistance (though they are commonly by the same sort of people), and occasionally the written sources give enough detail to identify a particular type of engine – but we must always be cautious.

The bolt-throwing weapons shot a bolt that varied considerably in size, from an ordinary crossbow bolt to something several feet in length – the one at Paris that skewered several men like a kebab in 885 was clearly extremely large. The term *'ballista'* was indeed used both for an ordinary crossbow and for larger engines. The larger weapons were very like large crossbows in any case, but required machinery to draw back the powerful string. Sometimes torsion in the form of twisted ropes was used to provide propulsion. The French on crusade used large weapons of this type made in such a way that they could be swivelled in order to aim better.

Many peoples used *ballistae,* including Romans, Arabs, Franks and Saxons. The normal weapon projected was a bolt, but sometimes these

A VARIATION OF *the mangonel, sometimes called a petrary, was also used for throwing stones in siege situations.*

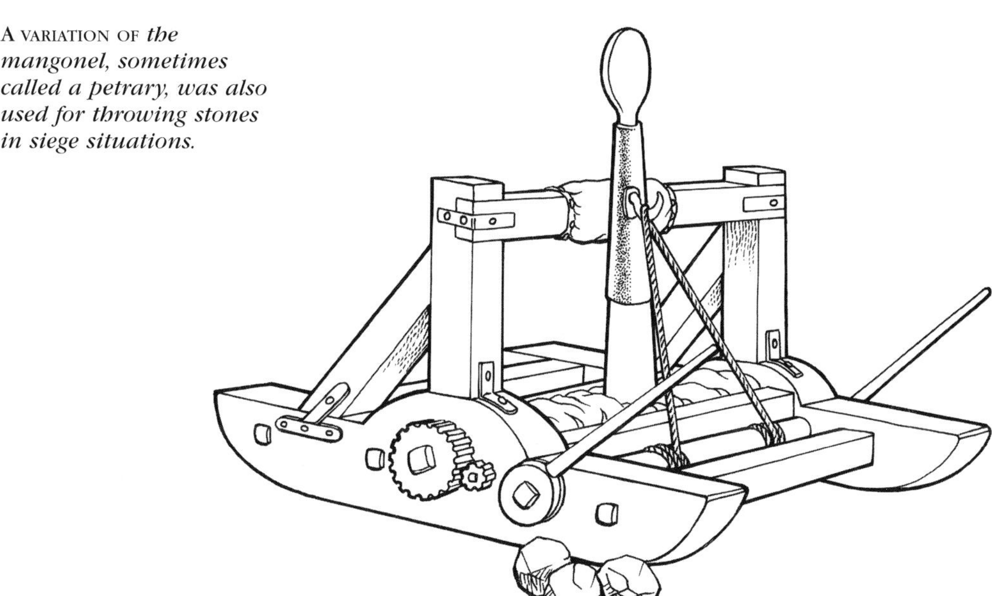

catapult-type weapons were used to hurl stones, as one would from the leather of an ordinary boy's catapult. Jaime I the Conqueror, king of Aragón, used catapults to shoot inflammable material. On occasion the severed heads of captured defenders were hurled back into a town or castle. At Auberoche the body of a captured English messenger, sent out by the garrison, was placed by the French on an engine with his message tied round his neck and hurled back inside. The English were 'much astonished when they saw him arrive'.

One of the most common engines was the mangonel. Again this term can be used in different ways, but it usually meant a hurling engine with a spoon-like arm. The arm was wound back on twisted ropes and then released so that torsion made it spring forward to hit a bar and release the object (usually a large stone) placed in the bowl of the spoon. A medieval Arabic writer said that he could not give all details of how the mangonel worked, since it involved 'secrets that must be well kept'. He did mention that cherry wood was best for the arm because it was flexible. The word probably derived from the Greek *mangano,* meaning 'to crush', becoming the Arabic *al-majanech.* We can therefore translate a mangonel as 'a crusher'. Another similar term for these engines was 'petrary', meaning simply 'a stone thrower'. Sometimes these engines were placed on a wheeled platform to move into position. A Turkish type of mangonel was described with a moveable bowl for the spoon so that the trajectory of the stone could be altered. That engine had a range of 110m (360ft). Stones were the usual objects hurled, but we hear of metal projectiles as early as the tenth century, Greek Fire slung by Geoffrey V at Montreuil-Bellay in the twelfth century, 'a rain of metal' (lead) hurled by Edward I against Edinburgh in the thirteenth century, manure at Karlstein in the fifteenth century and body parts at Malaga (1490).

Inevitably we can only examine the main engines in a single chapter, but the medieval terms for them suggest at least a fairly large number of variations on the theme. Hurling engines appear, for example, as *paterells, fonevols, fundae, tormenti, springalds, brigolles, algarradas, calibres* and *chaabla,* as well as mangonels and petraries.

Siege Towers

Belfries, or siege towers, appeared at almost every major siege in the central Middle Ages. They had long been used to approach walls. The basic idea was to produce a tower structure that could equal or overlook the wall so that men could be

THE DRAWBRIDGE ATTACHED *to the top of a belfry is being lowered on to a tower in a 14th-century illustration. The inside of the belfry contained ladders for attacking troops to climb to the top of the tower and assault the castle.*

stationed on it to attack or to mount the wall. Usually these towers were built at a distance from the wall, placed on wheels, and drawn up to attack positions, sometimes on a specially prepared ramp. The belfries might be simply pulled by ropes, but there were more sophisticated methods, such as the use of pulleys. We also hear of prefabricated towers, brought to the siege ready to assemble. Belfries were sometimes used to cover mining operations underneath them. They might also contain various engines such as rams, catapults or mangonels, but primarily their function was to carry men to the wall. Archers were commonly used to man the belfries.

Belfries typically had several storeys and might be mounted by internal ladders. They were normally made of wood and were often covered by hides to guard against fire - men were sometimes stationed on the top with water to put out possible fires caused by the enemy. As early as 885 the Vikings at Paris produced belfries with roofs, each with 16 wheels. A belfry made for Jaime I of Aragón in Mallorca had two platforms, one half-way up, one at the top, and was covered with hurdles. One at Lisbon was 29m (95ft) high, and one at Acre had five platforms. Often a ladder or bridge was ready at the top to use for mounting the wall.

Belfries were not immune to attack. Some got stuck in mud while being pushed forward, or even toppled over. Sorties were often aimed at damaging or destroying belfries. They were not always the most stable or solid of structures, and on occasions they were knocked apart or simply collapsed, killing the men inside - sometimes several hundred of them. A tower used by the Sword brothers during the Baltic Crusade simply blew over in a strong wind.

Deception in Siegecraft

Deception could be as important a weapon in sieges as armaments. Sometimes, the attackers could make an entrance into a castle by tricking the defenders into letting them through the gate, for example, by dressing themselves as harmless people or even as women. Sometimes a castle could be taken by working with a traitor already within the walls who would let the attackers in. Success could come through treachery or by dirty tricks. In the late thirteenth century, Geoffrey de Bruyères smuggled himself into the castle of Arakhoron in Morea. Once inside he managed to get the castellan drunk and then stole the keys to let in his men. At La Rochelle, the dim-witted and illiterate Count Philip Mansel was brought down by a trick. The French mayor of the town knew his man. He invited Mansel to lunch and produced a fake letter. This letter was supposedly from Edward III, and the mayor read it out. The missive ordered Mansel to bring his troops out of the castle the following day and put them on parade in the town square. Mansel fell for the trick and the following day obeyed the 'orders' of the king. His men were surrounded and had to surrender, as did the empty castle. Another method that often proved successful was through giving the appearance of massive strength and making threats that persuaded the enemy to surrender. Often, however, the walls had to be passed by force.

Concentric Castles

The constant struggle between attackers and defenders to gain the upper hand was moved on in the central Middle Ages by the development of expensive and complex castle designs. We have already noted the emergence of rounded towers. The next major step forward in castle design came with the improvement of outer defences.

The main idea of the concentric castle was that it had more than one line of outer walls. If there were two surrounding walls, the inner wall would be higher than the outer wall, so that the one could be defended more easily from the other. We

BEAUMARIS CASTLE, SEEN *from an aerial view, was built for Edward I by Master James of St George on the island of Anglesey, one of that king's series of great Welsh castles. It is concentric, with two surrounding walls and has rounded towers. It was never completed and never attacked.*

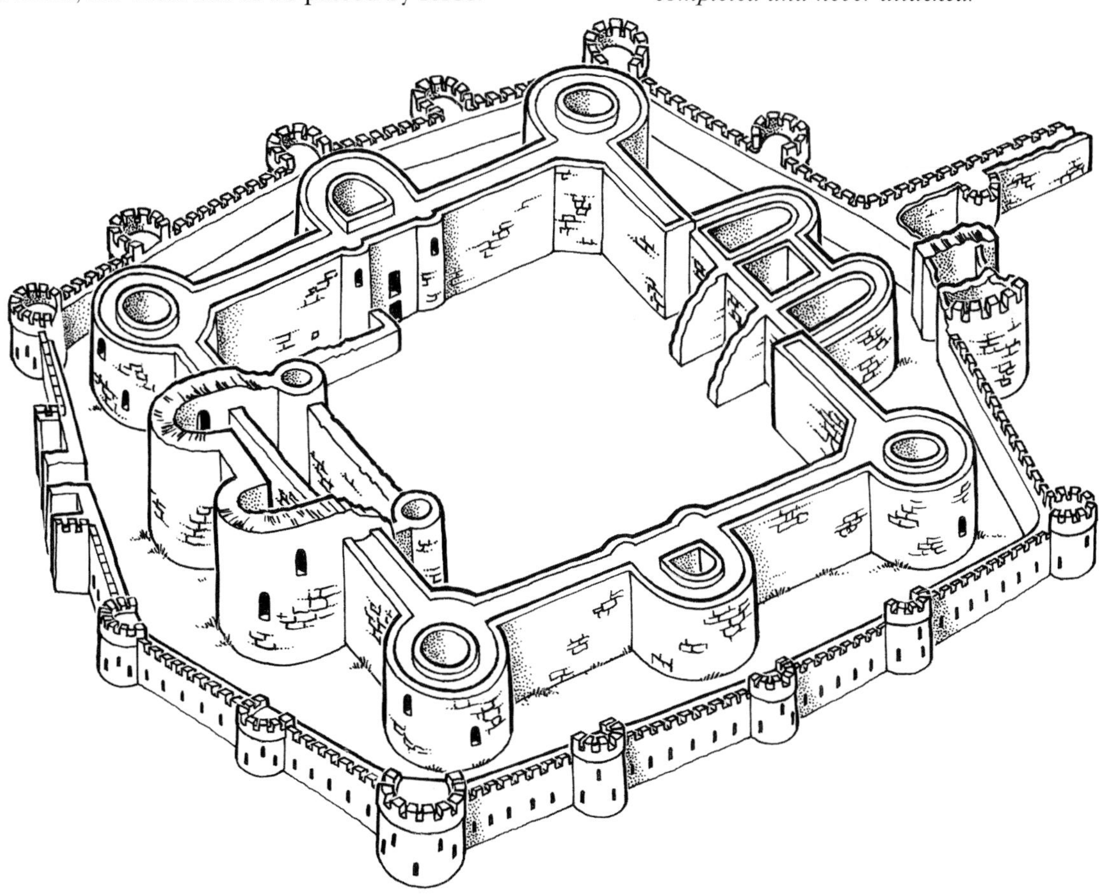

have seen some moves towards this concept, for example at Château-Gaillard, which was not concentric but did allow the defence of each of the two outer baileys from the one next in line. The idea of wall towers that projected beyond the wall was another relevant development that allowed the defence of the wall sideways on from the tower. The development of rounded structures for corner towers, wall towers and keeps also contributed to the new concept, moving away from the old rectangular design.

The emphasis in new castles tended to move to the outer wall rather than the keep. This may be seen in the polygonal French castles of the thirteenth century, for example, those built at Angers and Boulogne. Given this move, it was important to make sure the entrance was well defended and one sees improved gateways, often built within a tower or between two towers, perhaps with a double entry, a winding or angled entry, and possibly one or more portcullises.

One of the most important groups of improved castles was that built by Edward I of England during his conquest of Wales. These had all the marks of recent development and also brought the idea of concentric walls (more than one wall completely surrounding the castle) to a new level of achievement. The major concentric castles in this group are Rhuddlan, Harlech and Beaumaris. All three were built by Edward I's great architect, Master James of St George. Rhuddlan in Flintshire south of Rhyl was, like Harlech, built on a previously fortified site. Master James rebuilt it from 1277 on a concentric plan. It has a broad

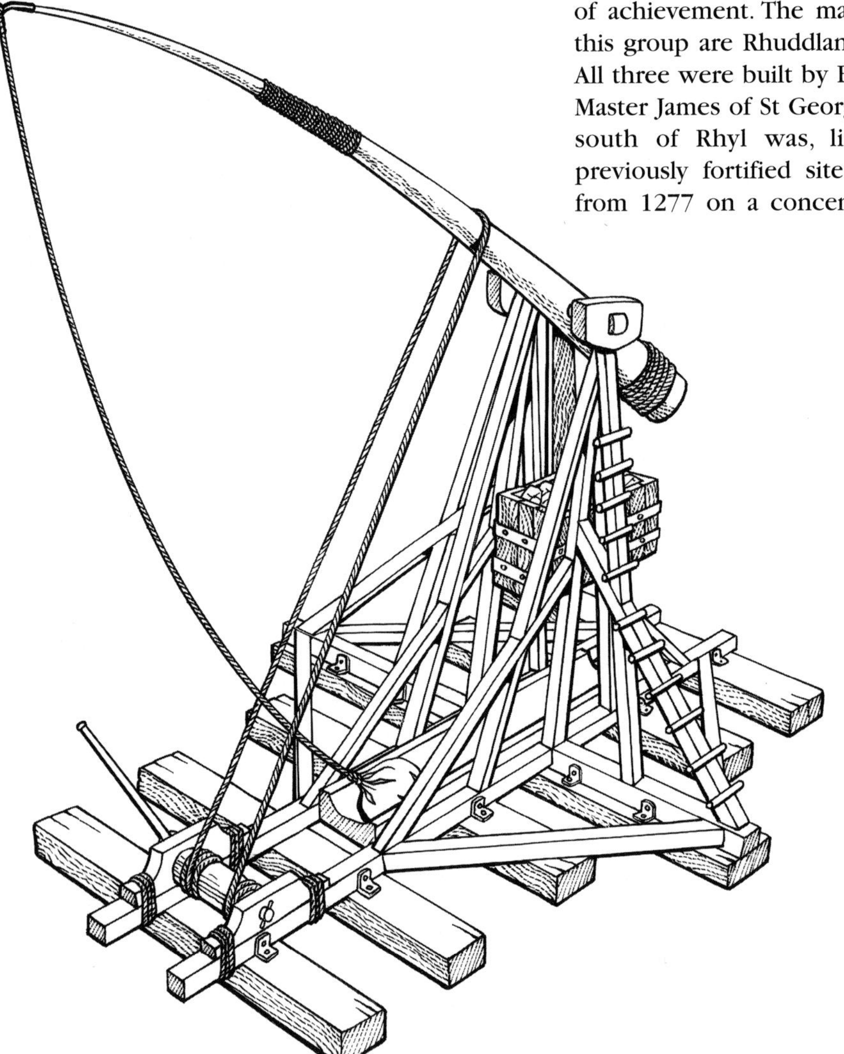

THE TREBUCHET WAS *one of the two major siege weapons invented in the medieval period. Its long tapering wooden arm was wound down and held in place. To the thin end was attached a sling in which the missile - usually a large rock - was placed. To the thick end was attached a very heavy weight - perhaps a crate of large stones. When released the weight dropped, the arm was flung up, the sling was thrown over violently and the missile hurled with great force.*

moat. The inner bailey is six-sided, with the two shorter walls on the east and the west having double towers. There are single towers in the north and south walls. The outer bailey wall is lower with a rampart around it. Harlech in Merioneth was begun in 1283. It was built on the River Dwyryd and cost £9500. Two sides were protected by a very wide moat. The gatehouse, facing east, has twin towers. The inner curtain wall has a rounded corner tower. The outer curtain is lower. Harlech castle replaced an older motte-and-bailey castle, and a moat separated the castle from the town. Beaumaris, perhaps the most imposing of the three, was built on the island of Anglesey from 1295. The inner bailey is rectangular with massive mural drum towers and two double-towered gates. The roughly octagonal outer bailey was never completed and it was never attacked.

One cannot omit a mention of Conway and Caernarvon, also built by Master James for Edward I in North Wales. Caernarvon was built from 1283. Like Harlech, a moat separated Caernarvon castle from the town. It had an unusual figure of eight shape and was never completed. It was not concentric but was a unique work said to be influenced by a view of the defences of Constantinople. Conway was also not concentric, having two main wards side by side. It did have double walls at the eastern and western ends, while the other sides (defended by water or moat) did not need additional outer walls.

New Siege Weapons of the Later Middle Ages

The massively strong castles that developed in the central medieval period made life difficult for besiegers. The old siege methods were still used and could be successful, but there was an increased demand for more powerful weapons to assist the attackers.

The first major original siege weapon of the Middle Ages was the trebuchet. The main point of difference with this weapon from others was that it worked by means of a counterweight. It remains uncertain at what date the trebuchet first appeared. The first clear evidence is from the thirteenth century, but it is probable that experiments with counterweights occurred at least in the previous century. Possible early appearances include at Lisbon in 1147, where we hear of Balearic *fundae,* William the Lion of Scotland's engine at Wark in 1174 (which had a sling), Richard the Lionheart's 'balearic slings' in the late twelfth century, and Jaime I of Aragón's *fonevols.* Any or all of these might have been trebuchets, but in no case does the literary evidence allow us to be certain.

The trebuchet depended on the use of a long and fairly flexible wooden arm, like that on the mangonel but supported by a pivot on a frame. The shorter and thicker end of the arm carried a crate, or something similar, that could be loaded with very heavy weights – perhaps stones or lead – to act as a counterweight. To the longer and thinner end of the arm was attached a sling. This end had to be winched down, thus lifting the counterweight into the air. The sling was then loaded with the missile, perhaps a large rock. A lever released the arm, which pivoted up into the air, carried by the counterweight dropping at the other end. The thin arm rose and the sling was thrown over and forwards, thus releasing the rock.

It is probable that there were experiments with the trebuchet in the twelfth century. By the thirteenth century the weapon had certainly arrived, and was soon recognized as the most powerful of all siege engines. The effect of the counterweight, and the extra power engendered by using a sling, meant that larger rocks could be hurled than had hitherto been possible, and they could be thrown with considerable force. Besiegers now had better hopes of battering down strong walls.

Egidio Colonna, who worked for Philip IV, king of France (1285–1314), could describe four different types of trebuchet. A later experiment, carried out for Napoleon III, produced a trebuchet that could hurl a stone weighing 11kg (25lb) some 182m (200 yards). A modern experiment showed that it took a 24-tonne (27-ton) counterweight to hurl a 1000-kg (2200-lb) stone, and that it was very accurate. The impact of the trebuchet on siege warfare was enormous. One trebuchet, used on behalf of Jaime I of Aragón against a castle in Ibiza, hurled just 10 stones. It was enough to make the defenders surrender. At Castelnaudry in the fourteenth century, three large stones were chosen for throwing. The first demolished a tower; the

SIEGE CANNONS WERE *developed from the 14th century and became increasingly efficient and important through the later Middle Ages. The word cannon comes from the Greek* kanun *via Latin* canna, *meaning a tube. The typical type was the bombard (right) made, for example, of iron and bound with iron hoops. A mobile chamber or breech was a common means of loading the gunpowder. By 1500 cannons were heavier and more powerful. An ordinary bombard could fire a shot of 136kg (300lb) but many were far larger.*

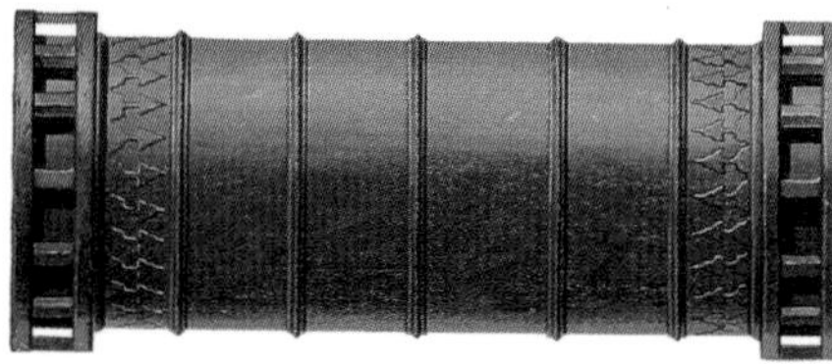

THE CANNON OF MEHMET II *(left) was cast in 1464 and used by the Turks to protect the Bosphorus Straits. The gun was divided into two parts for ease of transportation. It weighed 18.2 tonnes (18 tons) and was 5.25 metres (17ft) long.*

second destroyed a chamber; the third shattered on impact and killed many defenders.

The trebuchet could damage or destroy even massive walls and evened up the struggle between attack and defence. In the fourteenth century another new weapon made its appearance. At first it was not especially impressive. Gunpowder has a long history and was known to the ancient Chinese, though apparently used only to make fireworks. Roger Bacon, the western friar and scientist, described experiments with gunpowder in 1249. An Arab writer in the same century had also experimented with explosive powders, and gunpowder was used by the Moors in Spain in the fourteenth century. The *Milemete Manuscript* of 1326 illustrates a kind of cannon, shaped like a vase and having a touch-hole, ready to fire a bolt similar to that for a crossbow. In the first half of the fourteenth century there are several references to the use of gunpowder and cannons in western Europe, including in England, France, Belgium, Italy and Spain. Edward III of England used 10 cannons in the siege of Calais, and by 1345 there were no less than a hundred in the Tower of London. At first the noise of cannons seems to have made more impression than the firing of their shot, but by the fifteenth century they were more efficient and effective. They were built in increasing numbers and became the mainstay of besiegers.

The word cannon comes from the Greek *kanun,* meaning a tube. One early surviving cannon was an octagonal tube with a round bore. It had a breech block hammered in to place during casting. Cuprum and latten, both forms of brass, were used to make guns. But soon it was clear that cast iron was the best material. At first cannons were either placed on a mount to point them upwards or tied to a wooden board in order to tip

ILLUSTRATION OF THE *siege of Calais 1346–47. It was an early example of a siege where cannons were used by the attackers. Calais was besieged by Edward III after his victory at Crécy. Held by John de Vienne for French king Philip VI, the town was both blockaded from the sea and besieged from the land side. Smarting from his defeat at Crécy, Philip was reluctant to risk another engagement with the English, and little serious effort was made to relieve the city. The town surrendered in 1347.*

the weapon and aim it by placing wedges underneath. In the fifteenth century one finds trunnions (wheeled platforms) in use. Cannons were loaded either by a mobile chamber or thunder-box, or else at the breech. The chamber was filled with gunpowder and a heated touch applied to the hole in the tube or the touch-hole. The chamber was closed with a bung of soft wood to act as a wad between the charge and the shot. The bung would pop out like a cork, the idea being that the chamber itself should not explode. The mobile chamber was placed in the breech and clamped with an iron rod, then packed with tow. By the middle of the fifteenth century some very large cannons were being manufactured.

The Siege of Constantinople: 1453

Constantinople was a well-recorded siege. There are at least a dozen contemporary accounts of the famous event, including those by Doukas, Sphrantzes and Barbaro. The only problem is that the sources are nearly all Greek or western and inevitably provide a rather one-sided view. The main Arab account, by *Ashikpashazade*, is not so detailed, though it does give some balance.

Constantinople's position between Europe and Asia, and its growth into a major commercial centre, made it an inevitable target for attack. It possessed a marvellous position, protected by the sea on three sides – the Golden Horn to the north, the Bosphorus to the east and the Sea of Marmora to the south. The only land approach was from the west and was protected by imposing defences. Constantinople had withstood a myriad of sieges through the Middle Ages, from the Persians, the Arabs and the Rus to name but a few. It was ironic that the city first fell not to the barbarians or infidels from north, east or south, but to the Christians from the west, the outcome of the Fourth Crusade of 1203–4.

By this time, Christendom had divided into the Roman Catholicism of the West, and the Orthodox belief of the East led by Byzantium. Venice had seized control of the new crusade through the indebtedness of the other participants, and their need for Venetian naval transport. Under the blind doge Enrico Dandolo, Venice led the crusaders first, for commercial reasons, to attack Christian Zara until it surrendered. Then the crusade moved on to Constantinople, which was in chaos from internal political divisions.

The Fourth Crusade arrived before the walls of the city in June 1203. The walls were attacked and the Byzantines reacted in utter panic. The emperor, Alexius II, was deposed and Isaac II was restored with Alexius IV as co-emperor. There was another revolt within the city and this led not only to the deaths of Isaac II and Alexius IV but the proclamation of a new man, Murzurphlus, as Alexius V.

This series of changes weakened the unity and resolve of the citizens. The crusaders were now able to storm the walls by land and sea. Alexius V fled but was captured, blinded, and thrown to his death from the top of a column. Constantinople was sacked and a westerner, the count of Flanders, was named as the new Byzantine emperor, Baldwin I. A new Frankish Byzantine Empire was established. However, this only lasted until 1261, when Michael VIII Palaeologus restored Greek control. But the crusaders had ended forever the idea that Constantinople was invulnerable.

In the period leading up to 1453 Constantinople went through various further political crises. The greatest threat came from the Ottoman Turks. The city still resisted and survived, but around it Christian territory was falling into Turkish hands: Bulgaria by 1393, the Peloponnese by 1394, Belgrade in 1440. Constantinople was becoming increasingly isolated, an island in Turkish-controlled lands. Between 1393 and 1422 Constantinople withstood three major Turkish sieges while the city's population declined in numbers through the Black Death. Several times Byzantine emperors sought aid from the West. Constantine XI came to the throne in 1448. He was to be the last Byzantine emperor.

The Turks added to their own military expertise by borrowing from the West. They possessed a highly skilled army around the Janissaries, selected from the children of Christian slaves and trained purely for a military life. One area in which the Ottomans directed much effort was in siege weapons. A triumph for them was to win the support of the Hungarian engineer, Urban (Constantinople could not afford the salary he demanded). The Turks paid Urban and encouraged him to build a series of mighty cannons that were to be used in the great siege.

'The Turks brought up their artillery by the light of torches. They were screaming their war cries incessantly in an attempt to terrify us. Stones hailed from their engines like a dark cloud covering the sun and sky.'

– George Sphantzes, Greek chronicler

Mehmet II became the Turkish sultan for a second time in 1451. He had been sultan already from 1444 to 1446 as a boy. In 1451 he was still only 19. Mehmet was very studious and intelligent, and he liked to have histories of Rome read to him. He was young and ambitious, the son of a Christian slave girl. He was also fiercely hostile to Constantinople. Previous sultans had been content to let the city survive. Mehmet, however, began to close in on Constantinople by ordering the building of a new fort, the Rumeli Hisar (Cut Throat), on the European shore of the Bosphorus. When a Venetian ship tried to sail into the city it was shot at and sunk. Those who swam ashore were beheaded. These were the first actions in the siege. Mehmet raised an enormous army for the attack on the city, around 400 ships carrying some 258,000 men. They faced perhaps the best known defences in the world at the time. The city was surrounded by 14km (9 miles) of sea walls, and 6.4km (4 miles) of land walls fronted by an enormous ditch. There were 100 towers on the walls. The defences had fallen into disrepair in

THE TURKS ENTERED *Constantinople on 29 May 1453. The Byzantine emperor, Constantine XI, was killed. The sultan, Mehmet II, gave the city up to his troops to destroy and loot for three days.*

places, and desperate efforts were now made to repair them. A new boom was made from great timbers, joined by chains, and laid across the harbour of the Golden Horn to the tower at Pera. Appeals for aid were made to the West, but only some 700 Italians responded. As a contemporary writer records, there were 'hardly enough men to defend the circuit of the city'. Meanwhile, the Turks were using pen and ink to draw their own plan of the defences they were about to attack.

Mehmet examined the plans and decided to make his main attack in the Mesoteichion, through the Lycus Valley on the land side. There he made camp, setting up his red and gold tent. The engines were ordered up, including the new massive cannons made by Urban. The bombardment began. The first breach was made in the wall near the Charismian Gate, which shattered and collapsed, helping the Turks in their efforts to fill the ditch. The Greeks hastened to fill the breach in the wall with earth and timber.

Siege of Constantinople

1453

Sultan Mehmet II began to besiege Constantinople on 7 April 1453. The Turks already held much of Eastern Europe so the city was isolated and unlikely to receive more than minimal outside aid, which allowed the Turks to meticulously plan their assault. The Turks used large cannons made for them by the renegade Hungarian engineer, Urban. An Italian fleet broke through into the Golden Horn to give some relief to the city. Mehmet then by-passed the chain across the Golden Horn and took part of his fleet around Pera on rollers overland. They then took control of the Golden Horn and the city was completely blockaded. On 29 May they made a major attack in waves. The last wave was led by the crack force of the Janissaries. They got over the wall and at the same time broke through a small postern gate at Kerkoporta, which had been left open by mistake. Constantine XI was killed. The city was sacked for three days, after which time Mehmet halted the damage. Constantinople city became his new capital.

Constantinople, ancient Byzantium, stood at the point between Europe and Asia Minor and also between the Mediterranean and the Black Sea. It was thus important politically and economically.

1 Mehmet II established his camp outside the land wall from 7 April 1453. The city was cut off and the walls received a constant battering.

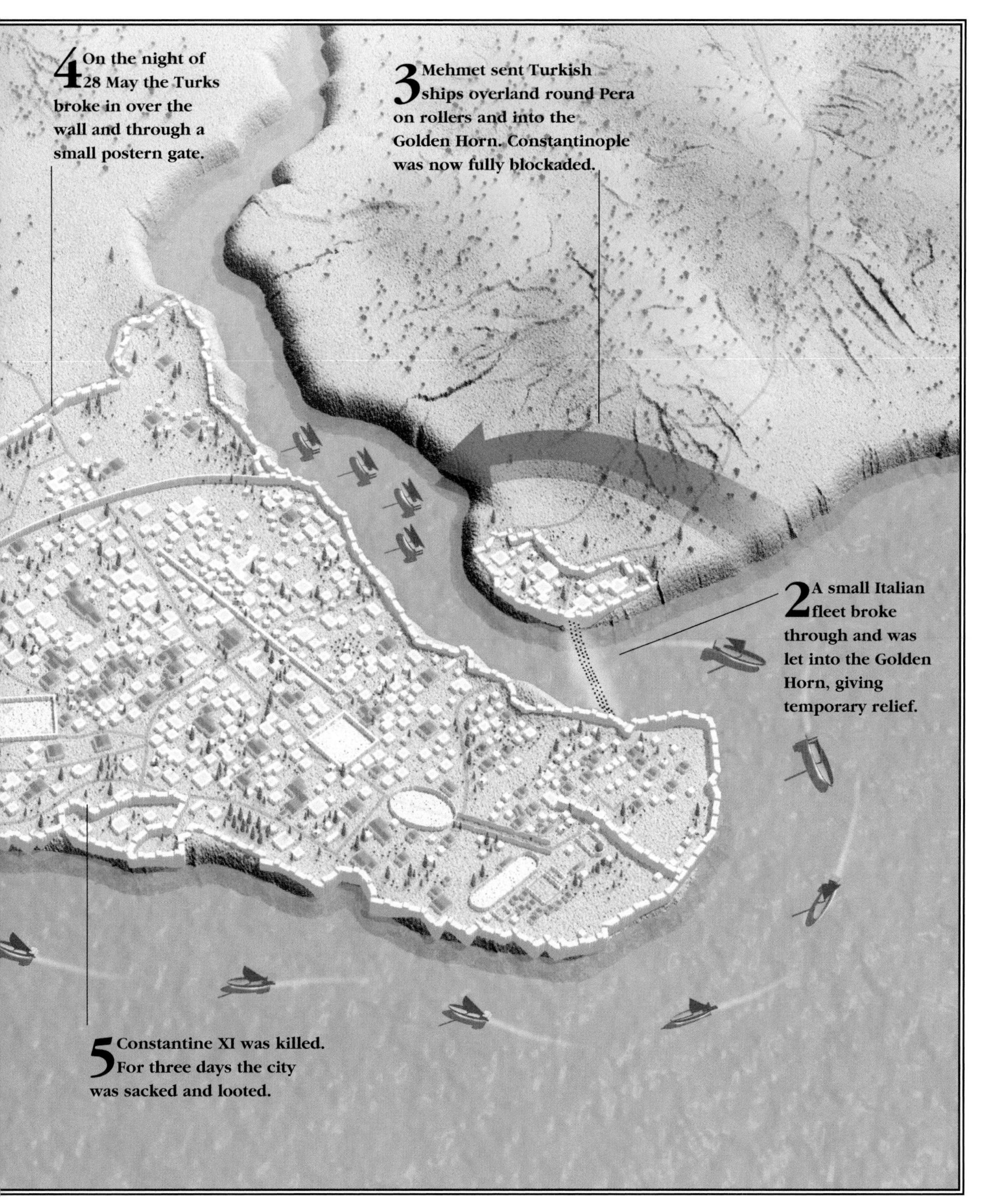
4 On the night of 28 May the Turks broke in over the wall and through a small postern gate.
3 Mehmet sent Turkish ships overland round Pera on rollers and into the Golden Horn. Constantinople was now fully blockaded.
2 A small Italian fleet broke through and was let into the Golden Horn, giving temporary relief.
5 Constantine XI was killed. For three days the city was sacked and looted.

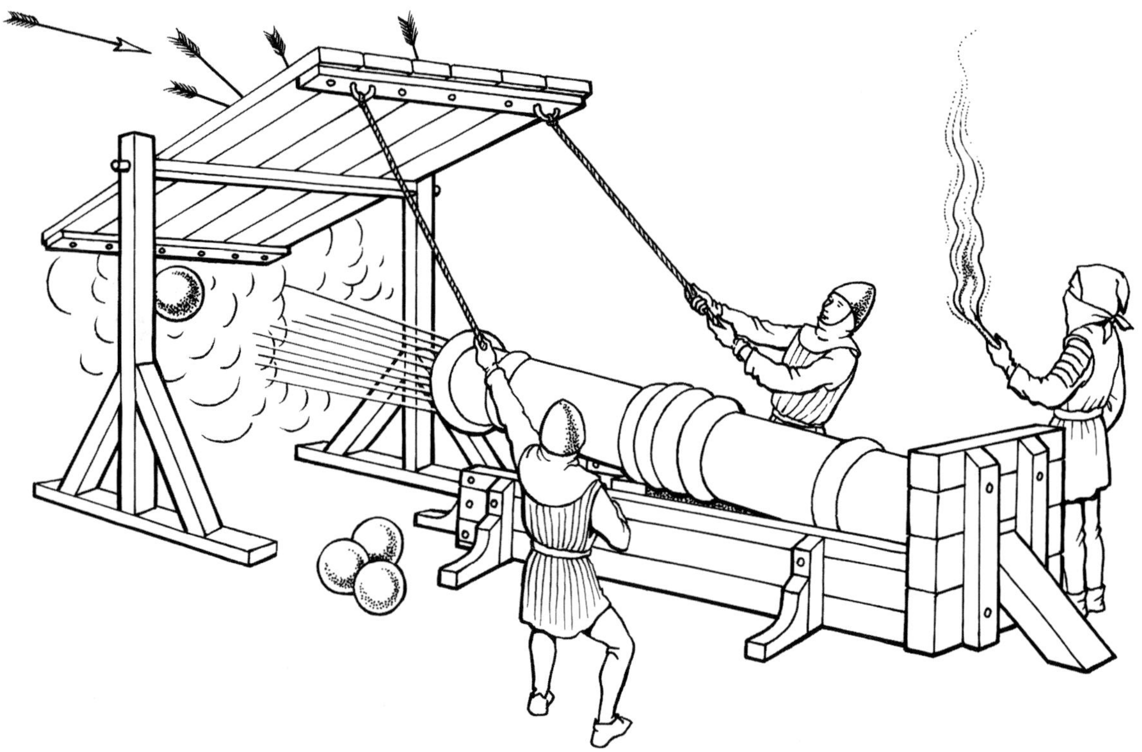

LARGE CANNONS BECAME *common by the late Middle Ages and some very large ones were used in 1453 at Constantinople. Here we see a wooden 'door' device used with a cannon. This was lowered to protect the men operating the cannon while emptying, cleaning and loading but it could be raised again for firing.*

Meanwhile, the Turks were tightening their hold. Two outer forts were captured along with an island in the Sea of Marmora. Prisoners were killed brutally, 'fixed by the fundament upon sharp stakes, which pierced them to the top of their heads', according to Jacopo Tedaldi, a Florentine soldier who was at the siege. On 18 April the Turks tried to cross the filled ditch, but again failed to break in.

There was a lull when a small fleet of Genoese galleys arrived. They survived a battering and were let through the boom at night. It was a small victory for the Christians. As a result the Turkish admiral, Balta, was ordered to be executed, though the sentence was commuted to the *bastinado* (beating with rods on feet and stomach) and dismissal. Now Mehmet decided on a new approach. He ordered ships to be taken into the Golden Horn overland, so by-passing the boom. A special track was devised and constructed via Galata. Cannons were fired to create smoke that would screen what was going on. In this way, seventy ships were hauled into the Golden Horn. Meanwhile, the Turks were carrying out preparations on land, including the construction of 14 mines. The Byzantines used Greek Fire to destroy the mines before they were used. Constantine XI, in company with George Sphrantzes, toured the walls to encourage the defenders. Treasure was melted down for coins to pay the troops.

The Turks constructed belfries and decided to make an all-out, concerted attack by land and sea. The Greeks made a procession around the walls carrying icons while bells were rung. The very last Christian service was held in Santa Sophia. The emperor climbed a tower on the wall and viewed the Turkish campfires in the Lycus Valley. The Turks prepared their artillery, bringing it up by the light of torches. The defenders took up their positions on the outer wall and the gates to the interior were locked behind them. It was to be a do-or-die fight. The attack commenced in the middle of the night, at 1.30 a.m. The Turks raised a massive noise with cymbals, pipes, trumpets and war cries. The attack came in waves, the weakest troops, the irregular *bashi-bazouks,* first. Orders were given by the sultan to kill them if they turned back. They reached the walls, but could not break in. After two hours the first attempt was abandoned. Now the cannons were fired in a tremendous barrage. A breach was made where the wall had been repaired. Dust and smoke filled the air. The second wave attacked into the breach, but were felled there or driven off. The dead filled forty carts and still bodies were left. The second wave had failed.

By now it was growing light. Mehmet prepared his final throw, the attack by his best troops, the Janissaries. Mehmet himself advanced to the edge of the ditch. One of the Greek commanders, the Italian Giustinian, was wounded and taken back through one of the gates, which badly damaged Greek morale. Others followed him and a panic ensued. At about the same time the Greeks attempted a sortie through a small postern gate in the wall. On their return they failed to close the gate and the Turks burst through it. The giant Hasan was first to make it on to the outer wall, which was soon captured.

The city was open. Many Greeks were killed, including Constantine XI. Later a body found wearing socks embroidered with eagles was said to be that of the emperor. In the massacre blood ran in rivers. Mehmet allowed the usual three-day sack - though he did rebuke one man for ripping up the paving. There followed an orgy of looting, seizing of valuables of all kinds and drinking of wine. At last it was over. A Greek described his city as 'desolate, lying dead, naked, soundless, having neither form nor beauty'.

Constantinople became Istanbul, a Muslim Turkish city and part of the Ottoman Empire. Mehmet II became known as Mehmet the Conqueror. Santa Sophia became the mosque of Aya Sofia. At first the Turks had difficulty in re-populating the city, but within 50 years it was larger than any city in Europe. Istanbul soon recovered as a commercial centre, but the Byzantine Empire was dead and the world had a new map. A great siege had altered history and its effect is still felt.

A Changing Battlefield

The trebuchet and the cannon had altered the balance in siege warfare. Walls and towers were no longer sufficient protection. The great age of the castle was coming to its end. Late medieval castles and towns did seek to improve their defences against the new weapons. This was done by building very thick walls and making ever broader moats so that weapons could not easily be brought up close.

Castle dwellers also improved their defensive weaponry. It was not easy to use trebuchets for defence, but cannons could be employed. Gunloops were made in the walls, smaller squatter towers were designed to be gun platforms, and special outer platforms were constructed beyond the walls to hold batteries of cannons.

These efforts had some effect, but they could not entirely nullify the force of artillery attack on the walls. Gradually men abandoned the hope of permanent defence of this kind, though new very powerful forts could protect small groups of men. Increasingly, however, the emphasis in warfare moved away from the siege to battles fought in the open. Fewer new castles were built, and those that were tended to place more emphasis on comfort for residence, with slighter walls and more windows to give light inside. Some were built in brick rather than stone, clearly for appearance rather than defence. In France the term 'château', which had meant 'castle', came to mean 'country house'.

The development away from castle building and siege warfare was never 100 per cent. Towns sought to make their defences as powerful as possible and new designs for shapes of towers and walls were tried. Town defences and forts, designed to hold and oppose artillery, were built with bastions, hornworks and ravelins. Sieges still had to be undertaken, but the switch was important and enduring. Warfare in the early modern age, and later, was fundamentally different from that of the Middle Ages.

CHAPTER 5

NAVAL WARFARE

Sea warfare in the medieval era is often dismissed as little more than rather soggy battles fought on the same principles as land fighting – hand to hand – with the ships playing little role except as floating platforms for marines. Such a view amounts nearly to a caricature of naval war in the Middle Ages.

The final stage of medieval sea battles consisted of grappling the enemy and fighting it out on deck. Leading up to that denouement, however, was a series of steps that, when viewed as a whole, make it plain that sea fighting was the most technically and logistically demanding side of medieval war, and was often played for the highest stakes.

The first element of medieval naval combat was providing ships, an enormous task calling for skilled carpentry and large resources. Even a ship

SPANISH SHIPS ATTACKING *the Earl of Pembroke's expedition, 1372, from a 15th-century manuscript of Froissart's* Chronicle. *Such illustrations, usually created by people who had no experience of ships or the sea, helped create the impression that medieval naval war was a disorganized free-for-all.*

as simple in plan as a Viking warship has been estimated to have cost something in the order of 4000 cattle to build and equip. For most countries of medieval Europe, this cost made a standing navy impracticable, but even so rulers strained their authority to force merchants to turn over their ships for use in war. Once equipped, navies had to have at least some maintenance system and organized supplies, unlike many armies of the era. In addition, while a land army could do without experienced commanders (although this was certainly undesirable), a ship would be lost without a captain who had undergone thorough training. The operation of a substantial fleet called for a large number of men with carefully honed technical skills, besides the ability to fight, which they shared with their brethren on land.

When a fight at sea took place, it was preceded by careful manoeuvring to gain the advantage of wind and wave. This positioning was vital since the most essential part of the battle was preliminary bombardment - with arrows, javelins, rocks, Greek Fire (perhaps even jars of scorpions or quicklime) - from a range of less than 100m (328ft) if the weapons were to be effective, and preferably with the wind assisting their flight. Medieval war at sea resembles nothing so much as two castles moving close and trying to take each other by storm. Effective defences aboard ship, quality of 'siege' equipment, favourable position, fighting ability and organization all made a difference.

Ships played an essential role in medieval war in both northern and Mediterranean waters. Besides use as warships to attack enemy fleets, ships could carry men to make surprise raids on enemy coasts. They transported men, horses and supplies. Privateering (and piracy) were very common, whether intended to deprive the enemy of needed supplies or just in attempts to get rich by seizing merchant ships. Medieval mariners even mastered the techniques of amphibious assault, beaching ships in the presence of the enemy and disgorging knights ready-mounted on their steeds, or sometimes mounting siege towers or battering rams on ships to breach the sea walls of land fortifications. Yet warships were *not* intended to sink enemy vessels, but rather to capture them. Mentions of waterline rams vanish from the sources from the seventh century on. In fact, the frame-built ships of the north were ill-suited to

RECONSTRUCTION OF A *7th-century Byzantine* dromon. *This ship was built for speed and manoeuvrability. Its single sail could be lowered and the oars relied upon during engagements. Note the syphon for Greek Fire in the bows.*

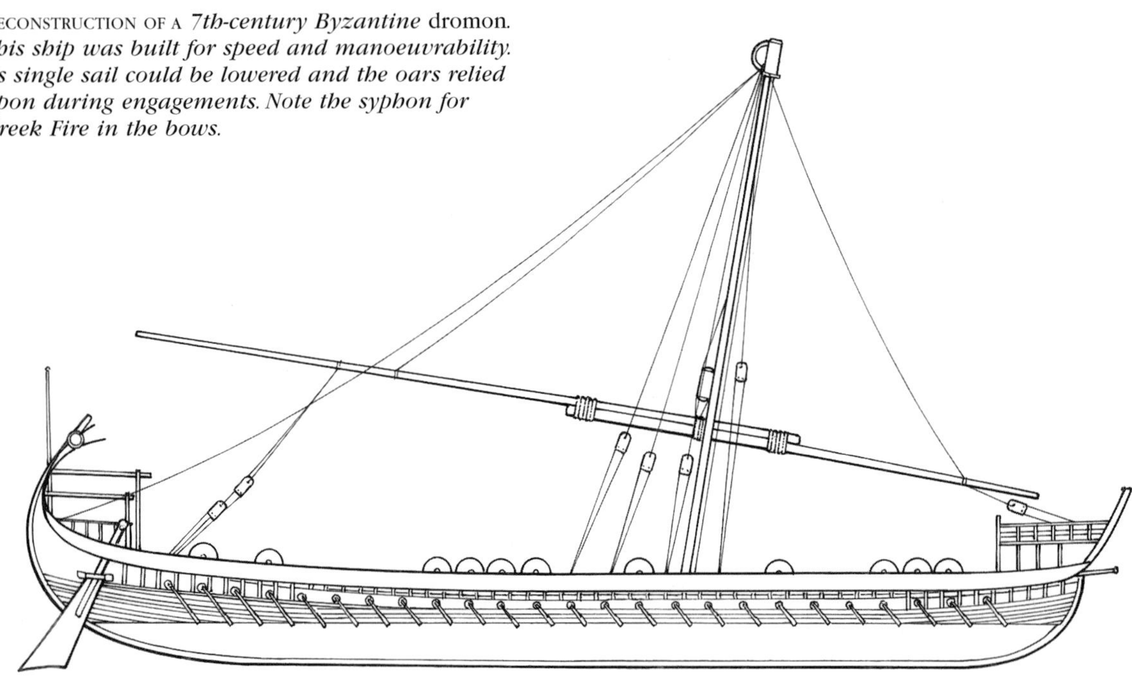

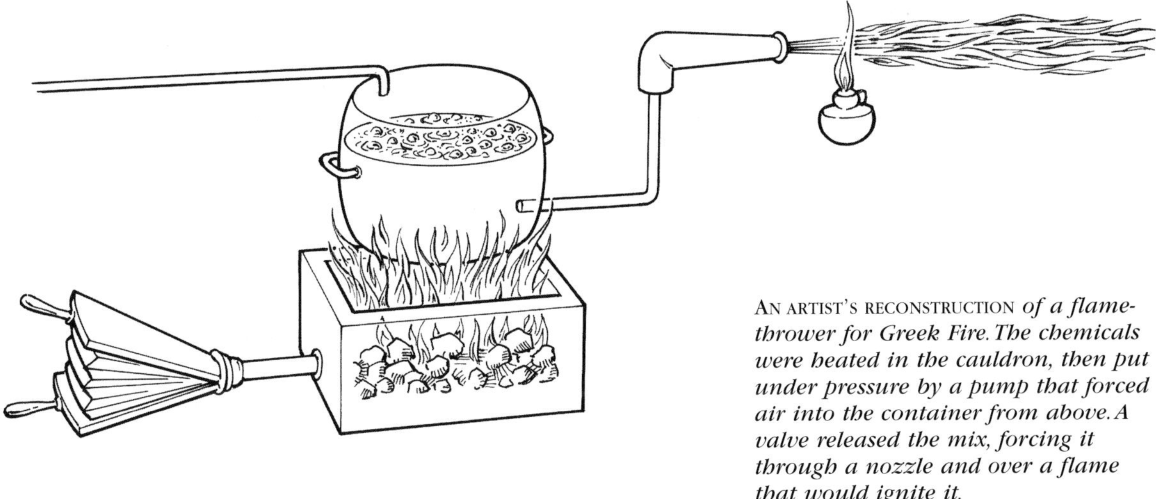

AN ARTIST'S RECONSTRUCTION *of a flame-thrower for Greek Fire. The chemicals were heated in the cauldron, then put under pressure by a pump that forced air into the container from above. A valve released the mix, forcing it through a nozzle and over a flame that would ignite it.*

ramming, and as more and more warships relied on sails rather than oars in battle, any attempt to ram would have been ludicrous.

As a last general point, it must be noted that the history of medieval naval war has many more unanswered questions than its terrestrial counterpart. Partly this is because of a traditional scholarly prejudice: naval war has seemed like alien territory, without the great deeds that enliven accounts of chivalric war. This prejudice was already present among medieval chroniclers. Few of these authors seem ever to have been to sea, or even to have talked to a seaman. It is impossible to reconstruct many of the great sea battles of the Middle Ages because the chroniclers sum them up with a couple of vague sentences or - worse yet - draw on classical authors like Vegetius to inform their imaginations about medieval war that was actually fought in very different ways. Written sources and drawings of ships are vague and impressionistic until the late fourteenth century, and there have been very few archaeological finds of medieval ships. So any study of medieval navies is very much a work in progress.

The Early Medieval Mediterranean

For centuries, Roman emperors maintained a fleet in the Mediterranean to suppress piracy and transport troops or important messages rapidly to the provinces of their far-flung empire. The ships were not needed for major fleet actions, so their rams were gradually replaced with a beak above the surface of the water. This was used to hold an opposing ship for boarding. These vessels evolved into the *dromon,* the main warship of the Byzantine Empire. The *dromon* was a simple galley, propelled in battle by one or two banks of oars with about 50 rowers on average, and also equipped with a square sail and a single mast that was lowered before a fight. Lighter, smaller ships were used for scouting.

As Roman administration collapsed in the fifth century, maintenance of this fleet proved to be impossible, and the Vandals especially developed a major competing navy that ravaged coastal areas. In the sixth century, however, the Byzantine Empire (the surviving eastern half of the Roman Empire), started to build up a standing navy again. The navy was developed by Emperor Justinian (527-565), who needed a fleet for his grandiose plans to reconquer North Africa and Italy. The Byzantine invasion of North Africa in 533 succeeded, despite the major Vandal navy, thanks to a ruse: Justinian stirred up a revolt in Sardinia, the Vandal king took the bait and sent his fleet there to suppress the rebels, allowing the Byzantine expeditionary force to land unopposed.

Soon a new and much more serious threat appeared in the Mediterranean: the Muslims, whose sweeping conquests starting in the year

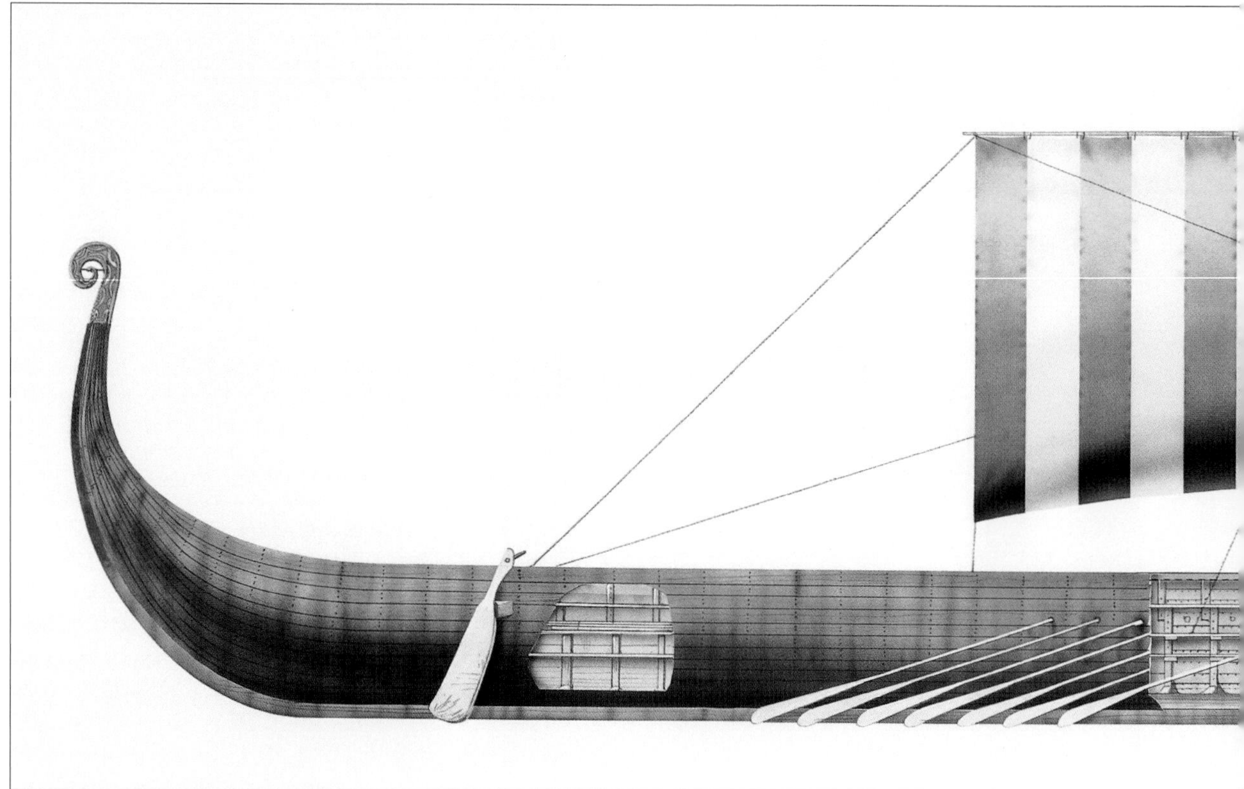

SIDE VIEW OF A TYPICAL *9th-century Viking longship. Deceptively simple in construction, such ships could penetrate far up rivers but were also strong enough to withstand travel on the open seas.*

633 soon gave them control of many coastal regions. The caliphs and their officials quickly recognized the benefits of the sea for conquest and effective rule of their new territories. Already in 648, Mu'awiya, at that time governor of Syria (he became caliph in 661), organized a navy, using his subjects' ships and crews.

The Muslims devastated Cyprus, and in 654 raided again and occupied the island. The alarmed Byzantines assembled a large fleet to stop this new scourge, only to be defeated in the following year at what is called *Dhat al-Sawârî* (the 'Battle of the Masts') off the south coast of Asia Minor. In this battle, the outnumbered Muslim force used unconventional tactics, chaining their ships together so their line could not be broken. They herded ships off one at a time to be boarded. Such a tactic would have made manoeuvring impossible, so they must have just sat and waited for the enemy to approach them. One account adds that the Muslim sailors used hooks to cut the rigging and sails of their opponents, which seems much less plausible, both because of the difficulty of wielding a blade very accurately at the end of an extremely long pole and because it is unlikely that the Byzantine *dromons* that opposed them would have had their sails up in battle. It is one of many cases where chroniclers' imaginations are suspect.

For the next three centuries, Byzantine-Muslim naval battles were common, each side jostling for control of islands and bases on the main sea routes. Of all these encounters, the most spectacular were the two Muslim sieges of Constantinople, in 673–679 and again in 717. Constantinople's land walls were impregnable; the key to conquest was blockade of the harbour and, if possible, attack against the weaker walls on the sea side. By 673 the caliphate had built up a substantial navy, making success a real possibility.

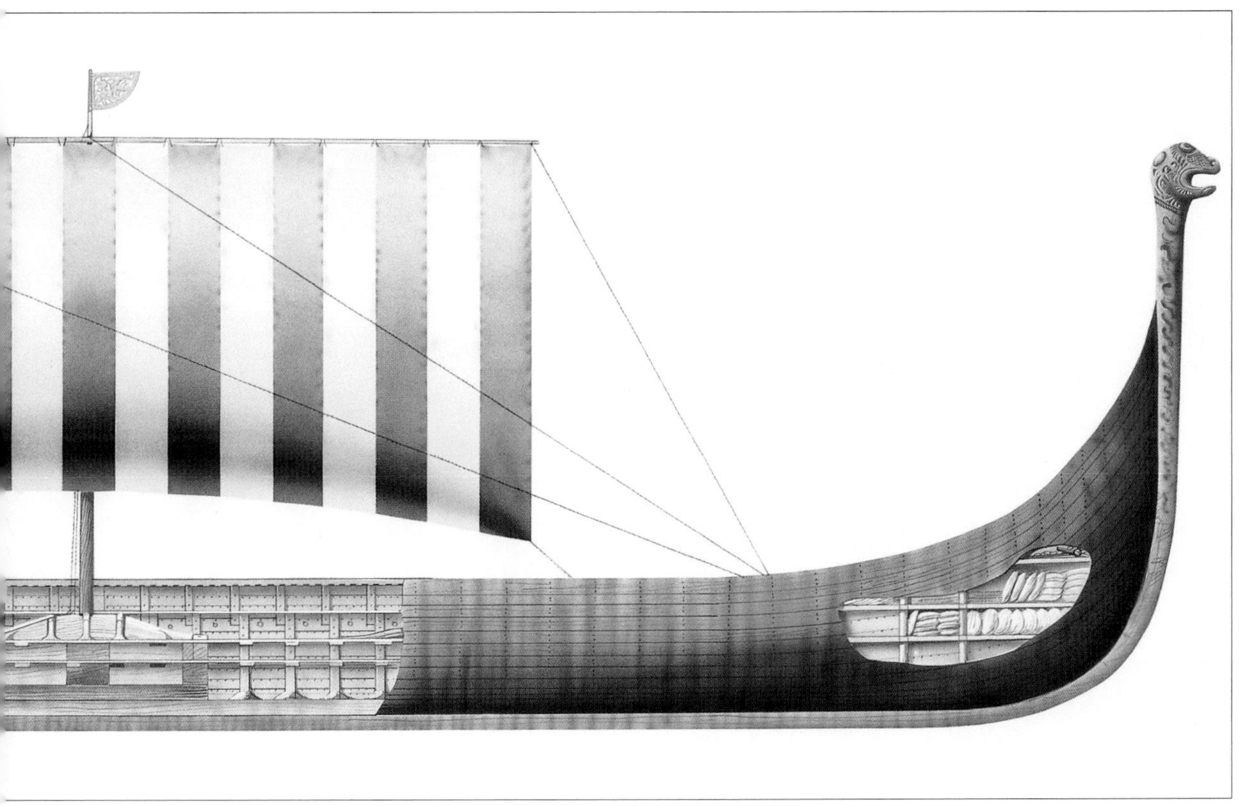

Nonetheless, the first siege ended when the imperial fleet broke out of the Golden Horn and turned the Byzantine secret weapon, Greek Fire, against the Muslim ships. Similarly, the 717 siege was broken when the Byzantine fleet sallied against the blockading navy, wreaking havoc with Greek Fire and, in the ensuing panic, providing the opportunity for the Christian crews of many caliphal ships to defect. The Muslim fleet had to withdraw. It was then mauled badly by storms and only about one-tenth of the ships made it home.

Greek Fire

Greek Fire was certainly the most exciting and evocative weapon of medieval fleets. Its recipe was a carefully guarded state secret, so well kept that today we no longer know how it was made. It was a flammable compound whose key ingredient was probably naphtha. Heated in a sealed cauldron under pressure, it was shot through a metal-sheathed tube mounted in the bows of ships. Placed in pottery jars, it was hurled at the enemy. It has been compared to napalm and reports say that only sand, vinegar or urine extinguished it. There are even descriptions of ships wrapped in vinegar-soaked felt for protection against it.

Greek Fire was an anti-personnel weapon, but it was not a 'ship-killer'. It was certainly effective in some circumstances, but must have been nearly as dangerous to Byzantine crews as to enemies. It is unlikely that a Greek Fire siphon could have had an effective range of more than a few metres. The great secret weapon was uncertain enough that no system of battle tactics was ever built around it, although Byzantine ships continued to use Greek Fire at least occasionally until the empire fell in the middle of the fifteenth century. There are also occasional mentions of Muslim navies employing it after they gained the secret in the ninth century.

More important than fleet actions, especially in the tenth century, was the use of ships for amphibious operations against enemy land positions. Thus in the Byzantine reconquest of Crete in 960 the fleet's most important role was to

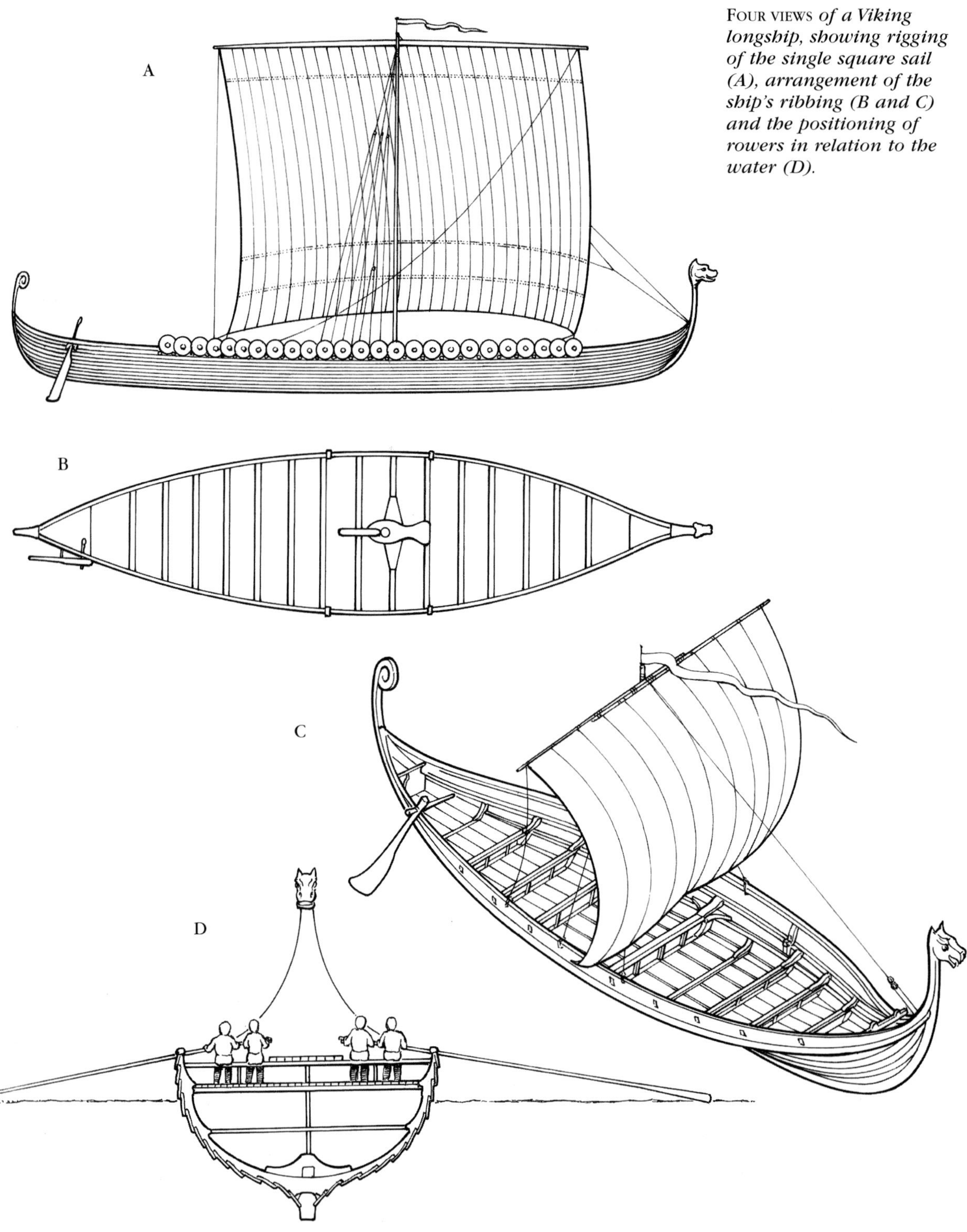

FOUR VIEWS *of a Viking longship, showing rigging of the single square sail (A), arrangement of the ship's ribbing (B and C) and the positioning of rowers in relation to the water (D).*

transport cavalry and troops. Ship ramps even allowed cavalry to land, already mounted, directly onto the beaches. By the eleventh century, however, the tide was turning against both Byzantines and Muslims in the Mediterranean, as the Italian city-states began to build navies and claim a role in both commerce and war.

The Viking Age

War at sea in northern waters in this early period was waged on very different terms. The ships employed were not all that different from those of the Mediterranean. Indeed, the warship of the early Middle Ages was a low, narrow galley, powered by a single bank of oars or a single square sail. The ships looked rather different to their southern counterparts since the wood most available for ships in the north was oak, a much harder wood that did not lend itself well to the mortise-and-tenon carpentry of Mediterranean vessels.

Instead, northern shipwrights created clinker-built ships, each strake of the ship's hull overlapping and nailed to the one beneath, after which the whole was caulked to make it watertight. The more important difference is that, after the Roman Rhine fleet dissolved in the fourth century, enemies who came by sea did not have to worry about counter-attack by an organized fleet. For centuries, there were no pitched battles at sea in the north. Ships did indeed play an important role in warfare, but primarily as transports for attackers who did most of their fighting on land.

The North Sea had a long tradition of piracy and raiding, involving most of the Germanic peoples whose territory bordered on the sea. In the third and fourth centuries, Frankish and Saxon raiders even reached the Mediterranean. For the most part, the preferred method of northern seamen was the hit-and-run raid. But warships also carried waves of Angles and Saxons to permanent settlements in what soon became known as England. While written accounts of the ships of this era are so vague as to be useless, a few archaeological finds suggest the capabilities of northern ships. The best-preserved ship - or rather, the mere outline of a hull - is the Sutton Hoo ship, used to bury an East Anglican king in the early seventh century. This ship was about 27m (89ft) long, 4m (14ft) broad, and 1.4m (4ft deep). It would have drawn about 0.6m (2ft) of water unladen, making it possible to travel far up major rivers. It was clinker-built, with nine narrow strakes per side, fastened with iron rivets. It probably had 20 pairs of oars, attached to the hull with *thole* pins. It is likely that the ship also had a mast and a single square sail that could be used to spare the rowers.

The feats of these early pirates were of a similar scope to those of the Vikings, Scandinavian raiders and at times conquerors who used their ships effectively against the land forces of western Europe. The earliest firmly dated Viking raid was the sack of the island monastery of Lindisfarne off the northeastern coast of England in 793. Over the next two centuries, the Vikings' ships took them to the British Isles, France, Germany and even Spain in a long series of devastating raids.

Charlemagne (768–814), the strongest ruler northern Europe had seen since the fall of the western Roman Empire, seems to have looked to Roman and Mediterranean models to fight these pirates. What he came up with was a two-pronged plan: coastal defences were constructed, and he also hoped to catch the raiders at sea. The Carolingian capitularies of 802, 808 and 810 ordered the construction of a war fleet. In 810 ships were ordered stationed on all of the major Frankish rivers, and in the same year a combined fleet was mobilized after Danes raided Frisia. They failed to meet the enemy at sea; in fact no Carolingian fleet ever met Viking ships in battle. Yet Charlemagne's efforts were very effective in convincing the raiders to concentrate on less-defended Ireland and England. Serious Viking damage to Francia only began after the Carolingian coastal defence system collapsed in 840, when Charlemagne's son Louis the Pious died.

Although there were no fleets to fight at sea, the Vikings' ships were essential to their success. They were, quite naturally a means of transport, carrying warriors and often horses surprising distances across the open sea. Such an accomplishment alone is impressive, considering the frailty and discomfort of Viking ships.

Viking Seine Campaign

Late 9th century

Viking raids were launched against most coastal areas of northern Europe throughout the eighth, ninth and tenth centuries. Ireland was an early target, followed by England and then Francia. Beginning in 885, a great Viking war band made a serious and concerted attempt to seize control of the rich heartland of Francia by sailing up the River Seine. In their first campaign (885-889) they met little opposition until they reached Paris, which they unsuccessfully besieged for nearly a year. Eventually they came to an agreement with the defenders before continuing upstream to pillage neighbouring Bugundy. They pillaged in central Francia (latter-day northern France) for more than two years, only withdrawing when they were paid a large Danegeld by the inhabitants. Further attempts followed, most notably in a great campaign of 890-92, during which the Vikings again attacked Paris as well as other northern towns. Note the large number of fortresses and fortified bridges along the major rivers.

SCANDINAVIA
IRELAND
BRITAIN
FRANCIA
MAGYARS
EMIRATE OF CÓRDOBA
BYZANTINE EMPIRE

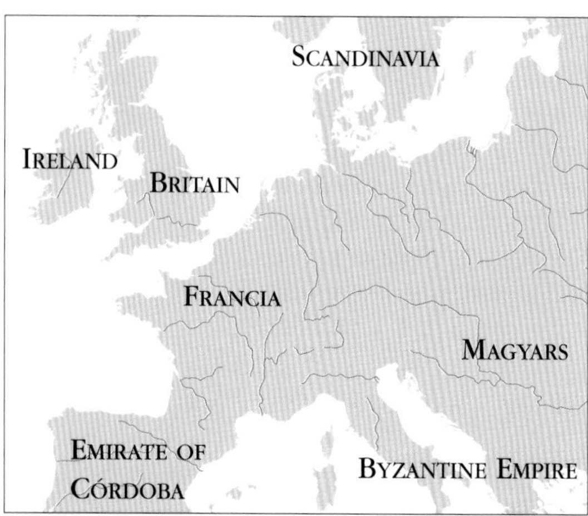

Vikings also raided southern France and Spain, even penetrating into the Mediterranean Sea as far as the southern coast of Italy. In 1057, the descendents of the Danish Vikings, the Normans, settled in lower Italy and Sicily.

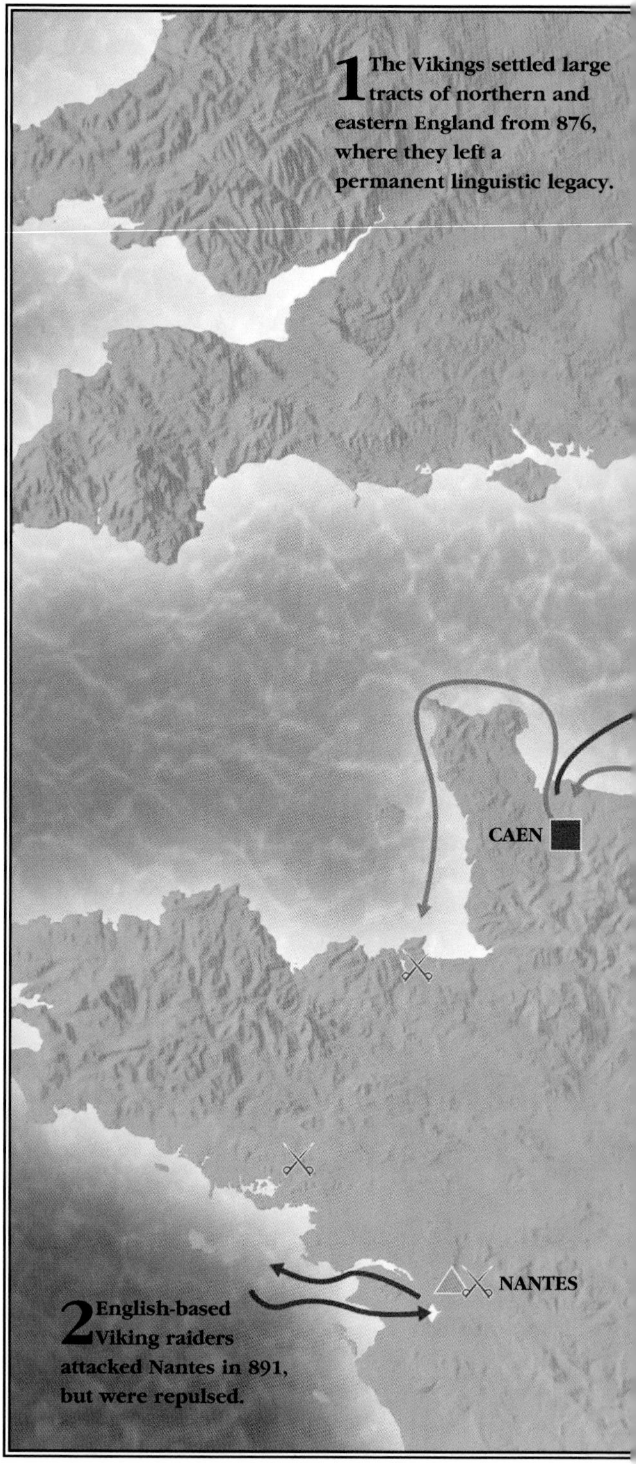

1 The Vikings settled large tracts of northern and eastern England from 876, where they left a permanent linguistic legacy.
CAEN
NANTES
2 English-based Viking raiders attacked Nantes in 891, but were repulsed.

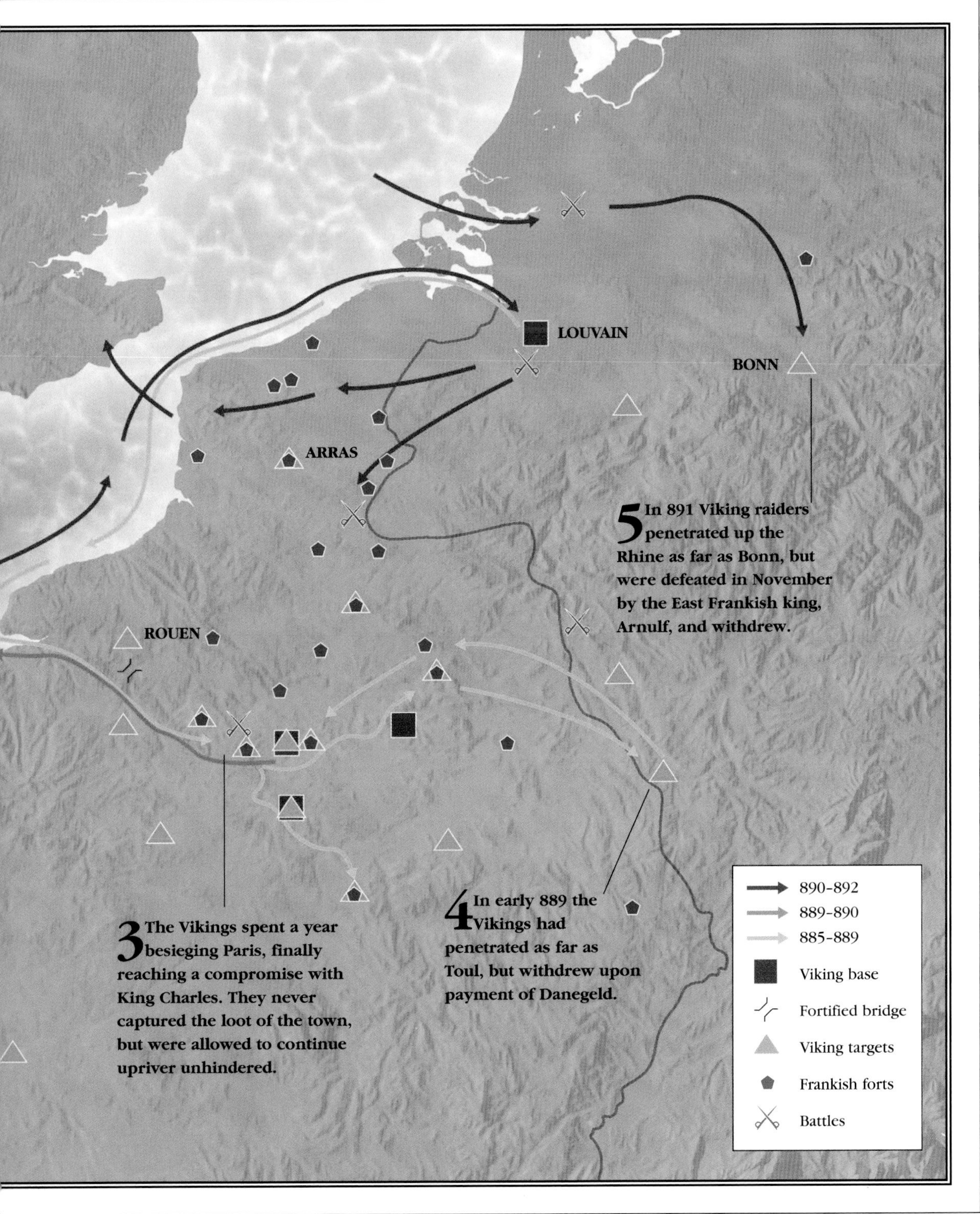
LOUVAIN
BONN
ARRAS
ROUEN
5 In 891 Viking raiders penetrated up the Rhine as far as Bonn, but were defeated in November by the East Frankish king, Arnulf, and withdrew.
3 The Vikings spent a year besieging Paris, finally reaching a compromise with King Charles. They never captured the loot of the town, but were allowed to continue upriver unhindered.
4 In early 889 the Vikings had penetrated as far as Toul, but withdrew upon payment of Danegeld.
890-892
889-890
885-889
Viking base
Fortified bridge
Viking targets
Frankish forts
Battles

They were essentially open shells, clinker-built, with no decking and almost no storage space. The men were usually forced to sit on their own sea chests while rowing. The vessels were long and narrow. An eleventh-century warship excavated at Skuldelev in Roskilde Fjord, Denmark, had a length to beam ratio of 7:1, making it speedy and flexible. Such ships were normally operated by 20 to 30 oarsmen, and the average ship probably carried between 30 and 50 men, although ships became larger over time. They could sail the open Atlantic – a replica of the Gokstad ship sailed from Norway to America in 1893 – but losses in heavy weather must have been frequent.

Viking ships also allowed a decisive element of surprise. The land forces they opposed were not professional armies, but were normally called to duty only for emergencies or war parties. Thus, by the time the opposition was mobilized, a Viking fleet could pillage a whole region and be safely on its way home again.

CONDITIONS ON A VIKING *longboat were cramped and crowded. Nearly every man would operate an oar, and skilled pilots would take turns at the steering oar and conning the ship from the bows.*

LESS EXOTIC THAN *the figures of Victorian romance, typical Viking warriors fought without body armour and were fortunate if they could afford a simple leather helmet. The wealthy had swords while the rest made do with clumsier weapons such as the axe.*

The Viking Seine Campaign: Ninth Century

The great Viking campaign on the Seine in the late ninth century, leading to the attack on Paris in 885, provides a useful example of how, at their most organized, Scandinavian raiders could use their ships in amphibious assaults - and also how land forces could stop them.

By 885 the Vikings were operating on a much larger scale than their earlier raids, amassing fleets that sometimes numbered hundreds of ships. Francia had suffered heavily, as by about 840 the Vikings had started establishing winter camps on small islands where they could protect themselves and their ships, using them as a base for further raids. In the 850s Paris was sacked twice. But King Charles the Bald finally developed an effective strategy to limit Viking mobility by constructing both forts and fortified bridges on the main rivers. So in the 860s most Viking bands had moved on to the easier pickings of England. However, England in turn had learned to resist them under the leadership of Alfred the Great. He ordered the construction of a fleet of large ships (which never met Viking ships in fights at sea, but may have had some deterrent effect) and, more importantly, established a series of fortified places to which people could flee for refuge during attack. So the Viking 'Great Army' looked elsewhere and went on to devastate much of Flanders. They raided the Rhine Valley in 882. And in 885 it was the turn of the Seine.

Perhaps as many as 600 Viking ships were involved in the 885-886 siege of Paris. At 30 to 50 men per ship, this would have constituted a very large fighting band for the era, a force well able to strip the lands bare along the Seine, although far from the 40,000 men the attackers were credited with by a frightened eyewitness who later wrote about the event. Since the Franks did not have a fleet able to stop the Northmen before they entered the river, defence relied on two elements: local drafts of troops that could fight the invaders on land, and a series of fortified bridges.

The logic of the fortified bridges was simple – they blocked all points upriver, unless the Vikings were willing to give up the advantage of their ships and travel on land. Those advantages were considerable, as ships provided an easy means to carry off slaves and other loot, provided easy and rapid transport and could be beached on an island that could easily be secured against attackers. In 885, however, the Frankish kings' policy of building such bridges was only partly successful. The Great Army was not stopped by the bridge over the Seine at Pont de l'Arche. The Paris bridge, however, was strongly held, even though its defences were not complete.

Consequently, the Vikings had to capture Paris to continue their raid into the heartland of the Frankish kingdom. Paris itself was a tempting prize for the raiders, but was not an easy nut to crack. Its population, only a few thousand strong, still lived mostly on the Île de la Cité, an island connected to the banks of the Seine by bridges defended by two forts.

The Vikings tried to take the northern fort by storm on 26 November 885, running their ships up to the base of the tower. This gave the fighters the protection of the gunwales as long as possible before they leapt ashore. The attack was only beaten off with great difficulty and the tower partly destroyed, but built again during the night. The next day the attackers tried undermining the tower's foundations with iron picks, only to be driven back by attackers who rained down on them both stones and buckets of a heated mixture of oil, wax and fish that got under armour and stuck to the skin. Despite being egged on by the Danish women with encouragement and mockery, the Vikings had soon had enough. They constructed and fortified winter quarters, protecting themselves and their beached ships with a ditch and simple rampart of stakes. They built battering rams and tried to craft a *ballista*. (Our witness gleefully reported that it collapsed and killed several attackers.) Apparently fearing that a Frankish army would soon relieve the Parisians, the Vikings then tried a desperate and expensive measure. They gave up three of their own warships for use as fireships, filling them with combustibles and hauling them upriver with cables pulled from the banks, hoping to ignite and burn down the bridge. This would have left the defenders in the tower cut off from any aid from the city. Unfortunately (from the Viking perspective), the ships crashed on the stone piers of the bridge, failing to do any serious damage.

> *'Then King Alfred ordered "long-ships" to be built with which to oppose the Viking warships. They were almost twice as long as the others.... They were built neither on the Frisian nor on the Danish pattern, but as it seemed to Alfred himself that they would be most useful.'*
>
> – ANGLO-SAXON CHRONICLE, *896*

The eyewitness to the siege of Paris, the monk Abbo of St-Germain, does his best to make the gallant success of his city sound like a Christian victory. He cannot disguise, though, that ultimately the Northmen broke through Paris's river defences. They took one tower after its bridge was destroyed by the flooding river, and the Frankish king, Charles the Fat, paid them tribute to get them to sail upriver and start looting Burgundy instead of finishing the conquest of Paris.

Standing Fleets

Ultimately, the key to ending Viking depredations was to maintain a strong fleet to discourage raiding. One can see the importance of a state fleet in the case of tenth-century England. King Edgar

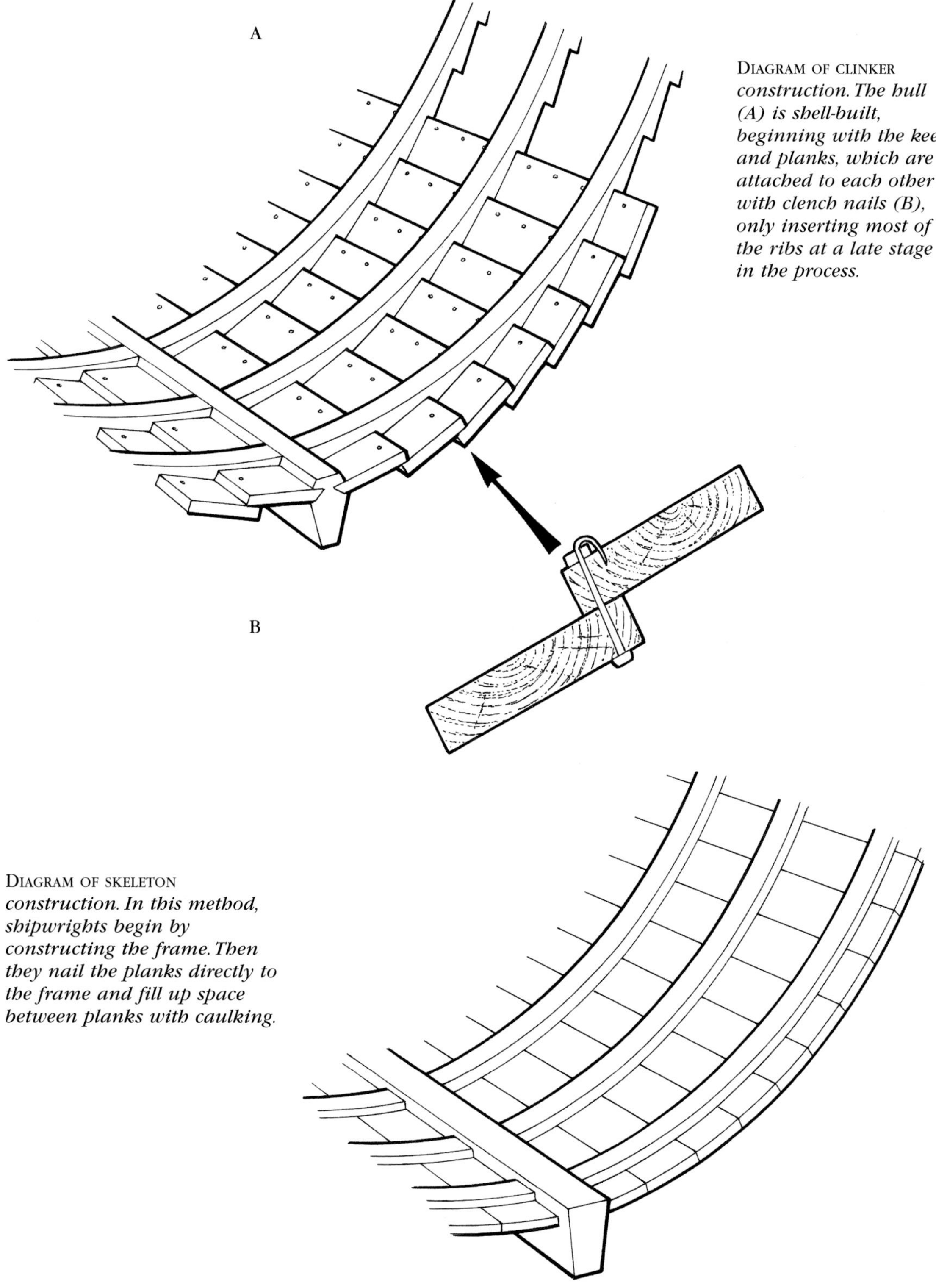

Diagram of clinker *construction. The hull (A) is shell-built, beginning with the keel and planks, which are attached to each other with clench nails (B), only inserting most of the ribs at a late stage in the process.*

Diagram of skeleton *construction. In this method, shipwrights begin by constructing the frame. Then they nail the planks directly to the frame and fill up space between planks with caulking.*

built up a significant fleet, building perhaps on the small squadron launched by Alfred the Great. Thanks to the ongoing danger of raids, the English were even willing to pay the heavy costs of a standing fleet, and Edgar was able to levy one warship and a crew of 60 from each 300 hides of land. As a result, there were no Viking raids after a major incursion was defeated in 937; pickings were easier elsewhere. But without strong leadership, a fleet was worthless, as in the time of Aethelred the Unready.

Large-scale attacks on England were launched by King Swein of Denmark starting in 991 and Aethelred, plagued by internal dissension and his own feckless leadership, could not stop them. He assembled a fleet in 992, but it was defeated - the Anglo-Saxon Chronicle says because the campaign plan was betrayed.

Another fleet gathered in 999, only to do nothing. A third fleet in 1008 broke up thanks to internal fighting before the Viking fleet even arrived. By the time of Cnut's final conquest of England in 1016, Viking ships were once again able to penetrate far up the major rivers, providing materiel, speed and protection against attackers with bows or stones. The importance of Danish ships can be seen in Cnut's siege of London in May 1016, when Cnut and his men got their vessels upstream of London Bridge by digging a canal parallel to the south bank of the Thames and then dragging their ships up it to flank the bridge.

The only fleet actions known from the Viking age come in 1044 and 1062, and were both waged between two Scandinavian navies. These battles, fought between Magnus of Norway and Earl Svein Ulfson on the one hand and between Harald Hardraada and Svein on the other, both took place in fjords on the east coast of Denmark. The second battle especially began with complex manoeuvring to gain the advantage of tide, wind and position of the sun. (It is important to bear in mind that even a slightly favourable wind is a major benefit when shooting lightweight arrows or throwing spears at an enemy's deck.)

The *Heimskringla,* a thirteenth-century history of Scandinavia, tells that in the second battle both sides roped together at least some of their ships in the centre of the battle line, creating large fighting platforms that would allow men to provide speedy reinforcements at the points of greatest danger. It is hard to see how this could have been carried out in reality, since linked ships would have been impossible to row and the fleets could not have moved close enough to grapple each other. Perhaps what was meant is longer cables, which left room between ships for rowing, although even that would have caused difficulties except in sheltered waters. The fighting then commenced

THIS ILLUSTRATION SHOWS *a hypothetical distribution of rowers in a Mediterranean galley of the high Middle Ages.*

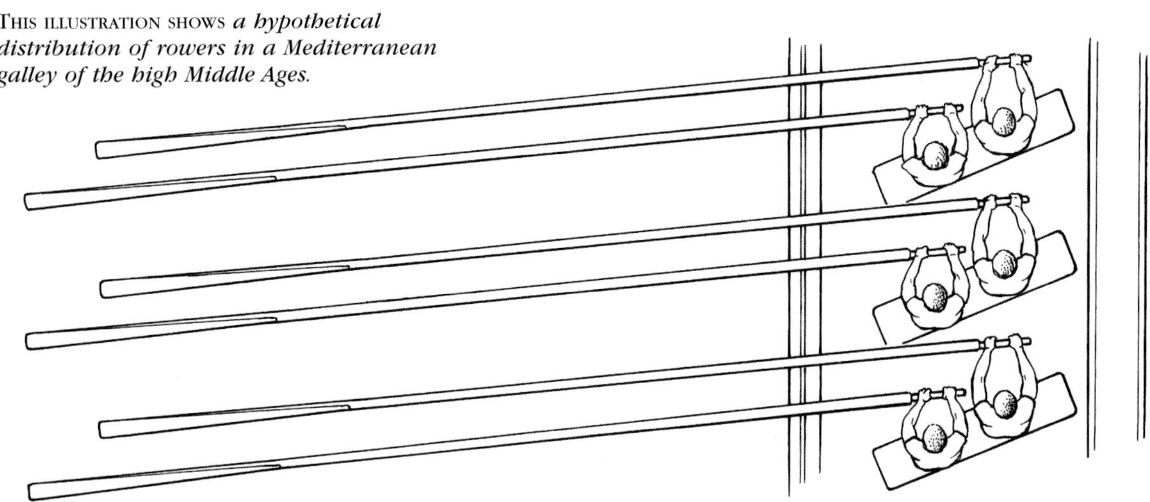

with the men on each side throwing or shooting missiles – javelins, arrows and perhaps stones – at the enemy, angling close enough to grapple and attack hand to hand.

Through the twelfth century, northern fleets remained most important as a means of transport, a function that became ever more important as rulers' ambitions and means became greater. The most famous northern invasion by sea was William the Conqueror's invasion of England in 1066, a vast enterprise that included transport of several thousand horses as well as fighting men. In this case, the war-like abilities of the ships were not tested, as the English king Harold did not muster a fleet against the invading Normans, and William and his men were able to land in England unopposed. William went on to show the utility of a fleet for logistical support in his invasion of Scotland in 1072, in which his land force was shadowed by a fleet that carried supplies.

> *'After our ships had blockaded within the harbour those vessels which had flocked thither to aid the enemy, our Franks moved wooden towers up to the wall and with great bravery leapt from them to the wall with drawn swords.'*
>
> – Fulcher of Chartres, referring to the capture of Beirut in 1110

The Crusades

Such northern enterprises, however, pale in scope beside the greatest ongoing fleet activity of the European Middle Ages – the Crusades. The crusading movement would have been impossible without the support of western fleets, above all those of the Italian states. By the end of the eleventh century, Italy had won naval superiority over both Byzantium and the Fatimid caliphate of Egypt. Rowed galleys remained the warship of choice, but a number of changes between the seventh and eleventh centuries had rendered the ships more manoeuvrable and easier to build. There had been a gradual transition from building a ship with the cabinet-making technique of mortise-and-tenon joints to a process, perhaps derived from northern shipbuilding, of constructing the ribs first and then nailing planks to them. In the same period, the triangular lateen sail replaced the older square sail, making it possible to sail in less favourable winds.

Ships were already important in the first Crusade (1096–1099). Several Christian leaders shipped their armies across the Adriatic instead of marching them completely overland. Italian ships bringing supplies saved the starving crusader army at Antioch. Moreover, during the siege of Jerusalem itself, Genoese ships provided the wood to build siege engines, some ships apparently even being dismantled for their timbers. Certainly Haifa was taken in 1100 thanks to a siege tower built from Venetian ships. From 1100 on, the majority of pilgrims and crusaders reached the Holy Land by sea, even though the Fatimid fleet continued to contest the Syrian and Palestinian coast for the next quarter of a century. The most important early goal of the Latin kings of Jerusalem was to gain control of Fatimid naval bases, often making use of naval assistance. Thus Genoese sailors helped take Caesarea, Acre, Tripoli, Beirut and Jubail, while King Sigurd of Norway's crusading fleet prevented the relief of Sidon in 1110.

The most significant naval intervention, however, was what has been called the 'Venetian Crusade' of 1123–1124, which broke Fatimid naval power. In May 1123 a Venetian fleet of galleys and merchant ships arrived in the east. The crusade objective was the port city of Tyre, but the fighters were hindered by a large Fatimid fleet that threatened to relieve the beleaguered stronghold. The Venetian fleet of about 40 ships, led by Doge Domenico Michiel, discovered a Fatimid squadron off the city of Ascalon.

The Venetians, who seem to have enjoyed numerical superiority, formed their ships into two groups, with the heaviest vessels in the van, including four merchant ships and some galleys that carried mangonels to help with the pre-contact bombardment of the enemy. The Fatimid fleet was routed. The historian William of Tyre reports that the doge's own ship rammed and sank the Fatimid admiral's vessel, although galleys had not been equipped with rams for centuries. More likely, the beak of the Venetian galley was crashed into the side of the enemy vessel, perhaps badly enough to spring its timbers. This engagement marked the end of Muslim naval power, although when Saladin became sultan in 1169 he devoted considerable effort to building up a new fleet. Interestingly, he used naval supplies purchased from Venice and Pisa. Although valiant crusaders, the people of Italy remained first and foremost merchants. Saladin's ships, with inexperienced crews equipped with light bows for the first shooting match, were unsuccessful in stopping the fleets of the Third Crusade.

While the details of the Battle of Ascalon cannot be reconstructed, several important points emerge:

1) The Venetians captured ten supply ships, denying vital supplies to the Muslim forces in Tyre;

2) Tyre had to surrender the next year because the caliph could not relieve the siege - Ascalon had been the final blow to Fatimid seapower;

3) It is clear that the Italians were already using mixed fleets - both galleys and merchant ships operating under sail - and that the merchant ships seem to have been regarded as an extremely valuable addition to the battle line.

Galleys were swifter and less subject to the vagaries of the wind than merchant roundships. To be rowed effectively, however, they had to be built low to the water. Merchant ships, by contrast, were much higher, a height that could be enhanced with more substantial towers in the prow, stern and even masthead than galley construction allowed. Height was a critical advantage, since the decisive part of most actions was the preliminary missile exchange. Although ship-board catapults figure in the chronicle account of the Battle of Ascalon, such mentions are rare and when they occur some historians doubt that they are anything more than chroniclers' fantasies. The difficulty of maintaining proper tension on catapults at sea, apart from their size and danger to the ship upon recoil, all make it unlikely that larger stone-throwing machines were ever used at sea - at least more than once. Instead, the missiles of choice were arrows and crossbow bolts, with javelins and hand-thrown rocks added as the ships closed. One need only compare the effect of throwing a rock down from a wall and up to the top of a wall to see how helpful a tall ship could be.

'And as the sea carried the ship forward again, it struck against this tower again, and as it did so one of the knights...[took] hold of this tower with hands and feet and got himself inside.... When he was inside...they rushed upon him and struck him fiercely, but, because he was in armour...did not wound him.'

– Robert of Clari, Constantinople, 1204

By 1200 the merchant roundship was playing a very important role in Mediterranean naval war and logistics. These ships could be very large. For his crusade in 1248 Louis IX built two-decker and even three-decker transport ships. The largest, probably able to carry 725 tonnes (800 tons) of supplies and equipment, had a crew of 80 and could transport 500 to 600 passengers or 100 horses. Such ships proved particularly useful in two great amphibious assaults, against Constantinople in 1203–1204 and Damietta in Egypt in 1221.

The Fourth Crusade: Constantinople 1203–1204

The Fourth Crusade, which took the Christian city of Constantinople in both 1203 and 1204, was

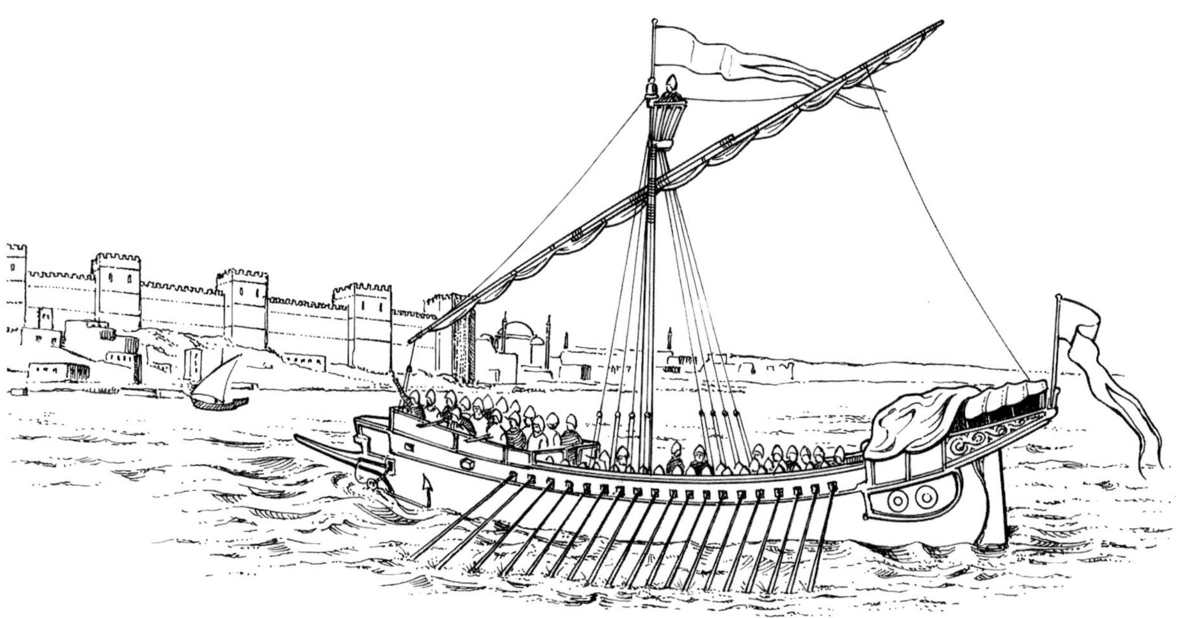

THE CONQUEST OF CONSTANTINOPLE, *1203. Shallow-draught Venetian-style galleys like this were well suited for attacks on beaches, and proved to outwit the defending Byzantines, who were not expecting a seaborne invasion.*

conveyed to the east in Venetian transports and accompanied by a fleet of 50 Venetian galleys. It is because of those ships that the crusaders came to be attacking a Christian city in the first place. The French leaders of the crusade made a treaty with Venice for transport, supplies and protection at sea, but fewer men than expected came and they found themselves unable to pay their commitments to the Venetians. In their quest for money, the crusaders agreed to restore an exiled Byzantine prince to his throne. The inhabitants of Constantinople, much to the crusaders' surprise, failed to welcome the son of their former ruler with open arms, so the Venetian and French crusaders decided to make him emperor by force. Thanks to the complicated state of the Byzantine Empire at the time, there followed not one but two of the great assaults of medieval war.

The Venetian seamen earned their pay, despite the fact that there was almost no Byzantine fleet to oppose them. As had been the case five centuries before, the key to taking Constantinople was the sea because the city was surrounded by water on three sides. The sea walls on the Sea of Marmara and Bosporus sides were nearly impervious to attack, rising as they did almost immediately out of the water and with the added protection of the rough water of the open sea.

The walls that faced the Golden Horn, the great harbour of Constantinople, were somewhat more accessible. Some areas had a little beach on which attackers could gain a foothold and raise scaling ladders. So for centuries the Golden Horn had been protected in times of danger by a great iron chain strung from two towers across the mouth of the harbour, effectively barring it to ships. The crusaders' first task was to take one of these towers, the Tower of Galata, which they accomplished on 5 and 6 July 1203. The assault was made from sea, with Venetian galleys towing transport ships towards the shore because of the navigational difficulties. The transports were then run aground, doors in the holds opening to ramps, so that the cavalry could disembark already mounted to meet the Greek soldiers who were trying to hold the beach.

FRENCH AND VENETIAN *forces succeeded in capturing Constantinople at the second attempt on 12 April 1204. Screens to protect their troops from missile fire helped the attackers get close to the wall and rudimentary belfrys allowed the crusaders to assault the mercenary troops assigned to defend city walls.*

A 14TH-CENTURY Venetian *galley was heavier and had more complex rigging than its 13th-century predecessor. Such ships ruled the Mediterranean for several centuries.*

These were soon driven off and the crusaders took the tower by storm. A reinforced Venetian ship then broke the chain, and the Venetians made short work of the decrepit Byzantine ships that tried to keep them from the Golden Horn.

Once in the Golden Horn, the crusader force had to face a city wall 9m (30ft) high, strongly defended by bowmen as well as stone-throwing machines. Some of the latter were so large that they could hurl boulders heavier than a man could lift and were capable of doing considerable damage to a ship. The crusaders divided their forces, the French crusaders attacking at the land wall some distance away, the Venetians approaching by sea. The Venetians prepared for their assault with considerable ingenuity. They covered their ships with hides for fear of Greek Fire and padded the vessels with timber and vines, so that stones thrown would have less effect. Most importantly, they constructed plank bridges broad enough for three men to stand abreast, and hung them so they could swivel from the masts of a number of the heavier roundships.

Like the bridges of siege towers, these devices were intended to be latched on to the wall, providing a route for the attackers. Galleys could operate closer to the shore thanks to their shallow draft. However, they were not built strongly enough and could not carry sufficient numbers of men to be used as mobile siege towers. The maritime siege tower was not a new idea - ships had been used as mobile siege towers at the siege of Salonika in 904 - but it is doubtful that any of the Venetian sailors or marines had been involved in such an assault.

Enrico Dandolo, the Venetian doge, personally commanded the assault despite his old age and

Constantinople

1203-04

The key to the first conquest of Constantinople in 1203 was an assault on two fronts: French crusaders attacked the land wall with siege engines and heavily armed knights and infantry, while Venetian seamen assaulted the sea wall. This meant that the defenders were spread thinly and not able to concetrate their forces. After taking the Tower of Galata and breaking the chain blocking the harbour, the Venetians sailed into the Golden Horn. Roundships had been specially padded and equipped with bridges for a direct attack on the sea wall; success was only possible because the Venetian galleys staged a diversion, landing and disgorging their oarsmen onto the beach. This distraction allowed a few men to leap from the bridges on to the wall. Once a tower had been taken, the victors opened the gates to admit the doge and his contingent. The Venetians successfully broke into the city, only to withdraw again when word came that their allies were hard pressed in their part of the assault. A second seaward assault, with the French crusaders onboard, proved more successful: on 12 April 1204 the city fell to the invaders.

Constantinople guarded the entrance to the Black Sea, the rich lands of which attracted raiders and would-be conquerors from as far back as the ancient Greeks.

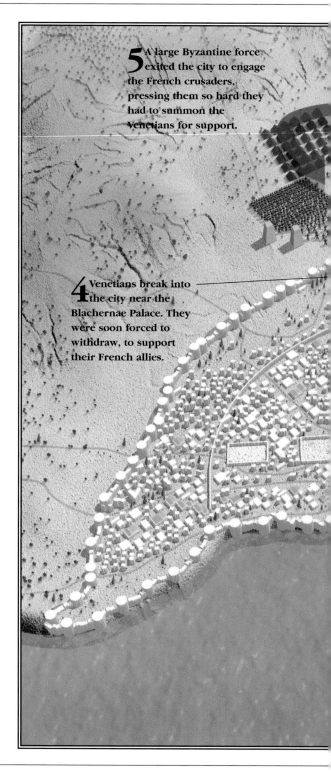

5 **A large Byzantine force exited the city to engage the French crusaders, pressing them so hard they had to summon the Venetians for support.**

4 **Venetians break into the city near the Blachernae Palace. They were soon forced to withdraw, to support their French allies.**

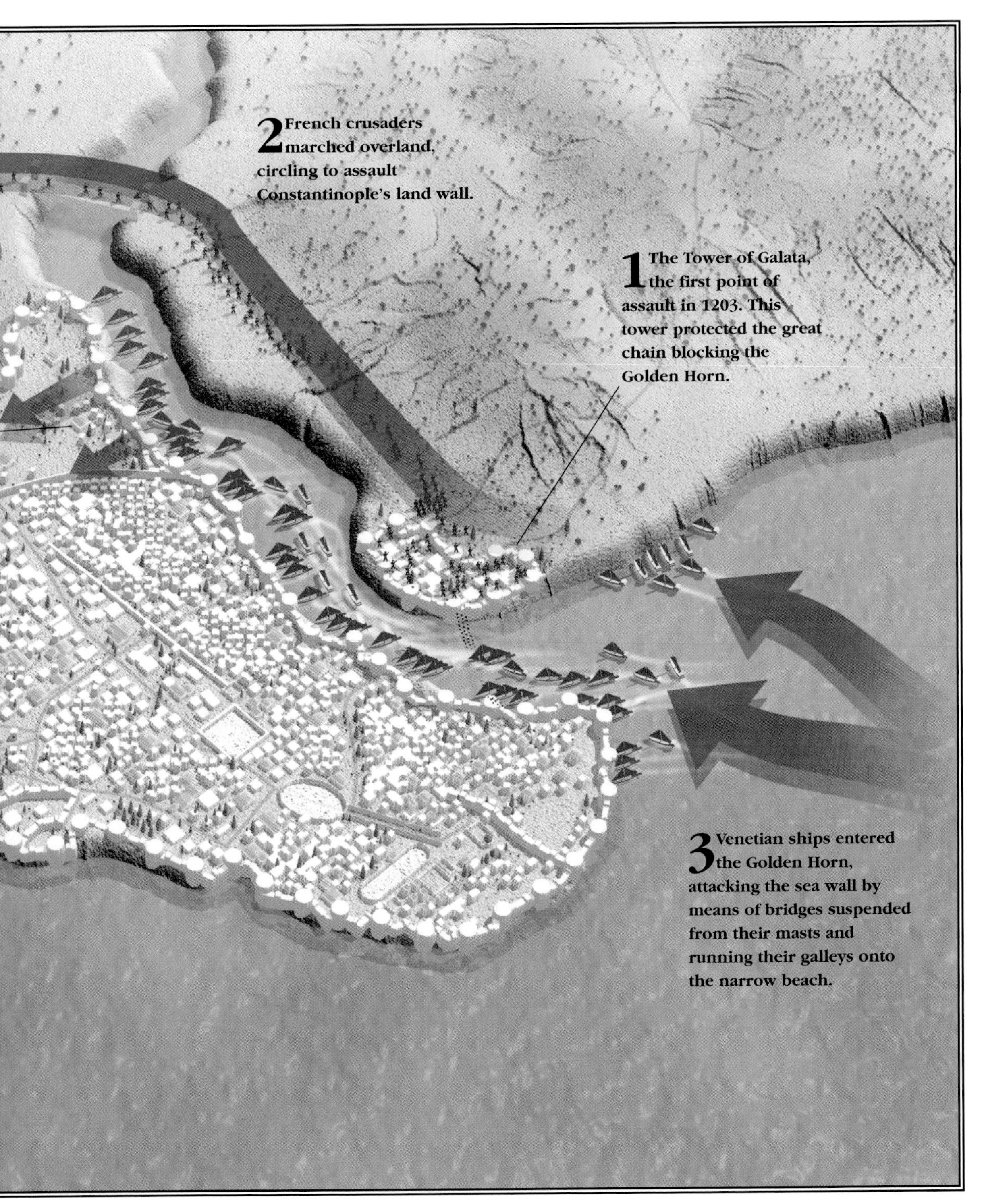
2 French crusaders marched overland, circling to assault Constantinople's land wall.
1 The Tower of Galata, the first point of assault in 1203. This tower protected the great chain blocking the Golden Horn.
3 Venetian ships entered the Golden Horn, attacking the sea wall by means of bridges suspended from their masts and running their galleys onto the narrow beach.

blindness. He drew the ships up in a long line, intending to assault as many points along the wall as possible. The larger roundships with their assault bridges led the way, thanks to a favourable wind that let them manoeuvre close to the shore despite the encumbrance of the bridges. Dandolo was desperate to draw off at least some enemy fire from the roundships, however, and ordered his crew to put him ashore.

The flagship was the first to beach, followed quickly by other galleys whose crews were eager to support their ruler and the standard of St Mark – galleys were rowed throughout the Middle Ages by free men, usually citizens of their city. The beach party raised scaling ladders on the narrow strip of land, while some of the roundships succeeded in hooking their bridges onto several towers. Once in the towers, the bridge crews opened the gates for their compatriots on the beach. The Venetians succeeded in winning a large section of the wall by this means, only to be forced to abandon the territory they had gained to reinforce the French crusaders, whose own attack had met fierce resistance. Nonetheless, the day was won. The usurping emperor, Alexius III, fled, and the exiled prince was taken into the city and soon crowned as Alexius IV, co-ruling with his father Isaac. The crusaders had accomplished their goal, and expected payment before their departure to fight Muslims.

'We forbid under penalty of anathema that that deadly and God-detested art of slingers and archers be in the future exercised against Christians and Catholics.'

– Second Lateran Council, 1139

Prince Alexius's promises had been completely unreasonable, though, and his half-hearted attempts to fulfil his obligations pleased neither Byzantines nor crusaders. He was soon deposed and an adamant opponent of the Venetians took the throne. When they saw that they had been cheated, the crusaders planned a second conquest of the city early in 1204.

This time, the whole force was concentrated on the sea walls, since the crusaders had discovered the impossibility of gaining the land wall during the first conquest. The sea walls had been heightened in the intervening period, so the swivelling bridges had to be slung higher on the masts. Once again the Venetian ships were prepared to serve as mobile siege towers, covered with timbers, vines and hides to protect them. A general assault was launched on 9 April, the ships moving forwards in line abreast, alternating transports, galleys and horse transports. The shallow-draught vessels ran up on the beach, while the men had to wade in from others, dragging their ladders and other equipment with them. Meanwhile, one bridge-carrying ship was sent against each tower. Unfortunately, roundships are moved by wind, and that day a rare south wind came up. Only five ships managed to reach the towers, and not a single one was able to attach its bridge. The attack was beaten off with heavy losses.

A second assault on 12 April had better success. This time 40 roundships were tied together in pairs, and a pair of ships sent against each tower. The pairings not only provided greater stability, but meant that a double-sized force was available to use each bridge that they succeeded in attaching to the wall. A north wind rose at about noon, sending the ships towards the wall – but still only four or five of these mobile siege towers managed to affix their bridges to a tower. That was enough. Once enough crusaders were in the towers, they were able to clear the nearby walls sufficiently so men on the beach could scale them by ladder. The city soon fell, the people of Constantinople suffering a devastating sack at the hands of their fellow Christians, who proceeded to divide up the territory of the empire in a way that gave Venice a great advantage in eastern Mediterranean trade.

Mediterranean War in the Later Middle Ages

With the Crusades, the fleets of the Italian city-states reached a high degree of technical skill that

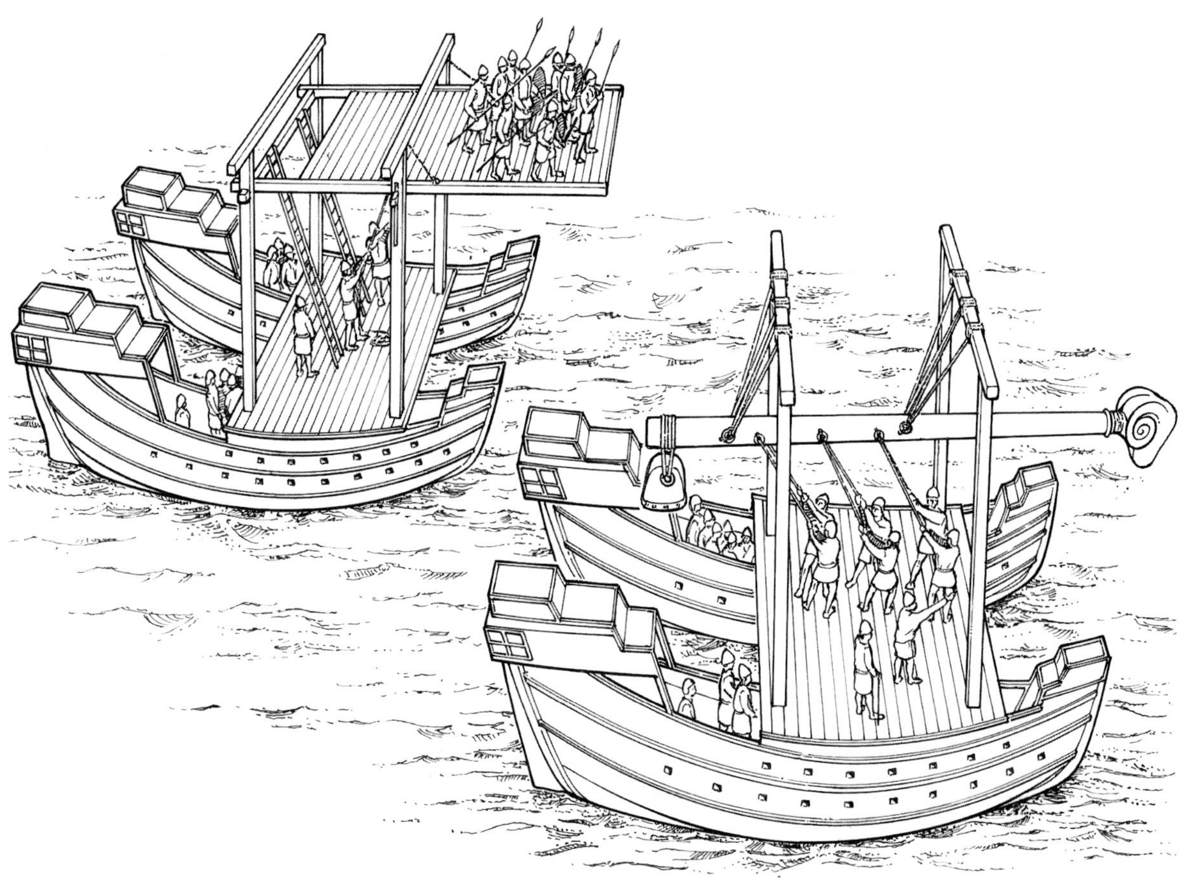

FLOATING SIEGE TOWERS *were sometimes used in the Mediterranean to assault sea walls. The ships were dismasted and joined in pairs to support an aerial bridge or battering ram.*

soon carried over to wars against other western Christians. The galley remained the dominant form of ship, as rulers were concerned more about manoeuvrability than height of ship, although galleys too came to be equipped with wooden castles. The decisive factors remained the same: ability to edge to a position of advantage, so more of one's own men could fire missiles at the enemy than the enemy could launch in return; the number and type of missiles, as well as the skill of the men who launched them; and, if all else was equal, the sheer murderous power of boarding crews. Accounts of later medieval war in the Mediterranean show clearly that commanders regularly worked to find the winning combination of factors, weighing manoeuvrability against protection for the men, and especially trying to come up with the sort of fighting men who could compete best on the plunging decks of ships. They experimented with throwing quicklime to blind the enemy and even with hurling jars of soap onto enemy decks to make them slippery, an especially effective device against men in heavy armour.

In general, though, the most effective weapon of naval war in the Mediterranean during this period was the crossbow. Use of the crossbow seems to have become common in the course of the eleventh century; the early twelfth-century chronicler Anna Comnena denounces the weapon as diabolical in terms that suggest it had not been seen in the Byzantine Empire before the crusaders arrived. The second Lateran council in 1139 denounced all use of crossbows against fellow Christians. However, the weapon was too useful for such proclamations to be heeded. Crossbows were standard equipment on Mediterranean ships for at least four centuries, testifying to their utility. Crossbowmen were normally equipped with two different sorts of crossbows. One required the use of both feet to prime them. The other type had a stirrup so it could be primed while standing. The former probably shot a greater distance, but took more time to load. Some ships also appear to have had large crossbows mounted on a stand that could be cocked with a winch. These were capable of shooting medium-sized stones and jars of noxious substances as well as bolts.

A long period of training was essential to learn how to fire a crossbow effectively under fire. Highly skilled warriors, crossbowmen were resented and feared. The value and killing power of a good crossbowman can be seen in the aftermath of the battle of Ponza, fought on 14 June 1300 between the Aragonese and the Angevins. After the Aragonese fleet won the day, their commander gave the order that the hands of the Genoese crossbowmen who had been captured from the enemy flagship should be cut off. He then ordered that they should be blinded for good measure. The most successful proponents of 'scientific' naval war in the Middle Ages were the Aragonese in their wars to claim the kingdom of Sicily.

This was called the War of the Sicilian Vespers, after the first big uprising of the Sicilians against Angevin rule was signalled by the ringing of the church bells for vespers. In these wars, the king of Aragon set himself against the cadet branch of the French royal house that had taken the kingdom of Sicily, and thus had to reckon at times with French royal forces. Aragon and its Catalan allies won a series of impressive victories beginning in 1282 when King Philip III of France resolved to invade Aragon. He collected a large fleet of support ships in the Bay of Roses, only to have them destroyed by a Catalan fleet on 2–3 September 1282.

Reconstruction of a *taride* *built for King Charles of Sicily in 1278. Roomier than a war galley, a* taride *could transport horses for amphibious assaults.*

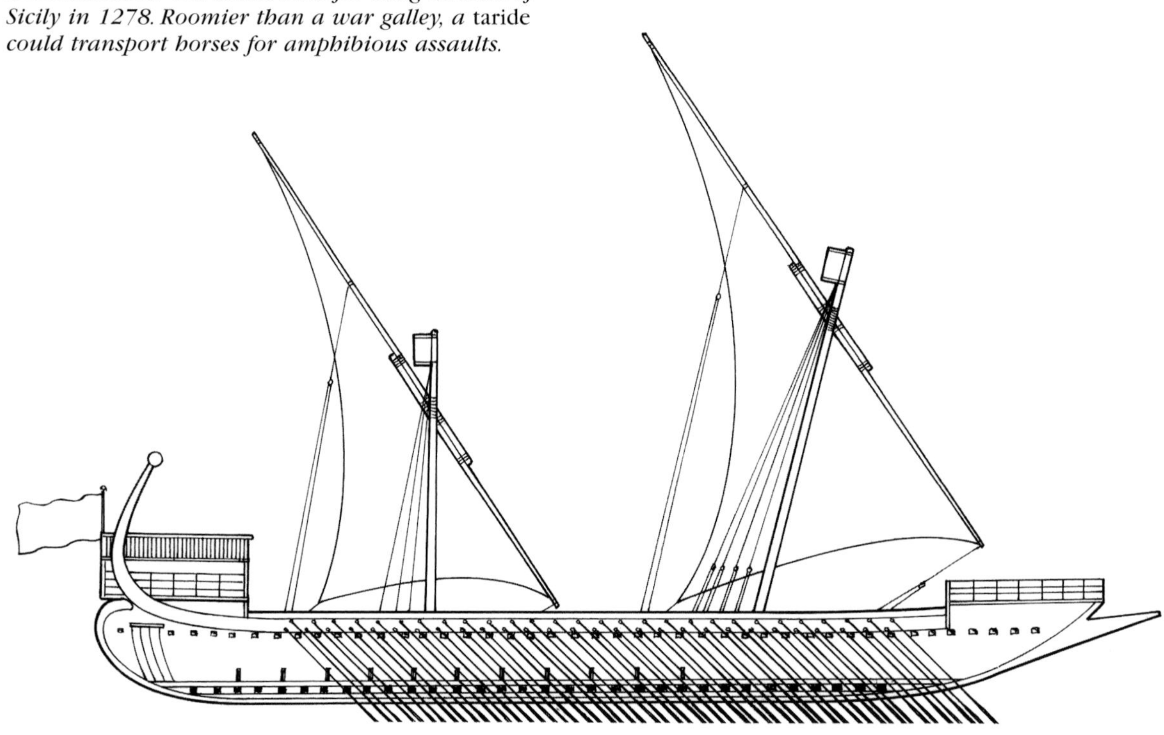

Battle of Malta: 1283

It is the Battle of Malta, fought on 8 June 1283, that shows Aragonese naval abilities most clearly. This was the first major victory of the admiral Roger of Lauria, who has been hailed as the greatest galley admiral of the Middle Ages. The Grand Harbour of Malta is one of the finest harbours of the Mediterranean and was vital to the strategy of both sides. An Angevin fleet of about 20 galleys probably reached the harbour on 4 June, followed by an Aragonese force of about the same size that arrived on the night of 7 June. Two small boats had been set to guard the harbour entrance. However, the two ships were tied up on either side rather than patrolling the whole mouth of the harbour. Because of this arrangement, an Aragonese ship was able to sneak into the harbour and spy out the Angevin plans.

Roger of Lauria then deployed for battle just before sunrise, in line abreast, with heavy cables strung between the ships. This was a tactic that the Genoese had developed in the twelfth century and that had become common by the thirteenth, apparently well suited to galley fighting. It was an open formation, leaving room for oars to operate, so the ships could row forward as a unit. The advantage was that men could be moved rapidly from one ship to another, reinforcing vessels that were boarded or that lost too many men to the initial missile barrage; the galleys probably had gang planks laid between them.

Once within the harbour, the Aragonese admiral had a challenge sounded to rouse his unsuspecting enemies. This action was probably not just a matter of chivalry. The Angevin ships were beached in the traditional fashion, stern first. This was an easily defensible position. Captured ships could not be floated away easily, and the crews could be endlessly reinforced from the land. The Angevins, once challenged, put out in their galleys and a battle commenced that lasted the entire morning. Both sides had mixed spearmen and crossbowmen, about 100 men per galley. As the battle opened, the Angevins fought in the usual way, throwing everything they had at the enemy in a large-scale missile barrage.

This is the point at which the battle took an unusual turn. Roger of Lauria ordered his men to stay under cover and respond with nothing but crossbows. Eventually the Angevins ran out of ammunition and then the Aragonese closed, using their remaining projectile weapons to very good effect to devastate the enemy's decks and throw them into disorder. The Aragonese then grappled and boarded, taking the enemy ships with hand-to-hand fighting. Only seven of the Angevin ships escaped, two of them so badly damaged that they had to be abandoned.

In the Battle of Malta, the Aragonese lost about 300 men, while the Angevin losses amounted to somewhere between 3500 and 4000 killed and captured, including the death of one of their two admirals. Several factors account for the magnitude of this victory. Certainly some credit has to be given to the skill of the Aragonese commander, but his tactics would not have been possible without some important Aragonese modifications in shipbuilding. The Aragonese ships were built higher and had high bulwarks behind which the men could hide during the missile barrage. These design features made the ships slower, so they were not generally adopted outside of Spain. However, especially thanks to the element of surprise, they had good success here. The ships they were fighting were probably similar to the galleys that the Angevin king Charles I of Sicily had ordered in 1275; the extant document provides our first detailed statistics about medieval galleys.

These ships were essentially huge rowing shells. They were long and narrow, with a proportion of 10.7:1 amidships. They were also very low; the height of the gunwale amidships was only 2.03m (6ft) above the keel. The Aragonese also had the advantage that their fighting men were better suited to naval warfare than the less-experienced Frenchmen. The Aragonese fleet was manned by Catalan crossbowmen, who were acknowledged as the best in Europe at the time. They also had very good light infantry known as *almogavars,* who came from the Moorish frontier. These men were lightly armed with leather cuirasses and were noted for their agility. The Angevin fleet, by contrast, was manned with knights in heavy armour and footsoldiers unsuited and unused to fighting on shipboard. The Spanish infantry proved much better at the fundamental task of staying upright on a shifting deck.

This victory was consolidated a year later in the battle of the Gulf of Naples, fought on 5 June 1284. In this encounter, Admiral Roger of Lauria drew out the Angevin fleet by feigning flight. The battle took place several kilometres from land. The fighting was hard, until the hidden Aragonese reserve ships came out and attacked the Angevin rear. One account says that in this battle Roger resorted to every known dirty trick, including throwing fire bombs, pots of sulphur and pots full of soap onto the Angevin decks. On 23 June 1287, the Aragonese won yet again against an Angevin fleet of more than 80 ships against Roger of Lauria's bare 40 ships. This battle, called the Battle of the Counts because several French counts were involved, again shows how vital knowledge of the sea was to winning battles.

Roger enticed the Angevins from port by shooting at the coast and shouting insults. When the Angevins came out from the harbour their ships soon got spread out, so they could be attacked by several Aragonese ships at a time, clearly better able to manoeuvre in the waters of Naples. The battle lasted most of the day, Roger apparently giving priority to targeting the French counts' ships, because they were unfamiliar with war at sea. By the end of the day about 40 Angevin ships were captured, along with 5000 prisoners.

Northern Waters: The Struggle for the English Channel

While galleys remained the dominant warship in the Mediterranean until the fifteenth century, a variety of reasons led northerners to rely ever more heavily on sailing ships in their military ventures. Surprisingly, these reasons do not seem to have included the rougher seas and tides of the open Atlantic, although both must have made it much more difficult to row a vessel than on the gentler seas of the Mediterranean. Instead, the vital factors in the transition to sailing ships for war were improvements in the type of ship, the expense involved and the crucial advantage of height when exchanging projectiles with another vessel in battle. An improved roundship design, the cog, came into use at some time around 1150. These ships started as bulk carriers; they were first developed in the harsh sailing conditions of the Baltic and soon spread to the North Sea. A cog was a high-sided, clinker-built ship, with a flat bottom and square stern. It was propelled completely by wind power, by means of at first two and eventually three square sails. Most cogs had a capacity of 90 tonnes (100 tons) or less, but some were able to carry 272 tonnes (300 tons) or even 362 tonnes (400 tons). Their height above the water, nearly 4m (14ft) from keel to gunwale in the excavated Bremen cog, compared to about 1.8m (6ft) for the Viking Gokstad ship. This gave fighters a great advantage. This was further increased by building wood castles both fore and aft, which could be filled with marines who could fire arrows and other missiles at the enemy beneath them.

The other great advantage of the cog was that it was the same structurally whether it was built for war or mercantile endeavours. Consequently, ships did not have to be specially built and maintained for occasional military purposes, although fourteenth- and fifteenth-century kings often commissioned small numbers of particularly large and impressive cogs as the centrepiece of their fleets.

Instead, merchants built and maintained cogs for their own purposes; the ruler claimed the right to 'arrest' these merchant ships at need, pressing them into crown service and compensating the owner and crew but not having to pay the whole cost of a ship. Usually all that would be necessary to militarize the ship would be to add the fighting castles, which were not a fixed part of the ships and could be added or removed as necessary. Although no merchant ship went unarmed for fear of pirates, large wood structures in the bow and stern, and perhaps even at the masthead, would have had a major impact on sailing performance and thus would be undesirable in relatively peaceful times.

One can already see the transition away from galleys in the thirteenth century. The northern Hanseatic League, for example, was essentially a trading consortium and never had war galleys. In war, however, member cities could put soldiers in cogs. This worked well and enabled the merchants to take on major states, as in 1234 and 1239 when the city of Lübeck successfully fought two naval battles against the king of Denmark. It proved nearly impossible for galleys to take possession of a cog at sea, as long as the men on the cog did not run out of weapons. It would have been quite a challenge to board a cog from the much lower galleys, to say nothing of the greater losses before boarding as the men on the cog had the protection of their castles and gravity fought against weapons thrown or shot from the galleys.

The basic technique of cog fighting was to manoeuvre to come at the enemy from upwind, controlling when and how the ships would engage - what is called the 'weather gage'. Ideally, the ship with the weather gage would hit the enemy at a right angle amidships, connecting to it with grappling irons. This would put the fighters in the forecastle in a strong position, overlooking the enemy deck. The ship under attack attempted in its turn to keep the stern to the enemy, so it could preserve the advantage of height. Still, up to the fourteenth century galleys remained a major part of the striking power in northern war fleets, especially since it was much easier to make a rowed vessel go where it was needed. There were few cogs that could tack closer than 80° to the wind. These northern galleys were clinker-built, with one square sail, much like Viking ships. They became bigger and heavier over time. King John of England had galleys with at least 70 rowers, while Edward I in the 1290s built some with 100 or more oars. By the 1290s there were even

FITTED FOR WAR, *this 14th-century merchant cog has castles at the fore, the stern, and the masthead. Later, this style of ship would be fitted with the world's first naval cannons.*

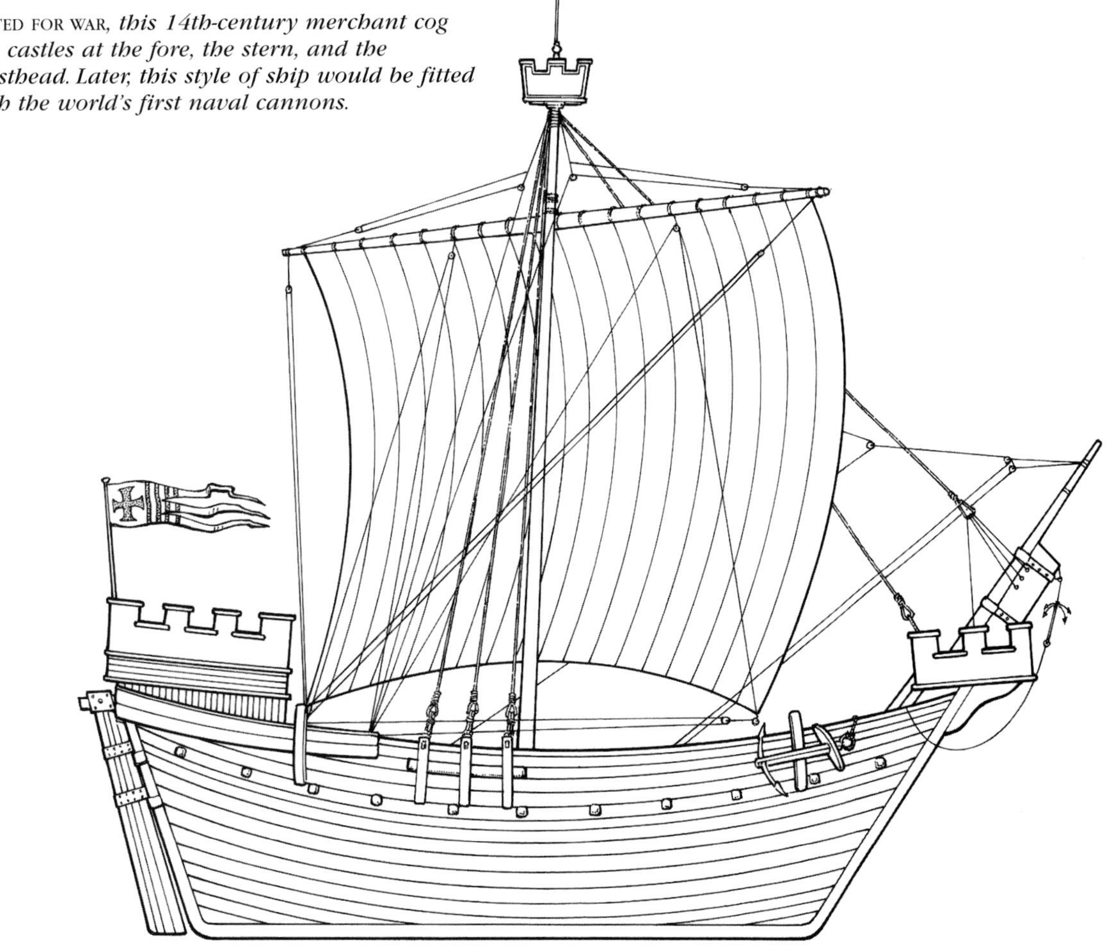

Battle of Malta

1283

An Angevin fleet held the Grand Harbour of Malta for the French-dominated Kingdom of Sicily. They were attacked on the morning of 8 June 1283 by a force of Aragonese galleys led by Roger of Lauria. Overnight, the Aragonese forces tied themselves across the harbour entrance. The Aragonese opened the battle by sounding a challenge to rouse the Angevins and bring them out of the harbour. The Angevins took to their galleys and rowed out to meet their attackers. In this unusual battle, the Angevin seamen were encouraged by their enemy to use up their entire supply of arrows and other missiles. The Aragonese barely responded until their enemies had virtually disarmed themselves. Then the Aragonese closed for hand-to-hand combat, inflicting absolute carnage on the empty-handed Angevins. In the ensuing chaos, Aragonese ships grappled their opponents and boarded, ending the battle with brutal hand-to-hand fighting.

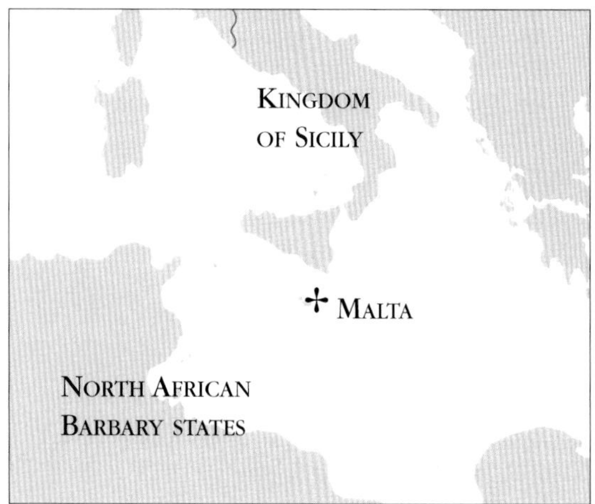

Malta's position south of Sicily in the middle of the Mediterranean made it highly desirable as a naval base. It was a key to control of the kingdom of Sicily, which included southern Italy.

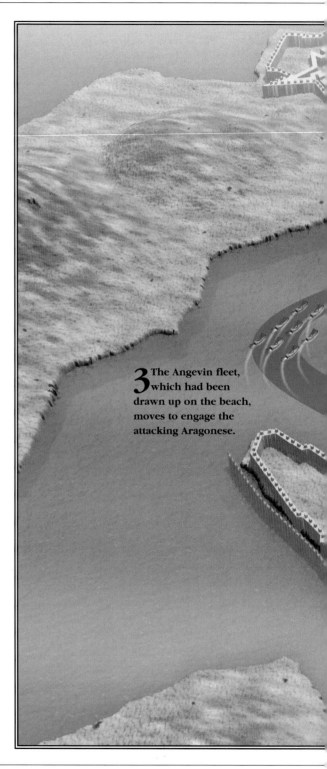

3 The Angevin fleet, which had been drawn up on the beach, moves to engage the attacking Aragonese.

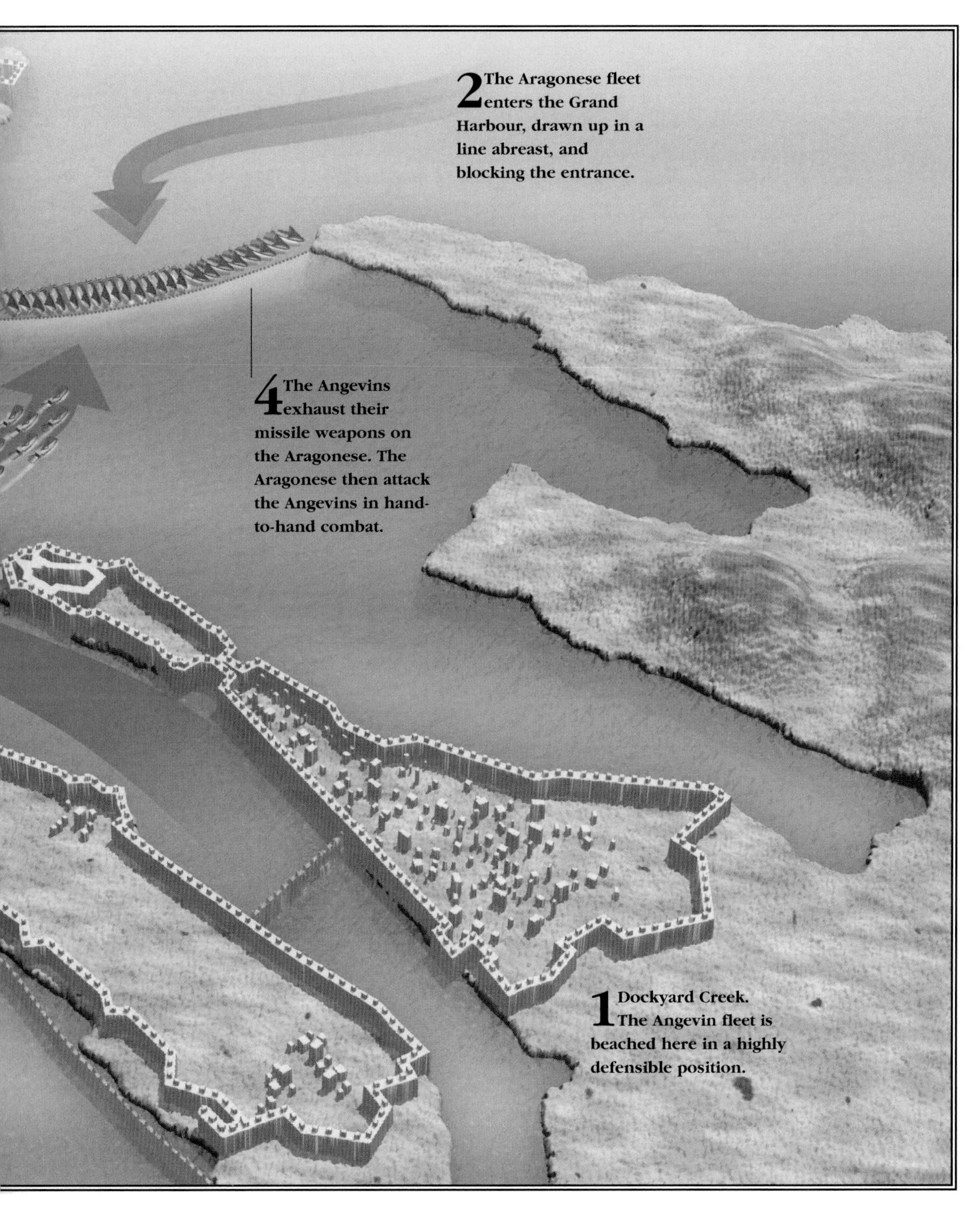
2 The Aragonese fleet enters the Grand Harbour, drawn up in a line abreast, and blocking the entrance.
4 The Angevins exhaust their missile weapons on the Aragonese. The Aragonese then attack the Angevins in hand-to-hand combat.
1 Dockyard Creek. The Angevin fleet is beached here in a highly defensible position.

experiments being tried out, such as equipping these galleys with fighting castles, in an attempt to combine the manoeuvrability of a galley with the height of a cog.

THE FINAL STAGE *of a sea battle between two northern European 14th-century cogs approaches. The cogs did not normally use oars, so sails had to be employed even during battle.*

Anglo-French Wars

The history of this transition in northern fighting method can best be seen in the frequent wars between France and England, which dominate European naval history in the thirteenth and fourteenth centuries. England had had little need for military ships since 1066, except for support vessels for occasional campaigns in Scotland and as transports for the invasion of Ireland in the 1170s. This situation changed dramatically when John of England lost Normandy. The French king, Philip II Augustus, for the first time controlled both the ports and the resources that would enable him to take war into the English Channel and beyond.

John, a bad ruler in many ways but with a sound grasp of military necessities, invested heavily in a fleet in the years 1209–12. It was a mixed fleet, including a new royal squadron of 20 galleys and 34 other ships, besides what he could take from merchants. The fleet was soon needed. Philip Augustus was eager to take advantage of John's poor international position (he was excommunicate at the time) and poor relations with his own subjects. So in 1213 he gathered a large fleet at Damme, at the mouth of the Zwyn. However, the French had forgotten vital lessons from the Viking era, including the basic fact that there was often very little warning of an attack from the sea in those days before radar. In blithe unawareness of the English fleet's proximity, the French commander had left his ships mostly unguarded at Damme, at least some of the ships drawn up on the beach, while most of the crews were on shore sacking the town nearby. The English squadron managed a complete and devastating surprise attack, carrying off all the ships that lay at anchor and burning those on the mudflats. King Philip had to abandon his invasion plan.

'He who rules on the sea will very shortly rule on the land also.'

– Khyr-Ed-Din, 1546

For all its success, the Battle of Damme hardly counts as a battle, since few enemies were present during the raid. More suggestive of what ships could do by the early thirteenth century was the battle of Dover in 1217, fought on the open sea off the coast of Dover. By this time, the affairs of the English and the French were in a hopeless tangle. King John's barons had disowned their fealty and invited the French king's son, Louis, to come and take England with their help. Louis had complied with a large force and had several successes. Then John died and baronial support of the French invasion dissolved when the leading baron took over the regency for the young king, Henry III. Prince Louis found himself in difficult straits but was still hopeful, and in 1217 his wife, Blanche of Castile, sent reinforcement troops with a supporting fleet under the command of Eustace the Monk, a famous fighter who had once spent time in John's service.

The French were already approaching the shore when the English fleet came up on their rear. Again the advantage of the weather gage was decisive, especially since descriptions make it clear that many of the ships engaged were cogs rather than galleys. The chronicler Matthew Paris tells of the cutting of halyards and shrouds so that the sails of enemy ships fell onto the deck. He also reports that the English flagship carried pots of powdered quicklime. As the fleets closed, the Englishmen threw these at the men on the French flagship, with devastating effects on the Frenchmen's eyes. The English won a decisive victory, capturing a number of French ships and driving off the rest. Among the captured vessels was the flagship; Eustace the Monk was summarily beheaded. Prince Louis was soon forced to make peace and return to his own country.

Essentially, there were no polite rules of war when it came to sea battles. When a ship was boarded, it was normal for the defeated enemy to be killed to a man. Certainly if the ship was damaged there was no line of retreat. It is quite possible that an English commander with classical tastes could have read about quicklime as a naval weapon in Vegetius's manual on warfare, and decided to try it out. Even if it was used at Dover, lime never became a standard-issue item on medieval ships; the chance of it blowing back and blinding those who used it must have been terrifying, rather like the dangers of using Greek Fire. Yet it is also possible that the chronicler of the Dover battle, who knew nothing of naval war, simply included a striking image from Vegetius in the belief that naval war *ought* to be waged in such a way. He also tells that the ships had iron rams, which they certainly did not. Interestingly, one of the French ships really was carrying a trebuchet, but this was apparently intended for the army in England, not for use at sea. There is no evidence of stone-throwing engines used on board ship anywhere in northern Europe in the Middle Ages.

After these invasion attempts, both the French and the English seem to have decided that naval fighting was too costly and risky to be sustained, although occasional fighting broke out on land. The

Quant le roy dan
gleterre z ses ma
reschaulx eurent
ordonnees leurs
batailles et leurs nauires
moult richement z saigement
Ilz firent tendre et traire
les voiles contremont et vin
drent au vent de quartier
sur dextre pour avoir lavantaige
du souleil qui en venant
leur estoit ou visaige. Si
sauiserent que ce leur pouoit
trop nuyre et detryerent vng
pou et tournoyerent tant quilz
leurent a leur voulente. Les
normans qui les veoient
tourner sesmerveilloient
pour quoy ilz le faisoient z
disoient ilz resoingnent et
recullent Car ilz ne sont
pas gens pour combattre a
nous. Bien veoient les nor
mans par les banieres que le
roy dangleterre y estoit per
sonnelement. Si mirent
leurs vaisseaulx en bon estat
Car ilz estoient saiges en

French did not make a serious attempt to create a war fleet again until 1284, and that was on the Mediterranean coast for war with Aragon, with effects that we have seen above. A crisis in the 1290s led Edward I of England to build galleys, but they achieved nothing.

In 1317 Edward II hired Genoese galleys for his Scottish war, apparently believing that professional galleys would be better than merchant cogs. The situation changed in the early fourteenth century when French and English relations deteriorated even more seriously than before. In 1337 war broke out on a scale that had not been seen anywhere in medieval Europe except for the Crusades. Over a hundred years of war, in fact, a war that seemed impossible to resolve because of English claims not only to land in France but to the French crown itself. Of course, the English and French were divided by the sea. Under these circumstances, northern naval warfare can truly be said to have come of age.

'They set out with their fleet... and sailed for England, coming into Southampton harbour one Sunday morning when the people were at mass. The Normans and Genoese entered the town and pillaged and looted it completely.'

– Froissart

The first stages of the Hundred Years' War were marked by an ongoing battle at sea between French and English privateers, pirates and merchants, each side hoping to profit and deny valuable supplies to the enemy. But already in 1338 Philip VI made use of a larger royal navy, mostly composed of galleys hired from Genoa. He launched several devastating raids against southern English ports, partly destroying several towns including Portsmouth, Southampton and Hastings. These raids effectively cut King Edward III's lines of communication, including supplies, between his continental possessions and England, and also destroying and capturing a number of ships, including Edward III's own great ships *Cog Edward* and *Christopher*. Philip and his advisors went on from there to organize a major invasion of England in 1339, only to have a storm scatter his fleet and spoil their plans.

From that point, France's naval position rapidly went downhill. The Genoese mercenaries enjoyed a series of impressive successes, but started fighting among themselves after their own admiral, Ayton Doria, tried to cheat them out of their pay. The oarsmen mutinied, seized several of the galleys and headed for home, losing Philip VI two-thirds of his battle fleet at one blow. By the end of 1339 the rest of the Italian oarsmen had been sent home. That left France with 22 royal galleys of its own, but an English raid on Boulogne early in 1340 burned 18 of these where they had been laid up for the winter.

Without this elite fighting force, the French seem to have lost confidence and in early 1340 decided on a defensive policy, blocking the English invasion fleet's access to the Flemish coast where they intended to land safely, since Flanders was England's ally. The French task could be accomplished with armed merchantmen, the 'Great Army of the Sea', as it was grandiosely named. It consisted of up to 200 ships, the largest grouping that could be found and therefore probably mostly cogs. The cost to equip them and hire crews was paid for with a heavy tax on Normandy.

In the meantime, an English invasion fleet was gathered. Made up of about 160 ships, most of them were privately owned and pressed into service to the crown. This fleet, commanded by Edward III in person, sailed for Flanders on 22 June 1340. They apparently did not expect to encounter the French fleet at the mouth of the River Zwyn two days later, the French determined to keep the English from landing upriver. At this stage, Edward had no choice but to go forwards. A

THIS 15TH-CENTURY MANUSCRIPT *illustration from Froissart's* Chronicle *shows the close, ship-to-ship combat at the Battle of Sluys, 1340* (Bibliothèque Nationale, *Paris).*

retreat could easily have turned into a massacre, French ships able to cut off the English one by one as they spread out on the open sea, not to mention what a crushing blow a retreat would have been to King Edward's honour.

Battle of Sluys, 1340

The Battle of Sluys began on 24 June 1340. The French decided on a battle strategy that suggests the French admirals, Hugh Quiéret and Nicholas Béhuchat, did not trust their ships' fighting capabilities and above all feared the English slipping by and landing their army. So the French blocked the mouth of the river completely, chaining the ships together in three long lines across the shallow estuary, about 5km (3 miles) wide at its entrance.

Apparently the most experienced of the French ship commanders advised against remaining in such a confined space, without room to manoeuvre and with the wind blowing into the mouth of the river, but the admirals did not listen. The chronicler Froissart tells that the ships, fortified with wooden fighting platforms, looked like a row of castles. The French strategy suggests either extremely poor seamanship, lack of information about the English fleet coming against them or reckless over-confidence. Some historians

A SHIPBOARD CROSSBOW *could be fitted onto a stand for greater stability while firing. Ships in the High Middle Ages were not typically fitted with onboard weapons, but the crew would add missile-throwers if the opportunity arose.*

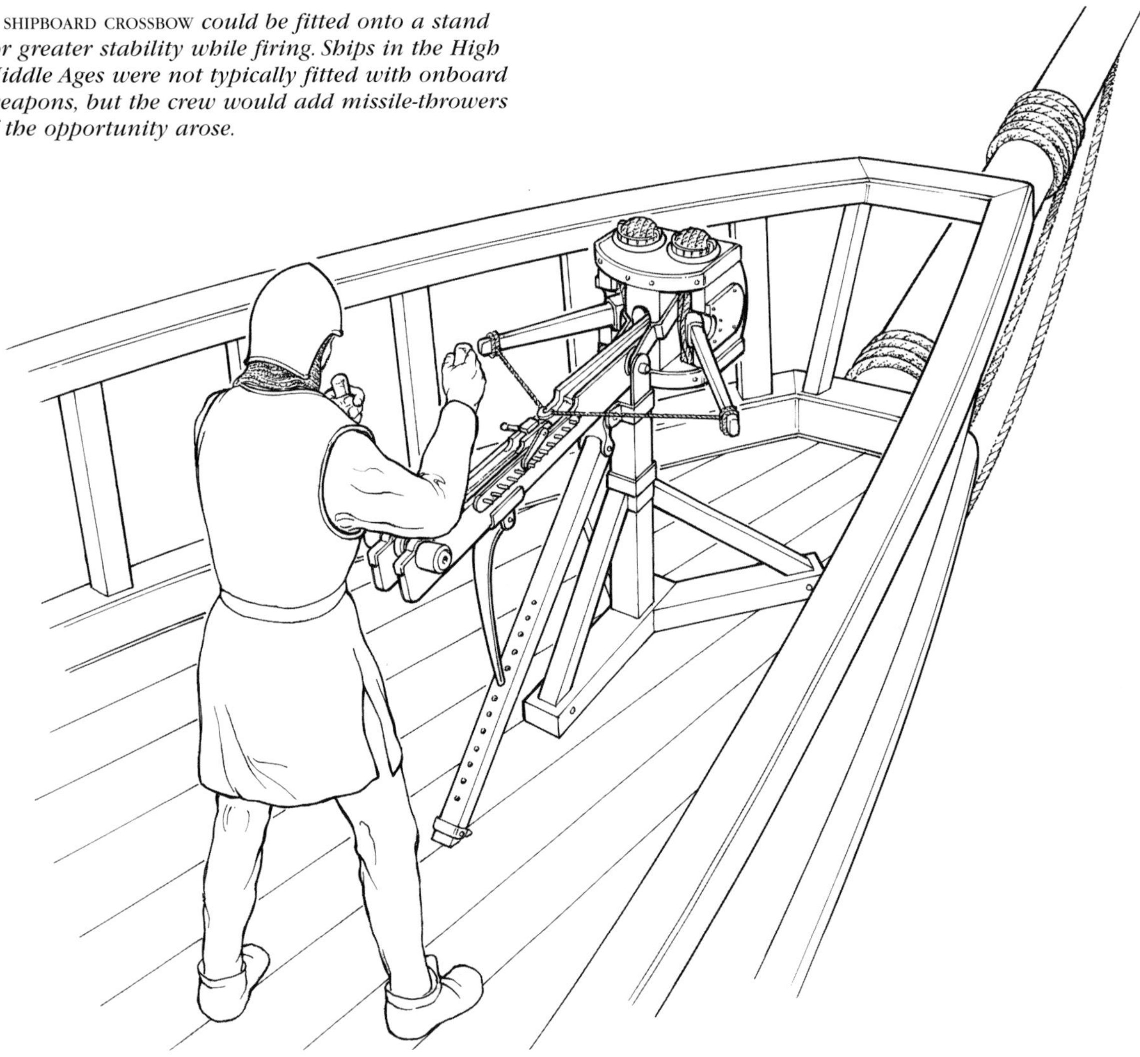

have questioned whether the French could really have chained their ships together; this practice of 'bridling' was described by the historian Livy and maybe medieval chroniclers were again borrowing from the past instead of observing the present. For sailing ships in a confined space affected by the tide, such a tactic was insane. Indeed, the French ships soon found themselves in difficulty, drifting east and fouling each other. The ships appear to have been cast loose at this point, but the French found themselves in serious disorder just as the English began to attack, taking advantage of wind and tide and not starting their final approach until early afternoon when the sun would no longer be in their eyes. The French were trying to edge west again when the battle began, adding to the confusion.

The English approached in three lines, with the largest ships to the front, including Edward III's own flagship, the cog *Thomas*. Height was once again an advantage, and the English had the manpower to exploit it to its fullest - a large army of men-at-arms and archers intended for the land army. Although often forgotten by chivalry enthusiasts, it was this Battle at Sluys, rather than the more famous Crécy and Poitiers, that showed for the first time the devastating effectiveness of the English longbow. The French marines were for the most part crossbowmen. They were much slower than their English equivalents in those crucial moments as the ships closed, and besides were probably understrength, since the French had lost most of their Italian mercenary crossbowmen. The French did what they could to compensate, including lashing boats full of stones to their masts and posting men at the masthead to hurl the rocks on enemy heads. By that time, however, many crews would have been too thinned to fight effectively.

The fighting was hot. Edward III himself was shot through the thigh with a crossbow bolt, and fighting raged from about 3.00 PM until nearly 10.00 PM (with two ships continuing to fight until the next dawn). But the English seem to have massacred the first French line in fairly quick order, gradually working to the second line, which was so tightly clustered together that the ships could not manoeuvre. A large force of Flemings, mustered on the west bank, then fell on the third line from behind, besides killing any Frenchmen who managed to struggle to the shore.

The result was a great English victory. No quarter was given, the English slaughtering the crews of captured ships. Between 16,000 and 18,000 French fighting men died that day. Among the dead were both admirals. Béhuchat was killed in the fighting; Quiéret was captured to be ransomed, but when it was discovered that he had commanded the French attacks against the southern English ports, Edward III ordered him hanged from the mast of his own ship. Not long after the victory, King Edward had his gold coinage redesigned to show himself enthroned on a ship.

> *'It was indeed a bloody and murderous battle. Sea-fights are always fiercer than fights on land, because retreat and flight are impossible.'*
>
> *– Froissart, on the Battle of Sluys, 1340*

Naval 'Arms Race'

Following the Battle of Sluys, a second English naval victory in 1350 shows that it was not just French ineptitude but English longbowmen and seamanship that had been decisive at Sluys. This battle was called 'L'Espagnols sur Mer' ('Spanish on the sea') since it was fought against France's Castilian allies in the open sea of the Channel off Winchelsea, on 29 August 1350. A Castilian fleet of 40 ships was sailing from Flanders for Spain when the English, again personally commanded by their king, attacked.

The Castilians had anticipated such an attack, so their ships were well loaded with stones and iron javelins to throw down on the English ships; they would also have been manned with well-trained crossbowmen. To add to their advantage, the Spanish ships were larger than those of the English. Despite such strengths, the English won

Battle of Sluys

1340

The French force was drawn up in three lines and perhaps tied together with cables, closing the mouth of the Zwin estuary to Edward III's English ships. Unable to manoeuvre, they could only wait to be attacked by the English fleet. However, maintaining their position in the ebb and flow of the tide and winds became increasingly difficult as the day progressed, as the English waited several hours before attacking. The English approached in three lines, led by their largest ships. The rapid fire of the English longbowmen proved superior to the outnumbered crossbowmen aboard the French ships, causing extensive casualties aboard the French vessels and giving the English the advantage as they closed for hand-to-hand fighting. Following the English victory, any French seamen who escaped from their ships had to face a hostile Flemish force on the bank, which helps account for the extremely high number of French casualties in this battle.

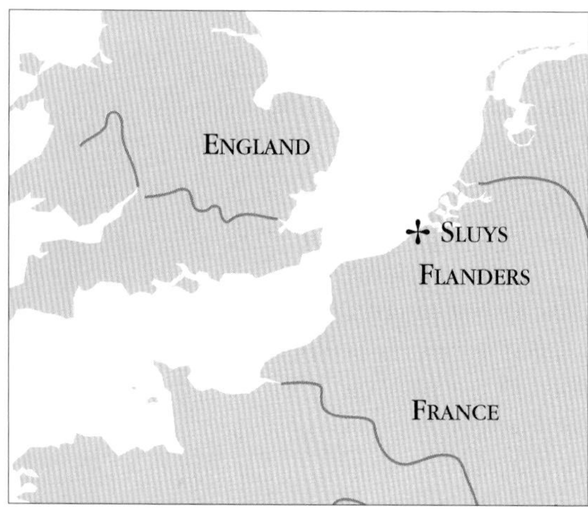

Flanders was Edward III's ally in his war against France. By landing his army there, Edward could join forces with Flemish troops for a joint invasion of northern France.

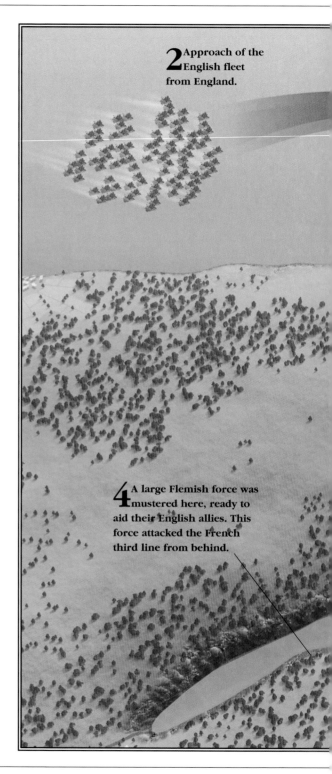

2 **Approach of the English fleet from England.**

4 **A large Flemish force was mustered here, ready to aid their English allies. This force attacked the French third line from behind.**

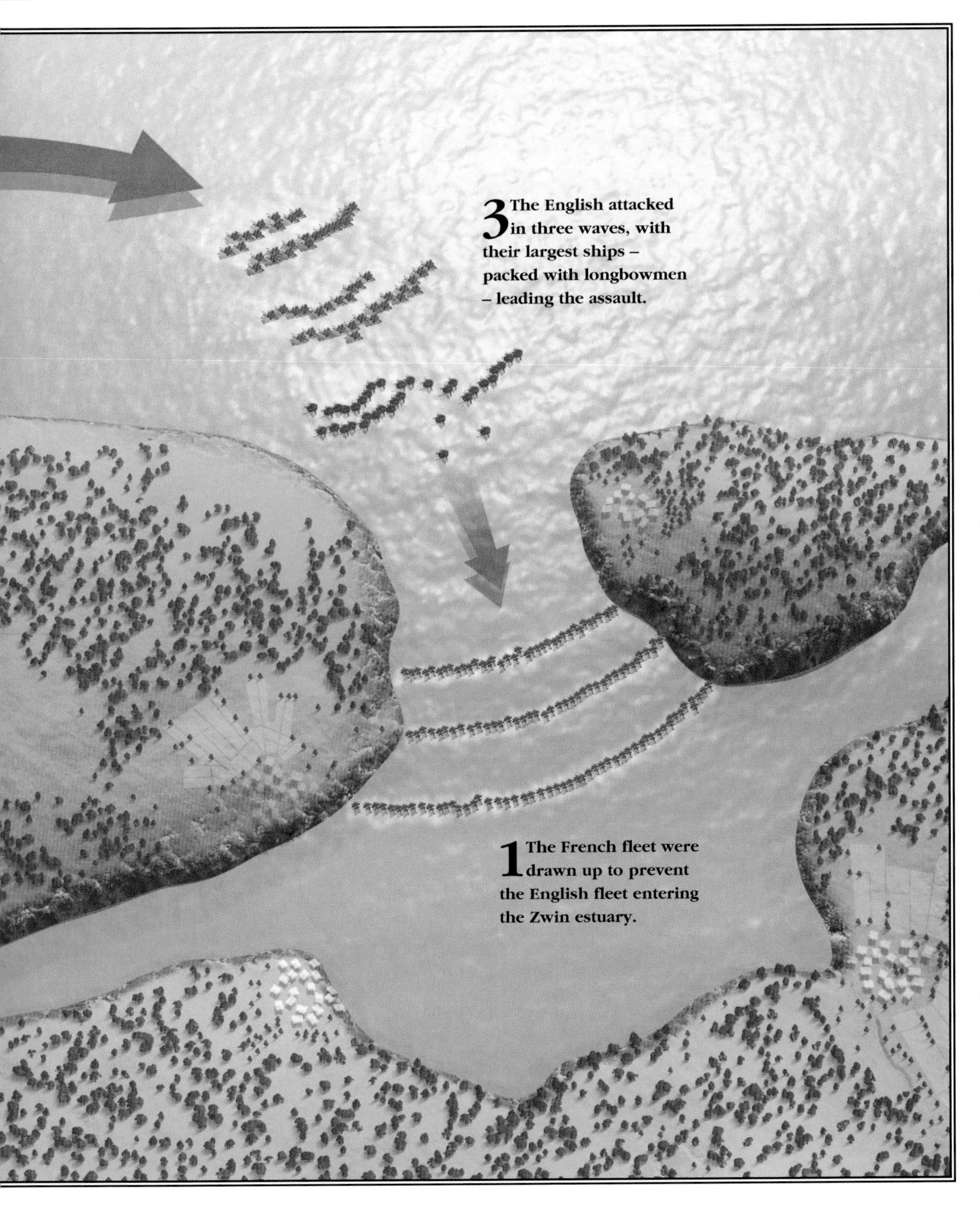
3 The English attacked in three waves, with their largest ships – packed with longbowmen – leading the assault.
1 The French fleet were drawn up to prevent the English fleet entering the Zwin estuary.

again. This was almost certainly because they could fire many more projectiles at the Castilians than the Castilians could return in the key moments when the ships closed. Froissart, always emphasizing chivalric virtue over military pragmatism, tells that in the thick of the action Edward ordered his flagship straight at a large enemy ship, shouting that he wanted to 'joust' it. Even Froissart recognized that a head-on collision at sea would do both ships serious damage, and tells that the seams of Edward's ship were sprung and it almost foundered (although, oddly, the quite thorough naval records extant from this period show no repairs to the cog *Thomas*). According to different accounts, the English took anywhere from 14 to 26 enemy ships.

When the English did suffer a serious defeat, at La Rochelle in 1372, it was because they had been caught napping, their ships beached in the harbour. The Castilian attackers set out to destroy as many as possible (it was a time-consuming task to get a beached ship to sea, and this was essentially a raid), spraying oil on the English decks and then shooting flaming arrows into them, besides probably also using fire ships at some stage of the attack.

By the early fifteenth century, northern navies seem to have consisted almost exclusively of sailing ships and there are signs of an 'arms race' to build the biggest and tallest. The French were still employing Genoese sailors and their ships, but by the time Henry V invaded in 1415 the ships they hired were tall carracks rather than galleys. Henry V responded by building four 'great ships' in the years 1413 to 1420, enormously large clinker-built carracks. The smallest of these, the *Trinity Royale,* was larger than most ships on the water at about 490 tonnes (540 ton). The largest, the *Grace Dieu,* must have been a marvellous sight to behold at 1270 tonnes (1400 tons). None were ever tested in a major naval battle, although two of these vessels played an important role in the English victory at Harfleur in 1416.

A 1420 inventory reported that the *Grace Dieu* included three guns among its armament. The cannon was still an exotic and largely untested weapon, included on ship as one of many anti-personnel weapons. The same inventory records that the ship had 144 gads, the iron darts that were commonly thrown at the enemy from the fighting tops. The first recorded shipboard gun was purchased in 1337 or 1338 for the English royal ship *All Hallows Cog.* This ship shot small lead pellets and crossbow bolts. In the course of the fifteenth century, ever more ships included at least some guns. They probably made little difference in battle, except by adding gunpowder smoke to the general confusion.

Shipboard guns had to be light pieces, otherwise the recoil could damage both crew and ship. Besides this, the weight of multiple guns, as long as they were placed on the upper deck and fired from gunwale or prow, could easily render the vessel unseaworthy. It was only in the early sixteenth century that shipwrights began to construct gunports and gundecks, moving the weight of the artillery closer to the waterline.

The Transformation of the Medieval Navy

In the fifteenth century there were many small conflicts on the North Sea, but no major naval battles. By contrast, the European states of the Mediterranean were more active at sea than ever before, fighting each other and also the rising power of the east, the Ottoman Empire. These late-medieval sailors had the advantage of two new types of ship, the trireme galley and the carrack. The shift to the trireme galley probably began in the 1280s during the War of the Sicilian Vespers. It involved an alteration in seating, staggering the rowers at three levels. This led to an increase in the size of galleys, paving the way for the 'great galleys' of Venice and Genoa in the fourteenth century. In the late thirteenth or early fourteenth century, Mediterranean lands also imported elements of northern ships, including the cog hull form and a one-masted rig with one square sail. They soon added a lateen mizzen sail to make the ship more manoeuvrable, creating the tall, powerful ship known as the cocha or carrack.

Venice and Genoa were the superpowers of the Mediterranean. They fought each other to a standstill in a war that raged from 1350 to 1400 that was marked by a series of fleet actions. (By 1400 Venice had control of about 3300 ships and 36,000 sailors, while the Arsenal, the great

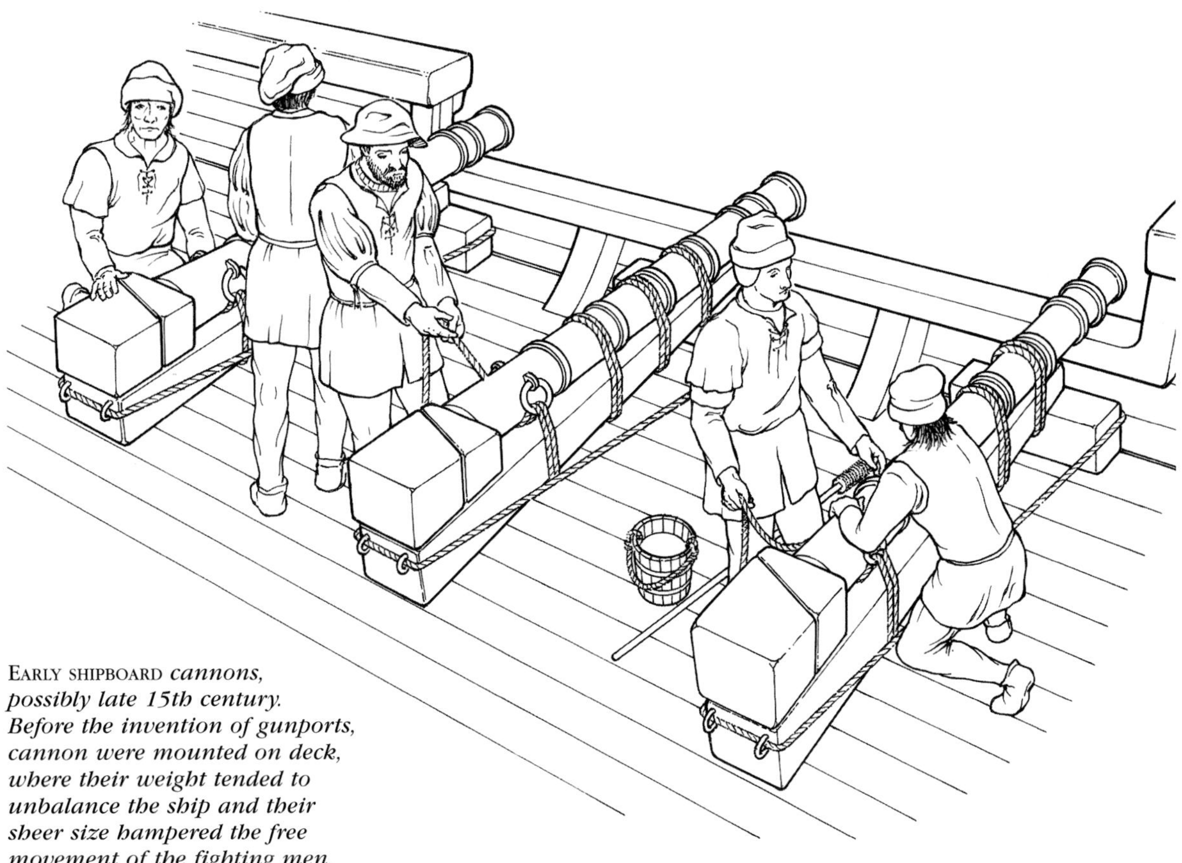

EARLY SHIPBOARD *cannons, possibly late 15th century. Before the invention of gunports, cannon were mounted on deck, where their weight tended to unbalance the ship and their sheer size hampered the free movement of the fighting men.*

shipyard of Venice, employed 16,000 workers.) They had a regular system of war galley patrols and also armed escorts for merchant ships. Their cut-throat competition for trade - and naval bases to support trade - won them many enemies.

Over the course of the fifteenth century, artillery became an increasingly important element of sea fighting, both in the form of anti-personnel guns aboard ship and shore batteries. For example, a fleet of Venetian galleys attempted to aid Constantinople during the Turkish siege of 1453, but the ships could not land because of Turkish guns mounted on the shore, some big enough to sink a ship. Yet the Venetians boasted that they could still defeat any number of Turkish ships at sea. It was true; in the Turkish-Venetian War of 1463-79, the Turkish galleys did not have a single success over the Venetians in an open battle. The Venetians were nonetheless driven out of the eastern Mediterranean, as the Ottomans conquered their land bases one by one.

In conclusion it can be stated that a new day was dawning in naval warfare. Cannon made the use of lightly built galleys more and more risky. This perhaps goes some way to explaining why sixteenth-century rulers began to place convicts and slaves on the rowing benches instead of free citizens. While 'ship-killing' guns did not appear on warships until the late sixteenth century, the trajectory to such armaments was already very clear by 1500, although boarding and seizing an enemy ship remained a common practice well into the nineteenth century. Longstanding medieval naval techniques, which were based on capture rather than destruction, only gradually became a thing of the past.

Select Bibliography

Abbo. *Siège de Paris par les Normands*. ed. H. Waquet. Paris: Société d'Édition 'Les Belles Lettres', 1942.

Bartusis, Mark C. *The Late Byzantine Army: Arms and Society, 1204-1453.* Philadelphia: University of Pennsylvania Press, 1992.

Bennett, Matthew & Hooper, Nicholas. Cambridge Illustrated Atlas. *Warfare: The Middle Ages 768-1487.* Cambridge: Cambridge University Press, 1996.

Bennett, Matthew. 'The Development of Battle Tactics in the Hundred Years War' in *Arms, Armies and Fortifications in the Hundred Years War,* ed. Anne Curry and Michael Hughes. Woodbridge, Suffolk: The Boydell Press, 1994.

Black, Bob. 'Leignitz' in *Miniature Wargames* magazine No 238. Bournemouth: Pireme Publishing, 2003.

Boardman, Andrew W. *The Medieval Soldier in the Wars of the Roses.* Stroud: Sutton Publishing Ltd, 1998.

Boss, Roy. *Justinian's Wars: Belisarius, Narses and the Reconquest of the West.* Stockport: Montvert Publications, 1993.

Bradbury, Jim. *'Greek Fire in the West'.* History Today, xxix, 1979, pp.326-31.

Bradbury, Jim. *Philip Augustus, King of France 1180-1223.* Harlow: Addison Wesley Longman Ltd., 1998.

Bradbury, Jim. *The Medieval Siege.* Woodbridge, Suffolk: The Boydell Press, 1992.

Bradbury, Jim. *The Routledge Companion to Medieval Warfare.* London: Routledge, Taylor and Francis Group, 2004.

Brown, R. Allen, ed. *Castles, A History and Guide.* Poole: Blandford Press, 1980.

Brown, R. Allen. *English Castles.* 3rd edn. London: B.T. Batsford Ltd, 1976.

Burl, Aubrey. *God's Heretics.* Sutton, UK: Stroud, 2002.

Burne, Alfred H. *The Agincourt War: A Military History of the Latter Part of the Hundred Years War from 1369 to 1453.* London: Eyre and Spottiswoode, 1956.

Burne, Alfred H. *The Crecy War: A Military History of the Hundred Years War from 1337 to the Peace of Bretigny, 1360.* London: Eyre and Spottiswoode, 1955.

Catton, Charles, ed. *Fighting Techniques of the Ancient World, 3000 BC - AD 500.* London: Greenhill Books Ltd, 2002.

Contamine, Philippe. *War in the Middle Ages.* Trans. M. Jones. Oxford: Basil Blackwell, 1984.

Chambers, James. *The Devil's Horsemen,* London: Cassell, 1988.

Delbrück, H. *History of the Art of War III: Medieval Warfare.* Lincoln: University of Nebraska Press, 1990.

DeVries, Kelly. *A Cumulative Bibliography of Medieval Military History and Technology.* History of Warfare, 8. Leiden: Brill, 2002 (update 2005).

DeVries, Kelly. *Infantry Warfare in the Early Fourteenth Century: Discipline, Tactics, and Technology.* Woodbridge, Suffolk: The Boydell Press, 1996.

DeVries, Kelly. *Medieval Military Technology.* Peterborough: Broadview Press, 1992.

Fahmy, A.M. *Muslim Sea Power in the Eastern Mediterranean from the Seventh to the Tenth Centuries.* London: Tipografia Don Bosco, 1950.

Forey, Alan. *The Military Orders: From the Twelfth to the Early Fourteenth Centuries.* Toronto: University of Toronto Press, 1992.

France, John. *Victory in the East: A Military History of the First Crusade.* Cambridge: Cambridge University Press, 1994.

France, John. *Western Warfare in the Age of the Crusades, 1000-1300.* Ithaca: Cornell University Press, 1999.

Friel, Ian. *The Good Ship: Ships, Shipbuilding and Technology in England 1200-1520.* Baltimore: Johns Hopkins University Press, 1995.

Gardiner, Robert, ed. *The Age of the Galley.* London: Conway Maritime Press, 1995.

Gardiner, Robert. *Cogs, Caravels and Galleons: The Sailing Ship, 1000-1650.* London: Conway Maritime Press, 1994.

Garmonsway, G.N. *The Anglo Saxon Chronicle.* London: J. M. Dent & Sons, 1975.

Gillmor, C. M. 'The Introduction of the Traction Trebuchet into the Latin West', *Viator*, xii, 1981, pp.1-8.

Gore, Terry. *Neglected Heroes.* London: Praeger, 1995.

Haldon, John. *Warfare, State and Society in the Byzantine World, 565-1204.* London: UCL Press, 1999.

Halsall, Guy. *Warfare and Society in the Latin West, 450-900.* London and New York: Routledge, 2003.

Hattendorf, John B., and Richard W. Unger, eds. *War at Sea in the Middle Ages and the Renaissance.* Woodbridge, Suffolk: Boydell, 2003.

Haywood, John. *Dark Age Naval Power.* London: Routledge, 1991.

Heath, Ian. *Armies of the Middle Ages, Vol 1.* London: The Wargames Research Group, 1982.

Heath, Ian. *Armies of the Middle Ages, Vol 2.* London: The Wargames Research Group, 1984.

Heath, Ian. *Armies of Feudal Europe 1066-1300.* London: The Wargames Research Group. 1978.

Houseley, Norman. *Crusading and Warfare in Medieval and Renaissance Europe.* Aldershot: Ashgate Variorum, 2001.

Hutchinson, Gillian. *Medieval Ships and Shipping.* Rutherford: Fairleigh Dickinson University Press, 1994.

Jenkins, R.P. 'A Second Agincourt', *Miniature Wargames* magazine No 3. London: Conflict Publications, 1983.

Kaeuper, Richard W. *Chivalry and Violence in Medieval Europe.* Oxford: Oxford University Press, 1999.

Keen, Maurice, ed. *Medieval Warfare: A History.* Oxford: Oxford University Press, 1999.

Keen, Maurice. *The Laws of War in the Late Middle Ages.* London: Routledge and Kegan Paul, 1965.

Kemp, Peter, ed. *The Oxford Companion to Ships and the Sea.* Oxford: Oxford University Press, 1976.

Kennedy, Hugh. *The Armies of the Caliphs: Military and Society in the Early Islamic State.* London: Routledge, 2001.

Kenyon, John R. *Medieval Fortifications.* New York: St. Martin's Press, 1990.

Lewis, Archibald R. *Naval Power and Trade in the Mediterranean, 500–1100.* Princeton: Princeton University Press, 1951.

Lewis, Archibald R., and Timothy J. Runyan. *European Naval and Maritime History, 300–1500.* Bloomington: Indiana University Press, 1985.

Mallett, Michael. *Mercenaries and their Masters: Warfare in Renaissance Italy.* Totowa: Rowman and Littlefield, 1974.

Marshall, Christopher. *Warfare in the Latin East, 1192–1291.* Cambridge: Cambridge University Press, 1992.

Montgomery of Alamein. *History of Warfare.* London: Collins, 1968.

Mott, Lawrence V. 'The Battle of Malta, 1283: Prelude to a Disaster', pp 145–172 in *The Circle of War in the Middle Ages*, edited by Donald J. Kagay and L.J. Andrew Villalon. Woodbridge, Suffolk: Boydell, 1999.

Newark, Tim, *Medieval Warlords,* Poole, UK: Blandford Press, 1987.

Nicolle, David C. *Arms & Armour of the Crusading Era, 1050–1350.* London: Greenhill Books, 1998.

Nicolle, David C. *Medieval Warfare Source Book. Vol. 1: Warfare in Western Christendom.* London: Brockhampton Press, 1995.

Nicolle, David C. *Medieval Warfare Source Book. Vol. 2: Christian Europe and its Neighbours.* London: Brockhampton Press, 1996.

Nicholson, Helen. *Medieval Warfare: Theory and Practice of War in Europe, 300–1500.* Houndmills: Palgrave Macmillan, 2004.

Oman, Sir Charles. *A History of the Art of War in the Middle Ages 378–1485* (2 vols.) London: Greenhill Books, 1991.

Prestwich, Michael. *Armies and Warfare in the Middle Ages: The English Experience.* New Haven: Yale University Press, 1996.

Pryor, John H. *Commerce, Shipping and Naval Warfare in the Medieval Mediterranean.* London: Variorum Reprints, 1987.

Pryor, John H. *Geography, Technology, and War: Studies in the Maritime History of the Mediterranean, 649–1571.* Cambridge: Cambridge University Press, 1988.

Queller, Donald E. *The Fourth Crusade: The Conquest of Constantinople, 1201–1204.* Philadelphia: University of Pennsylvania Press, 1977.

Robson, Brian. *The Road To Kabul.* Staplehurst, Kent: Spellmount, 2003.

Rodger, N.A.M. *The Safeguard of the Sea: A Naval History of Great Britain. Vol 1: 660–1649.* London: Harper Collins, 1997.

Rogers, R. *Latin Siege Warfare in the Twelfth Century.* Oxford: Clarendon Press, 1992.

Rose, Susan. *Medieval Naval Warfare, 1000–1500.* London: Routledge, 2002.

Runciman, Steven. *The Fall of Constantinople, 1453.* Cambridge: Cambridge University Press, 1965.

Smail, R.C. *Crusading Warfare (1097–1193).* Cambridge: Cambridge University Press, 1956.

Strickland, Matthew. *War and Chivalry: The Conduct and Perception of War in England and Normandy, 1066–1217.* Cambridge: Cambridge University Press, 1996.

Strickland, Matthew. *Anglo-Norman Warfare: Studies in Late Anglo-Saxon and Anglo-Norman Military Organization and Warfare.* Woodbridge, Suffolk: The Boydell Press, 1992.

Sumption, Jonathan. *The Hundred Years War. Vol. 1: Trial by Battle.* Philadelphia: University of Pennsylvania Press, 1990.

Tzu, Sun. *The Art of War.* London: Oxford University Press, 1963.

Vale, Malcolm. *War and Chivalry: Warfare and Aristocratic Culture in England, France and Burgundy at the End of the Middle Ages.* Athens, Georgia: University of Georgia Press, 1981.

Verbruggen, J.F. *The Battle of the Golden Spurs: Courtrai, 11 July 1302.* Woodbridge, Suffolk: The Boydell Press, 2002.

Verbruggen, J.F. *The Art of Warfare in Western Europe during the Middle Ages.* Woodbridge, Suffolk: The Boydell Press, 1997.

Index

Page numbers in *italics* refer to illustrations, those in **bold** type refer to information displays with illustrations and text. Abbreviations are as follows: (B) - battle; (NB) - naval battle; (S) - siege.

Picture and Illustration Credits

All maps and black-and-white line artworks produced by **JB Illustrations.**

AKG-Images: 6-7 (Biblioteque Nationale), 43 (British Library), 123 (Erich Lessing);
Art-Tech: 55, 63, 202, 214-215;
Bridgeman Art Library: 53 (Lambeth Palace Library), 205 (Musee des Augustins), 242 (Biblioteque Nationale);
Corbis: 72;
Mary Evans Picture Library: 48, 113, 115, 137, 145, 155, 210-211, 229;
MARS/Art-Tech: 46, 54, 59, 66-67, 86-87, 91, 107, 116, 122, 134, 170-171, 184, 203;
Topham Picturepoint: 130-131;
TRH Pictures: 24, 41, 98-99, 120, 132, 181.